The Habsburg Monarchy 1618–1815

Second edition

This is a revised and updated edition of a highly acclaimed history of the early modern Habsburg monarchy. Charles W. Ingrao challenges the conventional notion of Habsburg state and society as peculiarly backward by tracing its emergence as a military and cultural power of enormous influence. The Habsburg monarchy was undeniably different from other European polities: geography and linguistic diversity made this inevitable, but by 1789 it had laid the groundwork for a single polity capable of transcending its uniquely diverse cultural and historic heritage. Charles W. Ingrao unravels the web of social, political, economic, and cultural factors that shaped the Habsburg monarchy during the period, and presents this complex story in a manner that is both authoritative and accessible to non-specialists. This new edition includes a revised text and bibliographies, new genealogical tables, and an epilogue which looks forward to the impact of the Habsburg monarchy on twentieth-century events.

CHARLES W. INGRAO is Professor of History at Purdue University. He has held visiting appointments at Brown, Indiana, Washington and the University of Cambridge, and is currently Editor of the *Austrian History Yearbook*. He has published six books on central Europe and over forty articles both on the region's history and on present-day ethnic conflict.

New Approaches to European History

Series editors
WILLIAM BEIK *Emory University*
T. C. W. BLANNING *Sidney Sussex College, Cambridge*

New Approaches to European History is an important textbook series, which provides concise but authoritative surveys of major themes and problems in European history since the Renaissance. Written at a level and length accessible to advanced school students and undergraduates, each book in the series addresses topics or themes that students of European history encounter daily: the series will embrace both some of the more "traditional" subjects of study, and those cultural and social issues to which increasing numbers of school and college courses are devoted. A particular effort is made to consider the wider international implications of the subject under scrutiny.

To aid the student reader scholarly apparatus and annotation is light, but each work has full supplementary bibliographies and notes for further reading: where appropriate chronologies, maps, diagrams, and other illustrative material are also provided.

For a list of titles published in the series, please see end of book.

to *Bapoo*

Harold H. Beloin
1906–1999

The Habsburg Monarchy, 1618–1815

SECOND EDITION

Charles W. Ingrao

Professor of History, Purdue University

CAMBRIDGE
UNIVERSITY PRESS

CAMBRIDGE UNIVERSITY PRESS
Cambridge, New York, Melbourne, Madrid, Cape Town, Singapore, São Paulo

Cambridge University Press
The Edinburgh Building, Cambridge CB2 2RU, UK

Published in the United States of America by Cambridge University Press, New York

www.cambridge.org
Information on this title: www.cambridge.org/9780521780346

First published 1994
Reprinted 1994, 1995
Second edition 2000
Reprinted 2003

A catalogue record for this publication is available from the British Library

ISBN-13 978-0-521-78034-6 hardback
ISBN-10 0-521-78034-9 hardback

ISBN-13 978-0-521-78505-1 paperback
ISBN-10 0-521-78505-7 paperback

Transferred to digital printing 2005

Contents

Maps

Genealogical table – The Spanish and Austrian Habsburgs

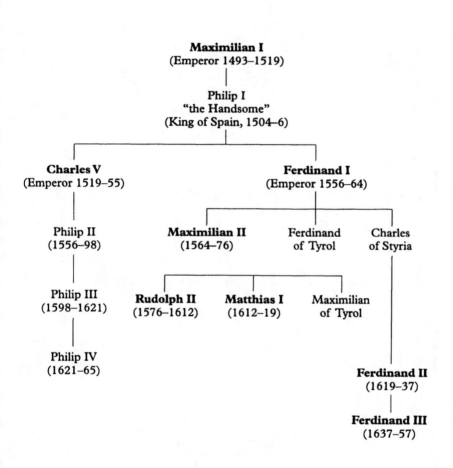

Maximilian I
(Emperor 1493–1519)
|
Philip I
"the Handsome"
(King of Spain, 1504–6)

Charles V
(Emperor 1519–55)

Ferdinand I
(Emperor 1556–64)

Philip II
(1556–98)

Maximilian II
(1564–76)

Ferdinand
of Tyrol

Charles
of Styria

Philip III
(1598–1621)

Rudolph II
(1576–1612)

Matthias I
(1612–19)

Maximilian
of Tyrol

Philip IV
(1621–65)

Ferdinand II
(1619–37)
|
Ferdinand III
(1637–57)

Genealogical table – The Spanish and Austrian successions

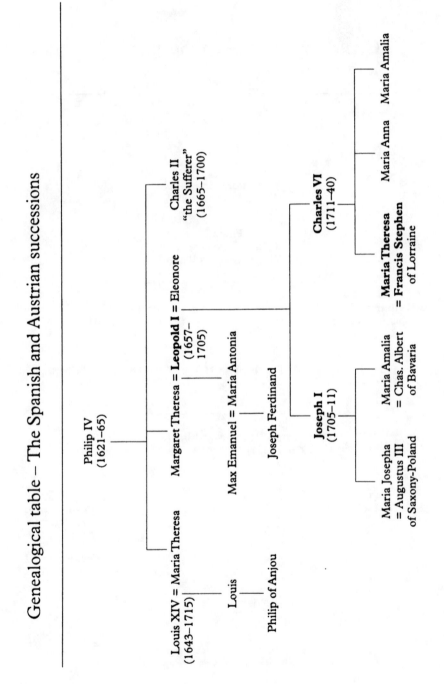

Preface

Neville Chamberlain spoke for millions of his British contemporaries when, at the height of the Munich Crisis, he lamented the prospects of going to war over "a faraway country" inhabited by "people of whom we know nothing." The prime minister was, of course, speaking of Czechoslovakia. But he could have just as easily used these same words to characterize his knowledge – or concern – about the other lands and peoples of the former Habsburg monarchy. A half century later even the educated public in western societies like Great Britain and the United States still know very little about the region, and even less about its history. Nor should this come as a surprise. Neither a bygone empire nor the small "successor states" that replaced it can inspire the same interest as great modern entities like France, Germany, or Russia. Yet, even before its dissolution in 1918, the monarchy's diversity made it much more difficult to comprehend, thereby discouraging anyone from investigating it in the first place. Part of the reason is that the monarchy was really three different countries at the start of the seventeenth century, each nested with several smaller, but distinct sub-societies. In many respects they remained disparate throughout its history. Of course, the same can be said of other European societies. But whereas it is possible to write Soviet or Russian history from the Great Russian perspective, and British history from an English viewpoint, the component states of the Habsburg monarchy were much too numerous, populous, and wealthy to be ignored, either by the Habsburgs or by those who study it. Finally, the monarchy's very diversity created a greater number of problems, many of which demanded solutions different from those applied in major nation states like France or Germany. Fascinating though they were, the monarchy's unique conditions and eccentric development make it a poor choice for anyone searching for a conceptually clean, "typical" example of an evolving nation-state.

What is even more surprising and unfortunate is that the peoples of today's central and east-central Europe – including the German-speaking populations of the *Bundesrepublik* and Austria itself – are themselves becoming less and less aware of their common heritage. The apparent diffidence of many modern Austrians may be explained by the country's longtime status as a neutral between rival power blocs. But is also true that the governments of the various successor states – including Austria – have endeavored for eighty years to instill in their peoples a new political culture modeled after the nation-state model of World War I's victors. Unfortunately, the process of imbuing their citizens with national pride has invariably come at the expense of a meaningful understanding and appreciation of the more complex challenges and achievements of the great Danubian enterprise that preceded them.

Such is the fate of the "losers" of great wars, that history is often written by their enemies. Yet neither the monarchy's ultimate extinction, nor its complex problems, nor even the current political agendas of the various successor states should deter us from studying it. By the second half of the eighteenth century it not only had the continent's most innovative government and largest army, but was also a leader in public education and the world of music. If the ensuing revolutionary decades laid bare the rottenness of Old Regime France, they also demonstrated the Habsburg monarchy's considerable military, political, economic and cultural resources, together with a remarkable durability. In a struggle between two systems, it was those of the supposedly "backward" Habsburg monarchy that fought the most land campaigns, weathered the most defeats – and still triumphed in the end. It subsequently played a leading role in turning back the French Revolution and crafting an international system that remained in place until 1914. When it finally collapsed four years later, it had already outlasted every other major monarchy in both longevity and dynastic continuity, despite having more natural enemies and less wealth with which to confront them. And, as we now know, the problems it confronted did not die with it, but persist today. Indeed, our ignorance of the Habsburg model and its legacy has inhibited our understanding of the tragic human and demographic catastrophes of twentieth-century *Mitteleuropa*.

This book will try to overcome some of these obstacles by presenting at the very outset several generalizations that can help unify and give purpose to the factual material, as well as to the monarchy's history beyond the volume's closing date of 1815. In keeping with the original Cambridge series' "new approaches" format, the rest of the volume will supplement the traditional narrative with additional generalizations and analyses that will hopefully give students cause for discussion, and scholars food for thought. From the very beginning of my research I have endeavored to afford social, economic, and cultural themes as much attention as possible, despite the relative dearth of published material on those subjects. By contrast, I have given minimal coverage to military campaigns, despite their immediate importance in defining the course of the monarchy's history. I have found it impossible, however, to write a book about the Habsburg monarchy and its people without devoting a great deal of attention to the political, and even diplomatic actions of its leaders. Indeed, given the highly artificial nature of their state and society, Habsburg statecraft played the most decisive and unifying role in determining virtually all aspects of its history, including its social and cultural evolution.

If the Habsburg monarchy is complex, so is its nomenclature. To avoid confusion, the text refers to it as "the monarchy" or "the Habsburg dominions," while reserving the terms "empire" and "Germany" for the lands and peoples of the Holy Roman empire. There are only two exceptions: in Chapter 4, I allude to a "second Habsburg empire" akin to the great dynastic conglomeration of Charles V; in Chapter 7, after the creation of the Austrian empire (1804) and dissolution of the Holy Roman empire (1806), the monarchy is finally accorded that designation. Although the word "Austrian" is occasionally used as an adjective to refer to the Habsburg monarchy's army or foreign policy, "Austria" itself is employed only to represent those provinces that comprise the so-called Austrian lands. Only after the creation of the Austrian empire does the term stand for the entire Habsburg monarchy. Another maddening ambiguity about the monarchy's terminology is the double connotation attached to the words "Hungary" and "Bohemia." When referring to all of the Hungarian or Bohemian crownlands, I often employ the terms "greater Hungary" and "greater Bohemia"; by contrast, "Bohemia proper" and "Hungary proper" (or "central Hungary") allude only to the individual component kingdoms of the same name. Unfortunately, there is no easy solution to the problem of place names. Given east-central Europe's mixed ethnic composition, many of its cities have two or three names. Whenever possible, the text uses the English-language names for towns, provinces, and geographical expressions. In those instances where there is no English equivalent, I have employed that designation which is most often found in other English-language histories, with other widely used alternative spellings in parentheses.

This is, without question, the most difficult writing project I have ever undertaken. Most of the problems have stemmed from the conceit that I could address university students, educated laypeople, and my fellow scholars in the same book. The greatest problem has been space. Whereas textbook publishers and their readers demand brevity, scholars crave a completeness and sensitivity to nuances that can only be addressed in a longer work. Trying to engineer both probably doubled the amount of time it took to complete the first edition. I am, however, grateful both to my first editor, Richard Fisher, for his willingness to expand the first edition a quarter beyond its contract length, and to Elizabeth Howard, for presenting me with the opportunity to prepare this enlarged second edition. Alas, one sacrifice that has carried over is footnotes. Editorial limits on the number of notes make it impossible to give proper credit to all the published authors whose work I consulted. Yet, as I soon found out, citing *some* of these scholars involves making arbitrary decisions that are unfair to those who are left out. One acknowledgment that I cannot forego is the dedication of this edition to the memory of my father-in-law, Harold Beloin.

1 The distinctiveness of Austrian history

On 9 June 1815 the representatives of the great European powers gathered in the Hofburg, the medieval city palace of the Habsburgs to sign the peace settlement that eliminated Napoleon's empire. The final act of the so-called Congress of Vienna was accompanied by no fanfare or celebration. Yet, as the last of the European princes and the other 100,000 visitors who had crowded into the city now departed for home, there was no mistaking the import of a treaty that would help define the European state system and preserve it from another great war for the next hundred years.

Although representatives of Great Britain, Prussia and Russia – and even defeated France – had played a major role in the peace negotiations, none had helped shape the course of the negotiations more than their Austrian hosts. And with good reason. Although it has always been fashionable to give the British Duke of Wellington the credit for defeating Napoleon at Waterloo, his fate had been sealed two years earlier when Austria entered the war. It was, in fact, the Austrian empire that had contributed the allied army's largest contingent and its commander-in-chief to the first conquest of France since the Franks. And it was the war aims of the emperor's foreign minister, Clemens von Metternich, that had served as the basis for the final peace settlement. Indeed, the so-called Metternich System that he directed from Vienna was destined to dominate the domestic and foreign policies of the continent until 1848.

It is with the Congress of Vienna and the subsequent Age of Metternich that many students' and historians' knowledge of Austrian history begins. As a rule they associate Austria's success with its great prime minister, while viewing the empire itself as a declining power that was destined for dissolution in World War I. Yet historians who credit (or criticize) Metternich for the system he helped to create forget his own characterization of himself as a mere helmsman who only followed the dictates of his Habsburg sovereign. In truth, Metternich adhered to many of the same principles that had inspired Austrian statecraft for most of the past three centuries. Moreover, our awareness of the Austrian empire's decline in the nineteenth century comes at the expense of ignoring its emergence during the seventeenth century as a powerful, at times innovative, force that often played a leading role in international affairs and coalition diplomacy.

But the Habsburg monarchy was also different from the other great states and societies of Europe. And it was because of its distinctiveness that it conducted its domestic and foreign affairs in ways that have encouraged western historians to visualize it as something of a European backwater, a political anomaly whose structural immaturity condemned it to a constant state of crisis and decay from the very beginning of its history. It is only by understanding the monarchy's inherent individuality that we can comprehend how it successfully dealt with problems that were present from the very beginning of its history and how it not only survived, but steadily grew in size and strength to the point where it had the military power and domestic stability necessary to resist and, ultimately, triumph over revolutionary France.

It is possible to identify at least five interdependent factors that were influential in determining the distinctive course of Austrian history after 1815, but which were already evident at least two centuries before: the impact of geopolitics and balance of power diplomacy; the diversity and individuality of the Habsburg dominions; the dynasty's close identification with Germany; its dependence on achieving a consensus among both domestic elites and foreign allies; the key role of the monarchs themselves in providing continuity and security for their state.

Diplomacy and the formation of the monarchy

In considering the monarchy's early history and emergence as a great power it is appropriate to recall the famous observation by the nineteenth-century publicist, František Palacký, that if the Habsburg monarchy did not exist it would have to be created. The monarchy was, in fact, created at the beginning of the early modern period, and continued to grow largely because its development was consistent with the needs of the international community. Indeed, it is difficult to underestimate the central role that dynastic diplomacy played in the monarchy's unique evolution. Most countries like England, France, or Spain can trace their eventual emergence as nation states to a geographical continuity that promoted a substantial degree of economic, political, cultural, and linguistic homogeneity. To a great extent their rulers and ruling elites merely acted out roles that had been largely predetermined by this underlying structural reality. By contrast, the Habsburgs used dynastic politics to assemble a conglomeration of otherwise disparate dominions, over which they might later superimpose domestic policies aimed at providing the continuity that their territories lacked. Yet the Habsburgs were also driven by geopolitical forces that greatly facilitated their success on the international stage. From beginning to end their monarchy's fate was shaped by the European practice of balance of power diplomacy, especially by the assistance of neighboring rulers and states that perceived it to be sufficiently strong to help resist more powerful enemies, yet weak enough not to pose a serious threat to their own security.

It was this double equation that had led to the election of the first Habsburg to the German imperial crown. The German princes who chose Rudolph I (1273–91) did so partly because, as the relatively obscure lord of several modest-sized southwestern territories, he was deemed insufficiently prominent to challenge their preeminent position within the empire. But they also valued his assistance in helping them to repel the threat posed by Germany's southeastern neighbors, Bohemia and Hungary. When Rudolph's forces killed the Bohemian king at the battle of Marchfeld (1278) he acquired his enemy's southeast German lands, including the duchy of Austria. By the middle of the following century his descendants had elevated themselves to the rank of "archduke" (with the help of a forged document) and had established their identity as the House of Austria.

But the dynasty acquired more than its Austrian identity at Marchfeld. It now assumed the possession of the empire's southeastern flank, which was exposed not only to Hungary and Bohemia, but ultimately to the growing menace of the Ottoman Turks. The Austrian lands' strategic position enhanced the Habsburgs' importance as defenders of Germany's frontiers and helped secure the election of a series of Habsburg emperors, beginning with the succession of Emperor Albert II (1438–40). Although the competing power of the other German princes greatly weakened the imperial office, the dynasty used it effectively to enhance its prestige and European profile. In a memorable flight of grandeur, Emperor Frederick III (1440–93) even adopted the all-vowel acronym AEIOU to represent his presumptuous, if prophetic, motto "Austria Est Imperare Orbi Universo" (*Austria is destined to rule over the entire globe*). Together with the acquisition of the Austrian lands, the Habsburgs' hold on the imperial crown also brought into play a second geopolitical factor that would help determine the course of Austrian history until the end of the monarchy: a strategic, central European location that exposed it to potential enemies and attracted an even greater number of solicitous allies.

Both of these factors – the Habsburgs' strategic position and their utility in achieving a balance of power among warring neighbors – played a decisive role in the dynasty's sudden emergence on the European stage at the end of the fifteenth century. Much of the individual credit belongs to Frederick III's remarkable son, Emperor Maximilian I (1493–1519), who was responsible for the conclusion and fruition of three key marriage alliances during the half-century 1477–1526. It was the first of these unions in 1477, between the then young Habsburg prince and Mary, the daughter and heiress of the duke of Burgundy, that inspired the famous refrain:

> Let the strong fight wars.
> Thou happy Austria marry.
> What Mars bestows on others,
> Venus gives to thee!

Its author, King Matthias Corvinus of Hungary (1458-90), could appreciate his Habsburg rival's good fortune. He had conquered most of the Habsburgs' Austrian lands from Maximilian's father and had even made Vienna his capital in 1485. The gap between the Habsburgs' dynastic pretensions and martial impotence even prompted the Viennese to mock Frederick III with their own version of AEIOU: "*Aller Erst Ist Österreich Verloren*" (*Austria has just lost everything*). But, five years later, Matthias's empire fell apart when he died childless. By contrast the progeny of Maximilian and Mary ultimately inherited both the Habsburg lands in southern Germany and Burgundy's holdings in the commercially rich Low Countries. This dual inheritance converted the Habsburgs from German territorial princes into a European dynasty of the first rank.

The next great match transformed them into a world power. When Ferdinand of Aragon and Isabella of Castile agreed to wed their daughter Juana to Maximilian's son Philip ("the Handsome") in 1496, they had no expectation that the Habsburgs would soon inherit the new Spanish empire that they themselves had done so much to create. Two elder siblings and, eventually, three nephews stood ahead of her in the succession. But the untimely death of all five of those heirs established Juana's claim. Thus it came to pass that four monarchies would be concentrated in the hands of Charles of Ghent, the Dutch-born, eldest son of Juana and her Habsburg husband Philip: Castile and Aragon through Charles's mother; Burgundy (including the Netherlands) and the dynasty's German lands through his father. His election in 1519 to succeed his grandfather Maximilian as German Emperor Charles V (1519–56) completed a stupendous dynastic coup far beyond the bitter expectations of Matthias Corvinus.

The Burgundian and Spanish marriages established a primarily western European conglomeration that included not only Spain and the Low Countries but also Aragon's extensive Italian possessions and Castile's emerging New World empire. It was not long before Charles V recognized his monarchy's Atlantic orientation and established Castile as its center. Given the relative remoteness of his Austrian lands, Charles ceded them to his younger brother Ferdinand in 1521. It was at this point that the consequences of a third, truly bizarre marriage compact involving Ferdinand led directly to the creation of a second major Habsburg state rooted in east-central Europe. In 1506 the two boys' grandfather, Maximilian, and the

Jagellon King Ladislas of Hungary and Bohemia concluded a highly speculative accord that foreshadowed a double marriage of Ferdinand to Ladislas's daughter Anna, and of Ferdinand's infant sister Mary to the as yet unborn (but, hopefully, male) child of Ladislas's pregnant wife. The subsequent birth of Ladislas's son and successor, Louis, enabled both weddings to take place, following the conclusion of a more definitive marriage compact in 1515. When the childless King Louis II died fighting the Turks at Mohács in 1526, his Habsburg widow Mary and brother-in-law Ferdinand were able to secure the latter's election as king of Hungary and Bohemia.

It is easy to attribute these three incredibly fortuitous unions to the frenetic matchmaking of Maximilian I, who actually planned and concluded numerous other, less fruitful marriage alliances during his lifetime. They came about, however, because Maximilian's dynastic partners shared a mutual concern over the growing threat posed by rival powers to the regional balance of power. In selecting Maximilian for his daughter, the duke of Burgundy was seeking assistance against his bitter enemy, the king of France, whose Swiss allies actually killed him in battle three months before the wedding. The union with Spain stemmed from Ferdinand of Aragon's desire to protect his own dynasty's possessions in Italy following France's sensational conquest of the peninsula in 1494. Although they produced no male heirs, two subsequent Anglo-Spanish marriage alliances were likewise motivated by England's historic rivalry with France. If Burgundy, Spain, and England envisioned the French as a menace to the balance of power in western Europe, the Jagellon kings of Hungary and Bohemia – and the noble diets that subsequently elected Ferdinand to succeed them as king – were driven by the need to enlist Habsburg assistance against the Ottoman Turks' relentless march through the Balkans. Indeed, their sense of urgency was not lost on the entourage of the ill-fated Louis II which literally had to fish the Hungarian crown out of the swamp in which their king had drowned while fleeing the Turks at Mohács.

The question arises why all these countries found the Habsburgs to be such desirable partners with whom to face these various foreign threats. Once again, the central location of the Austrian lands and the Holy Roman empire made Maximilian and his successors equally sensitive to the emergence of aggressive states all along the fringes of Germany, whether to the west in France, to the south in Italy, or to the east in the Balkans. Moreover, as each marriage bore fruit and added to the Habsburg patrimony, it steadily expanded the reach of their geopolitical interests and security needs, drawing them deeper in each direction until they embraced most of the continent. Moreover, although they were now the preeminent German dynasty and were invariably elected to hold the imperial crown, the Austrian Habsburgs were never regarded by Maximilian's contemporaries as great a threat to the regional balance of power as the French or the Turks. Hence they made ideal allies, in keeping with Machiavelli's famous dictum that one should always ally with weaker powers against stronger ones. Never again over the next four centuries would the Austrian Habsburgs reap significant territorial gains from dynastic marriages. But the reasons that had made Maximilian such a ready and desirable partner – the Austrian lands' strategic, central location, and the Austrian Habsburgs' usefulness as a benign counterweight in balance of power politics – remained more or less a constant in European politics to the end of the monarchy in 1918.

The problem of diversity

Acquiring an empire by inheritance was not, however, without its pitfalls. One of the unfortunate legacies of Maximilian's dynastic alliances was the diversity and individuality of the dominions that he brought together. As can happen in any arranged marriage, the subjects of these unions were sometimes incompatible, or at least unwilling to surrender their individual rights and independence to the dominant partner. Indeed, before they could receive the homage of their new subjects, the Habsburgs invariably had to swear to respect their privileges and autonomy – a constitutional nicety that would have been unnecessary had they acquired them by conquest. Hence both the Spanish and Austrian Habsburgs assembled a patchwork pattern of dominions in which the estates of their component territories retained a separate identity, as well as substantial control over the making and local enforcement of the law. Conditions such as these helped perpetuate each crownland's sense of independence at the expense of a common identity and loyalty to the monarchy as a whole. In the end these were fatal flaws that helped doom the Spanish Habsburgs to destruction in the seventeenth century, just as they ultimately contributed to Austria-Hungary's dissolution in the twentieth.

Whereas Spain's empire was scattered all over Europe and much of the globe, the Austrian Habsburg dominions at least had the advantage of being geographically contiguous. Nevertheless, as they entered the seventeenth century they were also, in the words of R.J.W. Evans, "not a 'state' but a mildly centripetal agglutination of bewilderingly heterogeneous elements." Ferdinand's union of Hungary and Bohemia with his Austrian lands had created an essentially tripartite territorial configuration that enjoyed limited economic ties and was linguistically, culturally, and constitutionally diverse. Much of this discontinuity stemmed from the lie of the land: with the singular exception of the Danube, which provided a solid link between parts of Hungary and Austria, the monarchy's unfortunate natural configuration of mountains and peripheral river systems had largely predetermined the separate development of its three components. Yet a century of Habsburg rule had done little to break down these barriers.

This lack of homogeneity was evident even within the monarchy's Austrian, Bohemian, and Hungarian dominions (see Map 1). The Austrian and other German territories that the dynasty had held since the middle ages were themselves little more than a disjointed cluster of over a dozen largely autonomous principalities that stretched over much of southern Germany. Over time the Habsburgs had done little to foster a common identity within these so-called hereditary lands, or *Erblande*. At his death in 1564 Ferdinand had renewed a common practice of his Habsburg predecessors by subdividing the Austrian lands among his three sons. This partition still obtained at the beginning of the seventeenth century. In addition to Bohemia and Hungary, the senior Habsburg line held only the two Danubian archduchies of Upper and Lower Austria or, more precisely, Austria above the Enns and Austria below the Enns (so named because of the small Danube tributary that separated them). Directly to the south, a second Habsburg court at Graz ruled a half dozen principalities that were nestled along the eastern fringes of the Alps: the three duchies of Styria, Carinthia, and Carniola, known collectively as Inner Austria, together with the much smaller Adriatic principalities of Gorizia, Istria, and Trieste. Finally, to the west a third Habsburg archduke at Innsbruck governed the most scattered and isolated lands of the Austrian lands: situated high in the Alps and almost totally detached from the other *Erblande* was the Tyrol; beyond it lay the *Vorlande*, or Outer Austria, the contiguous and equally mountainous county of Vorarlberg, roughly one hundred, widely scattered enclaves in southwestern Germany that included the oldest of the Habsburgs' ancestral lands. As geographically disjointed as these lands were, both the Tyrol and Inner Austria were further cut up by the presence of numerous enclaves belonging to a half dozen imperial prince-bishops.

Although most of the hereditary lands' roughly 2 million inhabitants (1618) were engaged in agriculture, their commercial economies were distinctive and largely independent of one another. The two archduchies were closely bound to the Danube river commerce that connected them with Hungary and Germany. The Upper Austrian capital of Linz was one of the monarchy's major commercial and manufacturing centers, specializing in the production and export of textiles, as well as the transshipment of wine and minerals from Hungary. The Lower Austrian capital of Vienna was also somewhat involved in the Danube trade, but was slowly assuming its role as the monarchy's administrative center. By contrast Inner Austria's largely agricultural economy also relied heavily on the mining of key minerals. Styria was one of the continent's foremost centers for the mining and crafting of iron, while Carinthia and Carniola were important producers of

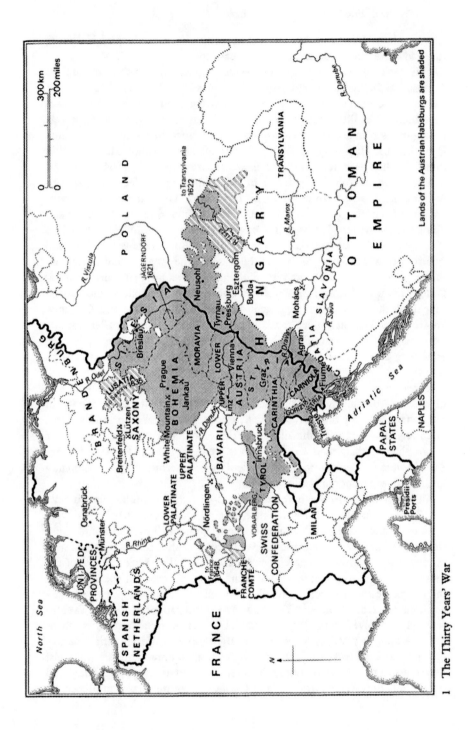

1 The Thirty Years' War

lead and mercury respectively. Although it also utilized the Danube as a conduit for its mineral exports, much of Inner Austria's commerce ran south to the Adriatic principalities which were, in turn, primarily influenced economically by their proximity to the sea and to northern Italy. The Tyrol and Outer Austrian lands enjoyed virtually no commercial links with the rest of the hereditary lands. Instead, the Tyrol served as an important route between Italy and southern Germany, to whom it exported glass, silk, and the extracts of its own metal and salt mining industries in exchange for food products. Meanwhile, the remoteness of the Outer Austrian lands rendered them an integral part of the economies of the Swabian and Alsatian German lands that surrounded them.

Ultimately the *Erblande* would be permanently reunited in 1665, following the extinction of all but one branch of the family. Nevertheless, these political, physical, and economic divisions encouraged each of the hereditary lands to develop a separate sense of regional loyalty (*Landespatriotismus*) and to focus more on its own selfish interests than on those of the other Austrian lands, or the monarchy as a whole. Moreover, their individuality was reinforced by the retention of their own governmental institutions, even after reunification. Every land was headed by a governor (*Landeshauptmann* or *Landesmarschall*) who was nominated by the estates and appointed by the crown. But real power resided with the estates themselves. Individual diets enjoyed a genuine right to negotiate with the governor over the crown's requests. More often they simply set their own legislative agenda. They alone were responsible for such things as the building and maintenance of roads, health care and sanitation, all levels of public education, and even regional defenses and militia. Except for the archduchies, the individual estates also levied their own tolls and tariffs, thereby accentuating the long-standing divisions between the hereditary lands. Even when raising money for the crown the estates did so by composing their own tax laws and then collecting them through their own army of officials. With the singular exception of Lower Austria, the estates' own bureaucracy invariably equaled or outnumbered the crown's until well into the eighteenth century. Indeed, the center of each land's power was not so much its diet but the officials whom it designated and paid, and who functioned continuously, even when the diet was not in session. As a nominee of the estates even the governor tended to be at least as deferential to the estates as he was to the crown.

Finally, one step beyond the estates' officials stood the local, landholding nobility, whose task – or privilege – it was to enforce all governmental decrees in their own jurisdiction, or *Herrschaft*. At this level parochial interests always held sway over the priorities of the government in Vienna. This was also the case with the numerous imperial bishops whose Tyrolean and Inner Austrian enclaves enjoyed considerable administrative autonomy.

Nor were those interests necessarily expressed in German. The southern-most hereditary lands may have belonged to the German empire, but they generally spoke a different language. The Carniolan, and much of the Styrian, Carinthian, and Gorizian countryside was Slovene. Istria spoke Croatian, while Italian was the dominant tongue in both Trieste and the southern Tyrol. More eccentric Romance languages could also be found along the western fringes of the Tyrol (Romansch) and Vorarlberg (Ladin). It would be misleading to suggest that this linguistic diversity somehow exacerbated the political, economic, or cultural divisions within the heredi-tary lands. The ruling elites and towns invariably spoke German, except in those areas where Italian dominated. Even then, language was of incidental significance unless it somehow reinforced a greater historical or political identity within the country's ruling class. This was not the case in the hereditary lands. It was, however, in Bohemia and Hungary.

Both Bohemia and Hungary had been established kingdoms for over five hundred years when the Habsburgs acquired them in 1526-7. Each was the creation of a conquering tribe: the Slavic Czechs, who may have arrived in Bohemia as early as the sixth century, and the Magyars, a Finno-Ugric people who subjugated the Slavic and other peoples of the Hungarian plain at the end of the tenth century. Though both nations' native dynasties had died out at the beginning of the fourteenth century, they had continued to prosper under a series of elected foreign rulers, culminating with the personal union of the two kingdoms under the Jagellon Kings Ladislas (1491-1516) and the ill-fated Louis II (1516-26). Indeed, as one of Germany's most prominent states and its only sovereign kingdom, Bohemia had played a major role in imperial affairs. Hungary had likewise been in the vanguard of the Christian defense against the Ottoman threat right up to the catastrophe at Mohács. Thus the two kingdoms already enjoyed a well-defined historical identity when their constituent nobilities elected Ferdi-nand of Habsburg king. Yet, as in the case of the *Erblande*, their natural configuration was somewhat more complex than their national histories might suggest.

Lying immediately north of the *Erblande*, the Bohemian crownlands consisted of five principalities, but are better visualized as two discrete regions. A series of heavily forested mountains encased the hilly terrain of the kingdom of Bohemia and its eastern neighbor, the margravate of Moravia. Only by proceeding north through the passes of the Sudeten Mountains was it possible to reach the largely flat, northern European plain and the other three Bohemian crownlands, the duchy of Silesia and the much smaller margravates of Upper and Lower Lusatia. The mountainous insularity of Bohemia and Moravia had rendered them a relatively homo-geneous region, especially by the standards of the rest of the monarchy.

Silesia was somewhat more diverse, composed as it was of no fewer than sixteen feudal principalities, only six of which were ruled directly from Vienna. Meanwhile, a half dozen princely families enjoyed substantial law-making and judicial privileges that afforded them varying degrees of independence from Habsburg rule. Nearly half of northern, Lower Silesia was ruled by two largely autonomous native dynasties, the Piasts of Liegnitz, Brieg, and Wohlau, and the Podiebrads of Münsterberg and Öls; in the south a junior branch of the Hohenzollern dynasty ruled the Upper Silesian duchy of Jägerndorf with the full status of imperial princes.

All five of the Bohemian crownlands were ethnically mixed. A Czech-speaking majority that included almost all of the nobility dominated central Bohemia and Moravia, while a large German minority held sway over the mountainous periphery. By contrast the nobility of Silesia and the Lusatias spoke German, as did the majority of Silesia's population. Southern, Upper Silesia did, however, have a large Polish minority as well as a small Czech population along the Bohemian frontier. If anything the Lusatias were even more distinctive, being the home of the Sorbs, Europe's smallest Slavic nation. The northern principalities' cultural and linguistic distinctiveness was not without political implications. Until 1616 Silesia and the Lusatias had a "German Chancery" at Breslau that enjoyed some autonomy from the Bohemian government at Prague. Even after its elimination the official languages of the northern principalities remained German, as opposed to Czech in Bohemia and Moravia.

What all of the Bohemian crownlands had in common was their human and economic wealth. In 1618 their 4 million inhabitants made them the monarchy's most populous component, as well as one of Europe's most densely populated. Moreover, a dearth of rich soil had inspired the development of manufacturing in all four crownlands. By the beginning of the seventeenth century greater Bohemia was one of central Europe's foremost producers of textiles. The mountains of Bohemia and Moravia were also a major producer of minerals, including iron, silver, and as much as two-thirds of the continent's tin. Prague itself had taken advantage of its strategic location to become a major transit point for the export to Germany of locally produced textiles and minerals, as well as livestock and crops from Austria, Hungary, and Poland, and iron from as far away as Styria. Silesia and the Lusatias were just as wealthy, but their remoteness militated against fuller integration into the monarchy's economy. Although Silesia was Hungary's principal supplier of finer textiles, the greater proximity of the northern European plain and the Oder and Neisse Rivers that ran the length of their territory inclined all three principalities to trade more with Saxony, Brandenburg, and Poland than with the rest of the monarchy.

During the sixteenth century Ferdinand and his successors had come to rely on the superior wealth of their Bohemian patrimony for most of their revenue. In return they deemed it wise not to disturb its political autonomy. They left untouched the autonomous treasuries that collected the revenues of each crownland. They also honored the indigenous nobility's right to fill government positions with native-born officials. Its central executive office, the Bohemian Court Chancery, was staffed by Czech-speaking nobles who answered to the estates and resided in Prague's Hradcany Castle, even if the residence of its Habsburg king was two hundred miles away in Vienna. Meanwhile, the estates enjoyed more than the extensive legislative and administrative powers found in the *Erblande*. Most notable among them was the traditional right of Bohemia proper to elect a king for all of the crown-lands upon the death of each monarch, generally after he had confirmed their rights and privileges. This was no idle instrument in the hands of the estates. During the Hussite religious revolt of the early fifteenth century Bohemia had refused to elect its late king's heir, and had prevented him from assuming the throne for seventeen years, until he and the pope had recognized its demands for special concessions. Two centuries later the country's Hussite past and the survival of the Czech language within the Bohemian and Moravian ruling elite reinforced the kingdoms' sense of distinctiveness and independence from the Austrian and Hungarian domin-ions, as well as from the German Habsburgs themselves.

Nowhere within the Habsburg dominions was the spirit of independence and tradition of opposition to the crown stronger than in Hungary. Located along the eastern borders of the Austrian and Bohemian lands and just outside the Holy Roman empire, Hungary consisted of three distinctive political entities, each with its own estates, laws, and variety of language groups. In the center stood Hungary proper. Most of the central kingdom comprised a rich plain formed by the Danube and several major tributaries. The one notable exception was northern, Upper Hungary (modern-day Slovakia) which was traversed by the western Carpathians. At the beginning of the seventeenth century the central kingdom held about 1.7 million inhabitants. In so far as generalizations are possible, the countryside spoke Magyar in the Danubian basin, Slovak and Ruthene in the Carpathians, and most frequently German in the towns. To the southwest, between the Drava River and the Adriatic, lay the closely associated Croatian-speaking king-doms of Croatia and Slavonia, a land of perhaps 250,000 people that had been bound in personal union with Hungary since the end of the twelfth century. To the east of the Danubian plain, within the curved eastern spur of the Carpathians, stood the hilly, but fertile principality of Transylvania. Transylvania was easily the most ethnically complex crownland. Its roughly 750,000 inhabitants comprised a Romanian peasant majority, together with the three politically enfranchised "nations" represented in its diet: the

Magyars; the closely related, Magyar-speaking Szekler; and the "Saxons," descendants of Rhenish-German settlers who, like the Szekler, had helped the Magyar kings defend the Transylvanian frontier during the middle ages.

As was the case in Bohemia, Habsburg rule in Hungary was circumscribed by extensive constitutional liberties that were defended by a proud and fiercely independent indigenous nobility. The institutional focus of their freedoms was the kingdom's bi-cameral diet and its independent Chancery, both of which claimed jurisdiction for the entire kingdom. Although the nobility as a whole enjoyed a virtual monopoly over all government positions, it was the great aristocratic landowners, or magnates, who held most of the key executive offices in all three crownlands. Chief among them was the palatine, whom the diet elected to preside over both the Chancery and its own upper chamber of magnates and high church officials. Within Hungary proper and Transylvania the nobility was dominated by the descendants of the original conquering nation. Although Romanian was still spoken by a few of Transylvania's generally landless, lower nobility, all of the Slovak nobility of Upper Hungary had long since become Magyarized. After five centuries of union with Hungary, it was also possible to find Magyarized Croatian aristocrats who had adopted their dominant partner's language and culture. Nevertheless, under the leadership of their viceroy, or *ban*, a united, Croatian-Slavonian diet jealously guarded its kingdom's separate identity and autonomy within both Hungary and the monarchy as a whole.

Beyond greater Hungary's magnate class stood the country's lower nobility, or gentry. Although much of the gentry was relatively poor and often landless, it too exercised considerable power, both as the dominant force in the Hungarian diet's lower chamber and at the local level through its control of all three crownlands' county governments. Moreover, the nobility as a whole enjoyed extensive individual privileges, including exemption from all taxes and the *jus resistendi*, its right to use force to resist any royal violation of its constitutional liberties. Finally, the noble-dominated diets of both Hungary and Croatia enjoyed the right to elect their king, once again generally after a redress of grievances. And, as in Bohemia, this was no empty prerogative.

The Habsburgs had learned this first hand shortly after Mohács, when the Magyar nobility split over the choice of a successor to the fallen Louis II. Whereas a Hungarian diet summoned by his Habsburg widow Mary had turned to her brother Ferdinand for protection against the Turks, a rival conclave had rejected the choice of a foreigner, choosing instead the native Magyar governor of Transylvania, Janos Zápolya. A similar division developed west of the Drava, where the Croatian nobility elected Ferdinand, while a Slavonian diet sided with Zápolya. Although Ferdinand soon drove

Zápolya from the kingdom, his rival made the fateful decision to enlist the aid of the Turks, who returned to Hungary in 1529, this time to stay. By mid-century the sultan had used his support for Zápolya's candidacy as a pretext for occupying more than half of the country, including its historic capital at Buda. The situation had changed little over the past fifty years, despite Habsburg efforts to reconquer Hungary in the so-called Fifteen Years' War (1593–1606).

Hence, Hungary at the beginning of the seventeenth century was not only a diverse land, but a divided one as well. The rich Danubian plain that stood at its center was almost wholly in Turkish hands. The Habsburgs retained only Upper Hungary, together with a slender corridor along the Austrian frontier where they established their new capital at Pressburg (Bratislava; Pozsony). Across the Drava only the western third of the Croatian-Slavonian kingdom, including its capital at Agram (Zagreb), remained under Habsburg control. To the east Transylvania was technically a Turkish protectorate, but managed to preserve a tenuous independence, thanks to its relative remoteness and its princes' ability to play off competing Habsburg and Turkish ambitions. It soon assumed the trappings of a sovereign principality by forming its own legislative diet and electing princes who quickly evolved from their former position of royal administrators to major players in east European politics.

The Turkish invasion and occupation had a devastating effect on the country. Even in the best of times the Hungarian crownlands constituted a modest economic unit that depended heavily on the raising and westward export of grain, wine, and livestock through the *Erblande*, Bohemia, or the Istrian Adriatic port of Fiume (Rijeka). The only significant exception to the country's agrarian profile was, once again, mountainous Upper Hungary, where the German-speaking mining towns of the Carpathian Ore Mountains produced most of Europe's copper, as well as silver, gold, and salt. Yet the kingdom's partition and the intermittent warfare that followed disrupted trade and the development of the towns that depended on it. As a result, by 1600 the sixteen royal towns that remained under Habsburg control contained only 40,000 people. The incessant warfare also drove tens of thousands of peasants from agriculture. Many became armed frontiersmen, or *hayducks*, for whom a nomadic lifestyle of animal husbandry and soldiering provided the only viable alternative to flight or starvation. It was a measure of the hardships confronting Hungary that a large portion of the population migrated from the areas under Turkish control, as well as from the most exposed areas on either side of the Habsburg-Ottoman frontier.

Even with migration from the Turkish south, the Habsburgs retained little more than a million of their Hungarian subjects at the beginning of the seventeenth century. What modest contribution a united kingdom might have made to the monarchy was more than canceled by the Turkish conquest. Truncated Royal Hungary was now hardly in a position to attend to its own defense and needed to rely on assistance from the other Habsburg lands. By mid-century the Bohemian crownlands had essentially assumed financial responsibility for defending nearby Upper Hungary. Meanwhile, what was left of Croatia-Slavonia was so weak that its diet reluctantly authorized Ferdinand to carve out a military border zone (*Militärgrenze*) along the Turkish frontier for resettling Serbian Christian refugees from the Balkans and employing them as soldiers for defense against Turkish incursions. Unfettered by the liberties or restrictions of the local estates, this unique institution and the *Grenzer* who served it were destined to provide the Habsburgs with a major portion of Hungary's overall military contribution over the next two centuries.

Significantly, the Military Border was primarily funded, supplied, and governed not by the emperor, but by the Inner Austrian regime at Graz, which stood in the greatest immediate danger from a Turkish thrust through Croatia. This delegation of Hungary's regional defense illustrates the decentralized nature of Habsburg authority at the beginning of the seventeenth century. During his reign Ferdinand had indeed established the skeletal outlines of a central government in Vienna. Policy-making had been entrusted to a group of the emperor's closest advisors, known as the Privy Council, or *Geheimrat*. The administration of ordinary, "cameral" revenue from crown domains, tolls, and mineral rights had become the responsibility of the Court Chamber, or *Hofkammer*. Meanwhile, the Court War Council, or *Hofkriegsrat*, had been set up to handle military matters, including the collection of extraordinary taxes such as the Contribution that the estates voted to support the army. But, with his subsequent subdivision of the hereditary lands and the extensive autonomy of the Bohemian and Hungarian regimes, both the *Hofkammer* and *Hofkriegsrat* were compelled to share functions with their counterparts in Graz, Innsbruck, Prague, and Pressburg. The only central organ that could claim competence for the entire monarchy was the Privy Council, but it was merely a consultative body without any bureaucracy to enforce its decisions. Moreover, all three bodies assumed a conciliar organization that was popular in the Spanish system of government but which suffered from the resulting diffusion of responsibility and power among their members.

Of course the monarchy's lack of unity manifested itself in many ways. One was in the total absence of a single, general assembly of the monarchy's peoples. By the middle of the sixteenth century the immediacy of the Turkish threat had enabled Ferdinand to reach an understanding with both the Bohemian and Hungarian estates by which they agreed to elect Habsburg kings so long as the dynasty could provide a legitimate male heir.

Their pretensions to independence were sufficiently strong, however, that they resisted attempts to assemble outside their own kingdoms. Thus, on only three occasions did representatives of as many as two Habsburg crownlands ever meet together: in 1530, when the Austrian and Hungarian estates convened at Linz; in 1541, when delegates from Bohemia and most of the Austrian lands assembled in Prague; and in 1614, when the Austrian and some of the Hungarian estates gathered again in Linz. However imperfectly attended these meetings may have been, they represent the only attempt at a general gathering of the monarchy's peoples until a truly comprehensive body convened for the first time in the middle of the nineteenth century.

The monarchy's lack of focus was also reflected by the ambiguous position of Vienna itself. The Habsburg dominions had no dominant administrative, economic, or population center. Prague, Pressburg, Graz, and Innsbruck all shared major governmental functions with Vienna. With 65,000 inhabitants, Prague was roughly the same size as Vienna. Even within the archduchies, Linz was a serious competitor to Vienna by virtue of its superior commercial position. Emperor Rudolph II (1576–1612) had actually moved the imperial residence to Prague for the last thirty years of his reign. Although his successors permanently reestablished the capital at Vienna, they did so principally because its central location between Prague, Graz, Innsbruck, and especially Pressburg (which was only forty miles down river) afforded it easier access to the dynasty's other capital cities.

The Habsburg monarchy and Germany

Finally, the monarchy lacked not only a common diet and administrative center, it shared no single crown or royal title. The Habsburgs of the seventeenth and eighteenth centuries wore a royal crown for Bohemia, another one for Hungary, and a series of lesser diadems for their various Austrian dominions. But their dignity of choice was the German imperial crown and the title of Holy Roman emperor. Which brings us to the final, and most complex piece of a very diverse puzzle. The Austrian and Bohemian lands belonged not only to the monarchy but to the Holy Roman empire, and the Habsburgs themselves were its undisputed leaders. By the beginning of the seventeenth century the dynasty had held the imperial title without interruption for nearly two centuries since the election of Albert II in 1438. But the new Austro-Bohemian-Hungarian monarchy that Ferdinand had brought together was far different from its fifteenth-century forebear. Through its control of the Austrian and Bohemian lands, the dynasty now directly ruled a third of the empire. Yet the acquisition of Hungary and subsequent Turkish invasion had saddled it with separate, extra-German commitments that increasingly forced it to divert some of its attention and resources from imperial affairs. The monarchy was, in fact, no longer an exclusively German state but an international combination facing both east and west. At the same time, however, the Habsburgs were determined to hold on to the imperial crown. At the beginning of the seventeenth century the imperial office still enjoyed some limited prerogatives, revenue, and prestige. More important, the Habsburgs prized their undisputed position as the leading German dynasty and continued to take their dominant role very seriously. Hence they continued to seek and uphold the imperial office as tenaciously as they did their rights in their own Austrian, Bohemian, and Hungarian crownlands.

The dynasty's Janus-faced attempt to manage both its own lands and German affairs was understandable, but ultimately beyond its resources. Its own diverse and disordered dominions were difficult enough to govern, especially in the face of foreign threats. By comparison it was impossible to rule the Holy Roman empire. Germany's constitutional and institutional framework was part of the problem, though they were not much worse than what the Habsburgs confronted in their own dominions. Each emperor's power was limited by his need to court the favor of those German princes who actually chose each new emperor. There were seven such electors at the beginning of the seventeenth century: the prince-archbishops of Mainz, Trier, and Cologne, the lay princes of Saxony, Brandenburg, and the Palatinate, and the emperor himself as king of Bohemia. In practice the electors enjoyed considerable leverage over each emperor, both at the time of his candidacy and near the end of his reign when he was eager to secure his designated heir's election as heir apparent with the title of King of the Romans.

Once elected, the emperor's constitutional prerogatives were virtually indistinguishable from those of many other monarchs. At the center of the government was the Imperial Court Chancery, which dispatched German policy in much the same way that the Bohemian and Hungarian Court Chanceries administered the business of those two kingdoms. A tri-cameral Imperial Diet, or *Reichstag*, served as the empire's legislative body, with the usual power to pass laws, raise taxes, and declare war. It was, in fact, only necessary for the emperor to obtain majorities in the College of Electors and the over two-hundred-strong College of Princes, but not in the essentially impotent College of Imperial Cities. The imperial judiciary was divided between two often competing courts. An Imperial Chamber Court (*Reichskammergericht*) was so hopelessly underfunded and paralyzed by princely rivalries that it could take over a century to decide some cases. By contrast, the relative efficiency of the emperor's own Imperial Aulic Council (*Reichshofrat*) afforded him more than a measure of power through its ability to adjudicate a wide range of legal matters. Finally, the empire's police and military functions were generally entrusted to a regional system of ten imperial circles, each with its own director and local assembly of princes belonging to that circle.

This was a complex, but not intrinsically unworkable system of government. The real trick to ruling the empire was not in winning majorities in the diet or judgments in the courts, but in enforcing their decisions at the regional and local level. Admittedly the smaller imperial principalities were more likely to comply with imperial directives, both because they were too weak to resist and because they relied on the emperor and the sanctity of imperial law to protect them against their more powerful neighbors. But the empire's great princes were capable of openly defying and acting virtually independently of the central authority. Many maintained their own armies and unofficial diplomatic relations with foreign powers, including the emperor's enemies. Hence, when they agreed with or were indifferent toward the emperor's directives, imperial government worked reasonably well. But, when they were in opposition, the emperor was powerless to compel compliance short of the use of force.

The power of the princes to defy and oppose the emperor eliminated any possibility that the empire itself would ever evolve into a governable state comparable to other European monarchies. By 1618 two turbulent centuries at the imperial helm had instructed the Habsburgs in the hopelessness of ever doing so. Hence they never really contemplated any attempt at "German unification" under a truly sovereign or hereditary ruler. Instead, as time wore on and the German princes grew stronger, the Austrian Habsburgs were increasingly compelled to deal with them more as allies and less as feudal vassals. In the process they realized that if they were to have a future as a great European dynasty it lay not in Germany but in its own, admittedly disparate crownlands. And it was there that they focused their attention. Although the Habsburgs continued to identify closely with Germany and to seek continued leadership through the imperial crown, they increasingly used it as a tool for serving the interests of the dynastic state that they had formed along and across the empire's southeastern border. Indeed, the dynasty – and many of its German-speaking subjects – retained this dual, though unequal identity well beyond early modern times until Bismarck expelled them from Germany in 1866.

Conflict or consensus?

Of course, the insoluble problems that doomed the empire and German unity made it all the more imperative that the dynasty complete the state-building process in its own dominions. If the Habsburgs were going to mold their disparate possessions into a viable state, they needed to reduce existing political, administrative, and cultural barriers by undermining the autonomy of their Austrian, Bohemian, and Hungarian dominions. They also had to acquire the right to implement taxes and other laws – and then enforce them at the local level, independently of the feudal nobility. That was the approach that most European monarchs took when confronted by similar circumstances. And that was also the path that the Habsburgs pursued from the beginning of the seventeenth century and, intermittently, thereafter. Furthermore, the same central European location that exposed them to aggression from several directions also facilitated their reception of new state-building strategies, especially from Germany and Italy. As we shall see, they did meet with a considerable degree of success. But the same geopolitical factors that had helped Maximilian and Ferdinand to acquire their dominions ultimately prevented their successors from converting them into a highly centralized, absolute monarchy. Elsewhere on the continent, countries like France, Sweden, Brandenburg-Prussia, or Russia could take advantage of opportune periods of peace or remoteness from foreign adversaries to strengthen royal authority and suppress the estates and provinces that opposed them. By contrast, the Habsburg lands' central European location almost always exposed them to at least one foreign power with whom their rebellious subjects might make common cause during a domestic conflict. Foreign intervention, or the threat of it, limited the extent of Habsburg attempts at centralization and absolutism, and left them incomplete.

This failure ultimately led the Habsburgs to pursue their domestic and foreign policies in ways that distinguished them from the continent's other great powers. For example, to the very end of the monarchy successive regimes tinkered with the central administration in the forlorn hope that, by rearranging or reconfiguring it in one way or another, they might attain through finesse what they had failed to gain through genuine reform. A second, still more crucial consequence was the Habsburgs' increasing willingness to govern by consensus. If the emperor could not wholly eliminate the distinctiveness of his dominions or overcome the power of the feudal nobility, then the next best solution was to earn their support by remaining sensitive to their political rights, social privileges, and economic needs. Such an approach mortgaged the central government's ability to integrate its dominions more fully. It also prompted the Habsburgs to strike deals with the most powerful social or national groups at the expense of those they deemed less likely to threaten domestic stability. But the sacrifice was worthwhile if the resulting symbiosis with the monarchy's major territorial and feudal elements eliminated internal unrest and enlisted their cooperation in achieving its most important dynastic objectives.

But the need to gain a consensus of ruling elites reduced more than the government's ability to pursue domestic reform or social justice. It also limited its freedom to fight wars, because these elites still controlled the financial means necessary to raise a large army. In practice this meant that the Habsburgs were unlikely to launch wars of aggression, both because they were aware of the monarchy's military weakness and because of the difficulties that they would have convincing their various dominions to make the necessary sacrifices. As a result they tended to be somewhat less impulsive or aggressive than the absolute rulers of France, Brandenburg-Prussia, or Russia, who were less dependent on gaining popular domestic support. In any event the monarchy's exposed central European location burdened them with a steady stream of likely attackers who rarely left them free to pursue aggressive designs of their own.

What the emperor *could* do was fight defensive wars that he could justify before the estates. In addition to mobilizing the monarchy's resources he was usually also able to continue the Habsburg practice of forming alliances with other powers that feared him less than his more powerful or aggressive enemies, especially when his attackers posed a threat to the international *status quo* and balance of power. Of course, by participating in such defensive coalitions the emperor was obliged to pursue only those goals that were acceptable to his allies. But that was a price he was generally willing to pay in exchange for the domestic and foreign support he received. Thus a Habsburg state that already depended on a consensus of domestic forces also came to rely on a consensus of other European powers in pursuing its foreign objectives. Indeed, patterns of Habsburg statecraft that later become associated with Clemens von Metternich, such as coalition and balance of power diplomacy and the maintenance of legitimate frontiers, were already evident by the seventeenth century.

The role of the dynasty

Needless to say, governing such a diverse state and enlisting support among domestic elites and foreign allies was far more difficult than ruling one of Europe's highly centralized absolute monarchies. Yet the Habsburgs have sometimes suffered by comparison with other dynasties. Historians have characterized them as a group of highly principled, conscientious, pious, and exceptionally moral individuals who nonetheless often lacked the foresight and decisiveness to bring their patrimony into line with the continent's other great monarchies. As a result they have been blamed for permitting the monarchy to proceed along what many historians see as a gradual, but steady decline extending from the reign of Charles V to its final collapse in the First World War. Even Austrian national historians have occasionally excused the Habsburgs' resort to moderation and half-measures as indicative of a certain "Austrian Clemency" that pervaded their character.

In reality the Habsburgs were temperamentally no less tenacious or aggressive than other rulers. As we shall see, they were capable of acting with the same mixture of determination, arrogance, intolerance, and brutality that has helped to saddle their Spanish cousins with the Black Legend. But, whereas the power and insularity of Spain might embolden its rulers to act with impunity, the Austrian Habsburgs could afford to do so only on the relatively rare occasions when they felt secure against potential adversaries at home and abroad. And, in those instances, immoderation usually proved counterproductive and ultimately compelled them to beat a hasty retreat. In short, "Austrian Clemency" stemmed not from some humane or docile mindset that was unique to the dynasty, but from its pragmatism in seeking to maintain its bridges to those domestic elites and foreign allies who offered the monarchy its greatest security. Indeed, even the few truly common personal qualities that united them, such as their conscientiousness and piety, were acquired traits that had been basically forced on them by the task at hand.

Nor were the Habsburgs necessarily the collective mediocrities of popular perception. Starting with the monarchy's creation in the sixteenth century they confronted the daunting task of governing a new dynastic state that was both diverse and difficult to defend. Instead of merely trying to hang on to what they had, they worked incessantly to strengthen their state and correct the flawed structure that Ferdinand had acquired in the sixteenth century. They succeeded in this role through persistence and hard work, imposing on their dominions integrated policies and a semblance of cohesion that would have otherwise been absent. The continuity that their policies provided did more to determine the development of their dominions than the actions of other sovereigns, whose responsibilities required less imagination and fewer emergency measures. Indeed, although some of the monarchs studied in this book were more talented and successful than others, all of them made a tangible contribution to the monarchy's development, even though they invariably left plenty to be done.

One indication of their pivotal role is the crucial part they played in resolving the great crises that periodically arose in the monarchy's history. It is possible to identify no fewer than eight occasions during its last three centuries when the monarchy faced dismemberment, whether through domestic rebellion, foreign invasion, or both: 1618–20, 1683, 1703–4, 1740–1, 1790, 1809–10, 1848–9, and 1916–18. It is no coincidence that all but two of these crises occurred at the end of one monarch's reign and the beginning of another's. This is because the mistakes or unresolved problems of one ruler tended to grow in importance until his successor was obliged to deal with them. That the monarchy's rulers quickly and successfully met all but the last of these challenges attests to their competence and – in the last case – to the high stakes that were involved. Nor is it mere coincidence that each chapter of this book is built around the first six of these crises that occurred before 1815. This is because each chapter deals with a major stage in the monarchy's development, and each stage hinged in turn on the resolution of a crisis, a turning point in the monarchy's evolution on which its very survival depended. In the end the monarchy emerged stronger and more secure from the successful resolution of each of these challenges. Indeed, the monarchy's greatest crises tended to precede its greatest achievements.

2   The Thirty Years' War (1618–1648)

The monarchy and the "general crisis"

The difficulties posed by the monarchy's diversity and exposed central European position preoccupied its rulers throughout its history. These problems were, however, compounded by other challenges that confronted it and much of the rest of European society at the beginning of the seventeenth century. Over the past generation most historians have accepted the notion that Europe was then in the throes of a "General Crisis" as it tried to adjust to the dramatic developments that had taken place over the previous century. The economy was changed forever by the dramatic expansion in trade and by the inflation, or "price revolution," caused by the influx of silver from the New World. Europe had heretofore had a predominantly barter- and subsistence-oriented agrarian economy controlled by land-owning nobles, but worked by their peasant labor force. It now began slowly converting to a money- and market-oriented economy controlled by the bourgeoisie and other capitalist elements seeking higher profits from trade and industry, as well as from agriculture. International relations were revolutionized by the sudden emergence of the new Habsburg world empire and the almost perpetual wars between it and its two natural enemies, France and the Ottoman empire. The need to feed the resulting arms race transformed domestic politics into a struggle between rulers and their people over the power to tax. Finally, the monarchs' concern for the security of their realms extended to their growing insistence on religious uniformity among their subjects, lest the growth of heresy inspire rebellion or civil war. The Austrian Habsburg monarchy faced all of these problems by the opening decades of the seventeenth century.

The economic crisis

As they entered the seventeenth century the Habsburgs needed to gain greater control over taxation, but first had to decide on whose shoulders the burden would fall. Whatever course they took the monarchy itself was not without the economic means to support an active role on the international stage. It is true that the Habsburg dominions never enjoyed either the commercial or manufacturing infrastructure of maritime societies such as England or the Netherlands, or the well-balanced economy of France. But they were not economically backward by the standards of the rest of the continent. The Bohemian lands provided the monarchy with a populous and productive manufacturing center that was complemented by the textile and iron industries of Upper Austria and Styria. The monarchy also enjoyed a firm agricultural base, especially in Silesia, the two archduchies, and its share of the Hungarian plain. Meanwhile, the mountains of the Tyrol, Inner Austria, Bohemia, and Upper Hungary made the monarchy one of Europe's foremost producers of over a half dozen different key minerals. Admittedly its regional economies tended to operate independently of one another and were not yet integrated by a single economic policy, but this was hardly as much of a problem as the monarchy's political, administrative, and cultural divisions.

The early seventeenth century was, nonetheless, a difficult time for the monarchy's economy. Although they may have been in the very heart of the continent geographically, the Habsburg dominions were no longer at the center of its trade routes. Expansion overseas had sharply reduced Europe's dependence on overland commerce originating in Italy and the Mediterranean in favor of the Atlantic sea lanes. The shift was felt most in the Tyrol, but also hurt the rest of the Austrian and Bohemian lands. The influx of American silver and gold also hurt the monarchy's mining economy, as did the increased extraction of Scandinavian copper and iron. Meanwhile, Hungary had been particularly devastated by the wars and constant border raids that followed the Turkish invasion. Losses in population, livestock, and crops were especially severe during the Fifteen Years' War (1593–1606), as the enemy began deploying armies of over 100,000 men, including thousands of particularly savage Mongol tribesmen. Nor was the damage restricted to Royal Hungary. Turkish attacks across the Austrian, Moravian, and Silesian frontiers were so frequent that towns typically erected bell towers, or *Türkenglocken*, to warn them of the approaching enemy.

Perhaps the most damaging development was the European price revolution. In the short term, inflation brought handsome increases in the profit to be made from exporting agricultural and other commodities to central and western Europe. In every part of the monarchy noble landowners endeavored to enter this market by increasing production of various products for export. Nowhere was this entrepreneurial spirit greater than in Hungary. Like their counterparts in the other sparsely populated lands of Christian eastern Europe, Hungary's landowners jumped at the opportunity by increasing the production of grain, wine, and livestock. By the middle of the sixteenth century the kingdom's *hayducks* were driving an average of 50,000 and sometimes as many as 100,000 livestock west each year. But the emphasis on commodity production came at the expense of ignoring investment in manufacturing. As a result the kingdom became wholly dependent on the import of finished goods, including all but the coarsest textiles, and even copper products that had been mined in Upper Hungary but refined and fashioned elsewhere. It ultimately paid dearly for its over-reliance on food production when, in the opening decades of the seventeenth century, a downturn in the central European economy brought a 50 percent decline in grain and livestock prices.

But the gravest consequences of the conversion to a market economy were borne not by Hungarian noble entrepreneurs, but by the entire monarchy's peasants and townspeople. In order to enhance profits landowners throughout the Habsburg lands strove to maximize productivity. This was by no means an unmitigated catastrophe since, among other things, it inspired greater efficiency in the organization and administration of increasingly large estates. It also led to the experimental cultivation of new crops, such as silk in Lower Austria and Moravia. In parts of Bohemia, noble entrepreneurs even constructed and stocked huge artificial lakes for the purpose of commercially breeding carp and pike. Estate owners in Lusatia, Silesia, and Bohemia also encouraged peasant households to supplement their income by spinning and weaving cloth for export to Germany. With the help of German, English, and Dutch middlemen, a small but productive cottage textile industry had evolved on many estates by the beginning of the century. But noble entrepreneurs also boosted production by arbitrarily placing greater burdens on their peasants. Hardest hit were enserfed peasants who were typically already prohibited from acquiring or selling their plots, or leaving the manor without their noble overlord's permission. In order to increase their profits noble entrepreneurs throughout the monarchy worked to reduce the amount of land that their serfs farmed for themselves, while increasing the size of their own demesne land. They then increased the obligatory labor service, or *robot*, that the peasants had to perform on those demesne lands. It is difficult to make precise generalizations because of the local variations in land tenure and labor obligations. Nonetheless, it is safe to say that conditions were most onerous in Hungary, where *robot* service rose from an average of perhaps one day a week in 1500 to three to six days a century later. Peasants in the Bohemian lands and Carniola appear to have suffered almost as much from this "new feudalism" that was now based largely on market forces and capitalist profit motive. By contrast, a few areas escaped these developments, most notably the largely free peasantry of the Tyrol and Vorarlberg, as well as the privileged soldier-colonists of the Croatian Military Border.

Nor were the exploitative effects of noble capitalism limited to matters of land tenure and labor obligations. Many a noble seigneur also tended to value his peasants as a captive source of suppliers and consumers. He might require them to process their crops at the manorial mill, brewery, or other facilities, and to sell all of their produce directly to him, often at a discount, so that he could then resell it directly to agents for export at the prevailing market rate. He might also insist that his peasants make all of their own purchases in towns and villages that lay within his seigneurial jurisdiction. Commercial imperatives such as these constituted yet another imposition on the freedom of the monarchy's peasants. It posed an even greater threat to the livelihood of so-called free towns that were neither owned nor subject to the authority of the local nobility but which now lost business to competition from the neighboring manorial towns or the nobility's foreign export agents.

Like the peasants themselves, the towns were not equipped to fight back without assistance from the crown. Indeed, as they declined under the impact of war, seigneurial competition, shifting trade routes, or the lack of industrial development, the towns were losing out to the landholding nobility in the competition for royal favor. Their relative position was evident in some of the regional diets, such as Lower Austria and Hungary proper, where all of the free towns shared only a single vote. By contrast, the political ascendancy of the monarchy's greatest landholders was most vividly illustrated by the crown's decision in 1608 to grant each of Hungary's roughly one hundred magnates individual representation in the upper table of that kingdom's diet. Given the economic and political trends set in motion by the new feudalism, it was virtually inevitable that the crown would avoid a confrontation with its resurgent aristocracy; instead, it would be easier to mortgage further the monarchy's economic development by shifting a greater share of the tax burden onto the backs of its free towns and unfree peasants.

Germany, Spain, and the threat of Habsburg hegemony

A second challenge that confronted the Austrian Habsburgs was their need to establish a secure position within the European alliance system. In the past they had benefited from close relationships with both the German princes and the Spanish Habsburgs. The two associations were, however, not necessarily compatible with one another. Nor were they strengthened by the dynasty's dramatic growth over the previous century. Both branches of the dynasty had originally risen to prominence in response to the need for a regional balance of power directed primarily against France in western and the Ottoman empire in eastern Europe. Yet it had been so successful that, by the middle of the sixteenth century, Spain had replaced its two nemeses as the principal threat to European security. As Christian Europe's second most powerful state, France could now count on receiving assistance from countries that had previously been in the Habsburg camp. Indeed, during the Protestant Reformation, several Lutheran German princes had enlisted French support against Charles V's attempts to maintain religious uniformity within the empire. The desire to rid Germany of Spanish influence was so strong that, when a defeated Charles abdicated in 1556, Catholic and Lutheran electors alike insisted on the succession of his younger brother, Roman King Ferdinand, rather than his own son, Philip II of Spain (1556–98). Emperor Ferdinand I (1556–64) and his successors managed to steer clear of Philip II's wars and, in the process, avoided crossing swords with the Spanish monarch's French, Dutch, and English enemies. Yet, as dynastic allies of Spain, the Austrian Habsburgs were still implicated in the Spanish threat to the balance of power.

The same prospect of Habsburg hegemony also troubled the dynasty's relationship with the rest of Germany. Despite gaining an upper hand in the middle ages the German princes had remained wary of the emperor's power. The dynasty's sudden emergence at the helm of not one but two large states had done nothing to assuage their fears. Indeed, many princes had used the appearance and spread of Protestantism as a weapon for undermining the authority of Charles V. Charles's troubled reign had demonstrated the need to reach an understanding with the major Protestant princes both in order to guarantee peace within the empire and to enlist their aid against the Turks. With his brother's abdication, Ferdinand I had immediately signed the Peace of Augsburg (1555), recognizing the equal right of Lutheran and Catholic princes to impose their religions on their subjects. By tolerating Lutheranism Ferdinand and his immediate successors ushered in a half-century of religious peace within Germany.

By 1600, however, the two confessions were again on the verge of open conflict. Both sides were at odds over the status of several imperial prince-bishoprics that had been declared Catholic by the Peace of Augsburg but which had since become Lutheran following the unexpected conversion of their bishops. They had also failed to resolve religious conflicts within several imperial cities. Nor had they anticipated the subsequent adoption of Calvinism by several German princes which, at the very least, added a more militant strain of Protestantism to princely politics. The prudent inaction of Ferdinand I and his successors had merely put off the inevitable conflict over the status of the disputed bishoprics and of Calvinism within the empire. Yet for the emperor to act would renew the Catholic–Protestant conflict, and at the same time excite fears that Habsburg power would be used to destroy Protestantism, if not German princely liberties altogether.

There was a sudden upsurge in Protestant paranoia when, in 1607, the emperor intervened on behalf of the Catholic minority of the imperial city of Donauwörth. The Protestants immediately reacted by forming the Evangelical Union, an armed association of nine princes and seventeen imperial cities led by the Calvinist Elector Palatine, Frederick V. Nor were princes without reason for concern. With the conversion of the lay electors of the Palatinate, Saxony, and Brandenburg the Protestants were only one vote short of controlling the next imperial election. Now, in response to the Evangelical Union, a competing Catholic League of twenty princes was created by Frederick's Wittelsbach cousin, the powerful Duke Maximilian of Bavaria. Both princely alliances were also in close contact with foreign powers. They needed only a just cause to push them over the edge into a religious civil war.

Religious conflict in the Habsburg dominions

In the end that push came from within the emperor's own dominions. The sixteenth-century Habsburgs had proven ineffective in opposing the spread of Protestantism within the monarchy. Their resistance had been tempered somewhat by humanist ideas that promoted free inquiry and Erasmian toleration. Indeed, Ferdinand's son Maximilian II (1564–76) had evinced Protestant inclinations in his own personal life and worship. His successor, the cosmopolitan Rudolph II (1576–1612), had actually turned his court at Prague into a center for unorthodox ideas and expression that ranged from unconventional art to alchemy and a genuine interest in scientific inquiry. His patronage of the Protestant émigré astronomers Tycho Brahe and Johannes Kepler constitute the monarchy's most significant contribution to the Scientific Revolution. But the principal reason for their timidity stemmed from what they perceived as a greater need to win the allegiance of their new subjects and mobilize popular support against the Turks. Hence, although the central government and the Habsburg archdukes who ruled Inner Austria periodically harassed their Protestant subjects, the threat of organized opposition prevented them from implementing a serious program of persecution.

By the second half of the sixteenth century the monarchy's peoples presented a confessional mosaic that reflected both Habsburg discretion and their own ethnic diversity: a majority of the German-speaking peoples of the Austrian, Hungarian, and Bohemian lands had adopted Lutheranism, as had most of Inner Austria's Slovenes and Upper Hungary's Slovaks; Vienna itself was mostly Lutheran. Hungary's Magyars had become overwhelmingly Calvinist. Although many Czechs remained nominally Catholic, most of them adhered to anti-Roman Hussite, or Utraquist, religious practices that had found an echo in the preaching of Martin Luther; meanwhile, many Czechs had converted to Calvinism or to the even more radical Church of the Bohemian Brethren. Although Croatia proper was largely Catholic, its Military Border was a haven for Orthodox Serbs. Indeed, of all the Habsburg dominions only the Tyrol remained essentially untouched by Protestantism. The Catholic Habsburgs were now a religious minority among their own people and had been compelled by their Protestant-dominated estates to grant varying degrees of religious toleration in every crownland except the Tyrol and Croatia proper. In most instances only the nobility and residents of free towns enjoyed freedom of worship. Yet, since most nobles were already Protestant, their peasants tended to be as well.

Toleration did offer some advantages. By accepting Protestantism the Habsburgs had removed religion as a source of conflict and promoted a certain degree of coexistence among the monarchy's different peoples, such as in Silesia, where Lutherans and Catholics actually took turns sharing churches on Sunday. By defusing the religious issue they also guaranteed the loyalty and support of their Protestant estates in the continuing struggle against the monarchy's foreign enemies. But all that changed with the coming of the Catholic Counter-Reformation. The reform and renewal of the Catholic church in the second half of the sixteenth century brought an intense commitment to reconverting the millions of Christians who had become at least nominally Protestant. At first this mission was borne independently by the various religious orders, most notably the Society of Jesus, which dispatched missionaries to preach and work among the monarchy's Protestant communities. With time, as the monarchy's Catholic laity became more committed to the spirit of the Counter-Reformation and convinced of its own righteousness, it became more impatient with the Protestant majority in its midst. Finally, during the closing years of Rudolph II's reign a previously reluctant central government committed itself to action.

A number of factors finally inspired the Habsburgs to confront their Protestant subjects. Their own religious principles doubtless played a role. So did the free hand they gained following the Peace of Zsitvatorok that ended the Fifteen Years' War in 1606. Indeed, both sides felt less inhibited about fighting each other once the common Turkish threat had subsided. Finally, Rudolph II and his successor, Matthias I (1612–19), were probably inspired by developments outside the monarchy. Both had been educated at the court of Philip II of Spain, where they could not have overlooked the terrible toll that religious conflict had inflicted on such confessionally divided societies as France and the Spanish Netherlands. Indeed, beginning with them the Austrian Habsburgs appear to have become convinced that only a uniformly Catholic society could be trusted to remain steadfastly loyal to the crown. At the same time they were doubtless encouraged by the example of their cousin, Archduke Ferdinand of Inner Austria, who had recently achieved some initial success in reintroducing Catholicism in his lands.

Whatever the causes, religious persecution began in earnest with the succession of Matthias. Although he encountered opposition everywhere, Matthias aroused the greatest resistance within Bohemia by attacking the religious concessions granted by Rudolph II's Letter of Majesty (1609). He began by rescinding the Protestants' prior right to construct places of worship on church- or crown-owned land. Then he started censoring religious publications and excluding non-Catholics from civil office. Finally, after Matthias had withdrawn their right to assemble and present grievances, Bohemia's Protestants decided to act. On 23 May 1618, following the government's destruction of two Protestant churches, a group of nobles marched into Prague's Hradcany Castle and confronted Matthias's two representatives, Vilém Slavata and Jaroslav Martinic, in their chambers. Following a heated exchange they hurled both men, plus their secretary, out of a window. As the three men fell sixty feet into the dry moat below, one of the conspirators taunted them by exclaiming "See if your Virgin Mary will help you now!" The survival of all three men, two with only superficial injuries, prompted a flurry of pamphlets claiming that eyewitnesses had seen angels swooping out of the heavens to break their fall to earth. Whether by divine intervention or sheer luck the three had, in fact, survived the celebrated Defenestration of Prague by falling onto a pile of manure that had been dumped directly under the window.

To be sure this was neither the first nor last defenestration in the city's history. The Hussites had launched their revolt by the same means two centuries earlier. Three centuries later the Communists completed their takeover by pushing Czechoslovakia's foreign minister to his death (though they claimed he jumped). Likewise the Bohemian rebels of 1618 intended their actions to symbolize a clean break with the established authority. A hastily convened diet promptly elected a new government and raised an army to defend the country. It was soon joined by Silesia and the Lusatias, which sent troops, and ultimately by Moravia as well. No less ominous for the Habsburgs were the reactions of their non-Bohemian crownlands. The nobility of both archduchies and then Hungary reacted to religious persecution in their own lands by aligning themselves with the Bohemians for mutual defense against the dynasty. As Matthias looked for help, only Catholic Croatia and the two Habsburg archdukes who ruled Inner Austria and the Tyrol remained loyal.

It was in the midst of this crisis that all of the Habsburg dominions suddenly fell into the hands of one man. The unmarried Archduke

Maximilian of Tyrol died during the course of 1618, followed by Emperor Matthias himself on 20 March 1619.[1] In other circumstances Matthias's demise might have mollified his rebellious subjects. But this was not the case in 1619. Before his death the childless emperor had designated as his successor his cousin, Archduke Ferdinand, who, after two decades of determined persecution, had virtually eradicated Protestantism among the general population of his Inner Austrian lands. Although a Bohemian diet had already elected Ferdinand as Matthias's heir in 1617, the nobility now refused to accept a sovereign who was certain to escalate the harassment of its own Protestant population. In August 1619, even as the German princes were electing Ferdinand to succeed Matthias as Holy Roman Emperor Ferdinand II (1619–37), the rebellious estates declared his earlier election as king of Bohemia null and void. They first offered the Bohemian crown to the Lutheran Elector John George of neighboring Saxony who, however, had the good sense to decline a confrontation with his new emperor. The estates found a more willing candidate in the young and adventurous Calvinist Elector Frederick V of the Palatinate, whose easternmost territories (the so-called Upper Palatinate) also bordered on Bohemia. Despite the advice of almost everyone, including the princes of the Evangelical Union, Frederick accepted his election and travelled to Bohemia, where he was crowned on 4 November 1619.

Posterity has justly criticized Frederick for irresponsible, if not treasonous behavior that helped transform the Bohemian revolt from a local, confessional conflict into a German civil war. At the time, however, he appeared to be in a far stronger position than his Habsburg adversary. In June 1619 Bohemian rebel forces had actually surrounded Ferdinand's new capital and only the timely arrival of some Styrian cavalry had saved him from capture. Moreover, in addition to 25,000 troops raised by the Bohemian crownlands and by his own means, Frederick could count on the active assistance of disaffected Protestants from elsewhere in the monarchy. At the time of his election the prince of Transylvania, Gabriel Bethlen (1613–29), had actually invaded Royal Hungary on behalf of the Protestant cause. By October Bethlen had joined forces with bands of Bohemian and Lower Austrian Protestant nobles in besieging Vienna a second time. Then, in January 1620 a group of Hungarian nobles assembled at Neusohl (Bansk Bystrica) and emulated the Bohemians by dethroning Ferdinand and electing Bethlen their king.

Despite their earlier commitment to Ferdinand I, the Bohemian diet and the rump assembly at Neusohl had used their kingdoms' elective privilege to

---

[1] The Tyrolean line established by Ferdinand I had actually died out in 1595, but Rudolph II had ceded Tyrol and Outer Austria to his younger brother Maximilian in 1602.

dethrone the Habsburgs and elect another dynasty in their place. Moreover, in Frederick V and Gabriel Bethlen the Bohemian rebels had enlisted foreign support in resisting the Habsburgs, just as had the Hungarian supporters of Janos Zápolya when they invited in the Turks in 1529. And, like his namesake a century earlier, Ferdinand II hardly had the resources to resist. Although the newly reunited Tyrolean lands were loyal and had sent some troops, they were too far removed to offer significant help. Likewise, Inner Austria continued to stand by Ferdinand, but the Protestant nobles who still controlled its estates were reluctant to mobilize against their co-religionists. By the beginning of 1620 even Croatia's heretofore loyal Catholic estates were in doubt, having threatened to seize control of the Military Border from Inner Austria and subjugate its free, Orthodox Serb *Grenzer*. Given the current constellation of forces within the monarchy, Ferdinand II seemed powerless to forestall the monarchy's dissolution or, at the very least, a complete capitulation to his Protestant subjects.

What saved Ferdinand and the monarchy in 1620 – and on numerous occasions thereafter – was the timely intervention of foreign allies whose interests its survival somehow served (see Map 1). The first armed assistance had already come at the end of 1619 from the Catholic King Sigismund of Poland, who orchestrated raids into Upper Hungary and Transylvania that forced Bethlen to withdraw from Vienna. At the same time Maximilian of Bavaria promised to mobilize the Catholic League, which was alarmed that Frederick's takeover of Bohemia would give the Protestants a four to three majority in the Electoral College. By the following March Ferdinand had also enlisted the aid of the Lutheran Elector John George, who was offended both by Frederick's militant Calvinism and by his wanton violation of imperial law. While Maximilian offered to conquer Bohemia proper, Elector John George undertook to pacify Silesia and the Lusatias. The price for their support was high, but worth the expense: Maximilian was promised the permanent transfer of the Palatinate's electoral dignity, as well as the right to acquire Frederick's German lands by conquest; at the same time Ferdinand agreed to pay for both invasions by pawning Upper Austria to Bavaria and the Lusatias to Saxony.

Aid from Spain came with fewer strings attached, and with good reason. King Philip III (1598–1621) saw the Austrian Habsburgs as a crucial ally in the continuing struggle with the Dutch and Frederick V, a natural enemy whose Rhenish territories threatened the supply lines between his lands in Italy and the Netherlands. Hence, by 1620 Philip had sent Ferdinand one army from each area, plus a third to conquer the Palatinate. With aid such as this the emperor hardly needed troops of his own. Nevertheless, generous subsidies from Philip III (1.2 million fl.) and an equally concerned Pope Paul V (380,000 fl.) enabled even Ferdinand to field an army.

While Ferdinand was building up this imposing array of forces, his adversary was becoming increasingly isolated. Frederick received no help from the kings of England and France, who regarded successful noble revolts against legitimate sovereigns as more dangerous than the survival of a far-off, demonstrably weak Habsburg emperor. By July their agents had even persuaded his own Evangelical Union not to come to his aid. Meanwhile, Frederick squandered his popularity within Bohemia by failing to curb his soldiers' depredations or his own contempt for his Lutheran and Utraquist subjects. With the coming of the campaigning season, the end came quickly for the "Winter King." First, Maximilian occupied Upper Austria and the Upper Palatinate. Then, the Spanish overran the Rhenish Palatinate. Finally, while the Saxons marched into the Lusatias and Silesia, a combined Spanish and Catholic League army under Count Tilly headed straight for Prague. On 8 November 1620 it took Tilly's veterans only one hour to rout the large, but poorly trained rebel forces at the battle of White Mountain. With Bohemia lost and his German lands already under Spanish and Bavarian occupation, Frederick was forced to flee into exile, never to return.

The Habsburg monarchy during the Thirty Years' War

The massive foreign assistance that culminated in the battle of White Mountain converted Ferdinand II from a virtual prisoner of the Hofburg to one of the most powerful and influential rulers in Austrian history. The new emperor was, in most ways, a typical Habsburg. He was a man of impeccable morality and piety, whose daily routine included two masses and at least two hours in meditation and prayer. No less typical was his dedication to the dynasty and the dominions it had acquired. What has always distinguished Ferdinand has been his reputation as an intolerant, almost fanatical, partisan of the Counter-Reformation, who stubbornly insisted on restoring Catholicism, no matter what the risks. In doggedly protecting his subjects from the evils of Protestantism he was convinced that he needed only to do God's work to insure His assistance, regardless of the temporal forces arrayed against him. This faith had been vindicated during his early years in Inner Austria, when he became the first Habsburg to restore Catholicism despite war with the Turks and the opposition of his Protestant estates. And it had been proven again by his miraculous survival following the Bohemian revolt.

There is a great deal of truth behind this characterization of Ferdinand II. Nevertheless, he was far less eccentric than his reputation suggests. Several of the seventeenth-century Habsburgs shared his faith in divine intervention and in the dynasty's providential mission. And, as we shall see, he was quite capable of flexibility and compromise when conditions required it. What made him unique were unusually favorable circumstances during the opening years of his reign that seemed to justify his sublime faith in Providence and the bold policies that emanated from it. In the East the monarchy was just beginning over a half-century of relative peace with the Turks. This was no accident. The outbreak of war with Persia inclined the Sultan toward peace. For his part, Ferdinand was committed to avoiding any provocation that might lead them to resume hostilities in the Balkans. Although both sides continued to launch devastating raids against each others' Hungarian lands, incursions were limited by prior agreement to frontier districts involving fewer than 4,000 men, no artillery, and immediate withdrawal from occupied territory. Though these conditions offered little solace to Ferdinand's Hungarian subjects, they posed no threat to the monarchy's overall security. Moreover, on those occasions when local Turkish commanders exceeded these self-imposed restrictions, the government in Vienna had the good sense to look the other way rather than risk drawing the Sultan into a two-front war that both monarchs wished to avoid. Having secured his eastern flank Ferdinand enjoyed the luxury of concentrating his attention in the West, where the triumphs of the Catholic League, Spain, and his own army afforded them hegemony in Germany for a full decade. Except for some military reverses during the early 1630s, the monarchy enjoyed a free hand in its Austrian and Bohemian lands until the end of his reign. It was the freedom afforded by peace with the Turks and his allies in Germany, rather than the zealotry inspired by his faith, that permitted Ferdinand II to put his stamp on the monarchy.

The triumph of the Counter-Reformation in Austria and Bohemia

During the Thirty Years' War (1618–48) Ferdinand II worked to restore Catholicism and enhance his own authority both in the monarchy and in the Holy Roman empire. We know far more about Ferdinand II's ambitious, but ultimately ill-fated imperial policies because of their long-ranging implications for Germany and their immediate bearing on the Franco-Spanish struggle for European hegemony. It was, however, in the Habsburg lands that the religious conflict had started, where the dynasty's primary interest lay, and where the emperor ultimately had the most lasting impact.

Ferdinand dealt most thoroughly with the Bohemian and Moravian crownlands. In June 1621 the government executed twenty-seven rebel leaders, whose corpses were then mutilated and exposed for several years on Prague's Charles Bridge. Several hundred more noble and burgher families were punished with the confiscation of their wealth. In addition to punishing individuals, Ferdinand also destroyed the underlying structures that had nourished the closely connected evils of political opposition and Protestantism. In 1624 he removed the Bohemian Court Chancery to Vienna, where he could control its officials. He then imposed the so-called Renewed Constitution (*Verneuerte Landesordnung*) on Bohemia in 1627, followed by a similar document for Moravia a year later. The law seriously impaired the Bohemian estates' ability to oppose royal authority. It replaced their right to choose future kings with an automatic, hereditary Habsburg succession. It also awarded the king various powers previously held or shared by the estates: although they retained the right to approve most taxes, he alone could maintain military forces, introduce major legislation, appoint and replace key public officials, and grant titles of nobility, even to foreigners. As a result of these changes royal administrators began to operate in the countryside for the first time, albeit in conjunction with commissions of local nobles. Ferdinand's restructuring of the country's religious constitution was equally far-reaching. Although the systematic persecution of Protestants had already begun within a year of White Mountain, it was the *Verneuerte Landesordnung* that officially ended Christian religious diversity in Bohemia. Henceforth only Catholics would be tolerated, except for a small number of privileged Jews. To underscore his commitment to the eradication of Protestantism, Ferdinand literally tore up the Letter of Majesty with two strokes of his own dagger.

By contrast, greater Bohemia's northern crownlands got off more lightly, mainly because of the intervention of Ferdinand's Saxon ally. Elector John George negotiated the Dresden Accord with Ferdinand in 1621, guaranteeing Lutheran religious freedom in Silesia in exchange for its declaration of loyalty and a subsidy of 300,000 florins. The Protestant cause was also defended by the Calvinist Piast and Podiebrad princes of Lower Silesia. Ferdinand had better luck in Upper Silesia, where he banned and seized the lands of the Protestant Hohenzollern margrave of Jägerndorf for his complicity in the Bohemian insurrection. Although the nobility continued to dominate politics at the local level, Ferdinand was also able to increase his administrative control throughout the rest of Silesia. Most notably, Silesia joined Bohemia and Moravia in placing its once independent treasury under the direct control of the *Hofkammer* in Vienna. In the end Upper and Lower Lusatia escaped Habsburg authority altogether. Originally pawned to Saxony, Ferdinand eventually accepted their permanent cession in order to keep John George tied to the Habsburg cause.

Ferdinand was also more lenient with the two archduchies, whose resistance had never led to an outright break with the dynasty. Perhaps it was their long association and close identification with the Habsburgs – or maybe just the greater proximity of Ferdinand's forces – that induced the Lower Austrian estates to make peace with him in the months before White Mountain. Whatever the motivation, they received from him a general amnesty and the retention of their privileges, including limited Protestant religious freedom. The Upper Austrian estates were less pliant and succumbed only under the weight of Bavarian occupation. Nevertheless, Ferdinand made no attempt to infringe their various other liberties following the end of the Bavarian occupation in 1628. His only meaningful innovation was the creation of an Austrian Chancery in 1620 to oversee the administration of the various hereditary lands that had been reunited by the recent deaths of Archduke Maximilian and Emperor Matthias. It was not long, however, before the archduchies' Protestants shared in the fate of the Bohemian and Moravian crownlands.

In his attempt to restore Catholic religious uniformity Ferdinand employed the same graduated process of persecution that had proven so effective during his early years as ruler of Inner Austria. Within his Austrian and Bohemian lands only Silesia was spared from such compulsory tactics. Persecution invariably began with the immediate expulsion of all Protestant clergy and schoolteachers, even in Lower Austria despite Ferdinand's recent promise of religious freedom. Protestant churches and other community property were seized or destroyed. Heretical works and other repugnant literature were consigned to the flames. One Bohemian churchman boasted of having burned as many as 60,000 volumes. Next came the implementation of forced conversion, first in the towns, then in the countryside. Burghers and nobles alike were generally given the option of conversion or expulsion, while peasants were essentially left with no choice at all. Only in Lower Austria were individual nobles permitted to remain Protestant, although they were subject to less overt forms of pressure. Enforcement was entrusted to "Reformation Commissions" that included representatives of the monarch, the local bishop, and often the local lord, together with a small troop of soldiers. Individuals were fined for not observing Catholic rituals such as mass, feast days, or fasts, as well as for less confession-specific trespasses like adultery or blasphemy. Finally, after a grace period had passed, recalcitrant Protestants received further punishment, such as the quartering of troops, the denial of Christian burial, and (in the case of burghers and nobles) ultimately exile.

Of course, compulsory observance did not guarantee inner conversion of the soul. The process of reeducating and reorienting the public was entrusted to a veritable army of priests who now fanned out into the towns and countryside, reappearing in many areas that had been Protestant for decades, including Silesia. Staffing such an enterprise posed a considerable challenge to the government. Ferdinand drew not only from his own priesthood, but from a truly international army of clerics that included Italians, Spaniards, Irish, and English exiles and, above all, Germans. Various religious orders contributed to the effort, though none more than the Society

of Jesus. Most important, the Jesuits established an instructional infrastructure that provided the monarchy with a continuous stream of teachers
for years to come. By 1640 two dozen Jesuit colleges were in operation,
including sixteen in the Bohemian lands, where an additional nine
institutions were also under development. By mid-century the Society also
ran or dominated all of the monarchy's major universities, including Graz,
Vienna, and Prague, together with the lone Hungarian university at Tyrnau
(Trnava). True to the Church's international mission, they attracted
students from all over Europe. The Jesuit University of Graz even gave
sermons in eighteen different languages.

The religious orders supported their instructional crusade by building
churches and other religious houses that showcased the triumph of the
Counter-Reformation. The wave of new construction was most evident in
Vienna, where they often built on land that had been seized from exiled
Protestant burghers. But the most pervasive instrument of conversion was
the steady regimen of clerical teaching, preaching, and devotional practice
that they fostered among the laity. The clergy's promotion of religious
rituals took several forms, most notably pilgrimages to shrines – many of
which had only been recently established – and the patronage of local cults.

In Bohemia the church sponsored pilgrimages to the White Mountain
battlefield and promoted the cult of its medieval king and patron saint,
Wenceslas. But throughout the monarchy it used popular devotion to
advance the belief that God had entrusted the Habsburgs with the divine
mission of protecting the True Church against its enemies. To support this
message it embraced Ferdinand's Providential interpretation of the miraculous survival of Slavata and Martinic, his own rescue from the two rebel
sieges of Vienna, and the subsequent victory at White Mountain. Above all,
however, the clergy and its Habsburg patrons looked to the distant past in
linking the dynasty with the saints and sacred symbols of the church.

They popularized existing legends that associated the Habsburgs with the
Eucharist, such as Rudolph I's gift of his horse to a priest who was on his way
to perform the Last Sacrament, and Maximilian I's escape from death while
climbing in the Alps because he was holding a sacramental monstrance. For
his part Ferdinand helped perpetuate the association by participating in
sacramental processions, such as Corpus Christi. The symbol of the Cross
was no less prominent in devotional preaching and literature, associating the
appearance of an illuminated, crucifix-shaped cloud with Rudolph I's use of
a cross and Ferdinand's rescue from the Bohemian rebels to his kneeling and
praying before one. Although veneration of the Virgin Mary was a common
ritual throughout Counter-Reformation Europe, Ferdinand and his apolo-
gists helped to forge an especially strong and historic dynastic link with the
mother of Christ. Hence their revival of the legend that Rudolph I never

undertook anything difficult without first appealing to Mary, and of true stories of Charles V's intense veneration of the Virgin. No Habsburg did more to strengthen the Marian cult than the emperor's son and successor, Ferdinand III (1637–57). His commissioning of a Marian pillar at Am Hof in Vienna at the conclusion of the war encouraged the erection of countless *Mariensäule* in town squares throughout the monarchy. He also began the lavish renovation of the pilgrimage church at Mariazell that soon became one of the monarchy's most cherished shrines. He even inserted allusions to the Virgin in the oaths of state officials. At Prague, so recently a hotbed of heresy and rebellion, university faculty annually swore to their belief in the immaculate conception.

Given the military superiority that Ferdinand II and his allies enjoyed after White Mountain, it is not altogether surprising that Bohemia, Moravia, and all of the Austrian lands meekly submitted to the inevitable triumph of the Counter-Reformation. The only major opposition came in 1626 when the Upper Austrian peasantry revolted against the appearance of Ferdinand's Reformation Commissions and the heavy taxes levied by the Bavarian military administration. It was, however, quickly suppressed by Maximilian and the forces of the Catholic League.

This is not to say that everyone converted. In Bohemia and Moravia Ferdinand's triumph and the massive restructuring that followed inspired one of the great mass migrations in European history. Perhaps 150,000 people – including at least a quarter of the nobility – left during the 1620s, to escape either immediate retribution for the rebellion or extended religious persecution. Although Protestant noble exiles who had not been implicated in the rebellion were normally permitted to hold on to their estates, many ultimately decided to sell them, often at bargain prices. Between government confiscations and private sales, over half of the two crownlands' manorial estates changed hands by the end of Ferdinand's reign. The new owners were mainly native Bohemians, most notably the prominent Lobkovic family and the previously obscure clan of the great Habsburg general, Albrecht von Wallenstein, but also Slavata and Martinic, whose fall from the Hradcany elicited a corresponding rise in their fortunes. Ferdinand also rewarded a large number of loyal Austrian and Hungarian families, as well as foreign-born soldiers and courtiers. It was this last element that infused the new Bohemian nobility with non-Czech names from all over Europe, such as Conway (Ireland), Gordon (Scotland), Bucquoy de Longueval (Low Countries), Marradas (Spain), Metternich (Germany), de Souches (France), and Piccolomini (Italy). To accommodate these families, as well as the country's large German-speaking minority, Ferdinand even elevated German to equality with Czech as the official language of Bohemia and Moravia. Although many foreign families resold their lands or died out, outsiders still comprised a large minority of the Bohemian and Moravian nobility at mid-century and lorded over perhaps 40 percent of their peasantry.

The turnover in the Austrian lands was much less extensive, but not insignificant. Several thousand Protestant nobles and townspeople left during the first decade of the reign. In Inner Austria alone, 754 noble families emigrated abroad during the three years following the belated removal of their religious freedom in 1628. Many Protestant Lower Austrian nobles chose exile, even though they retained the right of private worship. By mid-century, however, no fewer than 235 members of the Lower Austrian estates still identified themselves as Protestant. Although the government denied peasants the option of conversion or emigration, they were nonetheless well represented among those who left. At the end of the war came a final surge of perhaps 40,000 people from all social classes, including 20,000 Upper Austrians, once it had become clear that peace would not bring a restoration of religious freedom. Some resettled in Royal Hungary, but most migrated to Franconia, Swabia, and Saxony where whole towns sprouted up to accommodate Protestant exiles from the monarchy.

Of those who elected to stay, many secretly remained Protestant. Indeed, successful Catholicization depended heavily on the cooperation of the seigneurial nobility, whose participation in the Reformation Commissions and employment of the local clergy afforded them control over enforcement. Aside from those Lower Austrian nobles who remained Protestant there were Catholic nobles elsewhere who were less committed to implementing Ferdinand's policies. Moreover, many remote areas were beyond the effective control of government officials, nobles, and clergy alike. Indeed, clandestine Protestant communities survived for generations in remote mountain valleys, as well as in areas near the Saxon, Silesian, and Hungarian frontiers, over which passed a steady stream of itinerant Protestant preachers and prayer books. These exceptions cannot, however, obscure the extensiveness of Ferdinand's victory. By mid-century the overwhelming majority of his Austrian and Bohemian subjects had accepted his triumph and the restoration of Catholicism, a record of conversion without parallel in the history of the Counter-Reformation.

Hungary and the problem of Transylvania

While the Counter-Reformation made dramatic strides in Austria and Bohemia, its advance in Hungary was much more uneven. This was not because the Habsburgs made no attempt to convert the kingdom's Protestants. Rather, the key to the survival of Hungarian Protestantism lay in its continued ability to summon outside assistance. In the first half of the seventeenth century that role was filled by Transylvania. As the rulers of a multi-confessional society that tolerated Lutheran Saxons, Calvinist Magyars, Greek Orthodox Romanians, and even a large community of Unitarians, the princes of Transylvania were sympathetic to the plight of their Protestant countrymen living under Habsburg rule. When Rudolph II initiated systematic persecution near the close of the Fifteen Years' War, Prince Stephen Bocskai (1604–6) invaded Royal Hungary and compelled the king to reaffirm religious freedom at the treaty of Vienna (1606). At his death later that year Bocskai's testament explicitly urged his successor to utilize Transylvania's pivotal position between the Turks and Habsburgs to intervene on behalf of the kingdom's religious and other liberties. Beginning with Gabriel Bethlen a series of ambitious and aggressive princes did just that, frequently in tandem with the Habsburgs' foreign enemies. Bethlen invaded the monarchy three times in the first decade of Ferdinand II's reign, both to guarantee Royal Hungary's religious and other liberties and to enhance his own position and territory. Hence, although Transylvania was too far removed and its power too modest to reverse Ferdinand's victories in Austria and Bohemia, it compelled him to act in Hungary with a moderation to which he had elsewhere been unaccustomed.

Notwithstanding his reputation elsewhere for religious fanaticism, the emperor abided by the promise of religious toleration to which he had sworn in his election oath of 1617. He reconfirmed these guarantees and even ceded seven Hungarian counties to Transylvania at the Peace of Nikolsberg (1622) in exchange for Bethlen's surrender of the Hungarian crown that had been offered him at Neusohl two years earlier. He was also content to renew these terms despite subsequent Transylvanian invasions in 1624 and 1626.

Given these guarantees of religious toleration, the initial stages of the Hungarian Counter-Reformation employed tactics aimed at the voluntary, rather than coerced conversion of Protestants. As it did in Silesia, the government relied almost exclusively on the use of missionaries to provide a steady regimen of preaching, education, and devotional practice. The cult of the Virgin evolved quickly with the foundation of Marian societies in many of the towns, as did that of various medieval Hungarian saints, most notably the kingdom's founder and patron saint Stephen. Although other religious orders, such as the indigenous Paulines, played an important mediating role, it was the Society of Jesus that once again had the greatest impact. No churchman anywhere in the monarchy was as influential as the Jesuit archbishop of Esztergom and (after 1629) Cardinal-Primate of Hungary, Péter Pázmány (1570–1637). Exiled from his diocesan seat by the Turkish occupation, the Calvinist-born, native Magyar worked tirelessly from the Upper Hungarian town of Tyrnau to provide an instructional infrastructure for the kingdom's reconversion. He helped create seven Jesuit houses in Hungary (including two in Croatia), raised large sums of money to establish churches and schools, and in 1635 founded Hungary's oldest surviving university at Tyrnau. Writing in eloquent Magyar, Pázmány personally spearheaded an extensive literary campaign that reached his countrymen as no foreign-born cleric could. Even after his death the university press that he founded carried on his work with great effect.

Perhaps Pázmány's greatest contribution was his success in personally converting virtually all of Habsburg Hungary's hundred magnate families. Once converted, the kingdom's magnates generally exercised their prerogative to enforce the Catholicization of their peasants, whether by promoting the work of missionaries or by removing all Protestant churches and preachers from their estates. Given the choice between attending Sunday mass or no church services at all, many of them returned at least ostensibly to the Catholic faith. Not only did the magnates help propagate the faith, they also helped defend Royal Hungary against the dynasty's foreign enemies. With so much of the Habsburg military committed to fighting the Thirty Years' War, the magnates proved indispensable in raising and maintaining their own private armies against Turkish border raids and the constant threat of Transylvanian intervention. This was no mean accomplishment. For example, the 800-man garrison that the Batthyányi family employed at their main castle consumed 200,000 loaves of bread and 100,000 liters of wine each year. When added to the cost of the forces maintained by other magnate families, these expenditures saved the Habsburg king from paying considerable sums that would have otherwise been necessary for Royal Hungary's defense.

Toward a symbiosis of crown and nobility

After Ferdinand II's triumph and the changes that it brought in the Austrian and Bohemian crownlands, Hungary proper was in most respects the least typical component of the Habsburg dominions. Nevertheless, the role that its magnates played in introducing the Counter-Reformation and defending the country reflected the government's continued reliance on the landholding nobility throughout the monarchy. To a greater or lesser extent the central government still depended on local seigneurs to enforce religious uniformity, collect the Contribution, and administer justice in all three dominions. Given Hungary's easy recourse to externally supported domestic resistance, the Magyar nobility enjoyed the most control over local politics and, hence, the lives of the common people. But, this was still largely true not only in the Austrian lands and Silesia, but even in Bohemia and Moravia. After White Mountain, Duke Maximilian had urged Ferdinand to follow the example of Bavaria and install a centrally controlled bureaucracy in Bohemia that would reach right down to the local level. The *Verneuerte Landesordnung* did, in fact, destroy the Bohemian nobility's ability to oppose the king by eliminating its control over royal elections, legislation, the army, and key government officials. But, not unlike monarchs elsewhere, Ferdinand stopped short of ending its dominance over local politics, justice, or the manorial economy. Instead, he contented himself with purging what he saw as rebellious Protestant Austrian and Bohemian nobles and entrusting the monarchy's future to loyal Catholics. By leaving local affairs in their hands Ferdinand avoided the risk of alienating loyal nobles who would have resented being lumped with those who had actually opposed the crown. He realized how difficult it would be to rule without their support and cooperation, especially since he needed their help in meeting the challenge to his authority within Germany and Hungary, and the foreign threats that lay just beyond their borders.

And the dynasty was willing to offer a great deal in exchange for what it interpreted as the inseparable attributes of Catholicism and loyalty. As we have seen, loyal Catholic nobles from all over the monarchy had shared in the redistribution of confiscated Bohemian and Moravian estates after White Mountain. In addition, appointments to key government positions fell almost exclusively to Catholic nobles. This use of patronage was especially effective in confessionally mixed areas such as Lower Austria, Silesia, and Hungary, where the competition for lucrative and powerful positions enticed otherwise recalcitrant Protestant nobles to convert. Indeed, it may help to explain the ease with which Cardinal Pázmány was able to complete his work among the Hungarian magnates, who now strengthened their stranglehold over that kingdom's highest offices. No less persuasive was the monarch's bestowal of princely titles that often followed years of loyal service by the most wealthy and powerful Catholic aristocrats.

The crown also helped to strengthen the economic position of the nobility as a whole. Ferdinand II and his successors routinely approved the use of primogeniture to preserve the wealth, power, and prestige of noble families against divided inheritances. They also did little to impede the ongoing expansion of the nobility's growing commercial advantage over the peasantry and free towns. During the war landowners throughout the monarchy continued to extend their demesne land, often at the expense of peasant or common land. To compensate for wartime population losses, seigneurs were also allowed to increase the *robot* obligations and even to enserf other, previously free peasants. These victims of this so-called second serfdom now had to perform *robot* as well. The crown also awarded landowners various commercial privileges, such as the right to levy bridge tolls and market fees, that often came at the expense of local bourgeois entrepreneurs. By 1625 the gentry who dominated Hungary's county assemblies had even gained the right to set prices and wages. Noble seigneurs everywhere continued to exploit their peasants as both captive consumers and suppliers by compelling them to buy and sell from them, rather than neighboring free towns. These commercial advantages, plus the standard fruits of capitalist enterprise, helped to spur the growth of aristocracy throughout the monarchy. Thus, by mid-century just thirteen Hungarian magnates controlled 37 percent of the kingdom's villages, while the eighty-two aristocrats who sat in the Bohemian and Moravian diets controlled 62 percent of their crownlands' peasantry.

The tilt toward the landholding nobility – and the aristocracy in particular – was based both on traditional values that encouraged reliance on established elites and on the dynasty's perception that they could do it more good (or more harm) than the unprivileged orders. This spirit of accommodation came, however, at some cost to the monarchy's towns and peasantry. The towns progressively lost ground to the great landowners in the competition for both local consumers and foreign markets, most notably in Hungary, whose magnates gained a virtual monopoly over the country's livestock, wine, and grain exports. Their voice in the monarchy's diets eroded considerably during the war. The *Verneuerte Landesordnung* drastically reduced the number of towns represented in the Bohemian diet from forty to six, partly as punishment for their active role in the recent revolt. In the Bohemian, Moravian, and Styrian diets the towns were henceforth limited to a single collective vote, while in Carniola and Gorizia they were now excluded from participation in the powerful committees that helped govern each province. Frequently, they were not even allowed to take a seat, but were instead obliged to stand in the rear of the chamber for the purpose of receiving instructions from the representatives of the privileged estates. Indeed, as the Contribution necessary to finance the war soared, the crown permitted the noble and clerical majority to heap a disproportionate share of the burden onto the towns they represented.

It was the peasantry, however, that suffered the worst. By mid-century perhaps 90 percent of Hungary's peasants and virtually all of Bohemia's had fallen victim to the second serfdom. In Bohemia and Moravia serfs typically performed *robot* three days a week, with a quarter of them working the nobles' demesne land every day except Sundays and holidays. Contemporaries estimated that the combined discharge of labor service, rent, tithe and taxes consumed three-fifths of the average Bohemian serf's labor. Meanwhile the peasantry of rugged Upper Hungary may have suffered the heaviest labor services, given the relative scarcity of arable land and the large number of displaced Magyar nobles and border fortifications that they were called upon to maintain. Although the towns were scarcely in a position to do more than protest, the peasantry did resist *robot* by performing their compulsory chores in a desultory, almost mechanical fashion – hence the modern-day meaning of the word. They would also sell their draft animals, flee the manor, or simply refuse to work. Indeed, numerous peasant uprisings that broke out all over the monarchy during the years after White Mountain – and their savage suppression – had rather less to do with the religious aftermath of the battle than with its socio-economic effects.

The Habsburg defeat in Germany

Ferdinand II's triumph in the Bohemian and Austrian lands and the new spirit of crown–noble accommodation that accompanied it were critical developments in the Habsburg monarchy's evolution as a great European power. In the end they more than compensated for the dynasty's ultimate defeat in the Thirty Years' War. Although the emperor was always ready to serve God's cause, he entered the war in Germany with no preconceived plan or objectives. Instead, he was thrust into imperial politics immediately after his election by his allies' military successes. Although he ultimately devised his own policies, it was his association with their agendas – Maximilian's desire for Frederick V's territory and electoral privilege, the Catholic League's campaign against Protestant princely power, and Spain's search for allies against the Dutch – that helped prolong the war beyond its Bohemian origins. By tying himself to Spain and the Catholic princes, Ferdinand II divided his attention and resources between the empire and the monarchy itself. Most important, his renewal of the Habsburg dynastic alliance aligned the monarchy against the growing coalition of countries that were eager to reduce the Spanish threat to the balance of power.

The impending catastrophe was, however, hardly evident in the decade following Frederick V's defeat and expulsion from Bohemia. As a result, Ferdinand II acted in Germany with the same determination that characterized his treatment of the defeated Bohemian rebels. In January 1623 he fulfilled his earlier promise to Maximilian of Bavaria by banning Frederick V and transferring both his electoral dignity and possession of the Upper Palatinate to his Wittelsbach cousin. In order to legitimize the transfers, Ferdinand took the constitutionally dubious step of disinheriting Frederick's innocent heirs, just as he had done to the Hohenzollern relations of the margrave of Jägerndorf two years before. At the same time he permitted the Spanish to remain in possession of the strategic Rhenish Palatinate following the resumption of their war with the Dutch Republic. Although the Evangelical Union was soon intimidated into disbanding its own forces, the advance of Ferdinand's allies prompted several minor German princes and then, in 1625, King Christian IV of Denmark, to take up the Protestant cause. They were, however, no match for the forces arrayed against them. Although Spain's army was now committed to the war in the Netherlands, Ferdinand could still count on Tilly's Catholic League army. In addition, the emperor had raised a formidable army of his own on the strength of massive Papal subsidies and the resourcefulness of his own commanding general, Albrecht von Wallenstein, in tapping the wealth of the recently recovered Bohemian crownlands.

By 1628 the armies of Tilly and Wallenstein had scattered the renegade Protestant princes and compelled Denmark to make peace. With Germany at his feet Ferdinand II now availed himself of the opportunity to resolve the long-standing problem of those prince-bishoprics that had become Protestant since the Peace of Augsburg. In restoring them to the Catholic fold he doubtless felt that he was executing God's will. But he was also fulfilling his responsibility as emperor to enforce the compromise signed by Ferdinand I seventy-five years earlier. Not only did he seek the counsel of the other six electors. On the advice of the Privy Council Ferdinand II declined more radical requests by Mainz and Bavaria that he extend the decree to the confessionally mixed imperial cities and that he explicitly ban Calvinism.

The Edict of Restitution that he decreed on 6 March 1629 was no sinister master plan to destroy Protestantism or the imperial constitution. It was, however, a bold stroke that threatened to alienate many loyal Protestant states, most notably Saxony and Brandenburg, which had incorporated some of the bishoprics into their territory. Boldness was not a common attribute of the Habsburgs or their statesmen, but these were uncommon times in which they appeared to be firmly in control both at home and abroad. It was a measure of Ferdinand's sense of security that he unceremoniously dismissed Wallenstein and most of his 134,000-man army in 1630 in order to allay the widespread criticism of the general's ambitions and his troops' excesses. In naming Maximilian's general Tilly to replace Wallenstein, the emperor signaled once again his continued reliance on his allies.

Neither the emperor nor anyone else could have anticipated how quickly the situation would change following the intervention of Gustavus Adolphus of Sweden. Barely a year after Wallenstein's dismissal the great Swedish soldier-king was able to secure Saxony's defection and crush Tilly at the battle of Breitenfeld (17 September 1631). By the following spring Gustavus controlled much of central and southern Germany, and had either enticed or compelled the desertion of several of the Protestant princes. Meanwhile, with Tilly having died during the retreat, Ferdinand suddenly found himself without an army or a general to command it. Swallowing his pride, he did what had to be done. He again turned to Wallenstein, whose entrepreneurial skills quickly raised an imposing 100,000-man army that fought Gustavus to a draw at the Saxon town of Lützen (16 November 1632). For Ferdinand the best news was that the Swedish king had been killed on the battlefield. The worst was that Wallenstein had still not forgiven him for his earlier disgrace. In revenge this complex and intriguing figure purposely wasted the military opportunity raised by Gustavus's removal. Rather than drive an already wavering Saxony out of the war, Wallenstein withdrew his armies into Bohemia where his forces ravaged the lands of his sovereign instead. Worst of all he opened secret and treasonous negotiations with the emperor's enemies. Once confronted with proof of Wallenstein's treachery, Ferdinand rushed to remove him before he could secure the defection of the imperial army. A court faction headed by his son and heir, Ferdinand, finally persuaded the emperor to order Wallenstein's assassination, a sentence swiftly carried out by loyal officers on the night of 25 February 1634.

The monarchy had already lost the services of its best general months before the murder of Albrecht von Wallenstein. But, with his death, the emperor gained the use of two armies: the imperial army, whose loyalty he secured by appointing his son to command it, and a Spanish force of 15,000 men then marching north from Italy under the command of Philip IV's younger brother, the Cardinal-Infante Ferdinand. The two Habsburg generals symbolized the essential chemistry in the monarchy's earlier successes, both in their combined representation of state and church, and in their renewed expression of Habsburg dynastic loyalty. Indeed, the emperor's son had actually married the Spanish king's and cardinal-infante's sister, Maria Anna in 1631. Now, fifteen years after Spain's pivotal intervention in the Bohemian revolt, the younger Ferdinand had helped to recommit his Spanish brothers-in-law to the monarchy's cause.

Neither side could have imagined that the cardinal-infante's march constituted Habsburg Spain's last meaningful contribution ever to the Austrian monarchy. The crushing Habsburg victory at Nördlingen (6 September 1634) did, however, bring the emperor everything that he could have expected. Saxony and virtually all of the Protestant German princes made their peace with him at the Peace of Prague (30 May 1635). Ferdinand II again demonstrated his capacity for compromise, most notably by consenting to return to the Protestant princes all church lands that had been seized after 1627. He also acceded to Saxon demands for Lutheran religious toleration in Lower Silesia, although he was successful in limiting it to the largely independent Piast and Podiebrad principalities, plus the city of Breslau (Wrocław). In agreeing to these and other concessions, he adhered to the advice of his son, his councilors, the Spanish ambassador, and the Catholic German princes, while rejecting the pleas of his influential Jesuit confessor, William Lamormaini.

Both the monarchy and the empire needed peace. Meanwhile, Spain wanted the emperor's undivided assistance against France, which had just declared war eleven days earlier. Having long provided financial and diplomatic support for the dynasty's enemies, Louis XIII (1610–43) and his prime minister, Cardinal Richelieu, chose this moment to enter the war in order to keep the Swedes from following the Protestant princes to the peace table. France had long sought to weaken the emperor by supporting foreign enemies such as Denmark and Sweden, or domestic opposition from his German vassals. French intervention was, however, primarily aimed not at Austria but at Spain, whose destruction had been the main goal of French foreign policy ever since Richelieu's rise to power a decade ago.

For Spain and the monarchy alike the last phase of the Thirty Years' War is a dreary story of successive military setbacks. Once again it was Ferdinand II's good fortune to escape the consequences of his policies. With his not untimely death his son, Ferdinand III (1637–57), inherited the difficult task of coping with the monarchy's impending defeat. The new emperor deserved a better fate. He was as austere, pious, and dedicated as his father, but more gifted. He spoke seven languages, and found pleasing diversions in reading philosophy, conducting laboratory experiments, and writing music. If history has denied him a modern biographer and identity of his own, it is because of his bad luck of reigning at a time when the dynasty enjoyed very few choices. He did, however, make the most of what little opportunity he had. His decision to extricate the monarchy from the war was quick, appropriate, and painfully ironic. Having done so much to revive the Spanish alliance over the previous decade, he now recognized that the monarchy's survival depended on cutting its ties with his Habsburg relations. His decision to open talks with the French and Swedes within his first year as emperor was hardly a courageous decision, but necessity often compelled the Austrian Habsburgs to choose pragmatism before heroism.

Peace did not come quickly, however, partly because Ferdinand III was reluctant to abandon Spain to its fate, but also because he was unwilling to accede to his enemies' attempts to dismantle his imperial authority within Germany. The increasing toll that the war now took on his own dominions changed his mind. By 1639 the Swedes had reappeared in the Bohemian lands, parts of which they would continuously hold for the rest of the war. They delivered the key blow six years later when they occupied virtually the entire kingdom following their victory over a combined imperial-Bavarian army at Jankau (5 March 1645). Having just traveled to Prague to oversee Bohemia's defense, the emperor was compelled to return hastily to Vienna, thereby drawing unflattering popular comparisons with Frederick V's flight from Bohemia after the battle of White Mountain. In the weeks that followed, the Swedes entered the archduchies for the first time in the war, with advance units actually firing on Vienna itself. Nor did they come alone. Two years earlier the Transylvanian Prince George I Rákóczi (1629–48) had taken advantage of the dynasty's declining fortunes in Germany by demanding religious freedom for those Hungarian Protestant peasants who lived under Catholic seigneurs. Acting on cue, he now invaded Hungary and advanced on Vienna from the East for a possible joint siege. Although both the Swedes and the Transylvanians were soon obliged to withdraw – the latter at the behest of their Turkish overlord – the emperor now moved to save his own dominions from further destruction.

By the end of 1645 Ferdinand had capitulated to Rákóczi's demands at Linz by extending religious freedom to Hungary's Protestant peasantry and confirming the earlier cession of seven counties to Transylvania. At the same time, the dispatch of Austrian negotiators to the peace talks at the Westphalian towns of Münster and Osnabrück signaled Ferdinand III's willingness to surrender much of the remaining power of the imperial crown and to desert the Spanish Habsburgs. Although the German princes had been allied to the emperor since the Peace of Prague, they welcomed their impending triumph over imperial authority. Nor were they reluctant to abandon Spain to its fate. None of the princes had ever been comfortable with the emperor's Spanish ally, whom they still feared and blamed for over a century of conflict with France. In any event, by 1645, Bavaria, Brandenburg, and Saxony were all under enemy occupation and more than eager to end the war. For their part, the French, Swedes, and Dutch had no reason to regard the emperor as a threat once he had been shorn of meaningful power within the empire. Indeed, as Ferdinand's envoys signed the final articles on 24 October 1648 the Swedes were again knocking at the gates of Prague.

The Peace of Westphalia greatly reduced the emperor's authority in a number of ways. Above all it strengthened the position of Germany's Protestants. It undermined further the Edict of Restitution by restoring to the Catholic Church only those lands that had been conquered by 1624. It also guaranteed a confessional balance between the Protestant and Catholic princes by giving Germany's Protestant princely minority equal representation in the two imperial courts, as well as the right to veto all legislation by voting separately in the imperial diet on all religious matters. Finally, the treaty now recognized the rights of the Calvinist princes, who achieved equal status with the Catholic and Lutheran princes. Although their erstwhile leader had died in 1632, Frederick V's heirs were restored in the Rhenish Palatinate and given a new, eighth electoral vote to compensate for the one that had been transferred to Maximilian in 1623. Nor did the emperor necessarily derive comfort from the significant territorial gains of the three lay electors of Bavaria (the Upper Palatinate), Saxony (the Lusatias), and Brandenburg (eastern Pomerania and the bishoprics of Kammin, Halberstadt, Minden and, eventually, Magdeburg). Although they had remained loyal to the emperor through most of the war, their growth enhanced their ability to oppose him in the future. Indeed the treaty undermined imperial authority by officially recognizing the right of every prince to keep an army and negotiate alliances with foreign countries. Finally, France and Sweden also created new vehicles for frustrating the Habsburgs in the future. As signatories of the peace they became guarantors of the revised imperial constitution with the right to uphold the rights of the princes against the emperor. Furthermore, Sweden acquired western Pomerania and the bishoprics of Bremen and Verden along the northern coast, while France obtained the last of the dynasty's ancient holdings in Alsace – strategic territories along the empire's periphery that could serve as bridgeheads for subsequent invasions.

The impact of the Thirty Years' War

History has afforded the Peace of Westphalia its proper, prominent place in German history. It essentially defined the constitution of a divided Germany and its relationship with the Austrian Habsburgs for the next two centuries. Although neither Ferdinand II nor Ferdinand III had ever expected to Catholicize or control Germany as a whole, the war's reaffirmation of Protestantism and princely power dramatized the meager potential that Germany held for the dynasty. Thus 1648 marks a point at which the Habsburgs necessarily focused their attention and energy on the management of their own dominions. Although they continued to play a leadership role in German affairs right up to their defeat by Bismarck in 1866, they henceforth realized that their future lay in the fortunes of the monarchy itself.

Unlike the Holy Roman empire, the monarchy had suffered only minor territorial losses. The emperor's own subjects had, however, paid a fearful price, especially over the last decade. Three Swedish occupations in 1631–4, 1639–41, and 1645–8 had devastated the Bohemian crownlands as much as any other part of Germany. By mid-century a prewar population of over 4 million people had fallen by at least a third. Bohemia proper had been hit hardest, losing nearly half of its 1.7 million. Meanwhile, both Moravia and Silesia lost almost a third of their prewar populations of 800,000 and 1.5 million. Although many people succumbed to the atrocities of an undisciplined soldiery, the great bulk of civilian deaths resulted from the epidemics that tended to accompany the armies as they marched through the countryside. The steep population decline was bad news for the kingdom's farms and villages, many of which were deserted at war's end, but it was even more devastating for the country's towns and industrial economy. Not surprisingly the combination of wartime atrocities, epidemics, and exactions was felt hardest by urban dwellers, particularly males, whose weaker resistance to disease and eligibility for military service reduced them to roughly two-thirds of the female population. Thus, at one point in the war the Silesian town of Glogau had lost all but 122 of its 2,500 burghers. By 1648 both Prague and the principal Silesian city of Breslau had lost roughly 40 percent of their prewar population. Six years later 55 percent of Prague's buildings still lay in ruins. In Silesia, only 118 of Schweidnitz's 1,300 houses were left standing; the nearby textile center of Löwenberg counted only forty burghers and fourteen active textile workers from pre-war totals of 1,700 and 700.

The toll from the war was much lighter within the Austrian lands, where only those parts of the archduchies that lay north of the Danube had been exposed to foreign occupation. Nevertheless, perhaps 50,000 Protestants left the *Erblande*, including large numbers of artisans and miners whose departure dealt a blow to the Austrian economy. Although most of Hungary had avoided both the war and religious persecution, it did not escape wholly unscathed. Despite the half century of relative peace that followed the Peace of Zsitvatorok, Turkish raids had continued to spread devastation all across Hungary's exposed frontier, enslaving as many as 10,000 of the emperor's subjects a year and swelling the ranks of the country's *hayducks* to 100,000 strong. Yet even the simple herdsmen of the Hungarian plain were not immune from the ill effects of the Thirty Years' War. As the textile workers and miners of the Austrian and Bohemian lands had found out, the war had brought a general downturn in the central European economy that undercut the monarchy's export trade. Germany's demand for livestock had become so flat that Hungarian herders were sometimes obliged to return home with their animals from the Viennese fair. Finally, it is worth repeating that the *modus vivendi* that the dynasty reached with its nobles altered for the worse the underlying economic structures of the monarchy's free towns and peasantry.

Against the very real costs incurred by their subjects and their own ultimate defeat in Germany, the Austrian Habsburgs could measure the considerable progress that they had made in strengthening their position within their own dominions. By mid-century they had largely resolved the religious crisis that had sparked the Thirty Years' War. Whether by coercion, conviction, or simple expediency, the majority of the nobility had come to accept Catholicism. Aside from some Silesian and Lower Austrian nobles, only the Hungarian gentry remained Protestant. Moreover, the dynasty had helped to reestablish virtual Catholic religious uniformity among its Bohemian, Moravian, and Austrian subjects. The Peace of Westphalia had, in fact, confirmed the triumph of the Counter-Reformation there by reaffirming the emperor's right to enforce Catholicism in his own dominions, in keeping with the principle of *cujus regio, ejus religio* first enunciated at the Peace of Augsburg. Much of the work of conversion had, in any event, been achieved by 1648, as evidenced by the spirited defense of the Charles Bridge against the Swedes by the people of Prague in the closing days of the war. By then only Silesia and Hungary proper retained significant Protestant populations. At the insistence of Sweden and Saxony, Westphalia confirmed Ferdinand II's earlier commitment to tolerate their coreligionists in Breslau and the semi-independent principalities, but also won limited rights for other Lower Silesian Lutherans living under direct Habsburg rule. Meanwhile, in Hungary the treaty of Linz and the constant threat of Transylvanian intervention protected an uneasy Protestant majority.

Hand in hand with the dynasty's strides in re-Catholicizing its subjects was its establishment of a symbiosis with the landholding nobles that secured their loyalty to state and church in exchange for the retention of their economic, social, and local political privileges. Moreover, this loyalty was reinforced by the strengthening of royal authority in the Bohemian lands which remained, despite the ravages of the war, the monarchy's wealthiest and most populous component. Just as Spain had marshaled the wealth of Castile and Richelieu's France had increased the level of taxation in the *pays d'élections*, the Habsburg monarchy had now established in greater Bohemia a firm foundation for the projection of its power on the international stage. While focusing his attention on Bohemia, Ferdinand II also made some progress in overcoming the constitutional and administrative diversity of his dominions. Simply by reuniting all of the *Erblande* in 1619 he had begun the process of recreating a single, composite state, or *Gesamtstaat*, out of the dynasty's diverse dominions. He even drew up a testament in 1621 (and another in 1635) that declared the indivisibility of his dominions. Familial pressure obliged him to violate this principle just four years later by ceding the Tyrolean and Outer Austrian lands to his younger brother. Nevertheless, this new line of Tyrolean Habsburgs was destined to be shortlived. Ferdinand made another stride toward unifying his realm by creating an Austrian Chancery in 1620 and transferring the Bohemian Chancery to Vienna four years later. Together with the Hungarian Chancery, the highest administrative offices of the monarchy's three components were now concentrated in the same place. Ferdinand himself signaled his growing awareness that the dynasty's future lay with its own dominions, rather than with Germany, by beginning to shift the conduct and dispatch of foreign policy from the Imperial Court Chancery to the Austrian Chancery, a trend that would be continued by his immediate successors.

For all these achievements Ferdinand II clearly emerges as the most pivotal figure in the century since the monarchy's creation by Ferdinand I. It is worth reiterating, however, that his successes stemmed not so much from his religious zeal as from his ability to work with geopolitical and diplomatic realities over which he had little control. His willingness to tolerate Turkish provocations on his eastern flank and to make concessions to his Protestant adversaries in Hungary, Transylvania, and Germany illustrate his sensitivity to these forces. Of course, Ferdinand III was also subject to these same factors and, although history has chosen to ignore him, he also made a crucial contribution to the monarchy's destiny. Whereas his father had survived the great crisis of 1619 by appealing to his allies, Ferdinand III insured the monarchy's recovery from the events of 1645 by deserting them. By concluding a separate peace at Westphalia, the emperor forced his brother-in-law, Philip IV, to fight on alone in an already hopeless struggle against France. His was the right decision. Spain was doomed to defeat no matter what the monarchy did. At least Ferdinand III – unlike the Habsburgs of World War I – had the good sense to dissociate himself from the threat that his loyal, but all-too-powerful ally posed to European security before it dragged the monarchy down with it. Indeed, given the monarchy's exposed geographical position, it never could have risen as a great power so long as it had an ally with as many enemies as Spain. If there was a virtue to be found in the monarchy's capitulation at Westphalia, it was that the dramatic reduction of imperial power in Germany and the isolation and imminent collapse of Spain made it possible for the monarchy to remove the fears of its former adversaries. Only after these apprehensions had been allayed could the monarchy ever emerge as a great power by the traditional Habsburg recourse to coalition diplomacy.

3   Facing east: Hungary and the Turks (1648–1699)

The Westphalian aftermath

Notwithstanding the triumphs and accomplishments of the previous three decades, the Habsburg dominions confronted a number of challenges following the Peace of Westphalia. Above all they desperately needed a period of peace to recover from the wartime devastation wrought by a combination of invading armies and royal tax collectors. Although the dynasty had forged a working relationship with its landholding aristocracy based on loyalty, patronage, and a common faith, the central government still had to convert its essentially disparate dominions into an integrated state; Hungary in particular remained administratively, constitutionally, and confessionally distinct from the rest of the monarchy. Outside the monarchy the renewed emergence of France, and lately Sweden, as powerful and aggressive adversaries compounded the traditional threat posed by the Ottoman empire in the east. Given the impending collapse of Spain and deep divisions that the Thirty Years' War had engendered among his German vassals, the emperor needed to meet these new challenges to the monarchy's security by reestablishing or reviving an effective alternative to the alliance system of the past century. Each of these problems would be resolved by the end of the seventeenth century. Success would not, however, come easily.

Foreign affairs: isolation and insecurity

The monarchy's international position looked especially bleak at mid-century. By itself the Peace of Westphalia had done little to check the continued growth of French and Swedish power, or the emperor's own diplomatic isolation. Once they had suppressed the revolt of the Fronde in the summer of 1653, the young Louis XIV (1643–1715) and his prime minister Cardinal Mazarin were able to devote their undivided attention to the final stage of their war with Spain. The cession of the Habsburgs' Alsatian lands to France had already cut the Spanish Road between the Low Countries and Italy; with the surprise entry of Cromwell's England into the war in 1654, the Spanish Netherlands' encirclement was complete. Helpless as he was to assist his Habsburg brother-in-law, Ferdinand III's most pressing concern was the Swedes. They had not evacuated the Bohemian crownlands until 1650, after the emperor (or, more accurately, his subjects) had paid them 5 million fl. for the costs of their occupation. Nearly four more years passed before their forces had withdrawn from the rest of the *Reich*, following the satisfaction of all of the territorial, religious, and financial terms of the peace.

No sooner had the Swedes left the empire than their new king, Charles X Gustavus (1654–60), took advantage of a border conflict between Poland and Russia by invading Poland in the summer of 1655. By the end of the year he had occupied much of the country. Although Elector Frederick William of Brandenburg was troubled by this latest example of Swedish expansion, he joined forces with Charles in January 1656 in the expectation of balancing Charles's gains with his own Polish conquests. By December the new prince of Transylvania, George II Rákóczi (1648–60), had launched his own invasion from the south, after being offered southeastern Poland and the prospect of the Polish crown. By 11 April 1657 the combined armies of Charles X and Rákóczi met in apparent triumph at the Polish city of Sandomierz. Although Poland was not formally allied with the emperor, the impending partition of his northern neighbor represented a grievous blow to the monarchy's security, especially since it would be accompanied by a corresponding extension of the influence of the Habsburgs' Swedish and Transylvanian adversaries. Nevertheless, given the monarchy's current isolation and desperate need for peace, Ferdinand III could do little more than offer the Polish King John Casimir a mere 4,000 auxiliaries and a safe refuge in Austrian Silesia.

Although the triumph of France in the west and Sweden and Transylvania in the east seriously jeopardized the monarchy's international position and security, the greatest threat of all now arose in central Europe, where the Habsburgs suddenly faced the prospect of losing the imperial crown. On 2 April 1657, Ferdinand III died. The death of the 50-year-old emperor was not wholly unexpected. The strain of his earlier military campaigns and subsequent imperial responsibilities had long since taken their toll. Several years earlier he had attempted to insure the dynasty's retention of the imperial crown by having the eldest of his three sons, Ferdinand Maria, elected King of the Romans prior to his death. Yet no sooner had he secured his election (31 May 1653) and coronation as King Ferdinand IV (18 June 1654) than the 21-year-old heir died of smallpox just three weeks later. Ferdinand III quickly arranged for his next oldest son, the 14-year-old Leopold Ignatius, to succeed in the Habsburg lands by securing his election and coronation as king of Hungary (1655) and by having him crowned king of Bohemia (1656). But imperial law prohibited anyone from succeeding as German emperor before the age of eighteen.

The four-year wait for Leopold to become eligible for election gave the dynasty's enemies a golden opportunity to contest its control of the imperial crown. Mazarin was especially assiduous in cultivating alternative candidates for the imperial throne, including the elector of Bavaria and his own master, Louis XIV. Like the current military resurgence of France and Sweden, Mazarin's prospect of dethroning the Habsburgs was another unwelcome residue of the dynasty's defeat in the Thirty Years' War. He had little trouble nurturing the residual fear of Habsburg authority within the *Reich*. Nor had the three Protestant electors forgotten the Edict of Restitution and the Habsburgs' readiness to advance the Catholic cause within the empire. Finally, he played on the continued German fear that Leopold would renew his dynasty's alliance with Spain, either by intervening in the Franco-Spanish war or by inheriting Spain itself on the death of the childless Philip IV.

Yet, while none of the German electors wanted a Habsburg state capable of threatening them, they also appreciated the role it played in maintaining the empire's internal peace, or *Reichsfriede*, and protecting them against potential foreign enemies like France, Sweden, or the Turks. In fact, during the first years after the war, many German princes had formed a series of armed associations to protect themselves not only against Spain and the emperor, but against the anarchy into which parts of the empire had fallen following his defeat. Nobody better appreciated the princely dilemma than the influential archbishop-elector of Mainz, John Philip von Schönborn. As the ruler of Mainz, John Philip held considerable constitutional pre-rogatives through his position as imperial archchancellor. He presided over most of the empire's central organs, including the *Reichstag*, the imperial chamber court, and even the imperial chancery through his personally designated appointee, the imperial vice chancellor. He was also a true cham-pion of the smaller states that relied heavily on the emperor's policing power to retain their security against the ambitions of Germany's most powerful princes. Hence, while he too feared the specter of Habsburg absolutism, John Philip genuinely desired to preserve the effectiveness of imperial institutions, including its executive authority.

In the final analysis the German electors, together with the rest of the European powers, needed to make some refinements in the balance of power within post-Westphalian Europe, by defining the role of the imperial crown, the Polish commonwealth, and ultimately the Austrian Habsburg monarchy itself. By the spring of 1657 the successes of the dynasty's enemies compelled them to redress that balance at least somewhat in the monarchy's favor. Within a month of Charles X's junction with Rákóczi, Denmark compelled Charles X to withdraw most of his forces by invading Sweden proper. At the same time the Sultan expressed his own alarm over the ambitions of his Transylvanian tributary by dispatching Tartar auxiliaries to sweep Rákóczi's army from Poland. By July Rákóczi had concluded a separate peace with John Casimir and rushed back to Transylvania to face the Sultan's wrath. One month later Russia attacked Sweden's Baltic provinces, even though it was technically still at war with Poland. Then, in September, Frederick William switched sides in exchange for Poland's surrender of its claim to sovereignty over the Hohenzollern duchy of Prussia, and promptly attacked Swedish Pomerania. Although Leopold still hesitated to declare war formally on Sweden, these dramatic developments emboldened him to take a more active role in the war by providing John Casimir with a much larger force of auxiliaries for service against them. Although the war with Sweden dragged on for two more years, it was clear by the end of 1657 that Poland's integrity – and the monarchy's northeastern flank – had been secured.

While Poland's neighbors were moving to preserve its independence, the German electors were belatedly agreeing to perpetuate Habsburg control of the imperial crown. Victory did not come cheaply. Leopold was obliged to ply several electors with bribes raised by a combination of taxes, borrowing, and Spanish subsidies. The most costly vote belonged to Frederick William, whom Leopold paid 150,000 taler, ostensibly to compensate Brandenburg for Emperor Ferdinand II's seizure of the Hohenzollerns' Silesian duchy of Jägerndorf in 1621. In addition he was obliged to recognize Prussian independence from Poland and commit the monarchy to greater involvement in the war against Sweden. Much easier and even more pivotal was the vote of the new elector of Bavaria, who exhibited none of his late father's ambitions. By readily throwing its support to Leopold, Bavaria left France and the three archbishop-electors without a viable alternative Catholic candidate for the imperial crown, despite Mazarin's desperate attempts to promote Louis XIV.

Yet Leopold could not be sure of his election until he had won the outright support of the ecclesiastical electors and their leader, John Philip of Mainz. If anything, the archchancellor's desire to retain the Habsburgs had grown since the death of Ferdinand IV, since he saw in their Austrian and Bohemian lands the only critical mass capable of providing the empire with a *militia perpetua* to defend it against growing French and Swedish power. Four years later his only concern was the prospect of Leopold's perpetuating the Austro-Spanish alliance, especially if he were to inherit the Spanish empire on the death of Philip IV. To forestall that possibility John Philip had even queried Leopold's male Austrian relatives, including his uncle and Tyrolean cousins, about their interest in the imperial crown. The timely birth of a son to the king of Spain at the end of 1657 eased the archchancellor's concerns somewhat. Over the next six months, however, he attached a number of strings to his vote, each of which was intended to restrain Leopold from reestablishing the Austro-Spanish alliance of old. To reduce further the chances of his inheriting the Spanish crown, John Philip compelled Leopold to forego his anticipated marriage to Philip IV's elder daughter, Maria Theresa. He was also obliged to sign a neutrality treaty with Louis XIV. The archchancellor fortified this agreement with an electoral capitulation (*Wahlkapitulation*) signed by Leopold and all of the electors, which not only placed new restrictions on imperial power, but explicitly required the empire to remain strictly neutral in the closing stages of the Franco-Spanish war. Having made all of these concessions, Leopold was duly elected to succeed his late father as emperor on 18 July 1658, just one month after his eighteenth birthday. Even then John Philip was not finished in his search for guarantees. A fortnight after Leopold's ceremonial coronation in Frankfurt the archchancellor formed the so-called *Rheinbund*, an association of German princes that ultimately came to include not only the three archbishop-electors and several Protestant princes (including Brandenburg), but also Charles X of Sweden (as duke of Bremen and Verden) and Louis XIV. Its members agreed to prevent the emperor from infringing on the princely privileges guaranteed by the Peace of Westphalia or on its neutrality by sending troops across imperial territory to assist Spain in the Low Countries. The *Rheinbund* reminded the new emperor that he was still largely isolated and was valued by his vassals only as a counterweight against the emergence of greater threats to their security.

Leopold found out how alone he stood in the years immediately following his succession. On 7 November 1659 France and Spain ended a quarter century of hostilities by signing the Peace of the Pyrenees. Six months later the war in Poland came to a close following the signing of another peace treaty at the monastery of Oliva, near Danzig (3 May 1660). Although both France and Sweden made valuable acquisitions along their respective frontiers, none of their gains posed an overt threat to the monarchy itself. Yet, in exchange for French moderation, Mazarin compelled Philip IV to wed Maria Theresa to Louis XIV. There was a certain symmetry to Mazarin's policy: a decade ago he had compelled Ferdinand III to desert his Spanish brother-in-law at Westphalia; now Philip IV was reluctantly paying Vienna back by forsaking its long-standing Austrian marriage alliance. The match gave France the chance to inherit Spain itself should its king leave no male heirs. Admittedly Philip had obliged both the French and his daughter to renounce any claim she might have to the Spanish inheritance. Nevertheless, that renunciation was made contingent upon the payment of 500,000 crowns in compensation, an indemnity that bankrupt Spain was never able to pay. There was, in any event, considerable doubt in an age of divine right monarchs whether royalty could renounce inheritances granted by God.

Philip IV hastened to make amends by betrothing his second daughter,

Margaret, to Leopold, but her claim was correspondingly weaker than Maria Theresa's and she was, at age 9, still too young to marry and bear Leopold an heir. In the meantime Philip's infant son, Philip Prosper, died on 1 November 1661. Five days later his Austrian Habsburg wife gave birth to another boy. This, however, was the sickly Charles the Sufferer, whose numerous ailments could be traced to generations of inbreeding between the Austrian and Spanish Habsburgs – and perhaps to Philip's legendary sexual escapades, which had brought venereal disease into the king's family, together with thirty-odd bastards. Thus, despite having boasted four healthy adult males as recently as 1632 (to which could be added Philip's two newly born sons) the Spanish Habsburgs now stood on the verge of extinction. Remarkably, their demise foreshadowed an even more sudden and unexpected thinning of the dynasty's Austrian branch. As late as 1654 there had been no fewer than seven male Austrian Habsburgs about. But the deaths of Ferdinand IV (1654) and Ferdinand III (1657) had been followed in rapid succession by those of Leopold's uncle (1662), younger brother (1664), and the last two Tyrolean Habsburgs (1662 and 1665). When Philip IV died in September 1665, the 25-year-old bachelor Leopold and the sickly 4-year-old Charles were the only remaining male members of the once fertile dynasty. Thus, by mid-decade Leopold needed to produce an heir not only to stake a claim to the Spanish inheritance, but just to perpetuate his own line.

Domestic affairs: consolidation and centralization

The monarchy's continued isolation and the impending dynastic crisis placed a great burden on the new emperor's shoulders. Given the sad state of Spain's national economy and royal line, the old recourse to dynastic solidarity would clearly be insufficient, even if it did not inspire reflexive opposition from the German princes. For the time being he would have to rely on the monarchy's own resources for its security needs, and build on them accordingly. This remained, however, a daunting task, especially for a young and inexperienced ruler who had received no instruction in statecraft prior to his brother's unexpected death.

Leopold certainly had his gifts. He lacked neither intelligence nor intellect. He spoke five languages with an impressive degree of fluency. He was instinctively curious, an avid reader of history, science, and literature, and – like his father – a lover and gifted composer of music. A typical Habsburg, he was a man of great personal integrity and morality whose sense of duty made him a well-informed and diligent statesman. Leopold was, however, an unlikely hero. Like his cousin Charles, Leopold paid a physical price for having two Habsburg parents by being the ugliest member of his branch of the family. The outward jut of his jaw and lower lip was so exaggerated that he could not keep water from entering his mouth when it rained. Though he was an accomplished horseman who shared his father's passion for hunting, he had no interest in soldiering nor, for that matter, in war itself. More to the point, his naturally mild temperament prompted a phlegmatism and lack of resolve that often frustrated his advisors and allies.

Leopold's religious education doubtless accentuated his inertial tendencies. Originally trained by the Jesuits for a career in the church, he derived from his religious preparation not only an intense piety but also a faith in the decisiveness of divine guidance and intervention, rather than human action. Successive generations of Habsburg Marian devotion had, in fact, borne fruit in Leopold. He once exclaimed that "I want to have the most holy Virgin Mary as my commander-in-chief in wartime and my ambassador during peace negotiations." He acknowledged her favor by giving her name to seven of his nine daughters and by making numerous pilgrimages to the shrine at Mariazell. Yet it was this same search for guidance that often encouraged Leopold to delay or refrain altogether from making difficult decisions. Before long, even papal diplomats complained of his "excessive piety and fatalism."

The emperor's piety was also reflected in the makeup of his court. Leopold readily perpetuated the favored position of the Jesuits, from whose ranks he took a series of confessors. At the same time he depended most heavily for advice on a succession of intimate friends from other monastic orders, such as the Franciscan friar Hippolito de Pergine, and the Capuchins Marco d'Aviano and Emmerich Sinelli, who later became bishop of Vienna. Yet, as influential as these men were, almost all of the highest governmental positions remained the preserve of lay aristocrats. None was more important than the emperor's Grand Chamberlain (*Obersthofmeister*), often a close personal friend, who served as unofficial prime minister. Like his predecessors, Leopold also readily appointed (and frequently ennobled) talented and industrious commoners to staff the new and increasingly important Austrian Chancery, as well as numerous subordinate positions within the highest councils of state. These trained professionals were usually jurists and always Catholic, whether by birth or conversion.

From the moment of Leopold's succession until his death nearly a half century later the government's most pressing need was to raise the level of state income. The costly imperial election of 1658 and the Polish conflict had immediately dashed any hopes that the monarchy could receive appreciable fiscal relief from the heavy burdens of the Thirty Years' War. Moreover, the series of wars and foreign threats that surfaced during the reign obliged Leopold to enlarge steadily the 25,000-man standing army that his father had retained after the Peace of Westphalia, until it had reached 65,000 men by 1664 and 100,000 by the end of the century.

The government initially visualized two ways of raising the funds to support these forces: greater administrative efficiency and higher taxation. The Polish war had exposed the inadequacy of the monarchy's fiscal and military system, which was plagued by incompetent and dishonest officials who often staffed redundant administrative agencies that operated at cross purposes with one another. Unfortunately, Leopold's mild temperament was ill suited for administrative restructuring or the dismissal of expendable, but otherwise loyal officials. That Leopold was more inclined to appoint officials than dismiss them is illustrated by his handling of the Privy Council. Since its creation by Ferdinand I the Privy Council had served as the monarchy's highest deliberative body, a select group of no more than a dozen top state officials. Within a decade Leopold's patronage had swollen the Council to about sixty members, making it too unwieldy to perform its original function. By 1669 he had formed a new, smaller policy-making body, the Privy Conference, or *Geheime Konferenz* to replace the now useless Privy Council. It was not long, however, before Leopold had named so many of his favorites to the Privy Conference that it too had outgrown its usefulness. Aside from this dubious innovation Leopold did very little to reform the highest central offices. The council that most needed overhauling, the *Hofkammer*, remained a weak collegiate body that exercised little effective control over its supposedly subordinate provincial treasuries in the Bohemian and newly reunited Inner Austrian and Tyrolean lands. Meanwhile its notorious president, Georg Ludwig Count Sinzendorf (1656–79), used his position to embezzle 2 million florins in state funds – roughly the equivalent to 40 percent of the monarchy's annual revenue – despite years of rumors and charges of corruption.

Given Leopold's inability to overcome administrative inefficiency and corruption, he was forced to rely on the extraction of more and higher taxes from the estates. The level of the Contribution in the Austrian and Bohemian lands had already soared during the Thirty Years' War. Nevertheless, like his father before him Leopold was able to induce them to increase their support. Both men continued to visualize the nobility, together with the church, as key pillars in the state-building process. Thus, in stark contrast to the French Bourbons and English Stuarts, they preferred to work closely with the estates even to the point of accepting somewhat lower revenues than they wanted, so long as they could be sure of their loyalty to the crown. The success of this approach was most evident in the wealthier and more compliant lands of the Bohemian crown, whose estates met no fewer than fifty-nine times in the half century between 1648 and 1698. Already in 1650 Bohemia had agreed to maintain a fixed number of troops in Ferdinand III's newly created peacetime standing army. To pay for them, new land and tax registers were commissioned in Bohemia (1654) and Moravia (1664). For the next century greater Bohemia contributed between half and two-thirds of all the monarchy's income.

Ferdinand III and Leopold also achieved notable success in Silesia. Here they completed the consolidation of the semi-independent principalities that had begun with Ferdinand II's seizure of Jägerndorf in 1621. The Podiebrad dynasty sold Münsterberg to Ferdinand III, before dying out in 1647. In exchange for assisting John Casimir in his war against Sweden, Leopold reacquired the two Upper Silesian duchies of Oppeln and Ratibor that his father had pawned to Poland during the Thirty Years' War. Finally, in 1675 Leopold annexed Liegnitz, Brieg and Wohlau when the last Piast duke died (see Map 2). The central government did not retain all of the new domain lands that it acquired in Silesia, choosing instead to reward loyal aristocratic families such as the Austrian Liechtensteins (with Jägerndorf) and Auerspergs (with Münsterberg). In every case, however, it greatly reduced the extensive law-making, judicial, and other prerogatives that had heretofore rendered these principalities largely independent of Habsburg rule.

Leopold made fewer demands on the less wealthy and somewhat less compliant Austrian lands. He was especially patient with the Tyrol, which had been reunited with the rest of the *Erblande* following the extinction of its branch of the dynasty in 1665. A century of independence from Vienna had strengthened the sense of individuality that came with the Tyrol's physical and commercial isolation from the rest of the hereditary lands. Indeed, having been virtually untouched by the Reformation and the ravages of the Thirty Years' War, the Tyrolean estates offered little support for Leopold's requests for funds to rebuild the monarchy's economy and provide for its defense. Nevertheless, the emperor made no attempt to suppress the Tyrol's particularism. He scrupulously convened its estates, confirmed their privileges, and even retained the numerous administrative offices that both the Tyrolean and Inner Austrian lands had established following their separation from the rest of the monarchy in 1564. His appointment of German princes from Lorraine and the Palatinate to represent him as governor constituted another concession to their pretensions. At the end of his reign he even considered reestablishing its independence by ceding it to his second son. If Leopold respected the Tyrol's distinctiveness it was because its estates ultimately granted him some (though never more than two thirds) of the funds he requested and because both its confessional pedigree and loyalty to the dynasty were beyond question.

Indeed, if Leopold pursued one aspect of the state-building process with vigor, it was in continuing his predecessors' enforcement of religious uniformity, which he too visualized as a litmus test of loyalty to the monarchy. During his reign the Jesuits continued to tighten their grip over the monarchy's institutions of higher education. They also joined large numbers

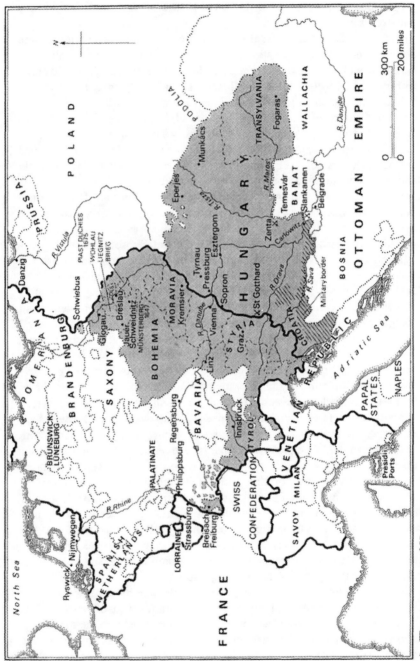

2   The reconquest of Hungary

of Dominican and Franciscan missionaries in pastoral work among the uncoverted. Like his father before him Leopold continued Ferdinand II's policy of sending Reformation Commissions into those parts of Austria, Bohemia, and Moravia where Protestant communities could be identified. Once again recalcitrant peasants were generally denied the option of emigrating and were compelled to demonstrate conversion, or at least attendance at mass and other Catholic observances.[1]

Within the Austrian and Bohemian lands both Leopold and his father devoted the most attention to converting Silesia's Protestant majority. At the Peace of Westphalia Sweden had not only compelled Ferdinand III to grant full religious freedom to Breslau and the semi-independent principalities, but also mandated the construction of three churches elsewhere in Lower Silesia just outside the walls of the Protestant cities of Schweidnitz, Jauer, and Glogau. Moreover, the treaty also forbade the expulsion of Protestants or their prevention from traveling to any of these locations (or across the Saxon or Polish frontiers) to worship their faith. These restrictions did not, however, forestall the reintroduction of Catholicism in areas not explicitly protected by the treaty. No sooner had the Swedes withdrawn their forces from the duchy than the Reformation Commissions made their appearance. By 1654 over 650 churches had been closed down or converted to Catholic worship, 500 preachers expelled, and their parishioners denied everything from baptism to burial services. The conversion process moved much more quickly in Upper Silesia, whose Protestants were effectively isolated from alternative places of worship. By 1675, however, the extinction of the Calvinist Piasts emboldened Leopold to extend Catholicization to Liegnitz, Brieg, and Wohlau either by expelling preachers outright or, more often, by preventing Protestant congregations from replacing their preachers when they died or retired. Over the next three decades attrition among Protestant clergy permitted him to close down over one hundred churches in the former Piast principalities. Indeed, by 1700 the entire duchy had only 220 Protestant places of worship left from among over 1,500 that had existed a century before. Meanwhile, arrayed against then were no fewer than thirty Catholic religious orders and Silesia's *Landeshauptmann* – who was invariably the bishop of Breslau!

Both Ferdinand III and Leopold I did encounter some limited popular resistance to their fiscal and religious policies within the Austrian and Bohemian lands. In Silesia so-called hedge preachers operating from hideouts in hilly and wooded areas continued to minister to the Protestant faithful, especially the majority of Lower Silesians who resisted conversion.

---

[1] Needless to say, compliance did not necessarily equate with conversion. In one Austrian parish, an ostensibly Catholic noblewoman registered her opposition to mandatory communion services by bringing along a pack of howling hunting dogs.

Clandestine Protestant communities survived elsewhere as well, most notably in the alpine valleys of Carinthia and Lower Austria. There were also occasional peasant uprisings against the steadily rising level of the Contribution, particularly during the second half of Leopold's reign. It is worth pointing out, however, that neither ruler encountered overt opposition to either their confessional or fiscal demands among noble or urban elites.

Their acquiescence was especially evident among the recently purged, but now steadfastly loyal and Catholic Bohemian and Moravian nobility. By mid-century their assimilation had progressed beyond politics and religion. The newly installed foreign nobility, as well as most native Czech nobles, adopted German as their primary language. Their rush to affect cosmopolitan tastes also inclined them to learn other languages, such as Italian and French, and to patronize artists, architects, and musicians from western Europe. Although neither the nobility nor the government had ever viewed Czech as a symbol of disloyalty, this process of acculturation further symbolized the nobility's acceptance of integration with the *Erblande*. The destruction of their homeland even impelled many Bohemian and Moravian aristocrats to maintain homes in Vienna, where they became increasingly welcome as major players in the central government. From his new residence there, the Bohemian chancellor ultimately joined his Austrian counterpart as an intimate advisor in foreign and domestic policy. There was, in fact, a significant increase in the number of native Bohemian aristocrats in the councils of state, a rise that complemented a corresponding decrease in the presence and influence of Germans from outside the Habsburg dominions. Perhaps the most eloquent indicator of Bohemia's assimilation into the monarchy was the transformation in the meaning of the word *Erblande*. By the end of the century Leopold and his counselors used it to describe not just the Austrian, but the Bohemian lands as well. It was, of course, technically accurate to refer to greater Bohemia as a hereditary dominion following the *Verneuerte Landesordnung*'s elimination of the elective crown in 1627. The change in nomenclature was, however, of more than semantic significance, representing as it did a real evolution in the way in which the dynasty now valued and trusted its Bohemian subjects, especially its ruling aristocracy.

The Turkish wars and reconquest of Hungary

Hungary was, of course, different. While the Austrian and Bohemian lands had borne heavy tax increases with minimal complaint, the Hungarian estates had steadfastly resisted similar attempts. Their opposition was partly justified by the kingdom's smaller population and relative poverty, but they were nonetheless resented in Vienna as deadbeats. Moreover, the Magyar nobility's proud retention of its native language, customs, and dress seemingly justified Leopold's tendency to treat them as outcasts at court, where they were generally denied access to key government positions outside the Hungarian Chancery. Although the kingdom's diet periodically accepted the stationing of troops from the Austrian and Bohemian lands for defense against the Turks, delegates frequently protested against the presence of such "foreign" troops on Hungarian soil. It was, however, the gentry's and masses' retention of Protestantism that did the most to undermine Leopold's confidence in their loyalty. The central government initially did little to challenge Protestant religious freedom in the decade following the Peace of Westphalia. In keeping with the treaty of Linz, Ferdinand III had immediately restored ninety of the Protestant churches that had been seized by Catholic magnates. Similarly, Leopold repeatedly confirmed the kingdom's religious liberties before its diet, albeit in the face of charges by Protestant delegates that individual Catholic magnates were still expelling pastors from their estates and compelling peasants to attend mass.

The Ottoman conquest of Transylvania

Given the sustained Magyar resistance to the emerging Habsburg *Gesamtstaat*, Leopold began his reign with the intention of maintaining his predecessors' focus on the monarchy's western dominions and the foreign threats that lay beyond. It was not long, however, before developments beyond Leopold's control compelled him to reassess and, eventually, reverse these priorities. The pivotal event was the decision of Sultan Mehmed IV (1648–87) in September 1656 to appoint Mehmed Kiuprili to the position of grand vizier. Although the new chief minister served barely five years before his death in 1661, he used it to undertake a thorough reform of the Ottoman empire's army and finances. He was, in any event, only the first of a succession of energetic grand viziers from the Kiuprili family who pursued an expansionist policy in Europe. Already by August 1657 he had induced the sultan to tighten his control over Transylvania by deposing the brash and ambitious George II Rákóczi. After a three-year struggle the prince was killed in battle in May 1660.

By then, however, the government in Vienna had been drawn into the struggle. As troublesome as Transylvania had proven in the past, the establishment of effective Turkish control there posed an even greater threat to the monarchy's security. Thus Leopold responded positively to Rákóczi's request for Austrian military intervention. At the same time, however, he was so intimidated by the prospect of war with the Turks that he initially did little more than occupy two Transylvanian counties that Rákóczi had ceded to him in exchange for his assistance. Leopold was more helpful once the peace of Oliva had freed up the Austrian forces that had been fighting Sweden. Even then, however, the 15,000 troops that he dispatched under Field Marshal Montecuccoli during 1661 was under orders to make "demonstrations" against the Turks in the hope that it might relieve pressure from the Transylvanians. In the end neither Montecuccoli's army nor several raids into Turkish Hungary by Croat and Magyar magnates proved effective in slowing the Turkish occupation of Transylvania. Although the Transylvanian diet had defiantly elected a new prince, Janos Kemény, to continue the struggle after Rákóczi's death, he too was slain by the Turks at the beginning of 1662 and the country occupied.

In the end Leopold's timidity failed to forestall Turkish retaliation. In April 1663 the sultan formally declared war. Soon thereafter the new grand vizier, Fazil Ahmed Kiuprili (1661–78), led an army of 60,000 into Royal Hungary. By November he had seized the formidable fortress of Neuhäusel, the only obstacle that stood between him and the Habsburg capitals of Pressburg and Vienna. By itself Montecuccoli's army was far too small to prevent the Turks from marching up the Danube. Moreover, Leopold could expect no help from the Hungarian diet, which had broken up the year before, following complaints against continued religious persecution by Catholic magnates and the recent influx of German soldiers sent to meet the Turkish threat. A desperate thrust into Turkish Hungary by the Croatian ban Miklós Zrinyi did, however, delay the Turkish onslaught until the summer of 1664. By then help had arrived from outside the monarchy. Aside from considerable Spanish and papal subsidies, the key aid came from the imperial diet, which convened in 1663 in response to Leopold's appeals. Although Mainz and its French allies initially blocked his attempt to vote taxes, they did commit the *Rheinbund* to provide an independent force that ultimately totaled 6,000 German and French troops. Yet as the Turkish threat grew, several other German states, most notably Bavaria, Brandenburg-Prussia, and Saxony, committed additional forces. It was with this motley force of only 25,000 men that Montecuccoli crushed a Turkish army twice as large as it attempted to cross into Styria near the ruined monastery of St. Gotthard (1 August 1664).

At the very least the victory at St. Gotthard saved the *Erblande* from invasion. To many Hungarians, however, it presented a rare opportunity to go on the offensive and liberate Hungary from Turkish rule. But Leopold and his advisers saw things differently. Despite his victory, Montecuccoli was still heavily outnumbered. Nor could they be sure of retaining all the forces under his command. It soon became evident that the French and many of the German princes who had rushed to the defense of the Empire's southeastern frontier were not interested in marching into the Balkans. They were also keenly aware that, except for the *Grenzer* provided by the Military Border and a few magnates, even Royal Hungary had contributed little to the war so far.

But they had another reason for pause. With the Spanish Habsburgs seemingly teetering on the edge of extinction, Leopold was reluctant to become deeply involved in a war with the Turks, lest it leave France free to seize the Spanish dominions after their demise. It was this combination of military weakness and interest in the Spanish inheritance that led him to sign a shameless capitulation just ten days after the greatest victory that the monarchy had ever achieved over the Turks. At the treaty of Vasvár Leopold surrendered several frontier towns, as well as the key fortress of Neuhäusel. He recognized the recently installed Turkish puppet Michael I Apafi as prince of Transylvania and even agreed to make an annual "gift" of 200,000 fl. to the sultan. In exchange Leopold received nothing more than the dubious promise of a twenty-year truce with the Ottoman empire.

The magnate conspiracy

If nothing else the latest Turkish war demonstrated the resilience of the monarchy's geopolitical *raison d'être*. Even its erstwhile French enemy and the independent-minded *Rheinbund* princes had come to its aid when it was threatened – and then promptly left its side once their purely defensive common goals had been achieved. Yet, at the same time, the unheroic peace of Vasvár had major consequences within the monarchy. The Hungarian and Croatian nobility had long resented the way in which Leopold's predecessors had ignored their need for greater security against the Turks. This had been especially true at the height of the Thirty Years' War, when Vienna was preoccupied with its interests in Germany. Now they seethed at a peace treaty that had been concluded without their advice or participation and had placed the prospects of a Spanish inheritance ahead of those of the kingdom's liberation from the Ottoman yoke. The magnates felt especially cheated because an offensive into Turkish Hungary would have afforded them the opportunity to enrich themselves, whether through plunder or the reacquisition of estates previously lost to Ottoman occupation. Several Hungarian and Magyarized Croat magnates now vented their anger by conspiring to overthrow Habsburg rule.

There was no doubting the pedigree of the conspirators themselves. The ringleaders included the Hungarian palatine Ferenc Wesselényi, the chief justice Ferenc Nádasdy, the dashing Croatian ban Miklós Zrinyi and his younger brother Peter, who expressed his contempt for the recent peace by launching a series of lucrative raids into Turkish Hungary. Other conspirators included Ferenc Rákóczi, son of the late prince of Transylvania, and Hungary's archbishop-primate György Lippay, whose estates near Neuhäusel had been signed away at Vasvár. Yet the conspirators' position and influence could not compensate for bad luck, compounded by their own incompetence and indecisiveness. Death soon carried off Wesselényi, Lippay, and Miklós Zrinyi, the latter in dramatic fashion after a fight to the death with a wounded boar. Although the new Croatian ban Ferenc Frangepáni soon joined their ranks, none of the conspirators proved particularly adept at intrigue. As Roman Catholics they failed to exploit fully the underlying Protestant discontent that existed within Hungary. Meanwhile, the Croatian conspirators naïvely counted on winning over the troops from the Military Border, despite Croatia's persistent attempts to deprive the *Grenzer* of their political autonomy and personal freedom. Equally misplaced were their hopes of receiving help from foreign powers. Although the French ambassador Gremonville provided some money and encouragement, Louis XIV was hardly prepared to sustain a Hungarian *Fronde*. The plotters received even less encouragement from Venice, Poland, Sweden, and the sultan himself, who declined their offer of Turkish vassalage, if only because he was too preoccupied with his recent invasions of Venetian and Polish territory to consider breaking his truce with Leopold. Indeed, before long both Gremonville and the sultan's chief interpreter betrayed the magnates' overtures to the emperor's agents.

The conspirators themselves were hardly more resolute or trustworthy than their foreign contacts. Some of them were determined to depose Leopold and even made plans to kidnap him in November 1667 when he journeyed from Vienna to meet his Spanish bride. But decades of generous patronage gave several others second thoughts about ending Habsburg rule. It was these doubts, tinged perhaps by contrition, that led Wesselényi, Nádasdy, and Peter Zrinyi to betray details of the conspiracy to Leopold at one point or another, as did Wesselényi's widow and several loyal magnates who were aware of the plot. If Leopold chose not to take immediate action it was because the conspirators' apparent lack of resolve and competence, as well as his own ignorance of their more radical plans, persuaded him that there was little to fear. The plotters finally forced his hand early in 1670 by belatedly appealing to Upper Hungary's Protestant majority and circulating pamphlets calling for Turkish rule. The poorly coordinated attacks that followed were easily repulsed by the strong garrisons that Leopold had recently moved into the kingdom. Moreover, while the Hungarian conspirators attracted a small following among Upper Hungary's Protestants, the Magyarized Croats Zrinyi and Frangepáni received no support in Croatia, where there remained strong feelings against Hungarian domination, heresy, and the prospects of Ottoman rule.

After a vain appeal for help to the Turkish pasha of Buda, Zrinyi and Frangepáni surrendered, followed shortly by Rákóczi. Leopold and his advisors initially intended to grant the conspirators' plea for clemency, if only to retain the kingdom's loyalty. But captured documents finally exposed the seriousness of the plot (including a plan to assassinate Leopold) and also betrayed the conspirators' continued duplicity when they tried to shift the extent of their involvement to others. Ultimately a special court composed exclusively of non-Hungarians condemned Zrinyi, Frangepáni, and Nádasdy to death, while fining Ferenc Rákóczi 400,000 fl. Still hoping for clemency, Leopold appealed the death sentences to the Privy Council. Instead, it upheld the penalty for all three men, who went to the scaffold on 30 April 1671.

Confessional absolutism in Hungary, 1671–81

The executions marked the end for Nádasdy, Zrinyi, and Frangepáni, but it was only the beginning of a much bigger crackdown in Hungary. Led by the Hungarian chancellor Tamás Pálffy and new archbishop-primate György Szelepcsényi, loyal magnates were now eager to demonstrate their commitment to the dynasty by punishing treasonous – and especially Protestant – elements within the kingdom. Pálffy spearheaded a broad investigation by a Hungarian tribunal that ultimately led to the arrest and interrogation of 2,000 nobles and the confiscation of three hundred estates worth 3 million fl. Leopold's other advisers wanted to go considerably further. Many shared Montecuccoli's opinion that the Hungarians were little more than a "nation of rebels, robbers, and restless men." No one despised them more than the Austrian Chancellor Johann Paul Hocher and the powerful grand chamberlain Prince Wenzel Lobkovic, who now spoke for the rest of the newly integrated Bohemian aristocracy in proclaiming his desire to "put the Hungarians into Czech trousers." Nor was the court's receding, but still influential German faction silent. Led by Margrave Hermann of Baden and the imperial vice chancellor Leopold Wilhelm von Königsegg, it urged that Hungary be placed under military occupation and Germanized, much as Bohemia had been a half century before. Leopold himself was hesitant to take action that violated his election oath or diverged from his predecessors' traditional cooperation with the monarchy's privileged orders. Yet, when combined with the country's widespread retention of Protestantism, the magnate conspiracy had so shaken his faith in the loyalty of his Hungarian subjects that he now attempted to introduce absolutism there.

Hungarian historians refer to the decade following the suppression of the magnate conspiracy as the "Ten Dark Years." From 1671 the emperor essentially ignored the kingdom's constitutional liberties. He left the office of palatine vacant and also failed to appoint a new Croatian ban following the execution of Frangepáni. He avoided calling the diet, which had not met since the delegates walked out in 1662. Leopold also considered, but resisted, his ministers' call for more drastic measures including the formal elimination of the kingdom's elective crown, together with its diet, independent treasury, judiciary, and county assemblies. He nevertheless now subjected Royal Hungary to a full-scale military occupation and a fivefold increase in the Contribution needed to pay for it. Although collection remained in the hands of the noble-dominated county assemblies, the presence of troops guaranteed full compliance as never before. Moreover, in a remarkable departure from the past, the kingdom's historically tax-free nobles were ordered to share half of the fiscal burden with their peasants. Nor did Leopold miss the opportunity to move against the kingdom's Protestants. Even though they had played only a minimal role in what was essentially a conspiracy of Catholic magnates, Archbishop Szelepcsényi initiated a campaign of religious persecution that included the closing of Protestant schools and churches, and the expulsion of their ministers.

It was not long before Leopold's actions elicited a violent response. Riots broke out in several Lutheran towns, such as Pressburg, where churches had been closed and the German magistrates replaced with Catholic Magyars. More ominous was the reappearance of thousands of Hungarian nobles and Protestants who had sought refuge from Pálffy's tribunal in neighboring Transylvania and Turkish Hungary. Upon their return they were joined by thousands of unemployed Hungarian soldiers whom Leopold had replaced with German and other "foreign" troops. By September 1672 these "crusaders," or *Kuruc*, had begun launching guerrilla raids against the isolated army garrisons that Leopold had stationed in Royal Hungary.

The government made an immediate concession to popular discontent by reducing the level of peasant taxation by 30 percent. Otherwise its principal response was to strengthen its grip on the kingdom. In February 1673 Leopold appointed the Grand Master of the Teutonic Order, a Hungarian-born ethnic German named Johann Kaspar von Ampringen, to govern the kingdom as head of a new *Gubernium* that would take orders directly from Vienna. Ampringen proved to be a conscientious governor who was genuinely devoted to minimizing the hardships caused by Leopold's policies. His office was, in any event, largely by-passed by the county assemblies and military garrisons that continued to communicate directly with the Hungarian Chancery and treasury. The *Gubernium* did, however, represent yet another violation of the kingdom's constitution and autonomy, as did Leopold's decision to place the Hungarian treasury under the direct control of the *Hofkammer*. Leopold also stepped up the pace of religious persecution. Backed by troops, Catholic clergy closed an estimated 800 Protestant churches and forced as many as 60,000 conversions. Protestant clergy who refused to convert were given the choice of exile or death. Whereas over two hundred agreed to leave and hundreds more converted, another ninety-three were condemned to death. Although Leopold promptly commuted their sentences, he sent forty of their number to row as galley slaves in Spain's Neapolitan fleet.

Even Hungary's loyal, *labanc* magnates were appalled by Leopold's contravention of the constitution.[2] They too resented the presence of "foreign" troops, tax collectors, and officials, especially when they themselves were still being denied patronage outside the confines of Hungary's own increasingly impotent state offices. Together with Ampringen, they protested that religious persecution and excesses committed by the military were progressively alienating the country. They urged Leopold to restore the constitution, appoint a new palatine, and replace German officers and troops with native Hungarians. Their concern was echoed by the growing intensity of the *Kuruc* raids, which continued every summer after 1672. With as many as 15,000 fighters the *Kuruc* raiders committed gruesome atrocities, which begot equally inhumane Austrian countermeasures. Yet, despite the size and ferocity of the *Kuruc* forces, they could not hope to overthrow Habsburg rule without foreign assistance. Transylvania had been at least temporarily neutralized by the Ottoman conquest. So long as Leopold remained at peace with the principality's Turkish overlord and with the French and Swedes in the West, he enjoyed the luxury of ignoring the voices of moderation and going ahead with his plans to forcibly integrate Hungary into the monarchy.

East versus west: The reemergence of the French and Ottoman threats

Yet, even as Leopold tightened his grip on the kingdom, his window of opportunity was rapidly closing. In the West, the monarchy was confronted by the emerging prospect of French hegemony. The French threat was, however, greatly exacerbated by the Habsburgs' own recent failure to resolve their own succession crisis. The military collapse and imminent extinction of the Spanish Habsburgs had suddenly converted Leopold and the Austrian monarchy into the dynasty's dominant partner. The two branches had renewed their centuries-old dynastic alliance in 1666, with the marriage by proxy of Leopold and Charles II's older sister Margaret. Yet Leopold's goals were different from those of past Austrian Habsburgs. Instead of seeking the security formerly provided by Spain's financial and military resources, he was merely trying to strengthen his claim to the Spanish succession following Charles's death. At the same time Leopold was desperate to beget an heir of his own. Yet, although Margaret quickly bore two boys and two girls, only a single female, Maria Antonia, survived the empress's own death in 1673. Two daughters by Leopold's second wife, the Tyrolean Archduchess Claudia Felicitas, also died, followed shortly by their mother in 1676.

[2] The term presumably stems from the German word, *Landesknecht*, or foot-soldier.

Meanwhile, Louis XIV could put forward a stronger claim, backed by the birth of a healthy son, Louis, in 1661; better yet, the Sun King had the power to press his pretensions. By 1668 he had made good part of his claim by seizing several Belgian towns in the so-called War of Devolution (1667–8). Given his own weak position, Leopold decided to cooperate with France and secretly agreed to a partition of the Spanish inheritance in the same year.[3] The emperor likewise ignored Louis's occupation of Lorraine in 1670, which further cut off the Spanish Netherlands, but posed no direct threat either to Germany proper or the monarchy itself. Vienna's policy of appeasement continued in November 1671, when Prince Lobkovic negotiated a neutrality treaty with Louis just prior to his planned invasion of the Dutch Republic. When Louis launched his attack five months later, Lobkovic not only initially maintained Austrian and German neutrality, but actually assisted France diplomatically.

Lobkovic's stance at the beginning of the Dutch War (1672–9) belied his "eastern" bias in favor of reducing Hungary at the expense of ignoring French aggression in the West. He did, however, incur significant opposition from a growing faction of "westerners" led by the experienced Austrian diplomat Franz Lisola and supported by the Spanish and several German and Italian envoys. By June 1672 the dramatic progress of French arms did, in fact, induce Lobkovic to conclude a defensive alliance with Brandenburg-Prussia to defend Germany's frontier and to dispatch Montecuccoli to the Rhine with a small observation force. Although Dutch and Spanish subsidies helped to increase the size of Montecuccoli's force, most of the troops came from various German states, rather than from the monarchy itself. When Leopold finally declared war on Louis XIV in May 1674, he directed Montecuccoli to use his forces only as a demonstration army to distract, but not engage, the French. Even this ploy was defeated by Lobkovic who secretly reassured the French that Montecuccoli's presence on the Rhine was no more than a bluff.

Leopold immediately expelled Lobkovic from court following the discovery of his duplicity in October 1674. Nevertheless, he was as yet ill prepared to assume a "western" strategy, not only because he would have to sacrifice his Hungarian policies, but also because the threat that Louis XIV posed to European security was still not sufficiently evident to inspire a broad European coalition. Indeed, French subsidies had enlisted England and Sweden as allies, and had secured the benevolent neutrality of several German states, including Bavaria and, ultimately, Saxony and the Palatinate. Leopold's own failure to provide a male heir undercut his own ability to build

[3] By which France was to receive Belgium, Burgundy, Naples, Sicily, Navarre, the Philippines, and Spain's North African enclaves, leaving Spain and its American and strategic northern possessions to Leopold.

a coalition since the extinction of both the Austrian and Spanish Habsburgs would remove the only obstacle to Louis's dynastic ambitions. Given the unlikelihood of defeating him, the meager anti-French coalition soon fell apart. The United Provinces opened separate negotiations at the Dutch town of Nijmwegen in January 1676. By the summer of 1678 both they and Spain had concluded a treaty that ceded the Franche Comté and additional Belgian territory to France. The following February Leopold also came to terms that included the loss of the strategic Outer Austrian city of Freiburg, as well as his acquiescence in the continued French occupation of Lorraine. Leopold's capitulation enraged Elector Frederick William of Brandenburg, who was now compelled to give back most of his conquests in Swedish Pomerania. In revenge he became a French client and joined Bavaria in agreeing to vote for Louis XIV in the next imperial election. Indeed, although Leopold had just produced a son by his new wife, Eleonore, the German princes had reason to be swayed by the prospect of French leadership were Leopold to die without leaving an eligible adult male heir.

Louis's gains at Nijmwegen did not slake his appetite for territory. Within a year he had created the notorious Courts of Réunion. These tribunals revived or concocted ancient territorial claims as a pretext for seizing various imperial principalities along the Franco-German frontier. Nevertheless, Leopold had no choice but to capitulate at Nijmwegen and acquiesce to the subsequent piecemeal annexations of German territory. Not only had his allies' desertion persuaded him that there was no prospect of stopping France in the West, but events in the East were pushing the monarchy toward a second, far more serious security crisis. By 1678 the *Kuruc* revolt had grown under the leadership of Imre Thököly, the 21-year-old son of a Calvinist nobleman whose estates had been seized following the magnate conspiracy. From his Transylvanian exile Thököly now commanded 20-30,000 fighters, including many Catholics alienated by the suspension of constitutional government. Nor was he fighting alone. The new grand vizier Kara Mustapha (1676-83) had resumed Turkish incursions into Royal Hungary following the successful conclusion of the wars with Poland and Venice. With his blessing, Michael I Apafi had concluded a subsidy treaty with France that permitted Transylvania to assist his fellow Calvinist Thököly's Hungarian operations. Leopold tried to isolate Thököly by dispatching four successive embassies to Constantinople during 1678 and 1679 in order to extend the twenty-year truce concluded at Vasvár. But all four ambassadors died before they could complete their mission, a coincidence that many of the sultan's advisors interpreted as a divine omen against renewing the treaty. Although the Ottoman empire had only recently begun a new war with Russia, Leopold had just cause to fear that the monarchy might be next.

Caught in a vise, Vienna was faced with the prospect of having to choose between fighting France in the West or the Turks and their Transylvanian clients in the East. Whatever the choice, both factions at court agreed that peace within Hungary was crucial. Their counsel was forcefully seconded by the monarchy's allies, especially the Dutch, whose sensitivity to Protestant persecution now became a new factor in restraining Leopold's attempts at confessional absolutism. Yet even the papacy soon began to urge restraint, fearing that the Hungarian rebellion would open the way for a Turkish invasion. As early as February 1676 Leopold responded to the beginning of Franco-Dutch talks at Nijmwegen by releasing all imprisoned Protestant clergymen. At the same time Spain was induced to free the remaining forty preachers from its Neapolitan galleys, albeit with some prompting from Dutch naval forces. Over the next three years Leopold made two abortive attempts to reach a settlement by convening the upper table of the Hungarian diet and then by opening direct negotiations with Thököly.

It was the mounting international threat posed by the French and Turks that finally persuaded him to restore the kingdom's constitutional liberties. In 1680 he appointed a new Croatian ban with expanded judicial and executive powers. The following year he convened the first full Hungarian diet in nearly two decades at Sopron. Meeting with the delegates in person, Leopold abolished the *Gubernium* and permitted the diet to elect the kingdom's first palatine since Wesselényi's death fourteen years earlier. He made several tax concessions, including the removal of the royal treasury's non-Hungarian members and the restoration of its independence from the *Hofkammer*. He also confirmed Protestant religious rights laid down seventy-five years earlier in the treaty of Vienna. Protestant clergy and teachers were to be restored, together with all churches that had not already been reconsecrated for Catholic use. To replace them he permitted Protestants to build up to two new churches in any county in which they no longer had a place of worship.

In return for these concessions the Hungarian diet joined its Croatian counterpart in mobilizing the kingdom's feudal levy, or *insurrectio*, to defend against the Turks. Nevertheless, Leopold's concessions to the Sopron diet proved insufficient to appease Thököly and his partisans. They did not trust Leopold's sincerity and doubted his willingness to abide by his promises once the foreign threats had passed. Nor did the government's religious concessions go far enough, principally because of the opposition of the kingdom's Catholic magnate majority. Although the agreement confirmed the religious freedom of nobles and burghers, the magnates refused to extend it to their peasants, despite the provision made for them in 1645 in the treaty of Linz. Indeed, they ultimately used their control of much of the countryside to block the restoration of all but fifty of the 888 Protestant churches seized over the past decade. They also supported Leopold's refusal to return the estates that the Pálffy tribunal had confiscated from Protestant nobles, especially since they had since acquired many of them from the crown. This was no small sticking point for Thököly himself, who sought the recovery of his family's lands as well as the creation of a sovereign principality for himself in northeastern Hungary.

Thököly's intransigence was also reinforced by Kara Mustapha, who had concluded peace with Russia in February and was now openly collaborating with the *Kuruc* and Transylvanian forces. Yet Leopold still hoped that he could somehow appease Thököly and the Turks. Ever since Lobkovic's fall eight years earlier, he had favored focusing on the growing French threat to Germany. He shared the view of "westerners" like Hermann of Baden who argued that land lost to the Turks could always be recovered in a future war, while territories taken by France would be lost forever. Moreover, France's seizure of the great imperial city of Strassburg in October 1681 had finally awakened much of the Empire and western Europe to the French threat. Within months several German princes, the United Provinces, Spain, and even Sweden had formed the so-called League of Augsburg to deter further Réunions. Although it was not easy for him to embrace a largely Protestant alliance and especially the Dutch, who had deserted him at Nijmwegen, the anti-French coalition held forth the promise of victory in the West. It was this prospect that moved Leopold to conclude a truce with Thököly. The emperor even permitted him to wed Helena Zrinyi, the daughter of Peter Zrinyi and recent widow of Francis I Rákóczi, whose massive estates would amply compensate Thököly for the lands his own family had lost. It was, however, a short honeymoon. Thököly waited exactly nine days after the June wedding before renouncing the truce and joining forces with Apafi and the Turkish pasha of Buda. By October their combined armies had seized control of most of Upper Hungary and begun raiding neighboring Moravia and Silesia. As late as August Leopold had advised his envoy in Constantinople to intensify his efforts to extend the monarchy's truce with the Turks. By now, however, the grand vizier had left Constantinople to join the main Ottoman army. His objective was Vienna itself. Like it or not, the monarchy would have to fight in the East.

The siege of Vienna and the Holy League

Kara Mustapha and his 100,000-man army began the long march to Vienna at the beginning of 1683. Along the way he was reinforced by the pasha of Buda and the Tartar Khan, though not by Thököly, whose forces continued to pursue the conquest of Upper Hungary. With the death of Montecuccoli two years earlier the task of defending the monarchy fell to his former lieutenant, the equally talented Duke Charles of Lorraine, who had entered the emperor's service following the French occupation of his duchy. With a field army of only 36,000 men, together with 12,000 men scattered in garrisons throughout Hungary and Croatia, Lorraine had no chance of stopping the Turkish march up the Danube. As news of their approach reached Vienna on 7 July, Leopold and his family hastily fled to Passau, 175 miles upriver. Their flight was punctuated at one point by a mob of frantic Viennese begging him to stay, and later by cursing peasants, some of whom blamed his Hungarian policies for the impending disaster. Thousands of Viennese followed Leopold westward, although their place was taken by even larger numbers of people seeking refuge from the countryside. Meanwhile, Lorraine positioned his outnumbered forces several miles to the north, on the other side of the Danube.

Appearances aside, Leopold's presence in Passau enabled him and his ministers to work for the city's relief by mobilizing a relief force. If nothing else the Ottoman threat facilitated the search for allies, especially among those neighboring countries which had the most to lose from a Turkish conquest of the monarchy. Poland's King John Sobieski had already concluded an alliance with him at the end of March, effectively reversing his pro-French foreign policy and occasional assistance to Thököly. He was now joined by Electors Max II Emanuel of Bavaria and John George III of Saxony, whose territories stood next in the Turkish path. Leopold also received commitments from the small imperial principalities of the Swabian and Franconian circles, whose own continued independence depended heavily on the protection of the Holy Roman emperor. No less valuable was the assistance that Leopold got from Pope Innocent XI, who had long dreamed of a Christian crusade in the Balkans. Innocent had played a decisive role in securing Sobieski's support by giving him subsidies and personally guaranteeing the alliance compact. He now supplemented this commitment by giving both Leopold and Bavaria's Max Emanuel the authority to raise money by taxing church property within their dominions.

While the monarchy's government in exile worked feverishly to gather a relief force, Vienna itself struggled desperately to hold out. Fighting was furious and nearly continuous. Kara Mustapha punctuated the ongoing bombardment and mining operations with no fewer than eighteen major assaults on the city walls, or about one for every three days of the two-month siege. In response the garrison made sorties to disrupt the siege operations. By August the stench of unburied bodies permeated the air of both sides of the ramparts. There was no shortage of atrocities. The grand vizier's cavalry and Tartar auxiliaries devastated broad stretches of the countryside. To demoralize the city's defenders, he had large numbers of captured peasants butchered in front of Vienna's walls. From the city's ramparts the garrison responded in kind by flaying captured Turkish soldiers alive and mounting the heads of their fallen comrades on pikes. But time was running out. The

Turks nearly took the city in a furious assault on 4 September, after their mines had breached the section of the wall nearest the Hofburg. That evening the garrison sent up flares to alert Lorraine that the city's fall was imminent. Somehow the defenders repulsed additional assaults for each of the next three days, even though only a third of the original garrison was still fit for combat. Finally, on 7 September bonfires on the Kahlenberg heights west of the city told the defenders that their deliverance was at hand.

The Christian army that attacked the Turks from the Kahlenberg on the morning of 12 September 1683 typified so many of the coalitions that played such a key role in the defense and expansion of the Habsburg monarchy. Although Lorraine's 20,000 Austrians constituted the largest single contingent, they comprised less than a third of the relief force. John Sobieski brought 18,000 Poles and, by virtue of his royal rank, won the overall command and the lion's share of the credit for the allied victory. No less important were the 11,000 Bavarians and 9,000 Saxons, led by their two electors, together with 8,000 troops from the Swabian and Franconian Circles. This considerable force was still numerically inferior to the enemy. But the Turks exhibited their customary weaknesses against disciplined troops, which were compounded both by Kara Mustapha's failure to fortify his position and by a well-timed sally from the besieged garrison. By dusk the remnants of his shattered army had fled, leaving all its supplies and artillery behind. Over the next few months the allies pursued the enemy into Royal Hungary, much of which was recovered by the end of the year. The close of the 1683 campaign also marked the end for Kara Mustapha. On orders from Mehmed IV, he was strangled and his severed head dispatched to Constantinople.

The sultan would have infinitely preferred Vienna as a trophy of war to the grand vizier's head. Yet, even had Kara Mustapha taken the city, he would probably not have been able to retain it, given the enormous difficulties in maintaining an army so far from its home base and the even greater Christian military effort that the city's fall would have likely inspired. But the Turks would have certainly made the most of their opportunity to devastate Vienna, together with much of the rest of the monarchy, and might have retained Habsburg Hungary in a subsequent peace treaty. Moreover, the monarchy's collapse would have forced Christian Europe to enlist the leadership of Louis XIV, who was eagerly waiting in the wings. With several of the imperial electors already in his pay, he would have even stood an excellent chance of being elected as Leopold's heir to the throne of Charlemagne.

The victory of Kahlenberg was no less decisive in orienting Leopold and his ministers toward expansion in the East. The day after the battle, Elector John George had returned home with the Saxon contingent, though not before personally lecturing Leopold on the evils of his religious policies. But the other German princes who had contributed to the city's relief now expressed a willingness to continue the struggle. Though he ultimately returned with his army to Poland, John Sobieski was eager to open a second front to reverse the recent Ottoman conquest of the Polish province of Podolia. Similarly, Venice was prepared to avenge its loss of Crete by attacking the Turks in the eastern Mediterranean. By March 1684 Innocent XI helped to join the Poles and Venetians to the emperor in a Holy League that he firmly cemented with considerable financial support. Over the next decade he taxed the church's wealth throughout Europe to finance what could justly be termed the last great crusade. Within the monarchy alone the clergy contributed a third of its income. Innocent also directed it to turn over a third of all the property it had acquired in the last sixty years and subsequently authorized the transfer of the sizeable estates of Archbishop Szelepcsényi and Bishop Sinelli following their deaths in 1685. However generous these initiatives may have been, Innocent was merely paying the dynasty back for the patronage and crucial support that it had given the church since the beginning of the century.

In return, the pope lobbied hard for peace with France in the West. Louis XIV had, in fact, suspended the annexation of German territories during the siege, if only because he did not wish to ruin his chances of assuming the leadership of Christian Europe once Vienna and the monarchy had been overrun. With his hopes dashed, he now resumed the Réunions, seizing much of Luxemburg by the end of 1683 and the archbishopric-electorate of Trier in the following year. To halt further French aggression, Leopold reluctantly came to terms with Louis at Regensburg in August 1684. Although he refused to recognize the permanent cession of other imperial territories, he did recognize Louis's acquisition of Luxemburg and his right to administer all the lands that he had seized before August 1681, including Strassburg, in exchange for the return of his more recent acquisitions and a twenty-year truce.

Leopold's decision proved to be as wise as it was painful and necessary. Freed from the need to defend against France in the West, the monarchy and its allies could devote themselves fully to the war in the Balkans. The Habsburg dominions were unusually forthcoming. As early as 1684 the Hungarians fielded 8,000 men under their new palatine, Pál Esterházy. In 1686 alone Leopold extracted 3.5 million fl. from the estates of the Austrian and Bohemian *Erblande*, together with another 2 million from the Hungarian lands. Nor did he want for allies. By 1685 there were nearly 40,000 German troops fighting in Hungary, including 8,000 Bavarians and 4,500 Swabians, as well as new contingents from Brunswick-Lüneburg (11,000), the Rhenish Circle (8,000), and even the pro-French archbishop-electorate of Cologne (6,000). In the following year the imperial diet voted an additional 2.75

million fl. (two-thirds of which was actually raised). No less significant was the return of 5,000 Saxons and Frederick William's dispatch of 8,000 troops from Brandenburg-Prussia. The great elector's support did not come easily. He still resented Leopold's capitulation to the French at Nijmwegen and his record of Protestant religious persecution. Nor had he forgotten the Habsburg seizure of Jägerndorf in 1621 or the more recent escheatment of the three Piast principalities of Liegnitz, Brieg, and Wohlau, to which the Hohenzollerns also had a claim. In the end, however, past grievances were overshadowed by the present behavior of his French ally, most notably the intensifying persecution of Huguenots that culminated in Louis's repeal of the Edict of Nantes (October 1685).[4] By 1687 the Christian crusade had embraced not only the emperor's once distant Protestant vassals but Orthodox Russia, which began its own operations on the edges of the Black Sea.

With peace in the West and allies in the East, Leopold's forces achieved a series of conquests unparalleled in the annals of the Turkish wars. Several German princes vied for the honor of humbling the infidel, most notably the Saxon and Bavarian electors, Prince Louis William of Baden (son of the new *Hofkriegsrat* President, Hermann of Baden), and Prince George Louis of Brunswick-Lüneburg (the future George I of England). Yet most of the laurels fell to Charles of Lorraine. By 1685 he had retaken all of Upper Hungary, including the formidable fortress of Neuhäusel, destroying a Turkish relief force and butchering its 3,000-man garrison in the process. By October virtually all of the *Kuruc* forces had deserted and sworn allegiance to Leopold after the pasha of Buda had seized Thököly in a clumsy attempt to trade him for peace. The next year the historic capital of Buda fell after a bloody 2½-month siege, as did most of southern and southwestern Hungary. By 1687 another crushing victory near the old Mohács battlefield yielded up much of Slavonia. By the end of the campaign Lorraine had also entered Transylvania and compelled it to supply and fund a large portion of his army. Although Apafi and the Transylvanian diet had hoped to retreat into neutrality, they had expressed as early as 1686 a willingness to accept Habsburg sovereignty in exchange for the promise of religious freedom and Apafi's retention as prince. Once Lorraine had strengthened his grip on the principality, he compelled them to accept these terms on 9 March 1688. Six months later Elector Max Emanuel captured Belgrade after a siege of only three weeks. By the end of the year his forces were marching into Turkish Bosnia and Serbia.

[4] Frederick William committed his forces in exchange for receiving the tiny Silesian enclave of Schwiebus as compensation for all outstanding Hohenzollern claims within the duchy. In the end Leopold avoided paying even this small price for Brandenburg's aid. Though he handed over Schwiebus in June 1686, the great elector's son, Frederick, secretly offered to return it to the monarchy after his father's death, a promise that Frederick somewhat reluctantly fulfilled in 1695, seven years after his succession in 1688.

The two-front war

In just five years the Holy League had helped Leopold to erase a century and a half of Turkish rule in Hungary. Yet the series of Balkan conquests came only at the sufferance of Louis XIV. The allies fully expected that the League of Augsburg and the Twenty Years' Truce that France had concluded at Regensburg would deter renewed French aggression. Louis XIV was, however, unwilling to allow the permanent destruction of the Ottoman empire as a useful ally in future wars against the monarchy. By the summer of 1688 he moved to relieve pressure from the Turks by sending his forces into Germany. In August 16,000 French troops occupied Cologne after the pope and emperor had helped thwart the seemingly certain succession of its pro-French coadjutor, Egon von Fürstenberg, as archbishop-elector. Leopold responded by joining the League of Augsburg in return for a commitment that included Dutch recognition of Austrian claims to the Spanish Succession. Leopold's accession to the League reached Versailles in mid-September, together with news of the fall of Belgrade. Ten days later his armies marched into the Rhineland, where they quickly seized the elector-ates of Trier, Mainz, and the Palatinate, as well as the strategic fortress of Philippsburg.

The monarchy was confronted once again with the threat of a two-front war and the agony of choosing between East and West. Leopold did not want for advice. Clerical intimates like Marco d'Aviano seconded the papal nuncio and the other envoys of the Holy League in urging Leopold to continue the crusade in the Balkans. Even Charles of Lorraine opposed opening a second front in the West, even though it offered the best hope of liberating his duchy from two decades of French occupation. Yet most of the German princes were unwilling to share in Lorraine's fate, especially now that the Turkish threat to the empire had been virtually eliminated. They soon joined the Spanish ambassador and many of Leopold's ministers in expressing the need to stop French aggression before it was too late. The emperor's decision was determined largely by the opportunities offered by the Grand Alliance now gathering in the West. With the exception of neutral Sweden, the League of Augsburg stood united against Louis XIV. Especially critical was the leadership of William of Orange, whose triumph in the Glorious Revolution had just placed him in control of both England and the Netherlands. Not only did he reiterate his earlier promise of support for Leopold's claim to the Spanish Succession, but he joined the German princes in backing the election of the emperor's 10-year-old son Joseph as Roman King. Armed with these incentives Leopold declared war on France on 3 April 1689.

During the course of the Nine Years' War (1689–97) against France the monarchy fought two wars, on two fronts, with two virtually distinct sets of allies. Only Leopold and the German princes were committed to both conflicts, although they now shifted most of their best troops and generals to the West. Louis XIV had begun hostilities in the Rhineland, which his forces systematically devastated before being pushed back by an imperial army led by Charles of Lorraine. Yet, the war ultimately spread to the Low Countries, Catalonia, and northwest Italy, following Spain's and Savoy's entry as belligerents in 1690. It was a measure of France's great strength that almost the entire war was fought on the territory of its many enemies, who could do little more than force a stalemate.

Meanwhile, Louis XIV was also able to accomplish his objective of saving the Ottoman empire from further catastrophe, and even emboldened the sultan to spurn Leopold's peace overtures. The massive diversion of forces west had, in fact, left the emperor with only 24,000 troops in the Balkans at the beginning of 1689. Despite these losses the new commander, Louis William of Baden, was initially able to retain the initiative, marching as far south as Albania and Macedonia. The Balkan peoples welcomed the imperial army at first, especially after Leopold had promised them religious freedom, tax exemptions, and national autonomy. Yet the proselytizing of the Jesuit missionaries who accompanied it soon cooled their enthusiasm and eliminated any chance of a general uprising against Ottoman rule. When the Turks counterattacked, Louis William was forced back to Belgrade, together with well over 30,000 Serb refugees who had already committed themselves to the Habsburg cause. The death of Michael I Apafi in April 1690 also emboldened the sultan to name the exiled Imre Thököly prince of Transylvania, dispatching him at the head of an army that quickly occupied much of the principality. Louis William hastened east and retook Transylvania by defeating Thököly one last time. But his absence permitted another Turkish force to surprise Belgrade and massacre its garrison. The Balkan front stabilized only a year later, when Louis William destroyed the main Turkish army at Slankamen, killing the Grand Vizier Mustapha Kiuprili and most of his commanders in the process. Although the German princes soon pressured Leopold into transferring the *Türkenlouis* to the western front, the emperor was able to maintain a virtual stalemate in the Balkans by enticing individual princes to contribute forces. In 1692 he secured troops and 750,000 fl. from Duke Ernest August of Brunswick-Lüneburg by promising to raise him to the rank of elector. Two years later he entrusted the new Saxon Elector Frederick Augustus with command of the imperial army in exchange for his commitment of 8,000 men.

Although both conflicts dragged on for several more years, the time for peace had come. Despite France's successes in the field, the strain of war on his kingdom ultimately moved Louis XIV to negotiate a settlement, even at the cost of disgorging some of his conquests. He was, however, able to minimize his losses by dividing his enemies, just as he had done during the Dutch War. Savoy was the first to defect in 1696, in exchange for some French territory. Soon afterward William of Orange entered peace talks at Ryswick. Although he invited Leopold to participate in the negotiations, the emperor proved a reluctant peacemaker. Admittedly there was no prospect of recovering more German territory than Louis XIV was already willing to give back. Yet Leopold was mindful of the delicate health of his Spanish cousin. Although Charles II had somehow survived into his fourth decade, he could not be expected to live much longer and was, in any event, incapable of providing an heir. Having already benefited from the combined strength of a great European coalition, Leopold now hoped the alliance would outlast Charles and guarantee Anglo-Dutch support for his own claim to the Spanish Succession. In the end his hopes were dashed by Charles II himself, who concluded a separate peace with Louis XIV in August 1697, following the fall of Barcelona. William of Orange followed suit one month later, leaving Leopold until 1 November to adhere to the treaty. In acceding to the treaty of Ryswick, the emperor formally recognized the loss of virtually all of Alsace, including the great imperial city of Strassburg. On the other hand the French restored all other annexations since the treaty of Nijmwegen, finally evacuated Lorraine, and actually returned the Outer Austrian city of Freiburg, together with the key Rhenish fortress of Breisach, which had been ceded at the Peace of Westphalia.

Peace in the West again afforded the monarchy the luxury of concentrating all of its forces against the Turks. Frederick Augustus continued to provide a considerable Saxon contingent in exchange for Leopold's help in securing the Polish crown after the death of John Sobieski in 1696. His conversion to Roman Catholicism at Baden bei Wien on 1 June 1697 guaranteed his election as King Augustus II by the Polish diet four weeks later. The king-elector's departure for Warsaw also permitted Leopold to replace a rather mediocre commander-in-chief with the brilliant young Prince Eugene of Savoy. Eugene had first served the emperor at the battle of Kahlenberg, only weeks after Louis XIV had denied him a commission in the French army. Yet, like so many of Leopold's best officers, he had eventually been transferred west, commanding the allied forces against the French in northern Italy. Now he returned east to fight against a less formidable enemy. On 11 September Eugene caught Sultan Mustapha and his grand vizier at Zenta, just as their army was crossing the Tisza River toward Transylvania. Although the sultan himself escaped, the grand vizier perished together with most of his officers and 30,000 men, a third of whom drowned trying to swim to safety.

At another time Zenta might have opened the way for a new round of Balkan conquests. Yet, once Ryswick had deprived the monarchy of its western allies, Leopold realized that he needed peace with the Ottoman empire in order to prepare for another conflict with France over the Spanish Succession. The prospects of further successes inclined his allies in the Holy League against a settlement. Yet, in the east it was the emperor who controlled the tempo of war and diplomacy. The Turks themselves enjoyed little more latitude than picking the precise moment of the treaty of Carlowitz, which was signed at exactly 11:45 a.m. on 26 January 1699, in keeping with the instructions of the chief Turkish negotiator's astrologer. The peace confirmed the monarchy's recovery of all of the Hungarian crownlands except for a small strip of eastern Slavonia near Belgrade and the Banat of Temesvár in central Hungary.

The legacy of Leopold I

The break-up of the League of Augsburg in the west and Leopold's decision for an early peace in the east foreclosed prospects for additional acquisitions for the empire and monarchy respectively. Nevertheless, his position in 1699 was infinitely better than the situation he had confronted in 1683. The monarchy was, in fact, more secure against outside threats than at any time in its history. Both Germany in the west and Hungary in the east were united behind the dynasty for the first time in over a century and a half. To the south, the Italian peninsula was still protected by the Spanish Habsburgs. Finally, to the north a weak, but massive Poland ruled by Leopold's Saxon vassal provided the monarchy with its most extensive *glacis*.

The monarchy had, of course, succeeded in crushing the Turks and stopping Louis XIV simply because the threats they posed were so great that they were perceived beyond the Hofburg. The Holy League was little more than a coalition of recent victims of Ottoman resurgence under the Kiuprilis. The frustration of French aggression could not have been achieved without a catharsis in the attitude of the Protestant German princes and the two Maritime Powers, who joined Leopold in burying their mutual suspicions on behalf of common security needs. Indeed, far from being dependent on Spain and the small league of Catholic princes who had saved it in 1620, the monarchy was now part of a broad international coalition that included major Protestant powers such as England and the United Provinces, as well as all of the more powerful imperial princes. One indication of the dynasty's emergence from diplomatic isolation and its renewed acceptance by the German princes was the almost effortless election in January 1690 of Leopold's son Joseph as king of the Romans. Even though Joseph was only 12 years old at the time, the electors not only granted him a special age exemption, but negotiated an electoral capitulation with Leopold that actually strengthened certain imperial prerogatives. Both concessions contrasted sharply with the tortuous four-year wait and humiliating capitulation that Leopold himself had had to endure three decades earlier. They also reflected more than the electors' fear of Louis XIV and the Turks. The close collaboration in the triumphant Balkan crusade had forged a strong German identity among all the German princes, especially those who had actually fought there. Whereas this spirit of patriotism was shared equally by the Protestant and Catholic princes, the dynasty's constitutional position within the empire was also further entrenched by a fortuitous shift in the confessional balance of the Electoral College. With the extinction of its Calvinist dynasty in 1685, the Palatinate had been inherited by the Catholic duke of Neuburg, whose daughter Eleonore had just become Leopold's third wife, and whose son John William was a close friend of Roman King Joseph. The recent conversion of the Saxon Frederick Augustus left Brandenburg and Brunswick-Lüneburg as the only Protestants among the nine imperial electors. The combination of Joseph's election and the overwhelming Catholic majority in the electoral college guaranteed Habsburg retention of the imperial crown for the foreseeable future. Moreover, the birth of a younger brother, Charles, in 1685 eliminated any immediate threat of the dynasty's extinction. Although Leopold owed his good fortune principally to outside support, these dynastic developments strengthened his position as a major player in European affairs. At the same time several domestic developments assisted in laying the foundations of a great power.

The integration of Hungary

After two centuries the monarchy had finally vanquished the Turks. Now it remained for Leopold to subdue his own Hungarian subjects. By the spring of 1687 the progress of the reconquest had emboldened the emperor and his Austrian and Bohemian counselors to institute constitutional changes that would bring the kingdom more into line with the rest of the monarchy. Yet Leopold had no intention of decreeing a Hungarian version of the *Verneuerte Landesordnung*. Instead he submitted his proposals to a combined Hungarian-Croatian diet. When it convened in October at Pressburg, he reiterated his intention of honoring his oath to uphold the constitution and the kingdom's liberties, including the diet's right to vote taxes, the nobility's control over local government, and the people's religious freedom. In exchange he sought only two constitutional changes. The diet readily agreed to abolish formally its right to elect its kings and to accept a hereditary succession, an innovation that it confirmed by recognizing his son, Joseph, as heir and his coronation as king. The diet also agreed to repeal the *jus resistendi*, albeit with some reluctance and only after repeated promises of religious freedom.

Leopold was no less successful in forging a new arrangement with the Transylvanian estates, which convened at Fogaras following the death of Michael I Apafi and the final defeat of Imre Thököly in 1690. His *Diplomum Leopoldinum* confirmed the privileges of the three nations represented in the diet, which agreed in return to pay a fixed annual contribution of just over 100,000 fl. (400,000 in wartime). He also recognized their right to elect a native governor, subject to confirmation by the crown. It was a measure of Leopold's moderation that he even recognized the late Michael I Apafi's son as prince until 1696, when the young man was finally brought to Vienna and induced to renounce his title in exchange for a pension and his elevation as an imperial prince. The emperor also recognized the principality's special status within Hungary by establishing an independent Transylvanian Chancery to represent it in Vienna. Finally, he confirmed religious freedom for the principality's Catholics, Lutherans, Calvinists, and Unitarians – though not for the Orthodox Romanian peasantry or a large Armenian refugee population that had fled there from Turkish Wallachia in 1672. Indeed, over the next decade Jesuit missionaries succeeded in convincing many of the Romanian and Armenian clergy to adhere to the Uniate (Greek Catholic) church, which recognized the authority of the papacy.

The settlements that Leopold offered the estates at Pressburg and Fogaras demonstrated that he had learned the lessons of previous Hungarian insurrections, but also that both sides recognized that future opposition would be less likely to succeed in the absence of an independent Transylvania or powerful Ottoman threat. Yet these efforts at forging a new relationship could not erase totally the mutual suspicion that continued to poison relations between crown and country. A notorious example had already surfaced in the months prior to the Pressburg diet, when Hungary's new military governor, Count Antonio Caraffa interpreted the idle gossip of some camp followers at the town of Eperjes as evidence of another plot against Habsburg rule. Although Leopold instructed Caraffa to abide by the kingdom's laws and a recently promulgated amnesty, he empowered him to establish a tribunal there to investigate and punish any treasonous activity. Over a six-month period seventeen prominent burghers and nobles were tortured into confessing to the groundless charges. In short order the unfortunate victims had their right arms cut off, were decapitated, drawn and quartered, and finally had their remains hanged from the city gate. By August the Palatine Esterházy and other magnates had prevailed on Leopold to discontinue the so-called slaughterhouse of Eperjes and eventually secured Caraffa's transfer to another position.

Moreover, in the aftermath of the Pressburg diet Leopold continued to rely almost exclusively on his Austrian and Bohemian counselors in making policy for the kingdom. Native Hungarians had virtually no voice in the country's reorganization, or *Einrichtungswerk*, which was instead placed in the hands of a commission headed by Leopold's grand chamberlain, Ferdinand Prince Dietrichstein. They were totally excluded from the so-called Commission for Newly Acquired Lands, or *Commissio Neo Acquistica*, a panel formed by the Dietrichstein Commission to ascertain ownership rights to recovered Hungarian lands. The Commission also disposed of much of sparsely inhabited southern Hungary and Slavonia without consulting the kingdom's authorities. Even the subsequent determination of the country's borders at the peace of Carlowitz was concluded without the participation of a single Hungarian negotiator.

This anti-Magyar bias was most evident in the policies that the government adopted in resettling the country. Before returning estates to their former owners, the *Commissio Neo Acquistica* demanded proof of ownership. Unfortunately, many of the deeds had been lost during the Ottoman occupation. Even when claimants could prove their claim, they had to pay a stiff administrative fee that was set at 10 percent of the value of the land recovered. In the many instances when nobles could not establish prior ownership, their estates reverted to the crown. As had happened in Bohemia after White Mountain, the emperor often gave newly acquired lands to non-native courtiers and generals who then resold them rather than establish roots there. This was, however, small consolation to those native nobles who could ill afford to repurchase their former estates. The Dietrichstein Commission also decided to repopulate much of the Hungarian plain with non-Magyar colonists who, it felt, would demonstrate greater loyalty to the monarchy. The area between the Danube and Tisza rivers was, in fact, already inhabited principally by Serbs whose ancestors had fled the Turkish advance over the past three centuries. By 1690 the Dietrichstein Commission strengthened their numbers by resettling the latest surge of perhaps 40,000 Serb and other Balkan refugees there, granting them religious freedom and a large measure of local autonomy. It also accepted Slovak peasants who had run away from their estates in Upper Hungary. The Commission's preference was, however, for Germans; by 1699 it had attracted them in such large numbers from the Bohemian crownlands that their former landlords persuaded Leopold to ban further emigration. Yet another source of friction was the government's decision to expand the Military Border beyond Croatia, despite the diminished Turkish threat. At Pressburg Leopold had, in fact, promised to restore much of the Military Border and new areas conquered by *Grenzer* forces to civilian rule, a pledge that he repeated to the Croatian-Slavonian estates in 1693. But a combination of pressure from the *Hofkriegsrat* and Inner Austrian regime, together with violent protests by the *Grenzer* themselves, forced Leopold to reconsider. In the end he retained the existing arrangement and established two new districts in Slavonia and along the

Tisza-Mures river valleys in southern Hungary, both of which were administered independently of Croatia and Hungary by the Inner Austrian offices of the *Hofkriegsrat* and *Hofkammer*.

Although the kingdom's nobility resented its continued exclusion from policy-making and from much of Hungary's newly recovered territories, the Habsburg regime generally abided by the spirit of the Pressburg settlement. In 1689 Leopold even rejected some of the Dietrichstein Commission's more controversial proposals in the face of strong opposition from the Hungarian diet. Within a few years, however, the stabilization of the Hungarian front emboldened him to contemplate additional steps toward integrating the kingdom with the rest of the monarchy. Ironically, the principal advocate for the consolidation of royal authority was the one Hungarian minister who did eventually emerge as an influential member of Leopold's inner circle. Born to a Magyarized Croat Protestant family, Leopold Cardinal Kollonics (1631–1707) had been converted and educated by the Jesuits. He had fought the Turks for much of his career, first in two expeditions to Crete as a Maltese knight, then as the director of medical services during the siege of Vienna. It was, however, as a thoroughly Germanized clerical and civil official that Kollonics earned Leopold's confidence. He was appointed president of the Hungarian treasury in 1672 and held a succession of high church positions before becoming archbishop-primate of Esztergom in 1695.

Even before Dietrichstein's death in 1698, Kollonics had become the most influential member of the Commission. By then he had also earned the hatred of many of his fellow Hungarians through his outspoken advocacy of confessional absolutism. At one point he is reputed to have predicted that he would "first render Hungary obedient, then destitute, and finally Catholic." Although the emperor never acted on Kollonics's appeal for wholesale Catholicization, the *Explanatio Leopoldina* that he issued in 1691 did warn that his extension of religious freedom to the reconquered lands was purely voluntary and only temporary. Two years later Leopold began levying indirect taxation on the nobility in exchange for discontinuing the outmoded feudal *insurrectio*. Over the next four years the kingdom paid 2 million fl. annually, which was increased to 4 million in 1698. Noble opposition forced Leopold to reduce their contribution to 250,000 fl., instead of the 1.25 million proposed by Kollonics. As was generally the case elsewhere in the monarchy, a far greater proportion of the tax burden now fell on the peasantry (3.5 million) and the impoverished towns (250,000). Nor did the peasantry's obligations stop there. By 1702 Leopold had instituted Kollonics's call for a largely native Hungarian army by rendering them subject to forcible induction into the army. Seemingly the kingdom's integration into the Habsburg *Gesamtstaat* was proceeding apace.

The economic recovery

In examining the half century after 1648, it is easy to focus on the crown's triumphs in Hungary, whether against the Turks or its own fiercely independent subjects. Yet, no less important for the monarchy's evolution as a great power was the recovery of the Austrian and Bohemian hereditary lands from the devastation of the Thirty Years' War. Their economic revival was, to be sure, less dramatic, more gradual, and ultimately just as incomplete. The constant turmoil in neighboring Hungary and the unwelcome succession of conflicts with Sweden, the Ottoman empire, and France deprived the peoples of the *Erblande* of any opportunity for peace. It did not, however, prevent the landed nobility from spearheading a postwar recovery and strengthening its position as the monarchy's leading entrepreneurial class. The creation of a standing army under Ferdinand III and Leopold I actually facilitated its evolution from a military caste to a capitalist one devoted to developing its estates. It was also in a better position to overcome the trials of war. Its control over local government left it free to compensate for increased wartime mortality and emigration by adding to the number and burdens of its serfs. Moreover, while the Contribution and other imposts continued to spiral, demesne land remained tax-free. The decline in rural population actually permitted the nobility to accelerate its ongoing acquisition of peasant plots by taking over deserted farmland. By the end of the century noble demesnes accounted for 20–25 percent of Bohemia's arable manorial land.

Estate owners also continued to hone their entrepreneurial skills. The second half of the century witnessed the introduction of several new crops in the Austrian lands. The two archduchies began planting tobacco after its value was brought to their attention by the Swedish invaders of 1643. Two decades later the Upper Austrian nobility was cultivating potatoes. By the end of the century a number of estates had reimported mulberry trees and silkworms from Italy to replace those that had been destroyed during the war. Italian influence was also responsible for the introduction of maize, which first appeared in Styria, but then spread to the other Austrian lands and Hungary before the end of the century. Inner Austria also made major strides in raising cattle, principally for export to Italy.

Greater Bohemia's recovery from almost constant military occupation was less immediate. Of peasant land abandoned during the war, a quarter of Moravia's was still uncultivated in the 1650s, a fifth of Bohemia's as late as the 1680s. The fish breeding and wine growing industries failed to achieve prewar levels of production. A postwar decline in export prices also forestalled a complete recovery of grain production until the end of the century. Nevertheless, the kingdom's estate owners compensated for these setbacks by stepping into the commercial vacuum left by the kingdom's towns. Wartime population and capital losses had, in fact, sharply reduced the towns' capacity for sustaining their export trade with Germany. The kingdom's landholding nobility responded by developing their own network of contacts, not only within Silesia and neighboring Saxony, but with Hamburg and the sea beyond. Although they sold a number of other products, such as iron ore, wool, glass, and various foodstuffs, they also derived considerable income by greatly expanding the small cottage textile industry that had evolved before the Thirty Years' War. The putting-out system not only supplemented their peasants' income from agriculture, but provided the seigneurs with licensing fees that they collected both from peasant cottagers and from the middlemen who collected and marketed their cloth.

Not surprisingly, the larger and wealthier landowners benefited most from agricultural and commercial innovations. They were not only better able to weather the initial shock of the war, but were then in the position to buy out those smaller landowners who did not have the resources to survive. Whereas the size of a typical Bohemian estate increased to thirty villages following the war, the profits and wealth of the greatest Austrian and Bohemian aristocrats reached enormous proportions. The net worth of a single member of the Austrian Schwarzenberg family tripled from 1 to 3 million fl. in the two decades following the siege of Vienna. By the end of the century, the Liechtenstein and Dietrichstein families together owned a quarter of all the land in Moravia.

Estate capitalism was not without its costs. The landholding nobility's increasing reliance on forced labor may have boosted production, but was also less efficient and humane than free labor. It virtually ignored the development of more profitable export industries in favor of foodstuffs and raw materials, such as unfinished cloth, that came under the control of foreign entrepreneurs. Nor were the benefits of estate capitalism evenly distributed among the emperor's subjects. In Bohemia and Moravia the gentry's inability to compete with the great latifundia of the wealthiest nobles led to their virtual disappearance as a class. The drastic decline in the number of noble families represented in the Bohemian diet from 1,128 in 1620 to only 238 at the end of the century reflected not only the purges of the Counter-Reformation but the economic shakeout that followed. The *Erblande*'s peasantry paid the stiffest price of all. A combination of increased labor obligations and sustained religious persecution led many peasants to emigrate, whether to the towns, other manors, various German states, or to the newly recovered Hungarian lands.

The towns also continued to lose ground to the aristocracy, particularly in the Bohemian crownlands. They were especially handicapped both by the continuing spiral of taxation and by the ever present competition from noble estate owners. As a result they recovered more slowly than rural areas, or even manorial towns. Fully two decades after the Peace of Westphalia the numbers of burghers in the major textile towns of Lower Silesia were still only a fraction of their prewar levels: Schweidnitz counted only 350 out of 1,800; Löwenberg barely 200 out of 1,700; Jauer, which the Swedes had burned to the ground in 1648, still had only 150 out of 1,400 burghers. In Bohemia proper, Prague itself had only 355 artisans in 1674, compared to 1,200 in 1620. Far from compensating for the loss of burghers and artisans, the influx of unskilled peasants from the countryside merely added the unwelcome financial burden of tending to growing hordes of beggars. Indeed, unlike most estate owners, the textile and mining towns of Bohemia and Moravia experienced difficulty paying off their wartime debts, a burden that prevented them from modernizing their equipment. Religious persecution also hampered the recovery of many towns in the hereditary lands. Merchants, artisans, and miners alike reacted to the Westphalian settlement and the unremitting persecution by Ferdinand III and Leopold I by emigrating to Protestant territories such as Saxon Lusatia and the relatively tolerant frontier towns of southwestern Poland. Meanwhile, the burghers and nobles of Lower Austria joined in persecuting the archduchy's small, but commercially important Jewish population. In 1669 the Viennese blamed them for a fire in the Hofburg, while Leopold's own Spanish wife Margaret attributed a recent miscarriage to their presence in the capital. Within a year a 100,000 fl. inducement from the city government had prompted the emperor to complete their expulsion from all of Lower Austria, although interests of state compelled him to exempt two court factors and later extend exceptional privileges to the talented financier Samuel Oppenheimer.

As late as 1700 the population and production levels of several free towns in the Bohemian crownlands had still not reached prewar levels. Some, such as Jauer, never regained their former positions. Most urban centers had, however, fully recovered by then. By the 1670s Breslau was once again a city of over 30,000 and had taken the lead in reviving the Silesian towns' wool and linen production. At the end of the century greater Bohemia's towns and rural cottagers were exporting 1.5 million fl. annually in cloth and linen and had established markets as far away as London and Britain's overseas colonies. The recovery of the *Erblande*'s sheep herds also keyed a rebound in the wool industry. Linz had already regained its virtual monopoly over Upper Austrian production by the 1670s, and was employing 4,000 full-time workers by 1700. As a group the mining towns were less fortunate, if only because of weaker prices and stronger foreign competition. Nevertheless, at least Inner Austrian metal exports had revived by the end of the century, principally by finding new markets in Italy.

While the *Erblande*'s economy had largely rebounded during the half century after Westphalia, Hungary measured its recovery only in terms of territory regained from the Turks. Unlike the hereditary lands, it had enjoyed no respite from military conflict and occupation. The most notable exception was Transylvania, which had escaped the heaviest fighting and was still relatively prosperous. Much of Croatia was also spared, although its economy was now based on little more than supplying the Military Border garrisons and ransoming Turks captured in cross-border raids. By contrast Upper Hungary had been devastated by almost continuous hostilities. At least half of the farmland in its eastern, Ruthene-speaking districts had been abandoned; by one count over 70 percent of the 1,180 homesteads on the huge Rákóczi estate near Munkács remained uncultivated until well into the next century. The thin strip of Royal Hungary that bordered directly on the Austrian lands had also been ravaged, especially in 1683, when an estimated 10,000 residents of the massive Esterházy estates were killed by the Turks. Those communities that survived the Turkish wars relied principally on raising livestock – which now outnumbered the native population by two to one – and producing modest quantities of wine and grain. Given the lack of healthy drinking water and grain (a third of which was grown on demesne lands), many Hungarians adapted to a diet of meat and wine.

Not surprisingly it was the newly liberated districts of the Hungarian plain that fared worst of all. Like other Ottoman dominions it had suffered throughout the century from outbreaks of plague and smallpox. During the reconquest, both sides had oppressed its inhabitants, not only by taxing and requisitioning supplies, but by resorting to the wanton pillage and violence that had long been common practice in the Habsburg-Turkish wars. Many peasants responded by fleeing to the towns, where they cultivated compact plots just outside the walls. Those who remained in the countryside were often *hayducks* who, having lost much of their livestock to the war, survived only as brigands or mercenaries of the emperor, individual magnates, or Michael Apafi. By 1685 the south-central plain between the Danube and Tisza rivers had lost most of its settled population; to the southwest, Slavonia was virtually uninhabited. The reconquered territories were further reduced by a new plague epidemic that claimed 30,000 lives between 1690 and 1692. By one estimate their population (excluding Transylvania) had dropped by the end of the war to as little as 10 percent of what it had been on the eve of the Ottoman conquest.

The devastation of war and the growth of estate capitalism were two phenomena that were common to both the first and second halves of the seventeenth century. One development that distinguished these two periods was the belated efforts of the central government to promote economic development following the Thirty Years' War. The evolution of a somewhat coherent economic policy was initially impelled by the need to raise money for Leopold's imperial election and for the wars with Sweden and the Turks. Later on it was sustained by the desire to match the economic growth of Colbertine France and, ultimately, by the need to rebuild Hungary. For the most part the monarchy was inspired by the contemporary German school of political economy known as cameralism. The emperor shared with his German vassals a compelling need to avert bankruptcy by a combination of economic reconstruction and the more efficient management of state finances. Most of the credit for the evolution of Austrian cameralism has, in fact, gone to three German émigré political economists: Wilhelm von Schröder (1640–88), whose studies of the British economic system had familiarized him with western models of mercantilism; Johann Joachim Becher (1635–82), who was the most original and influential theorist; and his brother-in-law, Philipp Wilhelm von Hörnigk (1640–1714), a propagandist whose famous tract Österreich über Alles, wann es nur will (Austria above all others if it only wishes) strove to rebuild the monarchy into an economically self-sufficient great power in the aftermath of the siege of Vienna.

Although both Becher and Schröder were already working in Vienna within a decade of Leopold's succession, theirs were neither the only nor the first voices to be raised following the conclusion of the Thirty Years' War. There were also government officials, such as the Bohemian Kammerrat Johann Christoph Borek and the Hofkammer secretary Christian Julius Schierl von Schierendorff (1661–1726), enlightened nobles and clerics like the Spanish Franciscan friar Cristóbal de Rojas y Spínola (1626–95), and numerous merchants and town magistrates, all of whom were genuinely concerned about the economic plight of monarchy's peoples. Like the cameralists in general, most struck a balance between the need to rebuild postwar levels of population and production both in the countryside and the towns. Yet, by leaning more heavily on trade and commerce they helped to shift attention to the problems of the monarchy's urban economies. Before his death Ferdinand III had already taken some remedial steps by attempting to alleviate the debts of the Bohemian towns and to limit some of the land-holding nobility's commercial privileges. Although previous Habsburgs had blamed the guilds for their restrictiveness, inefficiency, and the poor quality of the goods they produced, Ferdinand III intensified the pressure by extending privileges to independent artisans, who generally earned the protection of powerful local consumers such as nearby seigneurs, church foundations, universities, and military commanders. By 1689 a Leopoldine edict had given the government the right to control the number of masters and undercut the monopolistic effects of guild operations. Even before then Becher, who opposed all forms of monopoly, estimated that a third of the Austrian lands' 150,000 artisans were Schwarzarbeiter who did not belong to a guild.

Immediately after the war the Bohemian towns had petitioned Ferdinand to refine its own raw materials into more finished goods for export. Becher became the leading force in attempting this conversion. By 1666 he had inspired the creation of a Commerce Commission (*Kommerzkollegium*) in Vienna, as well as the reestablishment of the first postwar silk plantation on the Lower Austrian estates of *Hofkammer* President Sinzendorf. He subsequently helped create a *Kunst- und Werkhaus* in which foreign masters trained non-guild artisans in the production of finished goods. By 1672 he had promoted the construction of a wool factory in Linz. Four years later he established a textile workhouse for vagabonds in the Bohemian town of Tabor that eventually employed 186 spinners under his own (and later Schröder's) directorship. Although nothing ever came of Rojas y Spínola's visions of a trade concession with the Spanish empire, the treaty of Vasvár did implement Becher's plans for creating an Oriental Trading Company that used the Danube as a conduit for exporting finished goods to Constantinople from both the monarchy and western countries such as England and the Netherlands. At the same time a complementary Occidental Company was established to take over the western export of the monarchy's raw materials from foreign middlemen.

Some of Becher's projects met with limited success. In time Linz's new wool factory even became one of the largest and most important in Europe. Yet most of the government initiatives ended in failure. The Commerce Commission was doomed by Sinzendorf's corruption and indifference. The Tabor workhouse nearly collapsed after just five years owing to the lack of government funding, and was then destroyed two years later during the Turkish invasion. The Oriental Company was fatally handicapped by a combination of poor management, government export prohibitions against Turkey, the opposition of Ottoman (principally Greek) merchants, and ultimately by the outbreak of war. The *Kunst- und Werkhaus* also folded during the 1680s, partly because of the regime's unwillingness to import a significant number of foreign, Protestant teachers and skilled workers.

Government mismanagement, warfare, and religious persecution all contributed to these failures. A dramatic economic turnaround was, however, impossible in the absence of the necessary commercial infrastructure. The monarchy suffered from a dearth of banks and other credit institutions, as well as from an inadequate transportation system that was hampered by bad roads, internal tariffs, unnavigable rivers, and especially poor overland connections between the Austrian hinterland and the Adriatic coast. Whatever the underlying causes, the cameralists' mixed record emboldened their critics and cooled government support for the balance of Leopold's reign. Although they doubtless assisted in the *Erblande*'s recovery from the devastation of the Thirty Years' War, the monarchy as a whole remained an exporter of food and raw materials that it later reimported as finished goods.

Although the cameralists' agrarian programs also met with mixed results, they likewise promoted economic development, as well as greater social justice. The appeals of former Protestants Becher and Hörnigk for dramatic population growth and religious toleration bore fruit on the Hungarian plain, where the Dietrichstein Commission assisted the feverish pace of colonization with special grants of religious freedom. Schröder also played a key role in legitimizing the appeals of a growing number of public officials, nobles, and clergy who decried the suffering of the monarchy's peasantry. In one of his sermons, the prominent court preacher Abraham à Sancta Clara accused ruthless noble landlords of "sucking the blood of their peasants like leeches." Yet Schröder and numerous estate managers were motivated not only by humanitarian concerns, but also by a more sophisticated sense of enlightened self-interest: many of the German principalities had long appreciated the need to protect the peasantry as the primary source of production and tax revenue. This practice of *Bauernschutz* was an integral part of the thinking of cameralists like Schröder, who argued that a healthy and contented peasantry would be more productive and, therefore, enrich both the monarch and noble estate owners.

The government's belated inclination to protect its peasants was most evident within the *Erblande*. As early as 1657 Leopold issued a *Robotpatent* for the Bohemian lands that limited the demands that landlords could place on their serfs. Over the next two decades he ordered additional regulations which, among other things, empowered royal governors and local officials to adjudicate peasant complaints against their landlords. In 1679 he also issued a decree for Lower Austria that not only regulated and limited *robot* service, but even allowed peasants to commute service in exchange for a cash payment. Unfortunately, it proved impossible to enforce most of these initiatives at the local level against the passive resistance of recalcitrant landowners. Finally, in 1680 a major peasant uprising broke out in Bohemia and parts of Moravia. The army eventually crushed the revolt, executing more than a hundred peasants and sentencing over a thousand others to jail or forced labor. Yet Leopold also responded to its underlying causes by issuing a more sweeping *Robotpatent* on 28 June 1680. In addition to reaffirming every peasant's access to royal justice, the decree now limited *robot* to a maximum of three days per week,[5] and prohibited all service on Sundays and holidays, unless it was explicitly permitted by the parish priest. Finally, landlords were prohibited from arbitrarily raising rents or other fees, and even from compelling their peasants to buy products from seigneurial businesses.

---

[5] Except during harvest and other special occasions, when they could still be impressed for up to six days, but only if they were paid for their labor.

It is difficult to ascertain whether this latest *Robotpatent* proved much more effective than previous measures. Even where the three-day limit was observed, the patent may have led to an overall increase in *robot* service by establishing three days as a minimum standard for peasants who had previously enjoyed a lighter burden. Nor did a single peasant file suit against his landlord at any time over the next half century. Indeed, both the considerable emigration of colonists to Hungary after the reconquest and the outbreak of a second, smaller revolt in 1692 suggest that the *Robotpatent* was not a panacea for the Bohemian and Moravian peasantry. On the other hand, the final two decades of the century did witness a dramatic resurgence in their peasant populations, which finally reached prewar levels by 1700, despite the stream of emigrants to Hungary.

The government's attempts to improve the lot of the peasantry also extended to Hungary, though the opposition of the Magyar nobility presented an even greater obstacle to their success. As early as 1672, Leopold and his ministers had briefly considered reducing the Hungarian peasantry's manorial exactions as a means of undermining the appeal of the *Kuruc* revolt. Instead, they opted for the more conventional approach of confessional absolutism and Ampringen's *Gubernium*, perhaps because a direct attack on the nobility's privileges would have alienated even loyal Catholic magnates. After the Pressburg diet of 1687, the Dietrichstein Commission pressed for the same three-day maximum in *robot* service already in effect in Bohemia, together with a tax on noble demesne land. Yet, given the outcry that these plans raised when the diet met again in 1689, Leopold limited peasant relief to the establishment of regional, royal courts that enabled them to circumvent the seigneurial judges in filing complaints against their landlords. A short-lived peasant revolt in the eastern counties of Upper Hungary in 1697 attested to the need for greater intervention against the nobility – as well as to peasant discontent with increasing levels of royal taxation and recruitment.

The beginnings of cultural assimilation

Yet another ingredient in the monarchy's emergence as a great power was the shared identity and cultural unity that was beginning to evolve among its three most powerful institutions: court, nobility and Catholic church. Indeed, just as the crown had achieved a consensus with its foreign allies and German vassals, it had established a sense of common interest and interdependence with the ruling elites of its component lands. This was especially the case within the *Erblande*. Meanwhile, although Hungary's integration into the Habsburg *Gesamtstaat* had been both more gradual and less complete, both crown and country had grown more sensitive to each other's vital interests. The nobility had renounced the right to revolt and, as in Bohemia, its diet had formally acknowledged the dynasty's right of hereditary succession. For his part Leopold had purposely refrained from applying a Bohemian solution to Hungary. The nobility retained formidable constitutional limitations on royal authority, especially at the county level. Most of the kingdom's non-Catholic majority preserved at least a tenuous right to religious freedom. But these limitations in no way mortgaged the potential for a greater sense of unity and loyalty to the crown. If the Magyar nobility was still not totally committed to the monarchy as a whole, it was because it was still being denied the access to patronage and power that had been extended to the loyal Bohemian nobility after White Mountain. This too, however, would come with time.

Several instruments and symbols of the consensus between crown, nobility, and church were already evident by the end of the century. None was more obvious or important than the increases in the Contribution and the standing army that it supported. During the Thirty Years' War, Ferdinand II had been compelled to rely on Spain, the Catholic League, and military entrepreneurs like Wallenstein for the monarchy's defense. A half century later the steady growth in state revenue had promoted the establishment of a 100,000-man standing army. Although foreign officers and subsidies still comprised vital components, it was increasingly staffed by native nobles and outfitted by revenue drawn from all of Leopold's dominions, including large voluntary contributions from the monarchy's ecclesiastical foundations. The Bohemian and Austrian estates had cooperated most closely with the crown in steadily increasing their levies of troops and taxes. Even the Tyrol, which had earlier accepted reunification with the monarchy with a notable lack of enthusiasm, was moved to vote extraordinary sums during the closing decade of the war. Meanwhile, for the moment at least, the Magyar nation was acquiescing to increased levels of military quartering and taxation on a scale that likely exceeded those being levied within the *Erblande*.

Another integrating force crucial to the monarchy's development was the evolution of a common culture among its ruling elites. By 1700 the triumph of the Counter-Reformation was evident in several media. The crown continued to play a prominent role in propagandizing the link between the dynasty's destiny and the True Faith. Following the victory at the Kahlenberg, Leopold secured a papal declaration making 12 September a holy day throughout Catholic Europe in Mary's name. Although the cult of the Virgin continued to enjoy a special place in Habsburg hagiography, the emperor also promoted the veneration of other saints, such as Joseph (after whom he named his first son) and Leopold, his twelfth-century Babenberg namesake and founder of the great monastery at Klosterneuburg. Perhaps his most famous devotional monument was the *Pestsäule* that he erected in the

Graben, in which he attributed Vienna's deliverance from the plague epidemic of 1679 to his appeal to the Holy Trinity. As it had in the past the Society of Jesus led the monastic orders in carrying much the same message beyond the court. The graduates of its colleges controlled not only the monarchy's schools and universities, but censorship as well. It was also masterful in utilizing public dramas as a didactic tool. Some of its plays featured hundreds of actors and impressive scenery that depicted everything from heaven and hell to earthquakes and lightning. One Jesuit writer, Nikolaus Avancini, wrote no fewer than fifty-three dramas, many with historical themes that blended narration and praise of the dynasty and the Catholic faith. The religious orders also promoted processions in Protestant areas, such as the Lutheran towns of Lower Silesia, where they distributed leaflets predicting that spectators would "watch today, stand at attention tomorrow, [and] participate thereafter."

Their success is borne out by a dramatic increase both in the number of people entering the clergy and religious orders and other church-sponsored foundations. In Vienna alone, the second half of the century witnessed the foundation of 109 religious confraternities, together with over two dozen cloisters. The Jesuits accommodated would-be converts with extensive instruction, followed by mass conversion ceremonies conducted at their *Professhaus*. Government patronage continued to provide a potent argument for conversion, not only for nobles but also for the growing number of university-educated professionals seeking employment in the bureaucracy. These included a significant number of *Reich* Germans who, like the former Austrian Chancellor Hocher and Saxony's Frederick Augustus, saw conversion as a necessary prerequisite for the emperor's favor. Indeed, the closing decades of the reign witnessed the conversion of other key German-born officials, such as the cameralist Becher and both the future grand chamberlain and Austrian chancellor of Leopold's son Joseph. More remarkable was the return and conversion of several exiled Lutheran polemicists, who now turned their pens against their former faith. Among them were the Silesian Johannes Scheffler, who henceforth wrote under the politically correct pseudonym Angelus Silesius; Ferenc Otrokoczy, who was employed by the Jesuit press at Tyrnau; and his fellow Hungarian Stabaeus, who went so far as to pen an inflammatory polemic entitled *Martin Luther, come on out! The Cat will fight and eat the Mouse!*

The church also led the way in sponsoring construction projects and patronage of the arts throughout the monarchy, whether in the countryside, in major towns, or in Vienna itself. The building program was partly intended to propagandize its triumph over heresy and Islam, but also to accommodate the increased number of worshipers and clergy entering the church. In addition to new construction many existing churches were renovated in the new, baroque *Jesuitenstil* that became inextricably associ-ated with the Counter-Reformation. The newly prosperous landholding nobility followed suit with building programs of its own. The Bohemian and Moravian aristocracy distinguished itself through its support of the theater, the fine arts and especially music by retaining choirs, orchestras, and individual composers at their country estates. Many also built city palaces in Vienna, together with summer edifices beyond its walls. Whereas many were attracted to the city by the prospects of government patronage, others were drawn to the glamorous and stimulating lifestyle of the court, or even by the opportunity to compose and act in the court's dramatic and musical presentations. Despite its fiscal crisis, the court spent freely from the very outset of the postwar period. Ferdinand III's and Leopold I's sustained patronage of a musical establishment initiated the city's renowned associa-tion with the medium. Even when money was short, Leopold was known to pay his musicians first, before court officers. He celebrated his nuptials with Margaret Theresa in December 1666 with six weeks of celebrations that included various musical performances and an intricate equestrian ballet at the *Hofburg*. He also committed over 100,000 fl. toward the construction of a 1,500-seat *Komödienhaus* that was completed in 1667.

By the end of the century Vienna itself had emerged as another symbol and instrument for the integration of the monarchy's component lands. Its triumph over Prague, which had begun following the return of the imperial court after Rudolph II's death in 1612 and the transfer of the Bohemian Chancery twelve years later, was sealed by the losses subsequently inflicted by successive Swedish occupations. The extinction of the cadet Habsburg lines in Graz and Innsbruck, together with the progressive transfer of several Hungarian and Transylvanian offices, further entrenched Vienna's pre-eminent position within the monarchy. With a population of 80,000 it had already become the monarchy's undisputed administrative, cultural, and population center early in Leopold's reign. The massive toll in death and destruction wrought by the Turkish siege of 1683 temporarily set back Vienna's demographic and cultural evolution. Indeed, the city and the *Hofburg* itself were so devastated that Leopold was compelled to move the court to Linz for several months thereafter. Yet Vienna quickly recovered. The extended period of postwar confidence and prosperity witnessed one of the greatest building booms in the city's history, as government buildings, churches, cloisters, and aristocratic mansions rapidly filled the cramped space within its medieval walls, frequently in the place of burgher homes that had been damaged or destroyed in the siege. By 1700 it had grown far beyond its fortifications, housing a population of at least 100,000.

Church and aristocratic patronage embraced large numbers of native artists. Perhaps the most outstanding example in the field of music was the

Czech composer Josef Vejvanovský, whom Bishop Karl von Liechtenstein of Olmütz retained at his palace at Kremsier (Kroměříž). Yet they also drew artists from all over the continent, especially from Germany and Italy. The crown was no different. Ferdinand III and Leopold had revived Rudolph II's penchant for attracting artists from all over Europe, especially Italians. Italian symphonic and operatic forms established a century-long hegemony at court. In 1667 Leopold spent 100,000 fl. to put on a single Italian opera as part of the previous December's nuptial celebrations. Nor did he hesitate to use Italian forms in his own compositions, or the language itself in his speech and correspondence.

Yet the international ambience of Habsburg culture cannot obscure the emergence of German as yet another enduring, unifying cultural force in the monarchy's evolution. At first, its growing dominance among the monarchy's elites was not consciously promoted by the government. Quite to the contrary, the agents of the Counter-Reformation had often favored other tongues, especially in their attempt to subvert the influence of the monarchy's Lutheran towns. Thus Italian had gained the upper hand over German among the ruling classes of Gorizia and other parts of the Adriatic Littoral following the emigration of German-speaking nobles and burghers and their replacement by Italian Catholics. Similarly, the Leopoldine regime promoted the advancement of Slovak, and even Magyar, office-holders in the towns of Upper Hungary by reducing the special magisterial privileges of their Lutheran German oligarchies. In order to broaden Catholicism's appeal in the countryside, the Jesuit press at Tyrnau actually moved away from German in favor of Latin and the kingdom's other, indigenous languages. Thus it reacted to an existing Calvinist translation of the Bible by publishing a Magyar edition, even though vernacular editions were normally prohibited by the Papacy. It also made some inroads among the kingdom's Lutheran Slovaks, and Orthodox Ruthenes and Rumanians by translating and distributing catechisms and other religious literature among them. Nor was the picture altogether different within the Bohemian crownlands. In Upper Silesia several monasteries and other religious foundations were Polonized. Although Ferdinand II had granted German equal status with Czech in the conduct of official business, the latter remained the language of religious instruction among the Czech majorities in Bohemia and Moravia, as well as along the southern fringes of Upper Silesia. Moreover, by the second half of the century native Czechs had generally replaced the extranational army of principally German and Italian clerics first sent there during the Thirty Years' War.

The ultimate triumph of German was not due to coercion by the church or government, but rather reflected the voluntary acclimation of nobles, burghers, and professionals to the monarchy's increasingly dominant

German culture. The process of national acculturation had a long history within the Habsburg lands. Shortly after the Turkish occupation of most of Hungary, 60,000 Croat refugees fled to Lower Austria and the German-speaking areas of western Hungary and southern Moravia, where they ultimately adopted the local language; the parallel influx of Magyar nobles into Upper Hungary led the area's Slovak-speaking gentry to adopt Magyar. As we have already seen, many nobles residing in Habsburg Croatia, such as the aforementioned Zrinyi, Frangepáni, and Kollonics families, also became Magyarized by the mid-seventeenth century. Within the Bohemian crown-lands the Slavic Upper Silesian and Lusatian nobility had become Germanized long before the battle of White Mountain. Yet most important of all was the recent Germanization of Bohemia's and Moravia's foreign-born and native Czech nobility, if only because their rapid assimilation and steadfast commitment to the dynasty presented the government in Vienna with a vivid contrast to developments in Hungary. Following the un-successful magnate plot and Thököly revolt, Leopold and his Austrian and new Bohemian advisers concluded that the Magyar-speaking population was the least trustworthy element among the monarchy's diverse peoples. At the same time, they began to link German language and culture with Catholicism as another instrument for instilling greater loyalty to the dynasty. Hence the favor that the Dietrichstein Commission, its *Commissio Neo Acquistica*, and Cardinal Kollonics began to show German (and other non-Magyar) colonists following the recovery of the Hungarian plain.

However voluntary the process of Germanization may have been, it was effective largely because it offered nobles and other social groups greater access to wealth or power as members of the ruling elite. In this sense the regime's selective use of political privileges, patronage, and land grants was rooted in its quest for greater social control. Its noble protégés were, however, also motivated by a universal penchant for self-acclaim. Not unlike the French nobility at Versailles, their positions and very presence at court allowed them to share the limelight with the emperor, his court, and the church, especially when they joined them in patronizing builders and large numbers of fine and performing artists. The fabulously wealthy Karl Eusebius von Liechtenstein spoke for many aristocrats when he wrote a book on architecture in which he identified "the one and only reason for stately buildings: the everlasting name, fame and memory that one earns from the great edifices that he leaves behind."

This search for self-acclaim pervaded the entire ruling elite. The church used its patronage of the arts not only as a medium for religious education, but as a celebration of Catholicism's resurgence from the setbacks of the previous century. Leopold was no less driven by the need to celebrate his triumphs. Admittedly the monarchy's recent successes were due more to aggression by Louis XIV and the Turkish Kiuprilis that had united their enemies, than to Leopold or his impotent Spanish cousin; even as he entered the fifth decade of his reign, no one referred to "Leopold the Great" or spoke of an "Age of Leopold I." Nevertheless, the emperor used his patronage of the arts to promote the dynasty's image not only at home and abroad, but in his own eyes. His decision to emulate his French adversary by projecting an Austrian Versailles for his son at Schönbrunn reflected this personal quest – just as the shortage of funds that delayed its construction exposed the residual deficiencies that still separated the monarchy from France.

Ferdinand III and Leopold I had, in fact, achieved a great deal over the past half century. By continuing to service the interests of the aristocracy and church, they cemented the symbiotic alliance that their predecessors had forged earlier in the century. As a result the monarchy was now held together by an appreciably higher tax base, a reasonably effective standing army, and an emerging common culture that reinforced the hegemony of the monarchy's Catholic and German ruling elites. It is worth noting that each of these elements constituted a powerful integrating force that helped sustain the monarchy for the rest of its history.

Nevertheless, despite the new-found prosperity and confidence that energized all elements of the ruling elite, a number of problems still precluded the monarchy's emergence as a great power. One limitation was the monarchy's material resources. Over the past half century its population had grown by at least 2 million people from a low of perhaps 7 million in 1648. The bulk of these gains had come with the demographic recovery of the Bohemian crownlands and the reconquest and colonization of Hungary. Yet, its population was still dwarfed by Louis XIV's 20 million Frenchmen, and much poorer and less productive than those of France, England, or the United Provinces. In a world in which wealth was increasingly determined by industry and commerce, only 2 percent of the monarchy's population lived in towns. Meanwhile, the weakest link of all remained Hungary, which still needed time to recover from a century and a half of Turkish occupation. Even with the steady economic recovery of the *Erblande* and the tax increases that it supported, annual wartime revenue stood at only 9 million fl., or roughly an eighth that of France.

Another limiting factor was the crown's alliance with the church and land-holding nobility. Although it played a crucial role in uniting the monarchy and enhancing the dynasty's prestige, it did not come without some cost. As we have already seen, the remedial steps that Ferdinand III and Leopold had taken toward instituting a comprehensive economic program were undermined by the lingering legacy of religious persecution and by commercial privileges granted the nobility that hindered productivity among the monarchy's free towns and peasants. More important, its support for the

Counter-Reformation and feudal *Ständestaat* helped entrench values that were increasingly out of step with secular and rationalist ideas then sweeping western and central Europe. By the end of the century the Enlightenment had evolved in France and England, both as an outgrowth of the Scientific Revolution and as a reaction to the unpopular policies of Louis XIV and James II. Within Protestant Germany the growth of Pietism encouraged many states to adopt the economic, fiscal, and social policies preached by the cameral sciences.

There are at least three explanations for the monarchy's insulation from these trends. To a certain extent it was the victim of the ruling elite's own success. While the obvious shortcomings of Bourbon and Stuart regimes inspired French and English philosophers to seek different values represented by the Enlightenment, the monarchy's coalition of church, aristocracy, and crown was able to legitimize a system that had reestablished Catholicism, expelled the Turks from Hungary, and restructured and revived the *Erblande*'s economy. Rather than resort to skepticism and introspection, the ruling elites spread their own values through their patronage of the various media of the baroque.

A second factor was the Catholic ruling elite's persecution and expulsion of Protestants. Religious intolerance was never as extreme as in Spain, where the dynasty's senior branch could rely on a crusading zeal rooted in the peninsula's centuries-long struggle against Islam and pursue unbelievers without concern for civil war or foreign intervention. Still, many of the monarchy's greatest writers, philosophers, and scientists had already emigrated by mid-century. Perhaps the most noteworthy figure was the last bishop of the Bohemian Brethren, Jan Amos Komenský (better known as Comenius), whose wanderings after White Mountain embraced virtually every Protestant country in Europe, including Transylvania, where he joined several Magyar exiles pursuing philosophy and the natural sciences. Some stayed a bit longer, such as the rector of Eperjes's Protestant *Lyceum*, Johannes Bayer, who taught Bacon's inductive method for a decade before dying *en route* to his own exile in 1674.

Less overt but perhaps most effective in closing off the monarchy's cultural window to the West was the ruling elite's selective utilization of patronage. Whereas it did not overtly oppose science and humanism, these disciplines received much less attention than they had enjoyed before the Counter-Reformation. Thus, while several Jesuit thinkers and even Ferdinand III conducted experiments and studied the natural sciences, both church and state focused their support on propagating public loyalty to Catholicism and the dynasty. It was easy to find devotional books like two Magyar-language collections of Marian legends edited by Pál Esterházy in 1691 and 1696, or the Latin *Triumph of the Innocents* in which Stefan Székely glorified Hungary's past saints as the predecessors of the Habsburgs. Nor was there any dearth of descriptions, histories, and polemics devoted to the dynasty and its dominions. At the same time, however, it proved impossible for Franz Joseph Count Hoditz to find a publisher for his works on morality and law. The elder brother of the cameralist Schierl von Schierendorff even lost his judicial position in Moravia after prosecuting the Society of Jesus for violating local inheritance laws.

Some tenuous ties remained. The dynasty's retention of the imperial crown continued to serve as a magnet for German academics and other professionals – hence the valuable contribution of men like Becher, Hörnigk, and Schröder, all of whom hailed from Protestant states. The survival of at least partial religious toleration in Hungary and Silesia permitted both dominions to serve as intermediaries for the infiltration of new ideas from the empire and Western Europe. Indeed, while Catholic Hungarians and Silesians studied at Tyrnau, Olmütz, Prague, or the new Jesuit university at Breslau (founded 1702), their Protestant countrymen were exposed to rather different ideas being taught abroad at universities such as Utrecht, Leiden, Basel, Jena, Leipzig, and Frankfurt an der Oder. A century later, the German and Silesian connections would play a more significant role in the monarchy's political and cultural development. For the time being, however, the cultural hegemony of the monarchy's elite that manifested itself through self-promotion, limited persecution, and selective patronage took its toll. It is no coincidence that the monarchy did not produce a single major philosopher or scientist following the deaths of Tycho Brahe and Johannes Kepler early in the century; although the Silesian-born Christian Wolff brought the Enlightenment to an entire generation of Germans, he did so from university positions in Saxony, Prussia, and Hesse, while the Habsburg lands were initially unaffected by his teaching.

Nor is it surprising that the central government failed to take full advantage of the cameralists' attempts to reorganize its fiscal administration along more rational lines. To his credit Leopold did make limited progress in the face of constant pleas for reform. In 1680, with war looming on two fronts, he gave in to his creditors' demands for an investigation that eventually led to the dismissal of the corrupt *Hofkammer* President Sinzendorf. He not only recovered some of the 2 million fl. that Sinzendorf had embezzled, but issued a *Hofkammerordnung* in January 1681 that led to better record keeping, the drafting of roughly accurate annual budgets, and the subordination of the previously autonomous Bohemian, Silesian, and Hungarian treasuries to the *Hofkammer*.[6] Four years later the Capuchin friar Marco d'Aviano and the Papal nuncio urged him to reform the military's supply

---

[6] Although protests by the Sopron diet obliged him to restore the Hungarian *Kammer*'s independence four months later.

system after the 1684 campaign had exposed serious shortcomings. Although Leopold did little to address the structural defects in the system, he did replace the incompetent head of the War Commissar, Sigfried Breuner, by promoting him to a higher position.

Leopold's decision to promote Breuner rather than dismiss him outright lends credence to the conventional view that he was simply too mild, desultory, and indecisive to assert effective leadership. Throughout his reign he remained faithful to numerous loyal, but incompetent and often aged ministers who usually left their positions only when they died. Although Leopold acceded to some of his advisers' demands for change, he stopped short of the thorough house-cleaning that the monarchy's administrative apparatus needed. He was especially derelict in pursuing reform at the local level, where hordes of agencies run by the central government or the provincial estates either failed to collect or siphoned off a third or more of government revenue before it could reach the *Hofkammer*. Foreign governments were so suspicious of the *Hofkammer* that they were usually reluctant to supply Leopold with subsidies without having some oversight of the processing of the monies they provided.

The retention of this supremely irrational system limited the size and effectiveness of the Habsburg military. Montecuccoli had come right to the point when he stated that warfare required three things: "Money, money, and more money." Yet, thanks to chronic shortages of funds and the supplies they provided, the officers of his and Charles of Lorraine's generation often had to rely on their own resources to equip, provision, and pay their men, just as Wallenstein had done at the beginning of the century. As a result the Habsburg military often felt compelled to make "war pay for war" by living off conquered countryside. Although this system might work in time of war, it was counterproductive in peacetime, when much of the army was obliged to make sometimes excessive demands on the monarchy's own subjects, especially in Hungary. Moreover, even with the proceeds of foreign subsidies and the military occupation of Hungary, the army was not as well-equipped and only a quarter the size of the 400,000-strong French army. Thus, although the monarchy was virtually whole for the first time since 1529, it remained dependent on the support of foreign allies. Fortunately, Louis XIV's aggression had inspired an anti-French coalition not unlike the Anglo-Dutch-Spanish-German dynastic combination that had helped to create the first Habsburg great power at the turn of the sixteenth century. Now, two hundred years later, events in Madrid would put that coalition to the test.

4 Facing west: the second Habsburg empire (1700–1740)

The European powers had been preparing for Charles II's death for his entire thirty-five-year reign. Finally, at the end of the century unmistakable signs of his imminent demise encouraged a rash of diplomatic activity. Although the Austrian Habsburgs and French Bourbons were the main antagonists, all of the major, and several smaller, countries had a stake in the succession struggle. There were, in fact, initially three claims to Charles's inheritance, all based on the rights of Charles's two sisters. As the husband of the elder Maria Theresa, Louis XIV could put forward a claim on behalf of the Grand Dauphin and his three sons, especially since the Spanish government had never paid France the 500,000 crowns in compensation for renouncing its rights to the inheritance. Although Emperor Leopold had married the younger Margaret Theresa, their only surviving child was a daughter, Maria Antonia. Before her death in 1692, the archduchess had married Max Emanuel and borne a son, Joseph Ferdinand, whose rights the Bavarian elector now advanced. Leopold asserted his own rights as Margaret Theresa's widower, but his position as the head of the younger male Habsburg line gave him his strongest claim, especially in those parts of the Spanish empire where the laws of succession discounted the rights of female heirs. Moreover, as the father of two healthy sons, Leopold enjoyed the luxury of promoting the candidacy of the younger Archduke Charles, while the elder Archduke Joseph would rule the Austrian Habsburg monarchy after his death (see Genealogical Table on p. ix).

Bavaria's claim attracted immediate support from the Maritime Powers, who saw a Wittelsbach succession as an ideal counterweight in the balance of power. Joseph Ferdinand's candidacy was also popular in Spain, where the Austrian claim was undermined by the country's decline during two centuries of Habsburg rule and by Leopold's recent failure to send troops to prevent the fall of Barcelona. In a desire to forestall yet another war even Louis XIV was willing to recognize Joseph Ferdinand's claim, providing his dynasty received at least nominal territorial compensation. In October 1698 he concluded the so-called First Partition Treaty with William III that confirmed the Bavarian succession, while compensating Austria with Milan and France with the rest of Spain's Italian territories and parts of the Basque provinces. Leopold was willing to accept the agreement, which had the virtue of recognizing his rights through his grandson, placing Spain in the hands of his closest German ally, and protecting the monarchy's southern flank with the strategic duchy of Milan. Yet Joseph Ferdinand died suddenly just four months later, his demise attended by rumors that Leopold had had him poisoned. Although the stories were unfounded, Leopold was the immediate beneficiary of his grandson's death, if only because an Austrian succession seemed much less threatening to the balance of power than the prospects of a Spain dominated by Louis XIV. Indeed, William III and Louis XIV immediately concluded a Second Partition Treaty in June 1699 that awarded the bulk of the Spanish empire to the Archduke Charles, while compensating France with Spanish Italy.[1] Notwithstanding these favorable terms, Leopold and his ministers were less pleased with the second partition than they had been with the first. Although he felt entitled to the entire inheritance, Leopold was willing to settle for a partition, but only if it served the monarchy's strategic needs. In this sense Spain and its colonial empire were much less important than Italy, which they regarded as absolutely essential for defending the monarchy's southwestern flank. Similarly, they valued the acquisition of the Spanish Netherlands, but mainly because they hoped to use it to acquire neighboring Bavaria through an exchange with Max Emanuel.

All of these maneuvers ignored the wishes of Charles II, who shared his country's unwillingness to countenance the partition of its empire. He had, in fact, responded to the First Partition Treaty by willing all of his empire to Joseph Ferdinand. With the Bavarian prince's death, the king resolved to leave the entire Spanish empire to his Habsburg relations, rather than his French enemy. On 29 September 1700, he signed a will presented to him by his pro-Habsburg wife and the Austrian ambassador, Count Harrach, that designated the Archduke Charles as his only heir. But many of his ministers and grandees had other ideas. Led by the archbishop-primate of Toledo, Cardinal Portocarrero, they hoped to end a century of decline under the Habsburgs by turning toward France, the one country with the military resources to protect Spain against partition. Although Charles was never noted for his intelligence, he ultimately saw the wisdom of having Louis XIV as an ally rather than an enemy. Though barely conscious, he assented to a Bourbon succession on 30 October by scribbling the words "Yo el Rey" on a new will laid before him by Portocarrero.

Two days later the last Spanish Habsburg was dead. A startled Harrach learned of Charles's deathbed conversion only the next day, when he was

---

[1] It was understood that France would exchange Milan with the duke of Lorraine, thereby rounding off France's recent German acquisitions while at the same time reducing any strategic threat to the Austrian lands.

passionately embraced by a Spanish grandee who gleefully expressed his delight at "bidding farewell to the House of Austria." Nor did the humiliation end there. Leopold never received word from Harrach of Charles's death and testament because the ambassador's courier was thrown by his horse and killed while crossing the Alps. When he finally received the news it came from Versailles, where Louis XIV had already proclaimed his grandson, the duke of Anjou, King Philip V of Spain. To his credit Louis offered to set aside Charles II's will and abide by the terms of the Second Partition Treaty, if Leopold agreed to accept France's acquisition of Spanish Italy. Yet the emperor rejected this offer. With uncharacteristic decisiveness he ordered Prince Eugene and the monarchy's small field army over the Alps to begin offensive operations against Milan. Given Leopold's decision to fight, Louis XIV decided to accept the undivided inheritance instead of the Second Partition Treaty, since he would be better off fighting Leopold with a united Spain on his side.

Leopold's faith in the justness of his claim to the Spanish Habsburg inheritance was unshakable. Yet his seemingly reckless decision to fight both France and Spain hinged principally on his refusal to permit Italy to fall under Bourbon control after two centuries of Habsburg hegemony. His was a judgment that was shared not only by his ministers, but by successive Habsburg monarchs and statesmen for the next half century. Thus, just as Habsburg foreign policy had concentrated first on Germany and then on Hungary during the seventeenth century, it now refocused its attention westward on the Spanish inheritance, and especially the Italian peninsula.

The War of the Spanish Succession

As before, however, the emperor's prospects for success depended largely on his ability to attract domestic and foreign support. The *Erblande*'s estates expressed their support by voting a 50 percent increase in the Contribution. They even assumed nearly half of the monarchy's 40 million fl. state debt, thereby enabling the *Hofkammer* to take on extensive new obligations. A generation of French aggression against Germany also helped guarantee the loyalty of the imperial princes. Even before he had learned of Charles II's death, Leopold had secured a large military contingent from Brandenburg-Prussia by promising to recognize its elector as king of Prussia. Yet, if his quest for the Spanish succession was to succeed, he needed to reassemble the Grand Alliance that had fought Louis XIV in the Nine Years' War. At first, the Maritime Powers reluctantly accepted the legitimacy of a Bourbon succession in Spain, especially since it had been Leopold, rather than Louis XIV, who had refused to abide by the compromise proposed in the Second Partition Treaty. It was not long, however, before Louis XIV's arrogance rekindled the fear of French hegemony. At the beginning of 1701 he sent French troops into northern Italy and the Spanish Netherlands. In the process they unceremoniously expelled the Dutch from several "barrier fortresses" that the treaty of Ryswick had permitted them to garrison along the Franco-Belgian frontier. In August he concluded a commercial treaty with Philip V which threatened to exclude Anglo-Dutch shipping from Spanish America. When the deposed Stuart King James II died one month later at his Versailles exile, Louis XIV formally declared his 13-year-old son King James III. In addition to these provocations, the English and Dutch were also encouraged to take action by two quick victories that Prince Eugene won over the French at Chiari and Carpi in the spring and summer of 1701. Although neither battle loosened Louis XIV's grip on Italy, they reaffirmed the monarchy's traditional role as a useful instrument in maintaining the balance of power against more powerful and aggressive states like Ludovican France. On 12 September 1701 William III's diplomats at The Hague renewed the Anglo-Dutch alliance with the Emperor.

The Maritime Powers' financial resources quickly added bulk to the allied coalition. Subsidy treaties with several imperial princes committed large numbers of German troops to the 100,000-man Anglo-Dutch army then forming in the Netherlands. By 1703 a combination of territorial and financial incentives also enabled English diplomats to woo Portugal and Savoy from alliances that they had recently concluded with Louis XIV. Yet even more pervasive than money was the universal fear of French hegemony that prompted individual members of the Grand Alliance to champion one or more of the Habsburgs' claims to the entire Spanish inheritance. The Dutch insisted on Habsburg control of Belgium, lest it serve as a conduit for future French aggression. Both they and the English also visualized Habsburg control of Spain's colonial empire as the best guarantee of their continued access to American markets. Duke Victor Amadeus of Savoy and King Peter of Portugal switched sides in the war largely because they felt threatened by the prospects of Bourbon hegemony in their respective peninsulas; whereas Savoy sought to partition Milan with the Habsburgs, Portugal made the Archduke Charles's succession to the Spanish throne a precondition for its accession to the Grand Alliance. Even the German princes' desire for a stronger western frontier suggested that the monarchy might reacquire those Habsburg territories along the Rhine that France had seized over the past half century.

For the next decade this formidable constellation was able to invade Bourbon-held territory on as many as a half-dozen fronts at the same time (see Map 3). Nevertheless, a series of unexpected developments closer to home nearly resulted in the monarchy's defeat at the outset of the war. The first major setback occurred during the summer of 1702, when Elector Max

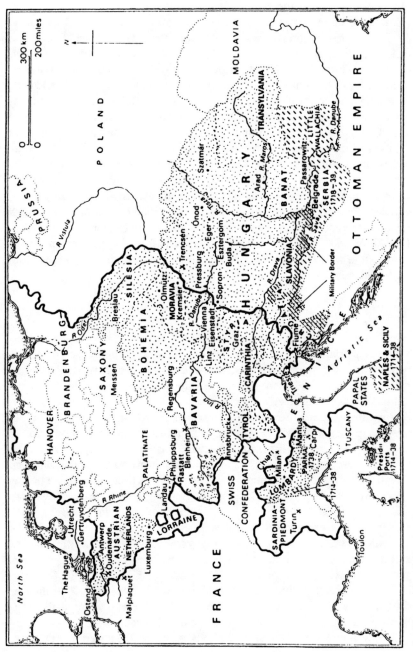

North Sea

The Hague
Gertruydenberg
Utrecht
Antwerp
Ostend ×Oudenarde
×Malplaquet
AUSTRIAN
NETHERLANDS
Luxemburg
LORRAINE
Landau
PALATINATE

FRANCE

R Rhine
Philippsburg
Rastatt
Blenheim×

SWISS
CONFEDERATION

SARDINIA-
PIEDMONT
Turin×

LOMBARDY
Milan×
Mantua×
PARMA
1738 Carpi

TUSCANY

PAPAL
STATES
Presidi
Ports
1714-38

1714-38

Toulon

NAPLES & SICILY
1714-38

HANOVER

BRANDENBURG

R Oder

SAXONY
Meissen

BOHEMIA

SILESIA
Breslau

R Elbe

Regensburg

BAVARIA

R Inn

TYROL
Innsbruck

MORAVIA
Olmutz
Kremsier×

R Danube
Vienna
Linz Eisenstadt
STY
Graz×

Trencsén×
Pressburg
Sopron
Buda
Esztergom

CARINTHIA

R Drave

SLAVONIA

CROATIA
Fiume
Trieste
×Carpi

VENICE

Adriatic Sea

HUNGARY

Szatmár

Ónod
Eger•
R Tisza
R Danube

BANAT
Arad
R Maros

SERBIA
1718-39

Passarowitz
Belgrade
R Save
Military Border

MOLDAVIA

TRANSYLVANIA

LITTLE
WALLACHIA

R Danube

OTTOMAN EMPIRE

PRUSSIA

R Vistula

POLAND

300 km
200 miles

N

3   The empire of Charles VI

Emanuel deserted to the enemy. Over the past century no major imperial vassal had been as closely tied to the Habsburgs as the Bavarian Wittelsbachs. Their close association had rested on a consistent coincidence of interests, including their parallel rivalries with the Palatinate and fear of Sweden during the Thirty Years' War, their perilous position as the empire's only two Catholic lay electors during the election crises of 1619 and 1654–8, and their close proximity to the danger posed by the Turks in 1683. Yet those interests had diverged since the death of Charles II. Having devoted over 40,000 men and 20 million fl. to the Turkish wars, Max Emanuel wanted to be rewarded with a royal crown like those recently acquired by the rival electors of Saxony and Brandenburg. Leopold had actively considered meeting Max Emanuel's expectations through an exchange of Bavaria for the Spanish Netherlands, where Max would succeed as king. But with the unwelcome surprise of Charles II's will, Belgium was no longer the emperor's to offer. Although Leopold continued to treat with Max Emanuel, the elector soon turned to Louis XIV, who was in a better position to hold forth the prospect of a royal crown, together with considerable territorial acquisitions in the Austrian lands and other parts of Germany.

The crises of 1703

Max Emanuel's desertion helped turn 1703 into one of the most disastrous years in Austrian history. It began with a Franco-Bavarian invasion of several neighboring German territories, as well as Upper Austria. With the monarchy's only field army already tied down in northern Italy, provincial militia units were the sole, insufficient obstacle to an invasion of the *Erblande*. During the summer Max Emanuel seized much of the Tyrol; only an uprising by the county's peasants and burghers compelled the elector to withdraw and prevented his junction with the French army in Italy. The emperor desperately needed to raise another army to meet the Bavarian threat. Yet, given the deficiencies in the monarchy's fiscal system, the money was nowhere to be found. Despite the recent increases in the *Erblande*'s Contributions and the heavy taxes being collected in Hungary, total government revenue still covered well under half of all expenses. The government was already borrowing heavily from its allies, wealthy aristocrats, and all ranks of state officials. Its biggest creditors were Jewish purveyors such as Samuel Oppenheimer, who delivered 11 million fl. worth of military supplies on credit during the first two years of the war. But Oppenheimer died in May 1703 and an audit of his bankrupt estate exposed the *Hofkammer*'s inability to repay even half of what they owed.

By autumn, the dual threat posed by Bavaria and the government's bankruptcy was compounded by a major anti-Habsburg rebellion in Hungary. Its causes constitute an all too familiar litany in the history of Austro-Hungarian relations. The most important provocations were the doubling of taxes and the military draft introduced by Kollonics. Tension remained, however, over intermittent attempts by some churchmen and magnates to convert the kingdom's non-Catholic majority, which now included nearly a million Transylvanians. Although the country's magnates were themselves Roman Catholic, they cleaved into two factions: *labanc* insiders, many of whom sought and benefited from court patronage to the point of losing touch with their Hungarian countrymen, and a majority who remained on their estates, where they harbored deep resentment over the effective suspension of their rights by a government that had not called a diet since 1687, excluded them from policy-making, and favored Germans and other foreigners through its *Commissio Neo Acquistica* and resettlement programs. Their natural leader was 24-year-old Prince Ferenc II Rákóczi. As the son of the Transylvanian Prince George II, maternal grandson of Peter Zrinyi, and godson of Imre Thököly, Rákóczi had the pedigree of a *kuruc* chieftain. He had only recently escaped to Poland after being arrested for plotting against Habsburg rule when a revolt broke out among the largely Ruthene peasants of his own massive estates in northeastern Hungary. He immediately assumed leadership of the rebellion, which quickly spread southward from the mountains of Upper Hungary into the central plain, where it steadily gained support among virtually all segments of the population. Within a year the *kuruc* controlled most of the central kingdom and Transylvania, where a rump diet actually elected Rákóczi as its prince.

Having entered the war in quest of Italy and the rest of the Spanish inheritance, Leopold now confronted the prospect of a crushing military defeat, followed by significant losses in territory and authority in both Germany and Hungary. The magnitude of the crisis finally convinced him to take remedial action. Yet much of what was now achieved was wrought not by the emperor and his inner circle, but by a growing reform party that was pressing for an immediate purge. Led by Leopold's elder son, Joseph, it included a number of junior officials, supported by many of the emperor's own generals, diplomats, German vassals, and foreign allies. By June 1703, the so-called Young Court had prevailed upon the emperor to replace the incompetent *Hofkriegsrat* and *Hofkammer* presidents with two of Joseph's protégés, Prince Eugene of Savoy and the *Hofkammer* vice president Gundaker Starhemberg.

The ministerial changes had little immediate effect on the monarchy's finances, which were further devastated by the loss of virtually all revenue from Hungary. With the government unable to fund more than a quarter of its needs, Starhemberg continued to depend heavily on borrowing. The purge did, however, encourage creditors to come forward in extraordinary numbers. While the new *Hofkammer* president set an example with an advance of 75,000 fl., his generosity was dwarfed by other aristocrats and public officials such as the Counts Sternberg (300,000), Przehorsowsky (400,000), and Czernin, whose 1.2 million fl. constituted the largest private loan in the monarchy's history. Meanwhile, the Maritime Powers lent over 3.6 millions, including a 500,000 fl. Dutch loan secured with collateral provided by the Elector Palatine John William and Margrave Louis William of Baden.

The war turns

The Young Court did have an immediate impact on the conduct of the war in the west. At the beginning of 1704 it devised and won Leopold's approval for a bold plan to concentrate allied forces against Bavaria. The duke of Marlborough immediately embraced the strategy, having already determined on his own that Germany's deliverance from the Bavarian threat be given top priority. His famous march into southern Germany and junction with an imperial army commanded by Prince Eugene led to the defeat of the Franco-Bavarian forces at the battle of Blenheim (August 1704) and their immediate expulsion from Germany.

Blenheim was a great victory indeed. More important, it was the first in a remarkable string of triumphs that make the next fifteen years the most illustrious in Austrian military history. As it had in the past, the monarchy benefited from the support of its allies in the anti-Bourbon coalition, especially from the English, whose support was personified by the increasingly close collaboration and rapport between Marlborough and Eugene. No less important was the leadership of Joseph I, who became emperor upon Leopold's death in May 1705. The 32-year-old Joseph was probably the least typical of the early modern Habsburgs. Unlike virtually all of his Austrian and Spanish relatives, he was a handsome man whose face showed no trace of the protruding Habsburg jaw and lower lip that were so prominent among his father's features. Significantly, the differences between Joseph and his line went more than skin deep. He was also unlike most of his forebears in his secularism. Every Habsburg emperor since the sixteenth century had received Jesuit tutors during childhood and grown up to become avid champions of the Counter-Reformation. By contrast, Joseph's childhood tutors and friends included several enemies of the Jesuits, as well as men of Protestant origin. Most notable among them was his grand chamberlain, Prince Salm, who was himself a former Protestant, and the cleric whom Salm entrusted with his religious instruction, Ferdinand von Rummel. Although Joseph was a devout Catholic, he exhibited his own hostility toward the Jesuits on a number of occasions, including one instance when he had a

Jesuit priest defenestrated after he appeared at his bedside disguised as a ghost to urge Rummel's dismissal. He and several of his ministers were also much more willing to tolerate religious minorities and were equally sensitive to the secular, rational, and scientific ideas that were just beginning to emerge with the Enlightenment.

Joseph also lacked the moral austerity and diligence that characterized so many of the Habsburgs. Unlike his father, who had been scrupulously faithful during forty years of marriage, Joseph was notorious for his drinking parties and casual trysts with noblewomen and servant girls alike. Although he was determined to discharge his obligations as emperor, Joseph often delegated affairs of state to his ministers, while devoting much of his spare time to various divertissements. His yearning for military glory led him to participate in the imperial army's successful sieges against the French fortress of Landau in 1702 and 1704. In an age when monarchs felled wild game in the company of numerous attendants while standing behind the safety of a barricade, Joseph reveled in exhausting hunting expeditions in which he pursued wild game in small boats, in wild horseback charges, and on foot without the protection of his bodyguards. Even when he attended meetings with his ministers, he often amused himself by drawing hunting and military scenes, as well as some remarkable vignettes of men hanging from gallows and heads stuck on pikes. Indeed, Joseph I was a typical Habsburg only in his love and talent for languages and the performing arts, which extended to his composition of music and mastery of the flute and violin.

If Joseph's diverse pursuits never interfered with the prosecution of the war it was because he provided decisive leadership to the talented and energetic ministers who now replaced the aging mediocrities of Leopold's regime. Moreover, they knew exactly what was expected of them. From the June 1703 purge to the end of his own reign, Joseph and his advisors identified their war aims and pursued them with dogged persistence. If they initially focused on Germany, it was because they realized that the Franco-Bavarian army posed an even more immediate threat to the monarchy's security than the Hungarian revolt or the French army in Italy.

The victory at Blenheim strengthened further the bonds between *Kaiser* and *Reich*. No one was more proud of his German identity than Joseph himself. As a youth he had forged close friendships with many of the imperial princes. After his succession he reinvigorated the imperial office through the energetic use of his prerogatives, often in collaboration with the other members of the Electoral College. In 1706 he placed Max Emanuel under the imperial ban. As punishment Joseph returned the Upper Palatinate to the elector palatine and placed Bavaria proper under imperial administration. He also immediately reorganized the Aulic Council, which he aggressively utilized to implement his policies within the *Reich*. Joseph's public expressions of German patriotism and his resurrection of imperial power have led some German historians to exaggerate the young emperor's commitment to the empire. However genuine these feelings toward Germany and his imperial office may have been, Joseph invariably subjugated them to the pursuit of distinctly Austrian interests. Much to the distress of his imperial vice chancellor, Friedrich Karl von Schönborn, he also emasculated both the Imperial Chancery and Chamber Court by shifting their responsibilities to his own Austrian Chancery and Aulic Council. The lesson of Joseph's German policies is, in fact, of the Habsburgs' continued use of imperial institutions to serve Austrian interests, albeit under a more powerful and energetic sovereign.

Once Germany had been cleared of foreign forces, Joseph shifted the focus of the war effort to other theatres. The conquest of Italy again became the primary objective, as it had been at the death of Charles the Sufferer. Joseph committed not only his own limited resources to this end, but even diverted imperial revenue and troops. The heavy taxation and forced recruitment that he authorized in occupied Bavaria even led to a brief peasant uprising at the end of the year. Thanks largely to the personal intervention of the duke of Marlborough, Joseph also secured major contributions from the Maritime Powers, who virtually doubled the size of Prince Eugene's army by providing 28,000 German auxiliaries. They also advanced nearly 3 million fl. in loans, including 400,000 fl. from Queen Anne's own personal fortune. These herculean efforts finally enabled Prince Eugene to take the offensive in the summer of 1706. His brilliantly executed march to the aid of Victor Amadeus of Savoy is reminiscent of Marlborough's thrust into southern Germany two years earlier. The resulting Austro-Savoyard victory at Turin was also the strategic equivalent of Blenheim, since it left the enemy without a field army to protect the isolated garrisons that remained in the peninsula. To hasten the achievement of his immediate objective, Joseph authorized Prince Eugene to sign a truce in March 1707 that allowed the French to withdraw their remaining 23,000 troops from northern Italy. The evacuation permitted him to complete the conquest of the peninsula with the dispatch of a 10,000-man army into Naples two months later.

Joseph's successes did not come without a cost. By permitting the French to extricate their garrisons and by committing many of his own forces to the conquest of Naples, Joseph effected a 30,000-man swing in the balance of forces available for service elsewhere in southern Europe. As a result, an allied attempt to seize the naval base of Toulon fell short of its goal and the main Anglo-Dutch-Portuguese army in Spain was overwhelmed and destroyed at the battle of Almansa (April 1707). Moreover, the emperor's withdrawal of so many Austrian and imperial troops from the empire also permitted the French temporarily to reoccupy and plunder much of southern

Germany during the summer of 1707. More frightening yet was a concurrent occupation of Saxony by a large Swedish army under its King, Charles XII. Fortunately, the invasion was directed not against the Grand Alliance, but rather Augustus II, who had joined Russia in attacking Sweden in the so-called Great Northern War (1700–20). Nevertheless, the reappearance of the emperor's old Swedish enemy along the Bohemian frontier further underscored his impotence outside the Italian peninsula. Having contributed so decisively to the victorious Blenheim and Turin campaigns, the Maritime Powers were understandably furious at the emperor's selfish pursuit of his Italian prize. Their pique could not, however, obscure the fact that two lightning campaigns had subjected Bavaria to Austrian occupation and the entire Italian peninsula to a century and a half of Habsburg hegemony. Nor did Joseph waste any time in exploiting his advantage. Using the Aulic Council as his principal tool, he immediately put the empire's old claims to sovereignty in northern Italy to good use. For the rest of the war, the Austrian army collected an average of nearly 5 million fl. annually in imperial taxes and quartering rights. Moreover, in 1708 an Aulic Council judgment placed the pro-French duke of Mantua under the imperial ban, thereby enabling Joseph to merge the strategic duchy with Milan.

The victory in Italy also permitted the emperor to devote more attention to ending the Rákóczi rebellion. He and his ministers initially hoped to achieve peace through negotiation. Even before his succession Joseph had attempted to placate the *kuruc* by announcing his father's offer to invest him with control of the kingdom and by promising to rule in strict accordance with the constitution. Yet even though Rákóczi and his lieutenants had no quarrel with Joseph, they were determined to secure structural guarantees that would not make Hungary's liberties dependent on the goodwill of individual sovereigns. Hence, the rebel leadership initially demanded the restoration of the elective crown, the *jus resistendi*, and an independent Transylvania ruled by Rákóczi himself. In reality Rákóczi was willing to settle for Transylvania, which would have resumed its historic mission as guarantor of the kingdom's liberties. But when the two sides met under Anglo-Dutch mediation during 1706, the talks foundered on Joseph's refusal to relinquish control of the principality.

With the failure of negotiations, Joseph was compelled to devote the rest of his reign to recovering Hungary by force. This was a formidable task, especially in the early stages of the revolt, when most of the Austrian army was fighting elsewhere and the *kuruc* forces comprised as many as 100,000 men. His father's recent victory against the Turks did, however, afford the emperor a number of advantages. The reconquest and resettlement of Hungary's southern frontier with non-Magyar settlers enabled him to follow a strategy of divide and rule that was to become so popular with later

Habsburgs. The Croatian estates and Military Border provided a steady flow of troops, as did the German and autonomous Serb immigrant communities that had recently settled along the southern edge of the Hungarian plain. Meanwhile, the bulk of Transylvania's non-Magyar populations remained loyal, or at least diffident to Rákóczi's appeals. The *kuruc* were also frustrated by Hungary's isolation now that the destruction of the Turks and conquest of Transylvania had deprived the *kuruc* of their traditional allies. Although Rákóczi approached Poland, Sweden, Russia, and even the Sultan, only far off France was willing to send any help at all. Even here the modest subsidies and 2,000 soldiers Louis sent were hardly enough. The *kuruc* force of peasants and *hayducks* may have been adept at guerrilla tactics, but their inability to besiege well-defended strongpoints enabled the Austrians to retain control of the central kingdom's western counties, Transylvania's urban centers, and a number of key fortresses in between. Eventually the arrival of regular Austrian army forces exposed its impotence in conventional warfare, as well as Rákóczi's own incompetence as a battlefield commander.

The rebellion's collapse was hastened by internal conflicts among Rákóczi's own supporters. From the outset, the prince had attracted such large numbers of fighters by exempting them from all tax and manorial obligations. He had also won over much of the country's non-Catholic majority by promising to restore religious freedom, together with those places of worship that had been seized under Leopold. Yet Rákóczi was never able to enforce these commitments. Most landlords ignored the exemptions, while Catholic communities and magnates often blocked the restoration of Protestant churches. Finally, the heavy taxes that he was obliged to levy to pay for the insurrection undermined support among those who had been incited to revolt by Leopold's own war levies. Here too the nobility undermined Rákóczi's popular appeal by refusing to assume their fair share of the tax burden. Indeed, many were less committed to achieving victory over the Habsburgs than to preserving their own estates in areas that were under *kuruc* control.

In the end it was the prince's determination to obtain greater foreign financial and military support that proved his undoing. In April 1707 Rákóczi formally assumed the Transylvanian throne in the expectation that foreign princes would be more willing to deal with a fellow sovereign. Two months later he induced a Hungarian diet at Ónod to depose Joseph and the Habsburgs, with the intention of using its crown to attract a foreign ally. Whereas Rákóczi's hopes for securing outside assistance went unfulfilled, his break with the Habsburgs weighed heavily on his war-weary countrymen, many of whom preferred peace and reconciliation to the prolongation of the rebellion. After the Ónod diet many of them were willing to accept Joseph, who sustained their hopes by pledging to abide by all of the promises that had been broken by Leopold.

Following the destruction of the *kuruc* forces at Trencsén (August 1708), the Austrian army began the long process of besieging and retaking those strongpoints that remained in rebel hands. When peace was finally restored in April 1711, it came on Joseph's terms. Although he offered a general amnesty and pledged once again to abide by the constitutional and religious settlement of 1687, the peace of Szatmár that his generals concluded with the *kuruc* general Sándor Károlyi offered none of the guarantees that the rebels had demanded. Rather than accede to the treaty or accept the offer of amnesty, Rákóczi opted to spend the rest of his life in exile. The rebellion that bears his name had lasted eight years, making it the longest civil insurrection in the monarchy's history. The Habsburg regime had poured tremendous sums and roughly half of its 100,000-man army into the "Hungarian labyrinth." This commitment constituted a considerable drain on the monarchy's military efforts elsewhere – as well as on the goodwill of the Maritime Powers, who sympathized with the revolt as a struggle for constitutional government and Protestant religious freedom. The reestablishment of royal authority over all of Hungary was, however, at least as crucial to the monarchy's future as the preservation of its German and Italian frontiers.

What was clearly less crucial was the rest of the Spanish inheritance. Yet, by 1708 Joseph was in the position to focus on the balance of the monarchy's war aims. His decision to transfer Prince Eugene to the Low Countries immediately yielded another decisive victory at Oudenarde (July 1708) and the allied conquest of virtually the entire Spanish Netherlands. One month later an Anglo-Dutch fleet seized Sardinia in the archduke's name. The emperor also committed the first Austrian troops to the Iberian peninsula, although only after the Maritime Powers agreed to defray all their expenses. Joseph even sent troops into the Papal States during 1708 in a successful attempt to force Pope Clement XI to recognize his brother as king of Spain. These efforts notwithstanding, the conquest of Spain proved beyond the allies' resources. Except in Catalonia, the Spanish people steadfastly supported Philip V against a Habsburg succession forced on them by the Portuguese and the Protestant Maritime Powers.

The peace settlements

What they could not win on the battlefield the allies nearly acquired at the negotiation table. At the first formal peace talks held at The Hague in April–May 1709, Louis XIV tentatively accepted their demand for the entire Spanish Succession, as well as much of Alsace, only to change his mind at the last second. The bloody victory won by Marlborough and Eugene at Malplaquet (11 September) persuaded the allies to moderate their demands. When talks resumed at Gertruydenberg the following March, they no longer insisted on the cession of Alsace. The United Provinces were even willing to let Philip V retain Sicily, which was still in Bourbon hands; it was only when their negotiators insisted that Louis XIV use his own army to eject his grandson from Spain that the talks collapsed.

Dutch wavering at Gertruydenberg was an unwelcome reminder that each member of the allied coalition was motivated by different war aims. The British were determined to place the Archduke Charles on the Spanish throne, from where he could guarantee their access to Spanish America. The emperor and his ministers were at least as interested in fortifying their hold on Italy with the acquisition of Sicily as they were in obtaining Spain and its overseas empire. By contrast the United Provinces had already achieved their primary war aim with the conquest of the Spanish Netherlands, where they intended to extend and strengthen their line of barrier fortresses against future French aggression. It made little sense for them to continue the war for their allies' sake, especially since the succession of French defeats now suggested that Louis XIV was no longer a threat to the balance of power.

The Dutch were eventually bought off with the promise of a greatly enlarged barrier in Belgium. Instead it was the British who proved the weak link that eventually broke the Grand Alliance. The end came suddenly with the landslide victory of the opposition Tories in the 1710 parliamentary elections. The Tories had exploited the public's dissatisfaction with the war in the wake of the bloody battle of Malplaquet and also capitalized on the widespread perception that the Austrians and Dutch were using Britain for their own selfish ends. The new Tory government immediately began secret discussions with Louis XIV with the intention of leaving Philip V in possession of Spain and its overseas empire. On learning of the Anglo-French talks, one of Joseph's ministers predicted woefully that "if the war lasts much longer, our allies will do us more harm than our enemies." Nine days later, the emperor's sudden death from smallpox guaranteed the fulfillment of this premonition. Although Joseph's ministers were able to keep his death secret from the Hungarian rebels until after the peace of Szatmár, they could not prevent it from hastening the breakup of the Grand Alliance. Since Joseph had no son he was succeeded by the Archduke Charles, who promptly returned from Spain. Were Charles to acquire the Spanish empire as well, he would rule an empire even larger than that of Charles V. Although the Tory government had decided on a separate peace several months earlier, Charles's succession and the threat it posed to the balance of power now gave them a compelling argument with which to persuade the rest of the allies to follow suit.

Although Charles's allies readily supported his election as Emperor Charles VI (1711–40), they now joined in separate peace talks with France. In April 1713 every member of the Grand Alliance except the Habsburg monarchy and the Holy Roman empire concluded peace with Louis XIV at Utrecht. Although the treaty recognized the monarchy's conquests on the Italian peninsula plus Sardinia, it confirmed Philip V's hold on Spain and its overseas empire, as well as the complete restoration of Max Emanuel. Even Charles's acquisition of the Spanish Netherlands was made contingent on his willingness to grant commercial concessions and a larger fortress barrier to the Dutch. In a final act of spite against their erstwhile ally, the British secured Sicily (together with its royal title) for its new Italian client, Victor Amadeus of Savoy. The new emperor initially refused to accede to the peace treaty, but soon realized the hopelessness of continuing the struggle without the Maritime Powers. With an invading French army once again on German soil, he directed Prince Eugene to conclude peace with Louis XIV on the basis of the peace of Utrecht. The monarchy received no additional gains in the treaty of Rastatt (March 1714); similarly the Holy Roman empire, in whose name a second treaty was concluded at Baden (September 1714), acquired nothing beyond the frontiers established by the peace of Ryswick. One year later Charles finally acquired the Spanish Netherlands by concluding a Barrier Treaty with the Dutch at Antwerp (15 November 1715).

By then Louis XIV had died and been succeeded by his 5-year-old great-grandson, Louis XV (1715–74). Yet neither the peace settlements with France nor the Sun King's death brought peace. Both Charles VI and his archrival Philip V were still unwilling to tolerate the Spanish partition that had been recognized by every other European power. After a decade in the peninsula, Charles could not accept the loss of Spain, especially Catalonia, whose people had championed his cause but whom the British had forced him to abandon after his brother's death. For his part Philip V had not reconciled himself to the loss of Spain's European empire. His resolve was bolstered by his second wife, the strong-willed Elizabeth Farnese of Parma, who was determined to secure an Italian inheritance for their newborn son, Don Carlos.

For the moment Charles and Philip were hardly a threat to each other since they were unable to launch an attack across the western Mediterranean without their former allies. This was not, however, the case in the Balkans. At the end of 1714 the Turks invaded Venice's possessions in the Peloponnesus and Dalmatia. Although they made no immediate move toward Hungary, past experience suggested that they would attack there next once Venice had been crushed. Rather than wait, the emperor and his advisors decided to enter the war while Venice was still available as an ally. In the resulting Turkish War (1716–18), Charles experienced for the first time the military glory that his father and brother had enjoyed. Prince Eugene promptly destroyed a vastly superior Turkish army at Peterwardein (5 August 1716), leaving the unburied bodies of the grand vizier and 30,000 of his men to rot in the midsummer sun. Shortly thereafter, Austrian forces entered Hungary's Banat of Temesvár for the first time in 165 years. The following summer Eugene besieged the key fortress of Belgrade, which surrendered a week after he had annihilated a Turkish relief army in front of the city's walls (16 August 1717). With the peace of Passarowitz (21 July 1718) the monarchy acquired the last pieces of Ottoman Hungary in the Banat and eastern Slavonia, the northern half of Serbia and western, or "Little" Wallachia.

The Turkish War of 1716–18 was the last conflict for nearly a century in which the monarchy would emerge as the clear winner. Indeed, although Charles VI had a nominal ally in Venice and was assisted by a few thousand German auxiliaries and Papal subsidies, it was the only war fought between 1526 and 1849 in which the monarchy achieved any kind of victory without significant outside help. Events then unfolding in the western Mediterranean proved more true to form. By 1717 Philip V and Elizabeth Farnese had managed to build a fleet capable of supporting a counterthrust against Italy. In August it transported Spanish forces to Sardinia, which fell within two months. One year later a second descent seized much of Sicily from its new Savoyard king. With Prince Eugene tied down in the Balkans and without a fleet of his own, Charles was once again dependent on the Maritime Powers. Fortunately, they and the new French regime were eager to establish a stable European peace. He now bowed to their will by quickly concluding peace in the Balkans and joining them in the so-called Quadruple Alliance against Spain. By the treaty of London (2 August 1718) Charles reluctantly recognized Philip V as king of Spain, as well as Elizabeth Farnese's son's right to succeed the childless rulers of Parma and Tuscany. In return, the allies helped him compel Victor Amadeus to cede Sicily to him in exchange for the much less valuable island kingdom of Sardinia. Meanwhile, the Quadruple Alliance made short work of the Spanish threat. The British Admiral Byng sank the Spanish fleet just eight days after the alliance was concluded, then transported Austrian and Savoyard forces to Sicily and Sardinia. Although the Austrians made poor progress in retaking Sicily, a French army crossed the Pyrenees and quickly compelled Philip V and his queen to come to terms.

Manifestations of greatness: the high baroque

Although Charles VI had refused to sign the peace of Utrecht, the six treaties to which he did affix his name during the first seven years of his reign afforded the monarchy unprecedented security. Whereas Szatmár and Passarowitz confirmed the monarchy's hegemony in the northern Balkans, the compromises at Rastatt, Baden, Antwerp, and London attained all of its strategic needs in the West. The Italian acquisitions of Milan, Mantua, and Tuscany's strategic Presidii Ports in the north, as well as Naples and Sicily in the south, rendered the monarchy's southeast flank every bit as secure as it had been prior to the death of Charles the Sufferer. Although a somewhat chastened Max Emanuel had been restored in Bavaria, his survival was more than compensated by the continued solidarity of the other German princes against their common enemies. Meanwhile, Sweden's total defeat in the Northern War removed it as a threat to the monarchy's interests in either Germany or Poland. Admittedly, the emperor had not won any part of Spain, a failure that he never completely accepted. Nevertheless, the priorities set by Joseph had determined both the extent and the limits of the monarchy's expansion, in keeping with its true strategic needs. With the recent Balkan conquests, a continuous natural barrier of mountains and rivers enclosed all of the monarchy's core lands, except Silesia and the Swabian enclaves. Moreover, for the first time in its history none of the *Erblande*'s four frontiers with Hungary, Italy, Germany, and Poland harbored a significant threat. Although a new, powerful enemy was destined to appear on the monarchy's borders after Charles's death, the thrust of Habsburg foreign policy during the rest of the century focused more on maintaining these buffer zones than on actually defending the monarchy's core from foreign enemies. Indeed, the historic nightmare of simultaneous invasion from both east and west would not materialize again until 1914.

At the same time, the monarchy's new conquests afforded it more than security. With the acquisition of the Southern Netherlands, Italy, and the Balkans, Charles VI essentially ruled a second Habsburg empire that was nearly as extensive as the European patrimony of Charles V and larger than any state in the history of the Austrian monarchy. Among Charles's contemporaries, only the tsar of Russia ruled more territory. Thanks to the addition of nearly 2 million subjects in the Low Countries and another 5 million in Italy, the monarchy embraced a population of over 17 million people; only the king of France could claim more subjects – and then only by discounting the millions of Germans governed by Charles' imperial vassals.[2] Furthermore, although southern Italy and the new Balkan marches added little to the monarchy's economy, Lombardy and the Low Countries considerably strengthened its commercial and industrial base.

Even before the advent of peace, the Habsburg court, clergy, and nobility had begun celebrating these triumphs with what was perhaps the greatest

[2] It is difficult to get an exact count of the monarchy's population or land area. Roughly speaking, the population broke down as follows: greater Bohemia and Hungary, 4 million each; Austria, 2.5. million; Lombardy (Milan and Mantua), 1 million; Sicily, 1.2 million; Naples, 3 million; the Netherlands, 1.7 million; northern Serbia and Little Wallachia, perhaps 150,000 total. The monarchy's land area was somewhat over 750,000 sq km, or about 90 percent the size of Charles V's European inheritance.

building boom in the monarchy's history. The first of the magnificent palaces, churches, monasteries, and assorted monuments of the Austrian high baroque date from the last decade of the seventeenth century, when the country was rebuilding from the Turkish wars. Leopold's appointment of the young architect Johann Bernard Fischer von Erlach (1656–1723) to serve his son Joseph represents something of a milestone. Fischer made some effort to emulate Leopold's French rival by employing the Ludovican sun motif in the triumphal arches that he prepared for Joseph in 1691, following his coronation as Roman king, and again in 1699, after his wedding to Wilhelmine Amalia of Brunswick-Lüneburg. The same conceit is evident in a huge fresco in Klosterneuburg, in which the painter Daniel Gran portrayed Joseph as a Habsburg sun god. Moreover, his grandiose plans for Joseph's palace at Schönbrunn represented a direct response to Versailles.

Yet, while competition with Louis XIV motivated Joseph and his artists, it was their celebration of the dynasty's triumphant leadership of a reunited Germany that dominated their thinking. All types of public and private edifices were adorned in the distinctive bright yellow of the German coat of arms. They were also built on a much larger scale that befitted the dynasty's imperial rank. The onset of construction on Schönbrunn in 1694 also inspired the aristocracy to construct their own massive palaces with extravagant artificial gardens and numerous outbuildings. At the same time the dynasty's military and religious triumphs were dramatized by the flamboyant motifs of its painters and sculptors, whose work routinely featured uncounted legions of trumpeting cherubs, trampled infidels, helmeted skulls, and assorted battle flags, swords, and cannon.

If anything, Joseph was even less hesitant than his father to divert scarce wartime funds to court festivities and the arts. In his six year reign he built a new opera house, two theaters, a fine arts academy, and the Viennese suburb that still bears his name. He tripled his staff of musicians to 300, and, at one point, even spent 30,000 fl. on a wintry sled cavalcade. Joseph's wartime patronage speaks volumes for the emphasis the baroque dynasty placed on display. Yet the emperor could not spend what he did not have. Most of his artisans, as well as Fischer himself, went unpaid until the decade after his death. Although wealthy private patrons could afford to begin various undertakings during the war, he was obliged to suspend work on what had already become a drastically scaled-down Schönbrunn palace. It was only with peace that the greater availability of funds enabled Charles VI to join the church and aristocracy in outdoing all their predecessors in the number, scale, and pretentiousness of their projects.

Although it is possible to find traces of Charles's nostalgia for Spain, the imperial style, or *Kaiserstil*, developed further the presumption already evident under Joseph I. But, unlike his more secular brother, Charles's patronage reestablished his father's focus on the dualism of crown and church. He spent very little on palace construction. Admittedly he renovated the *Stallburg*, which housed the Lippizaner horses of the famed Spanish riding school, and he built a massive imperial stable across from the Hofburg. His city residence remained, however, pitifully small and plain compared to those of other monarchs. Although Charles often spent the summer in his country residence at Laxenburg and the autumn months just outside the city walls at the Favorita, both were comparable in size and grandeur to an aristocrat's residence. Meanwhile he gave Schönbrunn to Joseph's widow rather than resume the construction that had been interrupted by the war. The emperor's most famous projects were religious in nature. He resurrected his seventeenth-century predecessors' devotion to the Virgin Mary. As early as 1706 he had credited her with delivering Barcelona from a Franco-Spanish siege and had planned to erect an obelisk in her name. He visited and renovated Mariazell shortly after his return from the peninsula. Moreover, the numerous religious columns that he commissioned around the monarchy included a great many *Mariensäule*, as well as a large number of monuments giving thanks for the end of a nationwide epidemic in 1713. Charles commemorated Vienna's deliverance with the construction of the great Karlskirche (1716–39). Named after his patron saint, St. Charles Borromeus, the church was framed by two enormous, free-standing columns that have been variously interpreted as representing Spain's pillars of Hercules, Roman triumphal columns, or even Turkish minarets. They are, however, inscribed from top to bottom with religious symbols and graced by the imperial crown. The religious and dynastic dualism of the emperor's patronage was also evident in the huge sums he spent on turning the great monastery at Klosterneuburg into an Austrian Escorial.

The emperor's patronage was motivated by the customary combination of religious devotion, dynastic propaganda, and unabashed self-acclaim. He was, however, also influenced somewhat by the emphasis that contemporary cameralist teaching placed on the public welfare. If churches and religious monuments attended to his subjects' spiritual needs, Charles also ministered to their health care by constructing hospitals and veterans' homes, and to their education by funding *Ritterakademien* and Fischer's lovely court library, whose façade bore an inscription dedicating it to the "publico comodo." Even less directly utilitarian expenditures on the court and the emperor's private quarters received the endorsement of men like Schröder because it recirculated funds that helped stimulate the economy.

The motivations of the clergy and aristocracy were more straightforward. During Charles's reign they celebrated the triumph of the Counter-Reformation by constructing or renovating hundreds of churches throughout the monarchy. In Hungary, the bishop of Eger and Vác alone built exactly ninety-nine. While the emperor was spending lavishly on Klosterneuburg, the Austrian abbots of Admont, Göttweig, Kremsmünster, Melk, and St. Florian renovated and expanded their own monasteries. As always the Society of Jesus was most active among the monarchy's Protestant populations. It sprinkled the countryside in post-Szatmár Hungary with Marian shrines, at one point declaring the kingdom's constitution to be under her personal protection. In Silesia, it continued to multiply the number of Jesuit colleges and churches, as well as the size of its new university at Breslau.

Art historian Hans Sedlmayr refers to the "inflated self-importance" of the many aristocrats who spent lavishly on palace construction under Joseph and Charles. Of course, some were more important than others. The Habsburg brothers readily shared their spoils with their key ministers, generals, and court favorites. In the closing years of his reign Joseph parceled out Max Emanuel's Bavarian domains and a number of confiscated Hungarian estates. Prince Eugene's Hungarian bequest was evaluated at 300,000 fl., the brilliant Bohemian Chancellor Count Wratislaw's at 400,000. The family of his favorite, Prince Lamberg, received 250,000 fl. even though his services amounted to little more than tending to the imperial stable and procuring women for his merriment. At his death Joseph bequeathed a legacy of 500,000 fl. to his last lover, Marianne Pálffy – exactly ten times the annual pension that he left his own mother. As in everything else, his younger brother was less spectacular, but no less generous as he routinely compensated his ministers and favorites with 40–120,000 fl. annually.

The emperors' favor guaranteed that these same men commissioned some of the greatest private palaces of the Austrian high baroque. Fischer's mammoth Palais Trautson was a suitable urban residence for the emperors' sometime chief minister. Both Imperial Vice Chancellor Schönborn and Prince Eugene employed another great master, Johann Lukas von Hildebrandt (1663–1745), for their palaces. Actually, the *Hofkriegsrat* president built two: a winter residence within the city walls and the famous Belvedere, which overlooked Vienna from the southeast. With its wonderful sense of proportion and scenic garden esplanade, the Belvedere easily outshone the palaces within the old city, which was already far too cramped to allow either architects to develop their plans or observers to enjoy the visual effect of their creations. In fact, the limited space led to several distinctly Viennese architectural traits, including the placement of shops on the ground level of many palaces, and the construction of four-storey houses with tightly curved stairways. With as many as 80,000 people crammed into the thousand residential buildings that lay within Vienna's walls, it even became necessary for aristocrats to admit rent-paying gentlemen as boarders within their city palaces.

As a rule, the smaller city palaces were less expensive than their generally larger suburban counterparts. Yet none of the 240 aristocratic residences that had sprung up in and around Vienna by 1730 came cheaply. Even a small luxury townhouse with a modest stairway and no ceremonial hall could cost 70–80,000 fl. Such expenses posed no problem for the wealthiest aristocrats. The Hungarian Palatine Pál Esterházy earned as much as 700,000 fl. each year from his estates. Although Prince Hans Adam "the Rich" Liechtenstein collected only half that amount, it was still sufficient not just to construct palaces but to purchase the tiny principality that still bears the family name.[3] Even Prince Eugene could supplement his relatively finite domainal income of 100,000 fl. with an additional 300,000 in various state salaries. Nevertheless, the high cost of prestige ultimately overwhelmed many less well-endowed nobles and obliged them to sell their half-finished palaces. Nor was such extravagance limited to Vienna or to the nobility. In Upper Austria alone no fewer than five monasteries spent themselves into bankruptcy and were forced to close down.

Of course, profligate spending did have its compensations. Although they all employed *robot* labor when possible, crown, noble, and church patrons also retained – and ultimately paid – thousands of skilled artisans. Hildebrandt's Belvedere employed 1,300 full-time workers. For forty-seven years the great abbey at Melk engaged roughly a hundred artisans, some spending their entire life on the project. By 1730 Vienna itself supported hundreds of master artists, including a remarkable 243 master goldsmiths, and ranked with Rome, Paris, and Venice as a major center of the arts. The influence of the north Italian baroque was evident in much of their work. It was no coincidence that Hildebrandt was Italian-born, while Fischer had studied under Bernini for sixteen years before coming to Vienna. Nevertheless, the monarchy's central position had always given it a facility for adopting, and then coopting, the ideas and culture of neighboring lands. Just as Italian missionaries had spearheaded the first wave of the Counter-Reformation, only to be replaced in later years by native priests, home-grown artists dominated a new generation of baroque masters that began after 1700. Although large numbers of German artists continued to find employment within the *Erblande*, native Austrians now replaced Italians as the dominant presence throughout the monarchy. A large contingent of Tyroleans also led native artists in bringing the Austrian baroque style to Catholic Germany, as well as to Saxony and Poland.

The Austrian baroque was less self-sufficient in the performing arts and letters. Italian composers and performers still dominated music and theater, both at court and on the estates of aristocratic patrons. The one notable

---

[3] In 1719, after Hans Adam had died, Charles VI formally created for his chief minister, Florian Anton Liechtenstein, what remains today the only surviving principality from the Holy Roman empire.

exception was the vernacular performances before popular audiences, whether at Vienna's new Theater am Kärntnertor (1712) or in the country-side, where Jesuit evangelists competed with traveling troupes by staging their own didactic presentations. Italian dominance in poetry was most evident in Vienna, where Charles VI employed first Apostolo Zeno and then Metastasio as his court poets. Even far-off Transylvania experienced a Latin cultural renaissance with the end of Ottoman rule. Except for the providential histories and apologies penned by the Jesuits, literature had few native sons writing in the vernacular. In 1716 the wife of the British plenipotentiary, Lady Mary Wortley Montagu, even claimed that the only writer she met during her prolonged stay in Vienna was a Frenchman employed by Prince Eugene. Two decades later, the prominent Italian historian Pietro Giannone claimed that he never bothered to learn German during his eleven years in the Habsburg capital because all of its educated elite spoke French or Italian.

Just as the court exercised a decisive influence over arts and letters, it also helped mold other aspects of elite culture, especially in Vienna. Unlike Prague or Linz, the capital had never made any pretense of being an industrial, commercial, or financial center. Moreover, the purges of the Counter-Reformation and the losses inflicted by the siege of 1683 had further stunted the growth of a moneyed bourgeoisie. Though the city's population and economy had recovered from these setbacks, it owed its prosperity solely to the patronage of the emperor and his court. As a result government service – or serving the government's needs – coopted the energies of enterprising commoners. Connections at court and a suitable noble or official title became more important than occupation or wealth, if only because they ultimately determined both. Small wonder that wealthy burgher families emulated the court nobility by constructing palatial townhouses. The attractiveness of aristocratic values may have made for greater social homogeneity and self-acceptance, but it did little to assist the evolution of a more productive urban bourgeoisie.

Behind the façade: government and economy

During the reign of Charles VI, aristocratic, clerical, and court patrons acclaimed the monarchy's triumph and emergence as a great power of the first rank. Yet, lurking behind the glamorous baroque façade was a reality largely unchanged since the days of Leopold I. The monarchy was more than ever a corporate society that was much better at displaying wealth than creating it. It was also still governed by an inadequate administrative system and a correspondingly weak military that was incapable of defeating any major western power without the intercession of powerful allies.

The monarchy had made a good start under the energetic and innovative Joseph I. He not only removed most of his father's ministers, but streamlined the size of key policy-making bodies such as the Privy Conference and Privy Council. The new emperor and his ministers were also much more deeply committed to the reform agenda of the cameralists. Working in tandem with Starhemberg, Joseph quickly streamlined regional administration by paring down excess personnel and subordinating Graz's and Innsbruck's independent administrative offices to the central government. In 1706 he founded the Vienna City Bank. Ostensibly run by the capital's municipal government, the City Bank was secretly directed by a Ministerial Bank Deputation headed by Starhemberg, under whose tutelage it assumed a fifth of the 60 million fl. debt that the *Hofkammer* accumulated over the next five years. Joseph was also willing to implement some of the projects proposed by the new *Hofkammer* secretary, the Austrian cameralist Schierendorff. True to cameralist dogma, Schierendorff advocated not only mercantile development and administrative efficiency, but also greater agricultural productivity by improving the living standards of those peasants who "sweat under the slavish yoke of serfdom." In order to reduce their taxes and increase overall state revenue, Joseph attempted to replace the inequitable and irregular Contributions voted by the estates with a "universal excise" that could be levied uniformly throughout the *Erblande*. He also directed the estates to investigate ways in which peasants could be freed from *robot* service. Near the end of the reign he actually commuted *robot* service on his own domains in the former Piast duchies of Liegnitz, Brieg, and Wohlau.

Ordinary "cameral" revenue more than doubled under Joseph to 8.5 million fl.[4] Nevertheless, the estates prevented him from carrying out some of Schierendorff's more revolutionary proposals. The Inner and Outer Austrian regimes retarded the subordination of their administrative offices in Graz and Innsbruck, and delayed the introduction of a universal excise by refusing to enact the new cadasters that it required. Opposition from the various Bohemian *Länder* also dissuaded the government from extending the *robot* pilot project to private land, even though it had dramatically increased crop yields in Liegnitz, Brieg, and Wohlau. Despite Joseph's energy and determination, he was no different from his predecessors in his desire to work with the monarchy's estates, especially in wartime. Such deference had proven advantages. The aristocracy had helped the government to finance the war with substantial loans, especially during the critical period before Blenheim. Vienna's town fathers had assumed equally imposing burdens through the City Bank. By increasing the Contribution by another 60 percent

---

[4] Whereas the Contribution was considered "extraordinary" income expressly intended for the military, "ordinary" income came from indirect taxes, crown estates, tolls, and other non-military sources.

shortly after Joseph's succession, the *Erblande*'s estates had effectively tripled their military taxes in a single generation to over 8 million fl. In Bohemia proper the nobility had even agreed to pay the bulk of the resulting 1.3 million fl. "Extraordinary" Contribution themselves. Yet the level of the Contribution actually declined somewhat after 1706, partly because the estates saw less urgency in making such sacrifices, but also because Joseph himself deeply appreciated the toll that taxes were taking on his subjects, particularly in the Bohemian crownlands.[5]

The succession crisis

At the very least, permanent structural changes in the monarchy's finances would have to wait until the end of the war. By 1720 that time had come. For the first time in its history the monarchy was free from immediate outside threats to its security that might impede the prosecution of internal reforms. The next thirteen years were, in fact, Europe's longest period of uninterrupted peace between the fifteenth and twentieth centuries. Hence Charles VI had ample opportunity to reform its government and build its economy without fear of upsetting the corporate pillars that supported the monarchy. But Joseph's premature death severely compromised these prospects in two ways. First, it created a new succession crisis. Although Joseph and his wife, Wilhelmine Amalia of Brunswick-Lüneburg, had had three children within their first four years of marriage, their only son did not live to see his first birthday. Shortly thereafter, the philandering emperor gave his wife a recurring venereal infection with symptoms that strongly suggest gonorrhea or herpes simplex. Henceforth, responsibility for prolonging the dynasty rested with Joseph's brother. Charles and his wife, Elizabeth Christine of Brunswick-Lüneburg, did have one son in 1716, but he too died within a few months. Over the next eight years Charles's supplications to the Virgin were answered – with the birth of Maria Theresa (1717), Maria Anna (1718), and Maria Amalia (1724). By the 1720s Charles's intensifying preference for his Spanish mistress and assorted young males further compromised his chances of providing a male heir. The empress herself did little to enhance the odds by becoming so obese that she could barely stand without assistance. Sadly, the last years of the reign were attended by rumors of Charles's hope that she would precede him in death, thereby permitting him to father a son by a second wife (see Genealogical Table on p. x).

Emperor Leopold had already made allowances for a female succession in

---

[5] The *Erblande*'s tax burden was generally apportioned as follows: Greater Bohemia, 66 percent (Bohemia 33 percent, Silesia 22 percent, Moravia 11 percent); Austrian lands, 34 percent (Inner Austria 17 percent, Lower Austria 11 percent, Upper Austria 6 percent). The Tyrol made only intermittent contributions.

September 1703, when he concluded the *pactum mutuae successionis* with his two sons on the eve of Charles's departure for Spain. The three men agreed that Charles and his male heirs would rule Spain and its empire, while Joseph would inherit the Austrian dominions from his father. Should either Joseph or Charles fail to provide a son, the surviving male line would succeed to both Habsburg realms. Female offspring would also be permitted to succeed following the extinction of both male lines. Finally, the *pactum* also decreed the unity and indivisibility of the Austro-Bohemian-Hungarian lands.

The settlement of the Habsburg inheritance was hardly attended by expressions of brotherly love. Joseph compelled Charles to cede the strategic duchy of Milan as a precondition for adhering to the succession pact. Although he then waived his claim to the rest of the Spanish empire in favor of Charles and his male heirs, Joseph appears to have insisted that his two daughters, Maria Josepha and Maria Amalia, would "everywhere and always take precedence" over any female issue that Charles might have. Whatever Joseph's intentions may have been, they lost all force with his death. Although the Pragmatic Sanction that Charles issued at court in April 1713 confirmed the *pactum*'s provision for a female succession and its insistence on the monarchy's indivisibility, it also placed his brother's two daughters behind any children that he might have, regardless of their sex.

The Pragmatic Sanction was a truly revolutionary document. Previous testaments, such as the *pactum mutuae successionis*, had also forbidden the monarchy's partition and allowed for a female succession. They had, however, remained largely hypothetical until now. By publicly enunciating these principles for the first time, the Pragmatic Sanction now necessitated their formal acceptance by the estates of the realm. This was particularly important in Hungary, whose diet still had the right to elect its king in the event that the dynasty failed to provide a legitimate male heir. From a practical standpoint Charles also wanted foreign recognition of the Pragmatic Sanction, lest it be treated with the same disregard as the will of Charles the Sufferer.

His exhaustive efforts to secure its acceptance at home and abroad have been criticized by many scholars, who often cite Prince Eugene's advice that a full treasury and well-equipped army would have served him better than the signatures of his fellow monarchs. Although the Pragmatic Sanction publicly laid the foundation of an indivisible, if constitutionally diverse, Habsburg *Gesamtstaat*, it was no substitute for administrative and fiscal changes that might have better enabled Charles's successor to defend her inheritance. Historians assert with some justification that the emperor's obsession with the Pragmatic Sanction diverted him from pursuing such badly needed domestic reforms. The fact is that the last male Habsburg had three decades to prepare the monarchy for his death – plenty of time to attend to state-building. Indeed, Joseph's reckless sex life and premature death compromised its future not only because it led to the succession crisis, but also because it placed Charles VI on the throne.

Administration and finance under Charles VI

Given Charles VI's prominence and the baroque pretensions that it inspired, it is not surprising that many historians have contemplated becoming his first modern biographer. Alas, further investigation persuaded every one of them to turn to other subjects. Surely contemporaries had no such illusions. He was a hopeless mediocrity – a rather reticent, stolid man who had inherited his father's phlegmatism and indecisiveness, but not his intelligence and conscientiousness. When he spoke he mumbled so fast that "the most skillful magician would not be able to understand him." His handwriting was so illegible that it took two centuries before anyone could decipher his diary. When the historian Oswald Redlich finally succeeded in doing so, what he found was a shallow and trivial mind that was hardly up to the challenges that the monarchy faced.

The task was needlessly complicated by Charles's nostalgia for Spain, an obsession that went far beyond his patronage of the arts. Instead of seeing himself as the sovereign of a greatly enlarged monarchy, he nurtured the illusion that he was the ruler of discrete Austrian and Spanish Habsburg states. He insisted on keeping the Spanish royal title long after he had departed the peninsula. Its escutcheon remained on the imperial coat of arms until the end of his reign. Even in death his ornate sarcophagus reminds us of his Spanish quest with a representation of a rare victory over Philip V at Saragossa. However fantastic Charles's conceit may have been, it had a real effect on the monarchy's organization. Upon his return from the peninsula, he established a parallel Spanish ministry and filled it with those Iberian and Italian exiles who had served him in Spain. Rather than take orders from the Privy Conference, this Spanish *camarilla* enjoyed direct access to the emperor through a wholly independent Council of Spain (*Consejo de España*). Charles even negated his brother's earlier transfer of Milan to Austrian rule by placing it under the jurisdiction of a new Italian Chancery that he subordinated to the *Consejo*. Among his Latin advisors, the Catalan Marquis de Rialp and the Neapolitan Count Rocco Stella enjoyed immediate access to the emperor. To his credit Rialp made an effort to work with his Austrian colleagues. Yet they could not hide their jealousy and mistrust for men like Stella, whom they nicknamed the "nighthawk" for his secretive, nocturnal visits to Charles's apartments.

Unfortunately, the Austrian ministers were unable to compensate for Charles's own lack of interest and vision. Unlike his brother, he refused to delegate authority, with the result that they waited around for instructions

and support that never materialized. Nor were they wholly without responsibility for the resulting ministerial muddle. Virtually all of Joseph's best
ministers had died or resigned within a few years of Charles's succession.
Those who remained were deeply divided by conflicts within their own ranks.
Most notable among the holdovers were Gundaker Starhemberg and Prince
Eugene, whose martial exploits helped make him the most influential court
figure during the opening years of the reign. Yet the greatest military genius
in Austrian history proved an indifferent *Hofkriegsrat* president. Like the rest
of the ministry, he worked only a few hours a day, while devoting most of his
time to playing cards and various other social pursuits. Even when his mind
turned to business, he expended far more energy in defending his reputation
in court intrigues than in improving the monarchy's military system or
training a competent field commander to succeed him.

By contrast, Gundaker Starhemberg was a much less political and more
diligent minister, who needed only the confidence of his sovereign to
continue the reform projects begun under Joseph I. He had, in fact, alerted
Charles to the monarchy's serious fiscal difficulties immediately after his
succession and had elicited from him a mandate for drafting a comprehensive
plan for restructuring state finances. In the end, however, the emperor
merely followed in the footsteps of many of the monarchy's rulers by making
minor adjustments in its byzantine administrative system at the beginning of
the reign, but doing very little afterward. He did, for example, create a
commission to discharge the mountainous state debt, and supported
Starhemberg's introduction of improved book-keeping methods at all levels
of the fiscal administration. Yet, far from encouraging Starhemberg's more
ambitious projects, Charles allowed the Spanish *camarilla* to make him a
scapegoat for the monarchy's chronic fiscal problems. Starhemberg eventually resigned as *Hofkammer* president in 1715, following the creation of the
so-called *Universal Bankalität*, a joint state–private investment vehicle that
challenged his control over the *Hofkammer* and the Vienna City Bank. He
stayed on as head of the Ministerial Bank Deputation and had the
satisfaction of witnessing the *Bankalität's* collapse one year later under the
weight of the Turkish war. But any chance of restructuring the monarchy's
fiscal apparatus ended with his departure from the *Hofkammer*.

Whereas the emperor showed little interest in changing the monarchy's
administrative system, he was firmly committed to retaining its constitutional
structure. As had past Habsburgs, he attempted to govern by consensus with
the monarchy's privileged elites, rather than through coercion enforced by
bureaucratic fiat. Even before his return from Spain he expressed his
determination to adhere closely to the traditional constitutions of all his
dominions. His establishment of the *Consejo de España* demonstrated his
distaste for continuing his predecessors' modest efforts to integrate and
centralize the government. Nor did he show any interest in Schierendorff's

suggestion that he assemble a diet of all the Habsburg lands for the dual purposes of adopting the universal excise and ratifying the Pragmatic Sanction. His decision spelled the deathknell of the universal excise and the uniform tax structure that it represented. Moreover, when he sought recognition for the Pragmatic Sanction, he negotiated separately with each of the crownlands, thereby entrenching further the notion of a constitutionally diverse Habsburg *Gesamtstaat*.

In Charles's defense, several of his Spanish dominions would have strongly resisted any move toward royal absolutism. Nevertheless, by failing to integrate any of them, Charles let slip an opportunity to add considerably to the state revenue. The administration and economy of Naples were so hopelessly mismanaged that the kingdom was actually a net drain on the treasury. Nor did the Austrian Netherlands contribute to the monarchy's coffers. Fully a third of its annual revenue was needed to reimburse the Dutch for the operating expenses of the eight barrier fortresses that they maintained along the French frontier; what was left was barely sufficient to defray the costs of its own administration and defense. Thus, despite the tremendous increase in the monarchy's size and population, it was the *Erblande* that still provided the bulk of its taxes. Given the paltry annual Contribution paid by the Austrian lands – 1 million fl. each from the archduchies and Inner Austria, and often nothing from the Tyrol or Outer Austria – the burden fell principally on Bohemia.

Nowhere, however, did the crown's reliance on mutual cooperation bear more positive results. Charles continued his predecessors' practice of rewarding the kingdom's loyalty by gradually extending its privileges. As had Joseph before him, Charles permitted the Bohemian and Moravian estates to revise parts of the *Verneuerte Landesordnung*. Their diets' activities also expanded to the point where they were in almost continuous session by the end of the reign. In return the Bohemia and Moravian estates did not disappoint Charles. Although they did expunge the *Verneuerte Landesordnung*'s references to the Bohemian revolt, their only substantive innovation was to expand the king's power over church lands, courts, and taxes. The Bohemian diet also readily adopted Charles's request for a "Decennial Recess" (1715) that bound it to provide a fixed Contribution without the need for annual negotiations, even though the grant compromised one of its most crucial remaining rights. Most important, they usually provided the same 6 million fl. Contribution that they had voted at the height of the War of the Spanish Succession.

The spirit of compromise was also very much in evidence in Hungary. Both sides had learned from the Rákóczi Revolt. Although the court continued to see the Hungarians as inveterate rebels, Charles kept the peace by generally observing the constitutional settlements of Pressburg (1687) and Szatmár (1711). The Magyar nation was no less willing to avoid confrontation with a dynasty that had fought and won three major wars in Hungary in little more than a generation. Nowhere was the spirit of compromise and cooperation more readily apparent than in the kingdom's diet. In 1715 it forsook two centuries of opposition to the presence of "foreign" troops on Hungarian soil by recognizing the need for a strong standing army, two-thirds of which was to be composed of non-native soldiers. To maintain the military it now accepted the need to vote a regular Contribution, which reached 2.5 million fl. by 1728. The diet also accepted the appointment of foreign-born officials when it affirmed the king's right to naturalize non-Magyar subjects. By the end of Charles' reign nearly 30 percent of the kingdom's magnates were foreign-born aristocrats with names like Auersperg, Liechtenstein, Lobkovic, Schönborn, Schwarzenberg, and Trautson. Few of these men actually became involved in the kingdom's affairs. Among those who did, the German Cardinal-Primate Sachsen-Zeitz, represented the Magyar nobility so forcefully in his capacity as president of the diet's lower table that one delegate boasted that "he could not have done better even if he had been the offspring of Attila himself." The kingdom's highest offices were, in any event, already subordinate to the government in Vienna. The Hungarian Chancery did little more than expedite policy determined by non-Magyar ministers in the Privy Conference. Although the kingdom continued to maintain a separate treasury in Pressburg, financial and military affairs were now run exclusively by the *Hofkammer* and *Hofkriegsrat*. Even the county assemblies, which remained active in the countryside, were increasingly dominated by *labanc* magnates.

The aristocracy's acceptance of Habsburg rule was also evident in its wholesale adoption of the Austrian baroque style. A half century had passed since the *labanc* magnate and later palatine Pál Esterházy built the kingdom's first baroque palace at Eisenstadt. Yet, although many church-built structures employed the baroque style, his countrymen had expressed their defiance and independence of Vienna by continuing to construct their own palaces in the Renaissance style. Now they competed with one another in hiring Austrian masters like Hildebrandt, the fresco painter Maulbertsch, and the prominent sculptor Georg Raphael Donner.

The crown's inroads extended well beyond the loyalty of the Magyar aristocracy. Whereas the nobility was densely concentrated in Upper Hungary, it was virtually non-existent elsewhere. Indeed, by 1720 the demographic losses of the past two centuries and the steady immigration of German and Balkan immigrants had reduced ethnic Magyars to less than half of the population of Hungary proper. They were even lower in those areas most recently wrested from Turkish control. Charles took advantage of these demographic peculiarities by keeping the southern half of both

Hungary and Croatia outside the jurisdiction of their respective diets. Despite the promises that he and his predecessors had made to the estates of both kingdoms, Charles kept the existing Military Border zones, even though some of them no longer adjoined the Ottoman empire. The Banat was also placed under direct military rule, as were the extra-Hungarian conquests in northern Serbia and Little Wallachia. Transylvania also remained a separate crownland. In deference to popular sensibilities, Charles refrained from assuming the princely title until the death of Michael II Apafi in 1713. Thereafter he ignored its diet and chancery, governing it instead through the Austrian Chancery and *Hofkriegsrat*. By detaching and ruling these areas directly, the government in Vienna was able to squeeze more revenue from Hungary.

Of course, in Charles's eyes the ultimate reward for his close cooperation with the estates was their rapid and unanimous ratification of the Pragmatic Sanction. In other countries, such a revision in the succession would have posed formidable problems and risks. The Hanoverian succession in Great Britain had only recently been challenged by Jacobite conspiracies and revolts. The late Louis XIV's testament had been invalidated by the Paris *Parlement* only days after his death. The will of Charles the Sufferer had been rejected by his Aragonese subjects. And in Russia, several monarchs had to contend with a seemingly endless parade of false tsars and very real revolts of their own palace guard. In the Habsburg monarchy, however, the deliberations over the Pragmatic Sanction were characterized above all else by loyalty and deference to the wishes of the last male Habsburg. The various estates of the *Erblande* quickly and unanimously accepted the Pragmatic Sanction, even though the Bohemian diet had serious reservations about the precedence afforded Charles's daughters and the Tyrol had heretofore refused to admit to a permanent union with the other Habsburg dominions. Croatia actually declared its willingness to accept a female Habsburg succession in March 1712, a full year before Charles had even issued the Pragmatic Sanction. A decade later the lower table of the Hungarian diet went so far as to prevent Cardinal Sachsen-Zeitz from presiding over its deliberations, because it feared that his previous close association with the late Joseph I would incline him to oppose the precedence that the Pragmatic Sanction gave to Charles's own daughters.

The monarchy's elites rewarded Charles's deference with a loyalty exemplified by the Austrian Prince Adam Franz Schwarzenberg who, when Charles accidentally shot him in a hunting accident near Prague, uttered the appropriate last words: "It was always my duty to give my life for my sovereign." As a rule, however, it was others who made the sacrifices and the privileged elites who benefited the most. In post-Szatmár Hungary the loyalist nobility actually persuaded Charles not to enforce his amnesty of the rebels too thoroughly so that it could keep the land it had seized from *kuruc* nobles. It also convinced him to replace the unpopular *Commissio Neo Acquistica* (which his brother had abolished in 1709) with a new body run by native officials whose decisions further benefited the growth of aristocratic latifundia. Even the diet's first-time grant of a regular Contribution in 1715 represented a victory for the nobility, which obliged the crown to recognize its own long-standing exemption from taxation. The *Erblande*'s nobility was only slightly more forthcoming. Although the Bohemian estates had agreed to pay substantial taxes during the recent war against Louis XIV, they had shifted most of the increases in the Contribution onto the shoulders of the peasantry, which saw its share quintuple under the last three male Habsburgs to 40 fl. per head. The Inner Austrian nobility was even more thorough, managing to shift all of its small share of the Contribution to the peasantry by 1728.

The peasantry also paid for the symbiosis between crown and aristocracy through the continuation of manorial obligations. In Hungary the crown permitted the diet to enact comprehensive legislation to stop peasant flight. It also acquiesced in the enserfment of large numbers of previously free *hayducks*, perhaps because so many had fought for Rákóczi and were no longer needed to fight the Turks. To his credit Charles responded to agrarian unrest in Bohemia by issuing *Robot* patents in 1717 and 1738 that forbade certain abuses and facilitated the peasantry's access to royal justice. Yet neither patent proved any more effective than those issued by his father.

Charles was only slightly less accommodating to the monarchy's largest landowner, the Roman Catholic church. For over a century the Habsburg clergy had demonstrated its loyalty by making large, voluntary contributions during wartime, including 1.2 million fl. during the most recent Turkish conflict. Yet Schierendorff and other cameralists had long argued that the monarchy's economic productivity and tax revenue had suffered from religious persecution, as well as from the enormous amount of tax-free land held in mortmain by the Catholic church. In fact, various monastic orders owned half of Carniola and nearly as much of Moravia. The emperor did make some perfunctory attempts within the *Erblande* to discourage the accumulation of church wealth. Yet he did nothing at all in Naples, Sicily or the Austrian Netherlands, where half of all arable land was held by a multitude of ecclesiastical foundations.

His position toward the church's cultural hegemony was more problematical. Though not as secular as his brother, Charles never exhibited his father's religious fanaticism. He also inherited from Joseph a group of advisors who subscribed to the secular, anticlerical views of the early Enlightenment. Although he did not share their interest in reforming the monarchy's educational system, he did make some effort to relieve the government's dependence on the church. He transferred primary responsibility for poor relief from the clergy to the police. He also embraced the cameralists' proscription against expelling productive workers, whatever their faith. Thus, in the years immediately after the archbishop of Salzburg's infamous expulsion of 20,000 Protestants in 1732, the emperor expressed his concern over the persistence of pockets of Protestantism within the Austrian lands by forcibly resettling a thousand Carinthians and Upper Austrians in Transylvania.

If he sanctioned the persecution of non-Catholics, it came partly at the behest of the estates. Having done so much over the past century to Catholicize the monarchy's privileged classes, the dynasty now felt constrained to heed their appeals against toleration. Even Joseph I had repeatedly refused to restore to Lower Silesia's Protestants all of the freedoms promised them by the Peace of Westphalia because he did not want to alienate the duchy's predominantly Catholic estates. Only Charles XII's occupation of neighboring Saxony and subsequent threat to intervene on their behalf ultimately persuaded him to relent. Even then, however, Joseph I hastened to console the "enraged and humiliated" estates by forbidding Lower Silesian Catholic converts to readopt Protestantism. Similarly, Charles VI failed to resolve Hungary's festering religious conflicts largely because of the opposition of the diet's Catholic magnates. Behind their leadership about seventy additional Protestant churches were closed down during Charles's reign. The *Carolina Resolutio* that he issued in 1731 limited full religious freedom to the few counties that were under Habsburg dominion at the time of the Sopron diet fifty years earlier. Elsewhere, he made a distinction between private and public worship by permitting Protestants to hold private services for immediate family members, but obliging them to celebrate all Catholic holidays. At the same time he continued the practice of appointing only Roman and Greek Catholics to government positions in Hungary and Transylvania.

For the first time the Military Border's Orthodox population also became subject to pressure to convert. The largely Serb *Grenzer* had always valued the crown's protection against the likely religious persecution and enserfment that they would suffer at the hands of the Hungarian and Croatian estates. Both Joseph I and Charles VI had confirmed their privileges and autonomy in exchange for their valuable military support against the *kuruc* and the Turks. But the crown had always regarded these arrangements as a temporary settlement that could be repealed once their Balkan homeland had been liberated from Ottoman rule. The Turks' defeat had, in fact, eliminated the need for at least some of the older Military Border districts. Although the crown intended to hold onto them for the troops and political leverage they afforded it within greater Hungary, it saw less utility in continuing to honor the Serbs' privileges. Within months of the peace of Passarowitz, Charles acceded to pressure from the Croatian and Inner Austrian estates by allowing Jesuit missionaries and Inner Austrian officials to seek the conversion of the Military Border's Orthodox priests, bishops, and monasteries. Unfortunately, their spiritual regimen included beating several priests and killing the prior of a monastery. By 1727 Orthodox bishops had been deprived of their secular powers. Further east, Serb *Grenzer* near Arad mutinied against a combination of Catholic proselytizing, foreign colonization, and the crown's repeal of their tax privileges. In the end, neither the persecution of the Military Border's Orthodox Serbs nor the enserfment of Hungary's *hayduck* frontiersmen ever led to a full-scale insurrection. They do show, however, the pervasive influence of the privileged estates, as well as the dynasty's own capacity for repression whenever the absence of foreign threats afforded it a free hand with its own subjects.

Economic initiatives and development

Charles's deference to the land-holding nobility and Catholic church was not without negative economic consequences, especially in the countryside, where he was generally unwilling to enact most of the agrarian reforms recommended by men like Schierendorff. The persistence of clerical mortmain and religious persecution continued to cost the economy productive land and subjects, just as the heavy exactions of landlords deprived peasants of the time, funds, and incentive that they needed to increase their productivity.

The economic picture was not, however, totally bleak. In contrast to the peasantry and religious minorities, the monarchy's small bourgeoisie was the one unprivileged element in Habsburg society that clearly benefited from Charles VI's attention. Admittedly he was not the first Habsburg to evince an interest in stimulating the economy. But, unlike his predecessors, Charles was able to combine a commitment to industrial and commercial expansion with a prolonged period of peace. He certainly needed little prodding: having spent his decade in Spain as little more than a British puppet, Charles had come to appreciate the power that a strong commercial economy bestowed upon countries like England and the United Provinces. It was during his reign that the writings of men like Becher, Schröder, and Hörnigk finally gained widespread acceptance; Hörnigk's *Österreich über Alles* went through sixteen editions and was employed in the instruction of Charles's three daughters. Schierendorff also found the emperor more willing to enact his mercantile projects than his other innovations. Not surprisingly, many of the emperor's economic initiatives took place within a few years of his succession. Yet, unlike the badly needed administrative reforms in which he quickly lost interest, Charles never relented in his efforts to develop new industrial and commercial enterprises to the point of personally inspecting and even investing his own money in them.

For the most part the emperor merely accelerated the introduction of conventional mercantile strategies that had already been adopted in other parts of Europe. Although his brother had recently reestablished a Commerce Commission in Vienna, he now created others in regional centers like Prague and Breslau for the purpose of creating a favorable environment for new industrial enterprises. At Schierendorff's suggestion he added an office for trade and manufacturing in 1718 to coordinate his mercantile projects. In response to decades of agitation that stretched back to Leopold's reign, the government also began using tariffs as a vehicle for encouraging the domestic production of finished products, rather than simply for raising revenue. After 1728 competing imports were taxed at rates as high as 100 percent. By 1735 the repeal of the excise on native (but not foreign) goods had given an additional edge to domestic production. Two years later a more comprehensive tariff law sharply lowered export duties, while retaining substantial imposts on imports. Charles also intensified his predecessors' efforts to remove the guilds' stifling effect on competition by attacking their monopoly over various trades and their right to set prices. Finally, a reform of the currency (1716) and the establishment of a state post (1722) helped provide a more congenial environment for industrial and commercial expansion.

As in other countries, the government attempted to create new industries that could either promote exports or reduce the monarchy's dependence on imported goods. Emperors Leopold and Joseph had already granted concessions for over a dozen such factories in the first decade of the century, producing everything from wax, lamp oil, glass, and various textiles to mirrors, silk, and even gold and silver thread. Several of those established during Charles's reign made exotic luxury products like porcelain, tapestries, and tobacco. The government was, however, most active and successful in promoting the expansion of existing industries, such as textiles, glass, and iron. By 1730 Vienna itself had no fewer than seven textile factories. Bohemia and Moravia added an equal number during the previous decade for producing wool, silk, and cotton products.

Although the government aggressively promoted the creation of various industrial enterprises, it actually owned or operated very few of them. Exceptions were the state-run workhouses, which continued to grow in number with the addition of facilities in Olmütz (Olomouc) (1702), Innsbruck (1725), Graz (1735), and Prague (1737). Otherwise, the government recruited private entrepreneurs by offering a host of incentives that might include the payment of subsidies, exemption from taxes and outside competition, or even complete religious freedom. No group was more important than the aristocracy, especially wealthy Bohemian and Moravian nobles who already had established patrimonial businesses and a ready supply of servile labor. It was, however, also necessary to attract foreign investors, entrepreneurs, and artisans, and the advanced business techniques and technology that they employed. Thus, Inner Austria's iron industry helped sustain its recovery from the depression of the last century by importing furnaces that permitted more efficient operation. The revolutionary steam engines that helped drain Upper Hungary's copper mines may have been installed by Fischer von Erlach's son, Joseph Emanuel, but they were the invention of the British engineer, Thomas Newcomen. Moreover, the mines themselves remained largely in the hands of Dutch agents. Nor would the *Erblande*'s porcelain industry have ever been competitive without hiring key entrepreneurs and artisans from Trier and the famous Saxon manufacturing center at Meissen. The growth and management of greater Bohemia's cottage textile industry were carefully nurtured by British factors who settled there during the first half of the century. One such agent in the town of Rumburg (Rumburk) managed to increase the number of looms from about 30 to 580 between 1713 and 1724. Moreover, the region's textile exports remained largely in the hands of German and English middlemen. With their help textile sales now reached beyond Germany to Great Britain and Spain as well as to their American colonies.

In fact, the promotion of overseas exports became one of the emperor's major goals, especially in the decade after the conclusion of the Turkish war. He did more than any previous Habsburg to create new and better commercial arteries that might fuel foreign trade. Like his father he expanded the monarchy's commercial waterways by building canals and dredging rivers. But he also devoted huge sums to an impressive road-building program that touched virtually every province of the monarchy. Charles attempted to open up three new avenues for trade. To the southeast the lower Danube became a conduit for exports to the Ottoman empire. Six days after the peace of Passarowitz he concluded a trade treaty with the Turks that afforded both countries free navigation of the river and, beyond that, access to each other's domestic markets. Ironically, it was the Turks who benefited the most. On the one hand, they proved reluctant to import foreign goods, except for those provided by the French. Meanwhile, Ottoman Greek and Jewish middlemen took advantage of Hungary's virtually nonexistent commercial infrastructure to establish themselves there for the purpose of exporting Turkish goods to the monarchy. So dominating was the Ottoman presence that the word *görög*, or "Greek," became a common Magyar term for "merchant."

Charles was much more successful in his efforts to develop a second export outlet through the Mediterranean. He literally paved the way during the 1720s with a complex network of roads. One traversed the Brenner Pass into northern Italy, another the Semmering Pass all the way to Trieste and the Adriatic littoral. He also spent 3 million fl. building a *Via Carolina* to improve Hungary's access to Fiume. The two Istrian towns were the focus of Charles's vision. In 1719 he made both free ports in the hope that they would encourage the *Erblande*'s merchants to circumvent the high Prussian tariffs that dominated the northbound trade route along the Elbe and Oder rivers. He even granted full religious freedom to skilled workers who relocated in either place, despite sustained protests from the littoral's Catholic estates. Many found employment with the Oriental Company that he set up in the same year. The company soon became a major enterprise with numerous industrial operations, including a textile manufacture in Vienna and another in Linz that ultimately employed 12,000 spinners and weavers. Despite its initial profitability, the Oriental Company went bankrupt in 1734. The Adriatic ports themselves also proved too distant to attract exports from the Bohemian lands. Yet the emperor's efforts were hardly in vain. For centuries Venice had enforced a monopoly on the Adriatic trade that limited the coastal populations of Istria and Croatia to little more than fishing and piracy. Under Charles VI the monarchy not only competed with the island republic but quickly surpassed it as the Adriatic's principal commercial power. Meanwhile, the Croatian littoral utilized its forests to become a center for shipbuilding and lumber exports. The roads that Charles built also greatly increased the volume of trade between the Adriatic provinces and the rest of the Austrian lands.

Charles focused his third overseas venture in the Austrian Netherlands. Belgium's economy had long been handicapped by ruthless Dutch competition. For the past 150 years the Dutch had used their control of the Scheldt estuary to blockade its main port of Antwerp. More recently they and the British had extracted far-reaching commercial concessions that had been written into the Barrier Treaty of 1715. Nevertheless, here was a crownland with the human and capital infrastructure to support the emperor's bold vision. The merchants of the crownland's principal port of Ostend had, in fact, already established themselves along India's Coromandel coast, from where they hoped to challenge the Anglo-Dutch monopoly in the Far East. In 1723 Charles offered them imperial protection from Dutch threats by chartering and funding the East India, or Ostend Company. The first colonial venture in the monarchy's history was an immediate success, paying its shareholders a 140 percent stock dividend after only four expeditions. It immediately expanded its operations in India, while launching new operations in North Africa and China. By 1730 the company's profits had matched the 6 million fl. originally invested by stockholders.

In keeping with contemporary strategies of political economy, the government focused its commercial initiatives on finding new markets for those dominions with an existing industrial base, such as the Bohemian lands, the two archduchies, and Belgium. Meanwhile, it took a rather different approach toward greater Hungary, which was classified as an agricultural area that would provide the rest of the monarchy with foodstuffs and assorted raw materials. As a result it made virtually no attempts to develop an industrial or commercial infrastructure there. Enterprising magnates tried to fill the void. Led by Sándor Károlyi, the diet of 1715 formed a commission to investigate strategies for mercantile development, including the creation of industries to refine the raw textiles, leather, and minerals that the kingdom produced. But the absence of support from Vienna foreclosed any chance for success. Károlyi ultimately created his own private company to carry through his plans, which included the construction of Hungary's first woolen factory in 1722, as did other magnates such as the Croatian ban János Pálffy and assorted members of the Esterházy family. All of these projects had, however, collapsed by mid-century. The kingdom remained very much an agrarian zone. Even its towns were typically inhabited primarily by peasant farmers, with craftsmen comprising only 10–20 percent of their population.

Charles and his ministers could be excused if they foresaw little else in Hungary's future. The Rákóczi Revolt had compounded the destruction wrought by two centuries of war and rebellion. Perhaps 85,000 *kuruc* had died in the fighting; famine and a devastating plague that broke out in 1708 may have carried off an additional 400,000 civilians. Fortunately, the prolonged period of stability brought by the peace of Szatmár enabled the kingdom to begin a remarkable recovery from an era of war and devastation that had begun two hundred years earlier. The government assisted the recovery of its agrarian economy through an ambitious program of peasant colonization. While it focused on those frontier districts that it ruled directly, individual ministers and other loyalist landlords worked to repopulate the central plain on lands they had received from the *Commissio Neo Acquistica*. They attracted tens of thousands of colonists with promises of land and tax exemptions, as well as personal and religious freedom. As always, German settlers from the *Erblande* and the empire were favored. Yet there also followed a significant redistribution of the kingdom's population with the attraction of Magyars, Slovaks, and Ruthenes from the more densely inhabited parts of Upper Hungary as well as Romanians from nearby Transylvania. Significant numbers of Balkan Serbs, Romanians and Bulgarians also settled in southern Hungary, as did a smattering of French, Italians, Catalans and even Russian Cossacks. At the height of the colonization the Banat spoke seventeen different languages, a pot-pourri of nationalities with ominous implications for the future. For now, however, the colonization was an unqualified success. German colonists led the way in draining swamps, clearing forests and employing new techniques and crops, such as corn, tobacco, and potato. The Hungarian plain resumed grain exports, while the Banat and the eastern reaches of Slavonia also converted their open stretches to large-scale cattle production.

It is difficult to judge precisely how successful Charles VI's economic policies were, at least in the immediate term. His initiatives benefited the well-established textile industry. Wool production increased dramatically in Bohemia (60 percent) and Silesia (100 percent) and Upper Austria; as early as 1725, the Linz woolen-stuffs factory had become one of Europe's largest, with a workforce of 4,400. Some new projects, such as the Meissen porcelain factory, the new commercial arteries, the Adriatic ports, and the colonization of Hungary brought immediate returns on the government's investment. Other enterprises remained dependent on government assistance or failed altogether. An estimated 30–50 percent growth rate in Austria's towns between 1660 and 1730 suggests growth, but is not conclusive given the likely flight of peasants from the countryside; certainly the tremendous increase of Vienna and its suburbs from 110,000 residents at the beginning of the reign to 160,000 at its end is due more to court patronage than commercial-industrial expansion. At the very least, Charles did help to establish a mercantile infrastructure, an inconspicuous but necessary first step in the monarchy's evolution as a formidable economic power.

He deserves less credit for his half-hearted attempts to resolve the government's chronic fiscal and administrative problems. Total state income had more than doubled to nearly 20 million fl. during the War of the Spanish Succession. There was, however, only a modest increase in either cameral or extraordinary revenue under Charles VI, even though the monarchy had nearly doubled in size. Instead the emperor made good use of the Vienna City Bank, which had assumed over half of the government's 100 million fl. debt by the end of his reign. Although they provided little in the way of revenue, the Austrian Netherlands also helped close the gap by loaning him over 10 million fl. during the 1730s. The rest, however, had to be financed by loans from foreign sources, his own ministers, and Jewish purveyors, just as his predecessors had done. Indeed, the 78 million fl. that the court Jews extended to the *Hofkammer* during the half-century 1698–1739 has prompted Ernst Wangermann to suggest that the monarchy owed as much to them as it did to the genius of Prince Eugene.

Manifestations of weakness: defeat and disillusionment

The monarchy's internal weaknesses were somewhat less critical now that its security zone extended so far beyond its center. Those threats that survived were directed primarily at its distant outposts in the Low Countries, Italy, and the Balkans, rather than at its core. Nevertheless, if the monarchy had enhanced its security, it had lost virtually all of its traditional allies. With its new acquisitions and the pretensions they inspired, it had outgrown its usefulness as an instrument against French or Turkish aggression. The new France that had emerged under Louis XV was, in fact, more cooperative and less threatening to the European balance of power. The French foreign minister, Cardinal Fleury (1726–43), was fond of pointing out that France was a "satiated power" that had no interest in wars of conquest. Rather than prop up the monarchy against France, countries like Great Britain were now inclined to nurture smaller states like Sardinia and Prussia as a counterpoise to any larger power, including the Habsburg monarchy.

Charles could still count on strong support within the empire, especially from those smaller and middle-sized states that relied on him for protection from their larger neighbors. Prince Eugene's most recent victories had further enhanced the widespread sense of Austro-German solidarity. Thus it was German auxiliaries returning from the Balkans who composed and first sang the famous *Prinz-Eugen Lied* and a duke of Württemberg who named all of his five sons after the Austrian generalissimo. With the able assistance of Imperial Vice Chancellor Schönborn, Charles VI exploited his prestige by continuing his brother's bold exercise of imperial prerogatives.

But even in Germany the fading French threat to the empire now encouraged Charles's most powerful vassals to focus more on their own selfish dynastic goals. In the north, Prussia's elevation as a kingdom (1701) and the Hanoverian succession in Great Britain (1714) rendered the two Protestant electors much more ambitious and less dependent on the emperor. Meanwhile, Charles alienated the Catholic electors of Saxony and Bavaria by his provisions for the Austrian succession. The Pragmatic Sanction had minimized the claims of Joseph I's two teenage daughters, Maria Josepha and Maria Amalia, especially after the birth of Maria Theresa (1717) and Maria Anna (1718). Nevertheless, both Augustus II and Max Emanuel eagerly sought the hand of Charles's nieces for their male heirs, both because of his daughters' tender age and because of the precedence that the earlier *pactum mutuae successionis* had awarded the Josephine archduchesses. Nor were the two electors alone in their faith in the "higher legitimacy" of the *pactum*. Upon reviewing that document, the Privy Conference actually urged the emperor not to wed either of his nieces to "two German princes whose pretensions can one day plunge this country into a long and unfortunate war." Yet Charles ignored their advice. Instead, he contented himself with a fifty-nine-page renunciation to which Augustus II, the Saxon Crown Prince Frederick Augustus, and Maria Josepha all swore on the occasion of their wedding in 1719; the same procedure was repeated by Max Emanuel, the

Bavarian Crown Prince Charles Albert, and Maria Amalia at the time of their nuptials in 1722. The recent fate of renunciations should have given the emperor pause, but he hoped that the two marriages would strengthen his ties with both electors. Instead, they immediately prompted Saxony and Bavaria to conclude a series of alliances with each other and with France that were aimed at making good their claims to the Austrian succession. By 1725 Max Emanuel had also concluded a family compact that enlisted the support of the Wittelsbach electors of Trier, Cologne, and the Palatinate. Once the elder Maria Josepha and her Saxon husband had produced the first of their fourteen children, Max Emanuel kept alive his hopes for a Habsburg legacy for the younger Maria Amalia by forging an "authentic and original" copy of a sixteenth-century Austro-Bavarian marriage compact that purported to award most of the *Erblande* to Bavaria upon the extinction of the dynasty's male line.

Two decades earlier, half of Europe would have rushed to support the Pragmatic Sanction as an absolute necessity for the preservation of the balance of power. Now Charles VI was obliged to press hard for its acceptance by the great powers. Unfortunately, his stubborn refusal to surrender his Spanish titles or to confirm a Farnese succession in Parma and Tuscany alienated not only Philip V, but also Great Britain and France. By 1721 the three countries had concluded a Triple Alliance to force the emperor's compliance.

In May 1725 Charles temporarily ended the monarchy's isolation by concluding an extraordinary alliance with his Spanish adversary. In return for meeting Philip V's dynastic agenda, the emperor secured two things close to his heart: recognition of the Pragmatic Sanction and commercial concessions for the Ostend Company in Spanish America. The so-called First Treaty of Vienna aroused so much suspicion among the other great powers that it quickly divided Europe into two hostile camps. By the end of 1726 the League of Herrenhausen (France, Great Britain, and the United Provinces) stood on the brink of war with Spain and Austria. Charles strengthened his position somewhat by concluding separate alliances with Russia and Prussia. He also extracted a promise of Spanish subsidies in exchange for the promise to marry his daughters to the sons of Philip V and the irrepressible Elizabeth Farnese. The prospect of his former Bourbon enemy succeeding in Vienna does not appear to have troubled Charles, especially since all of the children involved were still far from puberty. He was, however, jolted by the outbreak of limited hostilities between Spain and Great Britain, together with the massing of League forces in central Europe. Indeed, Charles had the good sense to realize that the monarchy lacked the financial and military strength to win such a war. During 1727 he attempted to mollify the Maritime Powers by suspending the Ostend Company's operations. His subsequent refusal to launch military operations or to conclude a formal marriage compact ultimately prompted Philip V to desert his ill-conceived alliance with the emperor.

The Anglo-Spanish Treaty of Seville (November 1729) isolated Charles once again and compelled him to capitulate to their demands. In the Second Treaty of Vienna (March 1731) he accepted the succession of Philip's and Elizabeth's eldest son, Don Carlos, in Parma and Tuscany. He also appeased the Maritime Powers by abandoning the Ostend Company altogether. In return for these concessions, the emperor did secure Anglo-Dutch recognition of the Pragmatic Sanction. As elector of Hanover, George II also endorsed Charles's testament when the Electoral College ratified it by a six to three vote at the beginning of 1732. Charles interpreted his accommodation with the Maritime Powers as a return to the "old system" by which the Habsburg monarchy and German empire had achieved great victories at the beginning of the century. Indeed, in seeking the electors' recognition of the Pragmatic Sanction, he had reminded them of the need to remain united against the historic French threat. The argument no longer carried any weight with Saxony or the Wittelsbachs of Bavaria and the Palatinate, all of whom had accepted French subsidies and voted no. Nor were the Maritime Powers overly concerned. Whereas Charles perceived the Second Treaty of Vienna as an alliance, they saw it only as a means of achieving a stable settlement that would leave them free to pursue their overseas commercial ventures in splendid isolation.

Unfortunately, the emperor's plans for the succession made war inevitable. With the end of the Spanish marriage alliance, he decided to wed the Habsburg heiress presumptive, Maria Theresa, to Francis Stephen of Lorraine. The match constituted a fitting reward for a loyal imperial vassal and a young prince whose own easygoing nature appealed to Charles VI. Yet Cardinal Fleury warned Vienna that France would not tolerate a match that would merge neighboring Lorraine with the Habsburg dominions. Even the Maritime Powers indicated that the interests of European stability would incline them to support French annexation of the duchy in the event of a Habsburg–Lorraine marriage. By 1732 Louis XV and Philip V had concluded a family compact with the intention of seizing the duchy, together with Charles's Italian possessions.

They were already mobilizing for an attack when the death of Augustus II in February 1733 provided them with an ideal pretext. The emperor and his Russian and Prussian allies initially opposed Frederick Augustus's attempt to succeed his father as king of Poland. The new Saxon elector won Charles over, however, by promising once again to renounce his wife's rights to the Austrian succession in favor of Maria Theresa. In September the Polish diet's election of Louis XV's father-in-law, Stanislaus Leszczyński, gave the emperor a strategic reason for supporting the Saxon candidate. Led by the gifted Privy Conference Secretary, Johann Christoph von Bartenstein, several of Charles's advisors cautioned that Austrian intervention in Poland would prompt a French counterthrust in Germany and Italy. Yet the emperor regarded the reality of a pro-French Polish king as a greater threat to the monarchy than the prospect of retaliation elsewhere, especially since he persisted in the belief that the Maritime Powers would eventually come to his aid. He was also aware that failure to support the Russians in Poland might cost him their assistance in the event of war with France.

The emperor did not have to wait long either to realize his objective or its consequences. A Russian invasion of Poland soon enabled the Saxon elector to succeed his father as King Augustus III (1734–63). In a futile effort to avoid French retaliation, Charles VI limited Austrian participation to a military demonstration in neighboring Silesia. By October French forces had overrun Lorraine. Over the next year they seized the key imperial fortress at Philippsburg and joined Spanish and Sardinian armies in overwhelming the Austrian garrisons in Habsburg Italy. Meanwhile, to Charles's dismay, France preserved Anglo-Dutch neutrality by pledging not to invade Belgium – the one crownland that the Maritime Powers were determined to keep in his hands.

It is not difficult to explain the monarchy's defeat in the War of the Polish Succession (1733–8). Except for Germany and Russia, the emperor fought alone. Admittedly Russia was now emerging as a powerful and committed ally. It was, however, preoccupied in Poland and too far away to assist its Habsburg ally in the West until later in the war. When 13,000 Russian auxiliaries did march to the Rhine in 1735, it was the local civilian population rather than the French enemy who panicked at their approach. Meanwhile, the empire's usually anemic military effort was further undermined by the Wittelsbach princes, who withheld their contingents from the imperial army pending Charles's satisfaction of their dynastic agenda. Nor did Charles receive sufficient support from his own estates, which provided considerably less money than they had during either the War of the Spanish Succession or the recent "cold war" with the League of Herrenhausen. The monarchy's generals proved incapable of overcoming their enemies' overwhelming numerical superiority. Although he took the field against the French at Philippsburg, the 71-year-old Prince Eugene was mentally and physically a mere shadow of his former self; his death in 1736 surprised no one. The commander of Austrian forces in Italy fared no better. Having recently been rendered nearly blind and deaf by a stroke, Count Mercy was killed in battle in a valiant, but unsuccessful attempt to save Milan from the enemy.

Given the army's collapse and the *Hofkammer*'s inability to finance another campaign, the emperor was compelled to conclude a preliminary peace with his enemies after just two years of hostilities. What was most surprising was the advantageous conditions that he received. The Peace of Vienna (30 October 1735) illustrates how cabinet diplomats like Clemens von Metternich used dynasticism, legitimacy, and compensation to achieve a stable peace. Whereas it confirmed the Saxon succession in Poland, the treaty compensated Stanislaus Leszczyński with Lorraine, which would then pass to France after his death. In Italy the monarchy surrendered Naples, Sicily, and the strategic Tuscan Presidii Ports to Don Carlos, as well as a western slice of Milan to Sardinia. In return, however, the Spanish prince ceded Parma to Charles VI and Tuscany to Francis Stephen. Finally, France joined its allies in recognizing the Pragmatic Sanction. Such a settlement pleased everyone in Vienna except Charles's future son-in-law, who proved reluctant to relinquish Lorraine. It was Bartenstein who finally won his acquiescence, though only after presenting him with the blunt *quid pro quo*: "No renunciation. No archduchess." In the end, three years passed before the Habsburg–Lorraine nuptials (February 1736) and the death of the childless Duke Gian Gastone of Tuscany permitted the signatories to sign a formal Treaty of Vienna (November 1738) implementing all of the territorial exchanges foreseen by the preliminary peace.

By then the monarchy was already on the verge of losing yet another conflict. Given its desperate finances, its leaders had little interest in fighting another Balkan war against the Ottoman empire. It was their Russian ally that forced a confrontation over a border dispute along the remote shores of the Caspian Sea. In the end the emperor and his ministers decided to join Russia simply because they feared losing their only remaining major ally. The Turkish War of 1737–9 involved the usual cast of belligerents: aside from Russia, the monarchy was assisted by troops from several German states, as well as by large sums raised by the *Reichstag* and the Papacy. The *Türken-glocken* rang throughout the *Erblande* each morning, calling the people to pray for victory and reminding them of the horrors of past conflicts against the Infidel. The estates gave early moral and monetary support for what everyone hoped and expected would be a quick and easy war. Instead, a series of five incompetent commanders managed to drag out hostilities for three campaigns, during which they steadily gave up territory despite winning every one of the four major engagements that they fought. The chief Austrian peace negotiator, Reinhard Wilhelm Count Neipperg, compounded their blunders by concluding the disastrous Peace of Belgrade (September 1739). In addition to recognizing the Turks' recent recovery of northern Serbia and Little Wallachia, the treaty actually compelled the Austrian army to surrender the virtually impregnable fortress of Belgrade.

The people of Vienna reacted to news of the treaty with riots and demands for Neipperg's head. The latest defeat was, in fact, much more of a shock than the recent setbacks against the Bourbon Powers. After all, this time the monarchy had had allies. The Russians not only had forced the Turks to divide their forces, but had conquered nearby Moldavia just as Neipperg was negotiating the surrender of Belgrade. Moreover, the men and money provided by the German princes and the pope eventually accounted for half of the emperor's own 45,000-man army. There were, however, a couple of parallels with the War of the Polish Succession that justified the court's sense of *déjà vu*. Once again, the monarchy had not been well served by its military commanders. The government was quick to punish them for not duplicating Prince Eugene's Balkan triumphs, even though the great general was himself responsible for the *Hofkriegsrat*'s failure to find a suitable successor. Of course, a larger field army would have compensated for the absence of a military genius. Yet, after the initial outlays and disappointments of the 1737 campaign, the estates had lost much of their enthusiasm for the war. As he prepared for the last campaign of his reign, Charles had actually been compelled to reduce the size of the army after they rejected his requests for money and supplies. Another, less evident parallel was the extent to which the government had been sucked into an unwanted war by the aggressiveness of its Russian ally. The emperor certainly needed to retain his allies, but not at the cost of making enemies and wars that he could not win.

It was a measure of the monarchy's new-found security that the recent campaigns and the territorial losses that followed occurred far from its center. If anything, the Treaty of Vienna had strengthened the monarchy's position in Poland and Lombardy at the expense of less defensible outposts in Lorraine and southern Italy. Although the loss of Serbia and Belgrade would have major ramifications in the twentieth century, none of the cessions made at the Peace of Belgrade seriously jeopardized Hungary's frontier with the Ottoman empire. The recent defeats did far more damage by exposing the monarchy's profound military weakness. The realization had a demoralizing effect on the court, which surmised that foreign adversaries might now be tempted to dispute Maria Theresa's impending succession. The nearly universal international acceptance of the Pragmatic Sanction was, indeed, of little benefit without the ability to defend it by force. Just before his death Prince Eugene had urged the emperor to neutralize Bavarian opposition by betrothing Maria Theresa to Elector Charles Albert's son. By then, however, Charles's antipathy toward his troublesome vassal and his daughter's own attachment to Francis Stephen made such a move impossible.

Of all the early modern Habsburgs, Charles VI contributed the least to the monarchy's development. This is not to dismiss the strategic and economic value of his territorial acquisitions, especially in light of his efforts to establish a commercial and industrial infrastructure. Nor should we downplay the role that his patronage of the arts played in enhancing his subjects' pride and identification with a unified Habsburg great power. In the end, however, the *Kaiserstil* proved to be as much a façade as the numerous foreign and domestic guarantees of the Pragmatic Sanction. Although his celebrated testament proclaimed the monarchy's indivisibility, the last male Habsburg did little to fortify it through constitutional, administrative, or military reform. In his defense, Charles VI had less immediate motivation to attend to these problems: unlike virtually all of his predecessors his realm never faced a crisis of survival that demanded drastic action. Of course, he should have anticipated the succession struggle that awaited his own demise. Instead, the monarchy's apparently secure position afforded him and his ministers a lengthy, fool's holiday that was sustained by a false sense of security and greatness. Thus he let pass a rare opportunity when the monarchy was in the position to attend to internal reconstruction while free from the threat of foreign invasion.

Defeat at the hands of the French and the Turks called attention to these deficiencies at a time when it was too late to take remedial action. Barely a year later Charles VI contracted a severe cold while hunting along the Austro-Hungarian frontier. At the first sign of a recovery, he gorged himself on a prodigious pot of mushrooms, stewed in his favorite Catalan oil. The mushrooms were either tainted or simply too much for his system to handle. Although his attendants rushed him back to Vienna, he expired at the suburban Favorita palace on 29 October 1740. Fittingly enough, the last word to pass his lips was "Barcelona."

5 The Prussian challenge: war and government reform (1740–1763)

It is one of the paradoxes of Charles VI's reign that he expended so much effort securing recognition of Maria Theresa's rights to the throne, yet did virtually nothing to prepare her for the awesome challenges that she would face. Her Jesuit education had been wholly bereft of instruction in the elements of statecraft. Her father had even excluded her (though not her husband, Francis Stephen) from the councils of state. Whereas she had no government experience, the ministers she inherited from her father had too much: at ages 67, 69, 70, 71, and 77, the five permanent members of the Privy Conference averaged more than three times Maria Theresa's 23 years. State finances were no less decrepit. Charles VI's last wars had obliged the *Hofkammer* to pawn nearly half of its annual cameral revenue of 10 million fl., with the result that part of the Contribution had to be diverted from the military to debt service. So severe was the fiscal crisis that barely half of the monarchy's supposedly 160,000-man army was actually under arms. With only 87,000 fl. of cash on hand and a 103 million fl. state debt, the archduchess was in no position to fight a major war.

The consequences were predictable enough. With the emperor's death Elector Charles Albert lost no time in presenting Bavaria's fraudulent claim to the *Erblande*. He was, however, in no position to act without the outside assistance of more powerful countries that had already recognized the Pragmatic Sanction. Although Cardinal Fleury immediately supported Charles Albert's candidacy for election to the imperial throne, he had every intention of respecting Maria Theresa's succession to all of the Habsburg dominions to the point of rejecting the French war party's call for the monarchy's final destruction. Surprisingly, it was the new king of Prussia who started the momentum toward a war of partition (see Map 4). Although he did not challenge Maria Theresa's succession, Frederick II (1740–86) pledged to help defend her against all enemies in exchange for Lower Silesia. The young queen and her ministers realized that the king's offer of protection was little more than extortion, since it implied that he himself would attack the monarchy should she decline his offer.

Frederick soon represented his claim to Lower Silesia as just compen-

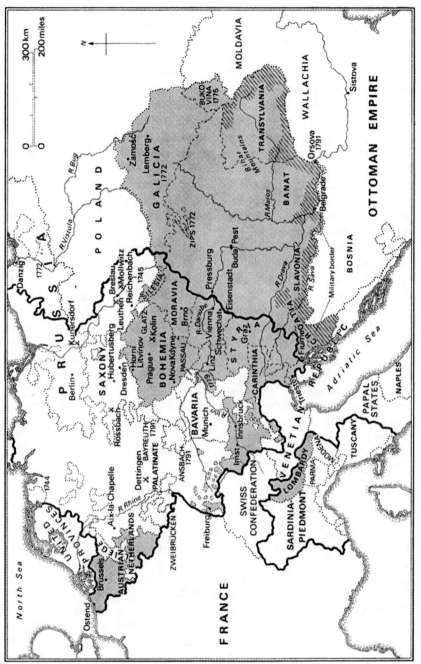

4 The monarchy in 1792

sation for the Habsburgs' earlier escheatment of Jägerndorf (1621) and Liegnitz, Brieg, and Wohlau (1675). His actions were, however, firmly rooted in recent history and *Realpolitik*. Austro-Prussian relations had deteriorated steadily since the beginning of the century, after Emperor Leopold I belatedly realized that the acquisition of a royal crown had heightened, rather than satiated, Hohenzollern ambitions. With the help of their imperial vice chancellor, Friedrich Karl von Schönborn, Joseph I and Charles VI had transformed their father's disillusionment into a comprehensive policy of opposition to further Prussian expansion within Germany. The final insult had come just before the deaths of Charles VI and his Prussian counterpart, Frederick William I (1713–40), when the emperor broke a long-standing commitment to support Prussia's legitimate claim to the prosperous Rhenish duchy of Jülich-Berg. Frederick William reputedly greeted this betrayal by pointing to his son Frederick, exclaiming "There is the man who will avenge me!"

The 28-year-old Frederick was certainly more inclined to deploy the formidable army and war chest that his father had left him. In contrast to his father's timidity and residual loyalty to *Kaiser* and *Reich*, Frederick was a brilliant opportunist who combined a youthful quest for glory with the realization that the Habsburgs were the principal obstacle to Prussia's continued expansion. Nor was he ignorant of the monarchy's recent displays of military incompetence, or of its current estrangement from the Maritime Powers. The new government in Vienna also knew how vulnerable it was. Although it had slightly more men under arms than Prussia, almost all were stationed far away from Silesia, having been committed to defend Hungary from the Turks, Italy from the Spanish, and the Low Countries from the French. For this reason several of Maria Theresa's advisors joined Francis Stephen in advising her to strike a deal with Prussia. In the end, however, the archduchess was so repelled by Frederick's crude attempt at blackmail that she rejected his overtures.

The War of the Austrian Succession

On 16 December 1740 Frederick led his army across the lightly defended Silesian frontier. By the beginning of January he had captured Breslau and virtually all of Lower Silesia. In Vienna, Maria Theresa pieced together an army to recover the duchy in the spring. It was a measure of the military's unpreparedness that she was obliged to entrust it to the hapless Count Neipperg, who had only recently been pardoned and rehabilitated for his role in the surrender of Belgrade. Neipperg performed better at the fateful battle of Mollwitz (10 April 1741), where his outnumbered forces came so close to defeating Frederick that the king fled the battlefield on horseback. A victory, followed by Frederick's expulsion from Silesia, might have preempted further attempts to contest the integrity of the Habsburg lands. Instead, the narrow defeat at Mollwitz opened the floodgates for a war of partition. At the end of May, France and Spain concluded the treaty of Nymphenburg with Bavaria, whereby they pledged not only to support Charles Albert's candidacy for the imperial throne, but also his claim to most of the *Erblande*. For their efforts, France and Spain would acquire Belgium and Lombardy, thereby stripping Maria Theresa of everything but Hungary and Inner Austria. By mid-June Prussia completed the coalition by adhering to the treaty.

Once again an ambitious German vassal posed a threat to the monarchy's existence. Twice in the past – at White Mountain and Blenheim – the monarchy had met the challenge with the timely assistance of foreign allies and loyal elements of its own ruling elite. But conditions were different in 1740, and for two reasons. First, the monarchy's allies were less convinced of its usefulness as a great power. Whereas its survival had been judged crucial by the other Catholic powers in 1620 and by the anti-French coalition in 1704, no one feared for the balance of power in 1740. Hence the German electors readily accepted French subsidies and agreed to support Charles Albert for emperor. Aside from promising Vienna a meager £300,000 subsidy, the British opted to remain neutral, both because the Walpole ministry wanted to focus on overseas expansion and because George II was reluctant to jeopardize Hanover's security by taking up arms against his long-time Prussian ally. Britain's decision preempted any chance of Dutch intervention. Indeed, both countries were quite willing to see Prussia strengthened, especially if it emerged as a useful, Protestant counterpoise to France. Second, Prussia's triumph at Mollwitz and the Nymphenburg coalition persuaded most of the monarchy's former allies that Maria Theresa and her monarchy were likely beyond help. The only exception was Russia, which offered substantial military assistance, but was then diverted in July 1741 by a French-inspired attack from Sweden. Indeed, news of the treaty of Nymphenburg and the diversion of Russia prompted Augustus III of Saxony-Poland to switch sides and join in the coming partition. Despite having concluded an alliance with Vienna in April, he now repudiated the Pragmatic Sanction and joined the Nymphenburg coalition in exchange for the promise of Moravia.

The same lack of commitment and confidence was also evident among Maria Theresa's own subjects. Here too Charles VI was partly responsible. By excluding Maria Theresa from governmental affairs and most public ceremonies, he had kept her an obscure figure among her own subjects, who now felt little obligation to support her. There also remained residual doubts about her legitimacy, especially in Bohemia, where many nobles continued to see the Josephine line as more legitimate and the German Charles Albert as a more appropriate consort than the French-speaking Francis Stephen. Nor was the archduchess helped by her colorless and unpopular husband, who had proven a mediocre *generalissimus* in the ill-fated Turkish War and had failed to father a male heir during the first five years of their marriage. Moreover, like the monarchy's former allies, many of her subjects were disinclined to support her so long as her cause seemed lost. Even among her father's advisors, only her Privy Conference Secretary Bartenstein and the 77-year-old Gundaker Starhemberg remained steadfastly loyal, while the rest were content to wait and prepare for a possible Wittelsbach succession.

Those prospects loomed larger during the summer of 1741, as the coalition's forces made swift progress through the *Erblande*. By October a Franco-Bavarian army had seized Upper Austria, whose estates promptly met at Linz to swear allegiance to Charles Albert. Two months later a combined Franco-Saxon-Bavarian force under the French Marshal Belle-Isle took Prague, where nearly half of the Bohemian nobility convened to pay homage to their new Wittelsbach king. As Joseph I's widow Wilhelmine Amalia contemplated Charles Albert's impending triumph, she urged her son-in-law to spare the Austrian countryside since "it is to your advantage that this country is not ruined." If the onset of winter temporarily saved Vienna itself from occupation, it could do nothing to prevent Charles Albert from breaking three centuries of Habsburg control of the imperial crown. It was a sign of Maria Theresa's isolation that the Electoral College's 24 January vote was unanimous, with even George II casting Hanover's ballot for the new Emperor Charles VII (1742–5).

By then, however, the tide was beginning to turn. Any explanation of the monarchy's miraculous recovery must begin with Maria Theresa. Unprepared as she was for the position into which she had been thrust, the Habsburg archduchess was blessed with several key character traits that would serve her well during her forty-year reign. She possessed great common sense, particularly the ability to identify those problems that afflicted the monarchy and find practical solutions for them, even when they contradicted her own rather traditional personal values. If her pragmatism helped save the monarchy, it was her sense of justice that made her the most beloved of all the early modern Habsburgs; her sense of fairness, ethics, and empathy for the unfortunate disarmed even adversaries like Frederick II. She was also an almost infallible judge of talent, capable of promoting and taking the advice of men like Bartenstein, while carefully withholding political responsibilities from less talented individuals, including her own, much beloved husband. Finally, Maria Theresa was more than willing to exploit her position as a female to manipulate the powerful men around her. Her ability to get her way by alternatively displaying her charm, vulnerability, tears, or anger was yet another weapon in her formidable arsenal of guile and grit.

The embattled archduchess had received some good news in March 1741, with the birth of her first son (after three daughters). Vienna had acclaimed the birth of the future Joseph II with a week of tumultuous popular celebrations. One banner declared boldly that "The enemy has lost his chance, for Austria now wears pants." Admittedly, the provision of a male heir somewhat strengthened popular support for the Habsburg-Lorraine succession, but that had proven of little consequence in preventing the conquest of much of the *Erblande*. In desperation Maria Theresa now sought relief from two unlikely sources. First she turned to Hungary. The decision was not taken lightly, given the government's traditional suspicion of the kingdom's loyalty. The Magyars did have their grievances. After having carefully observed the country's laws for the first two decades of his reign, Charles VI had not called a diet since 1729 and had permitted the palatine's office to remain vacant since 1731. His subsequent appointment of Francis Stephen to the extra-constitutional position of viceroy had helped neither man's popularity within the kingdom. Nevertheless, having survived a somewhat contentious coronation diet during June, Maria Theresa now recalled the diet to Pressburg with the intention of seeking their assistance. Nothing was left to chance. She carried with her the same crucifix that Ferdinand II had venerated during the darkest hours of the Bohemian insurrection. No less important were a raft of concessions that she made over several weeks of hard bargaining. In the end the Magyar nation did not disappoint its young queen. Before adjourning at the end of October, it pledged to raise an army of 55,000 which, together with troops raised by Croatia and directly by the crown in Transylvania, the Banat, and the Military Border, would raise Hungary's contribution to 100,000 men.

In pledging their support, the assembled Magyar nobility drew their swords and proclaimed their "life and blood" for their queen in one of Europe's last and most dramatic resorts to the feudal levy. The full story is somewhat less glamorous. The diet's declaration followed several weeks of hard bargaining and royal concessions, among them confirmation of the nobility's "eternal" exemption from taxation and eventual reintegration of the separately administered southern lands with the rest of the kingdom. For all their chivalry the Magyar nobility ultimately raised no more than 10,000 men, a force that was both smaller and slower to mobilize than the *Grenzer* and other troops raised along the kingdom's southern periphery. Hungary's declaration of support did, however, play a tremendous role in building confidence in Maria Theresa's prospects of success, especially within the *Erblande*. It also represented a major catharsis in the Magyar nobility's attitude toward the monarchy. Before 1740 its perspective had been dominated by its humiliating subservience to the dynasty's "German" lands.

The crisis of 1741 reminded it that Hungary also benefited from the larger, more powerful state that the *Erblande* helped provide and therefore had a definite interest in its preservation. In dispatching Hungarian forces outside the kingdom for the first time the Magyar nation endorsed the notion of a Habsburg *Gesamtstaat* as it never had before.

No less important than Hungary's intervention was Prussia's withdrawal from the Nymphenburg coalition. Frederick was eager to spare his army and war chest from further exhaustion. Yet he never would have come to terms with Maria Theresa had he not been convinced that she could prevent a total partition in which he would have certainly wanted to participate. One year ago Maria Theresa's sense of honor had kept her from acceding to Frederick II's demand for Lower Silesia. Now expediency compelled her to cede it in the secret convention of Klein-Schnellendorf (9 October 1741), so that she could concentrate her forces against Charles VII.

Nor did she wait for spring before striking back. During January the newly appointed Field Marshal Khevenhüller led a mixed force drawn from the Silesian front, Hungary, and Italy in the recovery of Upper Austria; Linz itself fell on 23 January, one day before Charles Albert was elected emperor. Then Khevenhüller took the Bavarian capital of Munich on 12 February, just as he was being crowned Emperor Charles VII in Frankfurt. Alarmed by the extent of the Austrian successes, Frederick temporarily re-entered the war by seizing most of Upper Silesia. Yet, despite this latest act of treachery, Maria Theresa bowed to necessity and accepted a British-brokered truce on 11 June that left Prussia in control of almost all of Silesia, as well as the Bohemian county of Glatz; when a formal treaty was signed at Berlin on 28 July, the monarchy retained only three Upper Silesian duchies: Teschen, Troppau, and, ironically, Jägerndorf. The peace did, however, permit Maria Theresa to resume the offensive, especially after Saxony's withdrawal from the war on 17 September. By year's end she had expelled Bavaria's French "auxiliaries" from Bohemia. Her coronation as queen of Bohemia in Prague in May 1743 confirmed her recovery of the kingdom's loyalty – and its all-important Contribution.

In recovering all but her Silesian lands, Maria Theresa had removed any doubt about her succession or the monarchy's survival as a great power. Thus, by the beginning of 1742 she had already reestablished the conditions under which the monarchy might again attract its old allies. In the past that had hinged not only on its being too weak to threaten the balance of power, but on its being strong enough to serve as an effective ally in maintaining it. Now that happy medium had been achieved. In February Sardinia agreed to cooperate in defending northern Italy from an impending invasion by France, Spain, and Naples. Together with the Sardinian army and the British Mediterranean fleet, Austrian forces were at least initially able to check the

Bourbon powers' advance. Whereas Sardinia proved to be an important factor in the peninsula, Britain's belated intervention was decisive everywhere. The Walpole ministry had fallen in February 1742, largely owing to popular pressure to join the war against France. By the beginning of 1743 George II and his new prime minister, Lord Carteret, had left for the continent to join what ultimately became an Anglo-Dutch-Austrian army reminiscent of the coalition armies that had once fought Louis XIV. The so-called Pragmatic Army's victory at Dettingen (27 June) – the last battle ever fought by a British king – virtually completed the expulsion of the French from Germany.

No less crucial was the reappearance of British financial aid. When combined with the monarchy's own resources, a very substantial £5 million subsidy quickly reestablished the military might that it had enjoyed earlier in the century. By the summer of 1744 Austrian forces had gone on the offensive by invading both Naples and Alsace. Maria Theresa's rising fortunes prompted Frederick II to attack her yet again, this time by invading Bohemia and seizing Prague. For the first time, however, she was able to repel the invasion, albeit at the price of recalling her forces from Alsace.

Yet another opportunity opened with the sudden death of the Wittelsbach Emperor Charles VII at the beginning of 1745. His 17-year-old son promptly concluded a peace treaty at Füssen by which he accepted the Pragmatic Sanction and pledged to support Maria Theresa's consort in the next imperial election, in exchange for the restoration of Bavaria. Despite the expected resistance from Prussia, Francis Stephen was duly elected by the electoral college on 13 September. Maria Theresa realized the significance of the imperial crown for a man who was grand duke of Tuscany, but had no authority within the Habsburg dominions. Hence she guaranteed that the coronation ceremony belonged to him alone, first by refusing to be formally crowned empress, then by limiting herself to watching his procession from a balcony as it wound its way through the streets of Frankfurt!

With Francis Stephen's succession as Emperor Francis I (1745–65), the house of Habsburg had regained control of the imperial throne, albeit through its Lorraine surrogate. Now only Silesia remained. Yet, Frederick prevented its recovery by thrice defeating the emperor's equally incompetent brother, Charles of Lorraine, when he led an Austro-Saxon army against the duchy, at Hohenfriedberg (4 June), Soor (30 September), and Kesselsdorf (14 December). Following Frederick's seizure of Dresden, Maria Theresa reluctantly acceded to British pressure and concluded a formal peace treaty at the Saxon capital on Christmas Day. In confirming the terms of the previous treaty of Berlin, the Peace of Dresden concluded hostilities in Germany.

For the rest of the war, she pursued the same strategic priorities that her uncle, Joseph I, had adopted four decades earlier by focusing primarily on

Italy, while entrusting Belgium's defense to the Maritime Powers. This did not prevent her from losing Parma to a late Spanish counterthrust. The British also obliged her to cede western Lombardy to Sardinia as compensation for its assistance against the Bourbon Powers. Nor was the Anglo-Dutch army able to prevent the brilliant French Marshal de Saxe from conquering the Austrian Netherlands and even the southernmost provinces of the United Provinces. In their separate peace talks with the French, the British made sure that the monarchy retained Belgium by compensating France with territories seized by its forces in the New World. But the Treaty of Aix-La-Chapelle (18 October 1748) also confirmed Prussia's possession of Silesia and, less significantly, Parma's cession to Elizabeth Farnese's second son, Philip.

When seen from the vantage point of 1741, Maria Theresa had reason to welcome the peace. The monarchy had survived, with her at its head, and her husband had kept the imperial crown under the dynasty's control. Although the empress attributed the "miracle of the house of Austria" to the intervention of the usual Habsburg deities, she owed her success to a more mundane combination. Certainly her own determination and political skill were important. But so was the customary, though largely voluntary, assistance of the monarchy's estates and foreign allies. However tardy her domestic and international support may have been, it had come in the end once she had demonstrated that she was capable of preserving the monarchy as an instrument for serving their own interests. Indeed, although it is easy to laud Maria Theresa's distinctive contribution to the monarchy's survival, her predecessors' successes in weathering similar crises suggest that a less remarkable individual might have achieved comparable results with at least some display of pragmatism and determination.

But a price still had to be paid for the dynasty's continued reliance on consensual politics. Within her dominions Maria Theresa grudgingly accepted the Hungarians' desiderata. She also deemed it wise to be lenient with the fickle Bohemian and Upper Austrian nobles who had deserted her. To be sure both estates had acted out of expediency and self-interest: the choice between the Habsburg and Wittelsbach claimants generally depended on whether an individual nobleman's landholdings or government offices were in areas held by Maria Theresa or Charles Albert. Though she initially ordered the expulsion of Prague's Jews for advancing money to her Wittelsbach rival and welcoming the brief Prussian occupation of 1744, she readily ignored the nobles' trespasses because she needed their support.

The cost of her allies' support was higher still. In successive negotiations she had been obliged to surrender almost all of Silesia, much of Lombardy, and even occupied Bavaria in exchange for the continued payment of British subsidies. The empress was likely correct in believing that she could have negotiated more favorable terms from Prussia, Sardinia, and Bavaria had she not had to depend on British negotiators. Indeed, they had even killed an Austro-Sardinian plan to swap Tuscany for Bavaria, because they feared that it would prompt Prussian re-entry into the war. Great Britain's stance was understandable, given its own interests. It was quite content to build up middle-sized states like Prussia and Sardinia as handy counterweights in the ever-changing balance of power; to earn its subsidies, its Habsburg ally would have to fight the common French enemy and no one else. The divergence between Austrian and British interests was clear enough to the empress, who protested her own diplomats' exclusion from the Anglo-French peace talks by exclaiming that "my enemies will give me better terms than my friends." In the end she refused to sign the treaty of Aix-la-Chapelle. Instead, the empress viewed it and the earlier peace of Dresden as no more than an interim settlement that she was determined to overthrow.

The first Theresian reform, 1749–56

It is easy to understand her resolve. Within the past fifteen years (1733–48) three lost wars had cost the monarchy most of the conquests of the century's opening decades. What it retained – Belgium, the Banat, and most of Lombardy – was materially less valuable than Silesia, whose million plus inhabitants had been the most productive and heavily taxed of all the Habsburg lands. Admittedly financial resources had never been at the heart of the monarchy's success. One is reminded of Prince Eugene's lament at one point during the War of the Spanish Succession that "if the monarchy's survival depended on its ability to raise 50,000 fl. at once, it would nonetheless be impossible to save it." Of course, it *had* repeatedly weathered such crises by receiving last-minute infusions of funds from its allies, estates, and loyal aristocrats. Yet recent events had demonstrated that, in the absence of a genuine threat to the balance of power, the monarchy could no longer count on the intercession of such traditional allies as the Maritime Powers and the German princes.

The loss was especially ominous within the Holy Roman empire, where Frederick II was now in the position to block the exercise of imperial authority. It was a measure of Prussia's sudden emergence as a counterpoise to Habsburg leadership that Francis Stephen had been unable to induce the *Reichstag* to declare war against France after his election in 1745. Despite having strengthened its ties within the empire over the previous half-century, the monarchy now resumed its reluctant, incremental retreat from German affairs. Indeed, with the loss of Silesia, German speakers now comprised no more than a third of the monarchy's 16 million people, a demographic shift pregnant with consequences for the next century.

Of more immediate import was the strategic impact of Silesia's loss. Until now powerful enemies like France, Sweden, and Bourbon Spain had been obliged to fight the monarchy from a considerable distance; although the Ottoman empire shared a long border with the monarchy, its military staging area near Constantinople was nearly three months' march from the Hungarian frontier. For a generation the monarchy had enjoyed an especially broad *glacis* of weak and benign neighbors that gave it time to react to any foreign military threat. Not unlike Great Britain with its English Channel, the central government could expend the time necessary to reach a consensus with its ruling elite and foreign allies before going to war. Now, with one blow Frederick II had breached these defenses and placed his armies within a short march of what was left of the wealthy Bohemian crownlands.

To survive the monarchy would need a more assertive and efficient central government, one that was capable of raising sufficient funds and troops to defend itself without having to rely on voluntary domestic or foreign support. The aging mediocrities who composed Maria Theresa's first cabinet were hardly the men to carry out such a reform. Luckily, most of them had died before the war ended. Among those who remained, only the relatively young Privy Conference Secretary Bartenstein played a decisive role in convincing the empress of the need for change. Theirs was never a cordial relationship. The Catholic convert from the Swabian *Vorlande* was too "prickly, precise, and pedantic" to inspire personal warmth. Nor did the empress easily overlook his common origins and the part he had played in her husband's earlier renunciation of the duchy of Lorraine. Yet personal considerations did not prevent her from seeking his counsel. If Bartenstein convinced Maria Theresa to reform the monarchy's administration, it was a new minister, Count Friedrich Wilhelm von Haugwitz, who actually devised the plan. Haugwitz was also a Catholic convert who had initially fled his native Silesia after the Prussian invasion. Ugly, unrefined, and colorless, he was nonetheless a perceptive, efficient, and tireless worker who first attracted attention in 1743, after he had doubled crown revenue within a year after being appointed governor of the three Silesian counties still under Habsburg control.

It was with the assistance of these two men that Maria Theresa now launched the first in a series of comprehensive administrative and constitutional reforms that are without parallel in the monarchy's history. Like all of her predecessors she began by recasting the central administration. None of the monarchy's highest offices went untouched. As early as 1742 a new State Chancery (*Staatskanzlei*), took over the formulation and dispatch of foreign policy from the Privy Conference and the rival Imperial and Austrian chanceries. Four years later the *Hofkriegsrat* relinquished all control over military supply to the General War Commissary, which now became a fully independent and equal ministry. Indeed, the total elimination of the Inner Austrian and Tyrolean War Offices in 1744 assured the War Commissary of greater authority than the *Hofkriegsrat* had ever enjoyed. The most dramatic move came in 1749, when the empress entrusted the *Erblande*'s affairs to a new Directory of Administration and Finance (*Directorium in Publicis et Cameralibus*) headed by Haugwitz. In practice the Directory was little more than a parent body for a powerful Court Deputation (*Hofdeputation*), soon renamed the Internal Conference (*Conferenz in Internis*), and a Supreme Judiciary (or *Oberste Justizstelle*). Together with the State Chancery, they now reduced such previously preeminent offices as the Privy Conference, *Hofkammer*, and Austrian and Bohemian Chanceries to virtual oblivion.

Although these administrative changes may have rendered the central government more efficient, they could not hope to improve the monarchy's position as a great power without increasing state revenue and the military forces that it supported. At the end of 1747 Haugwitz presented a plan for increasing the army to over 200,000 men, to be apportioned as follows:

108,000 *Erblande*
 25,000 Hungary
 24,000 Military Border zones
 25,000 Lombardy
 22,000 Austrian Netherlands

His expectation that the *Erblande* would fill out over half of the army was consistent with the perceptions and policies of his predecessors. What was radically different was the means by which revenue would be increased. His model was Silesia, which had protested the weight of royal taxation just three days before Charles VI's death, but which was now paying twice as much to Frederick II. Unlike the new Prussian regime in Silesia, Haugwitz did not propose to abolish the estates' right to approve taxes or participate in their collection. He did, however, expect them to double the Contribution and to commit themselves for ten years at a time, much as Bohemia had done in the Decennial Recess of 1715. Rather than squeeze all of the increase from the peasantry, the nobles' own domain lands would now shoulder at least part of the burden. Until now only the Bohemian nobility had ever agreed to such a tax, and then only as a temporary, wartime measure during the reign of Joseph I. Indeed, although the clergy had always volunteered considerable sums in wartime, it too was now required to pay a share of the Contribution on an annual basis. Finally, once the estates had collected the taxes, they would immediately turn them over to crown administrators for safer keeping.

By inspiring the most dramatic fiscal reform in Austrian history, Silesia continued to serve as a conduit for new and innovative ideas, even though most of it was no longer part of the monarchy. But Haugwitz's proposal did not go unchallenged. The Bohemian Chancellor, Count Friedrich Harrach, led the majority of ministers in opposing such a radical innovation. Yet the empress readily recognized the necessity for such a reform. Even as she overrode their objections she ridiculed their unrealistic conservatism by predicting that, "in fifty years, no one will believe that these were the ministers whom I alone created." When Harrach refused to present the proposal to the Bohemian estates, she sent Haugwitz in his place; Harrach resigned soon thereafter.

The question remained, however, whether the estates themselves would give their consent. Haugwitz had assured the empress that they would comply, if only to escape Silesia's fate of Prussian conquest and absolutism. That had doubtless been his experience during his brief term as governor of rump Silesia. This was one reason why the government approached the Bohemian estates first; another was that it realized that Bohemia would be eager to reassert its longstanding loyalty to the dynasty after having cavorted with Charles Albert early in the war. In the end both the Bohemian lands and the Austrian archduchies readily acquiesced to the government's requests.

Inner Austria and Tyrol proved more resistant, as befitted their relative remoteness from the Prussian threat. Carniola and Styria refused to commit themselves to a Decennial Recess, but they did agree to pledge taxes in three-year increments and regularly renewed them thereafter. Having already doubled its Contribution during the past war, Styria, was soon paying 1.1 million fl. annually, or quadruple its Contribution under Charles VI. Only Carinthia rejected Haugwitz's plan outright, despite Maria Theresa's repeated demands that it comply "voluntarily"; after 1750 she simply imposed and collected the duchy's share of the Contribution without bothering to consult its estates. Maria Theresa expected somewhat less from Tyrol, which agreed nevertheless to pay a regular, annual Contribution for the first time in its history. It also acquiesced in her separation of the Swabian lands from its jurisdiction, so that their taxes now flowed directly to Vienna, instead of Innsbruck.

Finally, although the crown never directly challenged the estates' right to collect the Contribution, Haugwitz established a system of crown deputations (1748) to monitor its local allocation and collection within the *Erblande*. Within three years the government had essentially coopted the estates' own agents, first by subordinating them to the deputations, then by assuming responsibility for their salaries.

Not surprisingly the empress and Haugwitz were less willing to challenge the existing privileges and corporate institutions outside the *Erblande*, where the collaborative relationship between crown and country was less firmly established. The empress did discard her father's delusions of a separate Spanish realm, first by renaming the *Consejo de España* the *Consiglio d'Italia*, then by subordinating it and the council for the Netherlands to the new State

Chancery. Otherwise she did nothing to infringe on the autonomy of her Italian and Flemish subjects. Nor did she attempt to subvert any of Hungary's governmental institutions. Thus, whereas she had emasculated the Austrian, Bohemian, and Imperial Chanceries, she left their Hungarian and Transylvanian counterparts intact, even though the latter was so insignificant that it conducted its business at a Viennese tavern.

The government's continued reliance on its Austrian and Bohemian lands increased the already unequal tax burden between the monarchy's German and Hungarian lands. Admittedly, Hungary was much poorer than the rest of Maria Theresa's other dominions. Nevertheless, by mid-century a prolonged period of peace and colonization had increased its population to over six million, making it far more populous than either the Austrian lands (3.9 million) or what was left of Greater Bohemia (3.1 million). Even when counting troops drawn from the Military Border, Greater Hungary was still expected to provide less than half as many recruits as the *Erblande*. Maria Theresa's acute sense of realism and her genuine gratitude for Hungary's crucial assistance in the recent war induced her to accept this disparity. Hence she abandoned the coercive and extra-constitutional tactics of the past in favor of a relationship based on greater trust and collaboration. She patiently endured one diet after another in which her Magyar subjects presented and vociferously debated hundreds of gravamina, while slashing her own requests for modest tax increases. Even after agreeing to half of the increase she requested, the 3.2 million fl. approved by the diet of 1751 implied a per capita tax rate of less than half that imposed within the *Erblande*.

The empress was able to compensate somewhat for the diet's niggardliness within those southern parts of the kingdom that were administered directly by the army. Thus, in Transylvania her military governor completed the process of emasculating that principality's diet at least a decade before it held its last meeting in 1761. By 1764 the principality's annual Contribution of 1,365,000 fl. was among the highest per capita collected anywhere in the monarchy. Perhaps the most important changes came in the Military Border. Here progress was measured not so much in money, as in the quantity and quality of troops provided. Indeed, the wartime performance of 45,000 *Grenzer* emboldened the empress to delay implementing her earlier promise to restore the kingdom's southern districts to the diet's control. Although she did return most of the Tisza-Mures Military Border to the estates, she devoted her energy elsewhere to improving and extending the entire system. Whereas the *Grenzer* had enhanced their reputation as ferocious fighters, inconsistent supply and pay by the Inner Austrian estates had sometimes reduced them to an undisciplined rabble. In 1750 the central government resolved the problem by assuming full responsibility for supplying, paying, and staffing the Military Border. The replacement of native commanders with regular army officers soon completed their integration with the rest of the Austrian army. The government also extended the Military Border 500 miles eastward across the full extent of the Hungarian-Turkish frontier by creating new districts in the Banat (1742) and Transylvania (1762–4).

These innovations did not come without opposition. Quite aside from the futile protests of the Inner Austrian estates, the largely Orthodox *Grenzer* themselves initially opposed the appointment of Catholic German officers, fearing that it presaged the loss of their religious and other privileges. Their fears were allayed somewhat by a special "Illyrian" Commission (1745) that looked after the interests of all Orthodox Serb communities, even those that were situated within Hungary proper. Not surprisingly, the Commission's extraterritorial rights inspired protests from the Hungarian and Croatian estates. Nor did the new Transylvanian Military Border gain ready acceptance among local nobles and free peasants, including several hundred Szekler who were killed in 1764 in a vain attempt to forestall its creation. Nevertheless, the Military Border, the Banat, and Transylvania constituted the few places in the monarchy where the Habsburgs could rule like absolute monarchs.

By contrast, Maria Theresa's expectations were probably lowest in Milan and the Low Countries, principally because both dominions regularly financed their own administrative and military expenses with a minimum of acrimony. She also appreciated the large loans that Belgian and Milanese merchants regularly floated for the central government. Moreover, both provided modest increases in revenue without the need to introduce major constitutional changes like those carried out in the *Erblande*. Much of Belgium's larger contribution stemmed from a rare Austrian success at the Peace of Aix-la-Chapelle, where the Dutch agreed to renounce the annual 1.5 million fl. subsidy that they had collected for the upkeep of its barrier fortresses. Meanwhile, Milan's revenue also rose immediately after the war, following the first significant administrative and fiscal restructuring since the Renaissance, including a new land cadaster completed in 1755.

The fruits of Haugwitz's project were both immediate and dramatic. By 1754 the Venetian envoy was reporting that total crown income had doubled from 20 to 40 million fl. within the past decade. Despite losing most of Silesia, Bohemia's Contribution actually increased from 6 to 7.4 million fl. by 1763, while Austria's more than doubled from 2 to 5.1 millions. Although the *Erblande* fell somewhat short of Haugwitz's quota of 108,000 troops, the increased and more efficient levy of taxes and troops throughout the monarchy nevertheless raised the army to perhaps 180,000 by 1756. Of necessity, the growth of the military paralleled an equally dramatic increase in the army of civil officials who now administered the Habsburg state. Within the core lands alone the central bureaucracy nearly doubled from 6,000 (1740) to 10,000 (1762); two decades later it would approach 20,000.

Not only did the military and civil services grow in size, they also evolved in ability and outlook. Led by Prussia, many of the German states had taken steps to professionalize their military and civil officialdom. By contrast the Habsburg army and officer corps had changed little from Montecuccoli's day. Every regiment was trained and equipped differently by its commander. The officers themselves were still appointed and promoted by favor or purchase, rather than by merit. Deficiencies in the officer corps were most notable at the top, where both Francis Stephen and his brother, Charles of Lorraine, had recently assumed places in the long line of hapless commanders-in-chief that had followed Prince Eugene's death. Beginning in 1748, the monarchy's new *Hofkriegsrat* President, Field Marshal Daun, improved and systematized the army's training and equipment by following the proven example of Prussia. All ranks received higher and more regular pay. Civil service reform began at the same time on the insistence of Haugwitz, who assured the empress that if divine intervention had indeed saved the monarchy in the past, it had done so by compensating for what had already been lost by incompetent ministers and bureaucrats. Civil officials were henceforth evaluated on merit and awarded better remuneration, including a comprehensive pension system that had long been common among their German counterparts.

If the Theresian regime was bent on professionalizing the military and civil services, it was also determined to make the entire ruling elite more secular in outlook. This dramatic break with the culture of the Counter-Reformation was partly motivated by a desire for greater autonomy from the Papacy and the rest of the Church establishment. Yet it stemmed primarily from the belated recognition that the monarchy's close adherence to the values of the Counter-Reformation had retarded the evolution of the kind of rational political culture that had made Prussia such an imposing threat.

Whereas the empress heartily endorsed secularization as a practical necessity, the impetus for cultural reform came from elsewhere. Just as the Counter-Reformation had entered the monarchy from Italy, secular reformation now came from the peninsula's great Catholic reformer, Lodovico Antonio Muratori (1672–1750). Not unlike the Theresian regime, Muratori had been inspired by the desire to counteract his country's economic and cultural backwardness by restricting the church's authority and influence to spiritual matters. He abhorred the lost productivity caused both by the large number of holy days and by the excessive devotion of religious confraternities and public ceremonies. He also blamed the prevalence of ignorance and superstition on the Jesuits' scholastic methods, which relied heavily on

Latin and the rote memorization of impractical knowledge. By mid-century Muratori's advocacy of human knowledge and reason, as well as German theories of natural law, had had an impact on many of the monarchy's leading churchmen, most notably consecutive archbishops of Vienna, Johann Joseph Trautson (1751–7) and Christoph Anton Migazzi (1757–1803). Both men were eager to assist the government in reducing the power of the papacy and its Jesuit paladins. Other Viennese reformers had a more radical agenda. Half of the State Chancery's six ministers had been educated at Protestant German universities, where the rationalist doctrines of Christian Wolff had been instilled into a generation of future civil servants. Meanwhile, the empress's influential personal physician, Gerhard van Swieten, wanted to introduce an even more secular cultural regime similar to that of his native Flanders.

Whatever their agenda, the men around Maria Theresa focused most of their efforts on the Jesuits. They wasted no time stripping the Society of its century-long monopoly over censorship. Within a year of her succession they had already begun to shift the responsibility for non-religious works from the lay faculty of the Jesuit universities to civil officials. By the end of the decade they had stripped the Jesuit University of Vienna of its authority over the production and sale of books within the city. In 1751 censorship was formally in the hands of a new Censorship Commission (*Zensurkommission*) directed by van Swieten. Instead of aristocrats or high government officials, the commission was dominated by some of central Europe's most innovative thinkers, including the German cameralist J.H.G. von Justi (1720–71) and the political theorist Karl von Martini (1726–1800). Although the commission initially included two Jesuits, who were responsible for religious and philosophical works, their competence was progressively reduced until 1759, when they were expelled at the insistence of Archbishop Migazzi. At the same time the archbishop also induced the Censorship Commission to ban all Jesuit publications. The Commission did, however, encourage individual Jesuit writers to continue to publish independently by depriving their superiors of any editorial control over their work.

The Theresian regime also initiated the process of wresting control of the monarchy's educational system from the Jesuits and other religious orders. The first stage, which consumed the first half of the reign, focused only on the educational and vocational needs of the noble and professional classes. Led by van Swieten, the government quickly asserted control over the University of Vienna's curriculum by establishing new faculties for history, geography, science, civics, and natural law. It also reformed several existing disciplines. Van Swieten personally overhauled the medical faculty in 1749, after discovering that large numbers of medical students were enrolling in foreign universities in order to receive adequate training. By 1753 the philosophy, theology, and law curricula had also been restructured to reflect the influence of German natural law theorists like Christian Wolff. Meanwhile, parallel curricular changes were instituted in the *Erblande*'s other universities at Prague, Graz, Innsbruck, and Freiburg. No less important was the childhood preparation of the monarchy's elite, especially those intended for government service. Although the government did not yet have the resources to challenge Jesuit control of education below the university level, it did establish several preparatory schools. The most famous was the *Theresianum* (1746), an academy for future civil servants that was housed in the old Favorita palace. There was also a military school established at Wiener Neustadt in 1751 and a so-called Oriental Academy, which was dedicated in 1754 for the training of diplomats for service in the Balkans. Significantly, both the *Theresianum* and Oriental Academy were staffed primarily with Jesuit faculty, but soon provided a forum for a new generation of educational reformers.

By their very nature, Maria Theresa's early cultural initiatives did not bring immediate results like those effected by Haugwitz's tax reforms. Rather they constituted a long-term investment in the monarchy's future. To some extent the same could be said for the mercantile policies that she pursued during the opening three decades of her reign. After the war she redoubled her father's efforts to strengthen the economic base that supported the monarchy's taxes and troops. Above all, she intensified past efforts to make the economy more independent from foreign exporters – only now the competition included the former province of Silesia. Its loss had suddenly deprived the rest of the Bohemian lands of their major domestic outlet for finishing raw textiles, such as unbleached linen. The government hoped that the Bohemian lands could fill the gap themselves, thereby avoiding a most unwelcome dependence on Prussia, while also ruining the Silesian economy by depriving it of its Bohemian suppliers. Not surprisingly, the resulting postwar factory boom took place mainly in the Bohemian lands, with Upper Austria a close second. As in the past the state relied on private, mainly aristocratic entrepreneurs and investors, except when bankruptcies forced it to intervene. It also continued to provide subsidies and reduce guild restrictions, especially when they hampered the growth of export industries. In an effort to encourage new technology, the government imported foreign experts and awarded prizes for using the latest methods – while penalizing those entrepreneurs who failed to employ them. In addition to factory construction, the government also endeavored to protect new and existing industries from Prussian Silesia and other foreign competitors by erecting higher tariff barriers in Bohemia (1751), Hungary (1754), and Austria (1755). It also redirected the flow of commerce southward through the Adriatic and the Balkans, at the expense of the former northern route that passed through Silesia. As part of this strategy it founded and nurtured new trading ventures, including a Trieste-Fiume Company, with the help of investors from the Austrian Netherlands and Italy.

The next two decades yielded some impressive results, especially in those cottage industries that dominated Bohemia's proto-industrial landscape. For example, the town-run concern of Nova Kdyne that was founded in 1769 employed 300 workers on site, but also 1,500 home spinners and weavers. There were, however, also major manufacturing establishments employing advanced production methods, such as at the textile mill at Horní Litvínov, where each of 400 workers performed just one step in a forty-five-stage wool production process. According to historian Herman Freudenberger, the Moravian town of Brno became "the Manchester of central Europe" following establishment of a large fine-woolen factory in 1764. To the south the Trieste-Fiume Company also flourished. Thanks to a monopoly for refining foreign sugar (1755), it was soon running a refinery that employed 700 workers. Indeed, the government's overall effort to redirect its trade routes away from Prussia was rewarded by impressive growth in the business of both Adriatic ports.

As before, the government's industrial strategy ignored Hungary, which was still valued only as a producer of food staples and a captive market for the *Erblande*'s finished goods. A new Universal Commercial Directory that supervised mercantile operations even redefined its competence to exclude Hungarian affairs within just three years of its establishment in 1746. The only notable exception to this bias was the promotion of mining in the Bihar Mountains of Transylvania, which had now replaced Silesia as the monarchy's most mineral-rich province. Otherwise the Theresian regime limited its efforts to promoting agriculture, most notably by dispatching a second and, ultimately, much more successful wave of 43,000 German colonists to southern Hungary.

The limits of reform

By 1756 Maria Theresa had already earned an honored place in Austrian history. In less than a decade she had virtually doubled state revenue, restructured the administrative and military system, and begun the process of entrusting it to a more competent, professional elite. Yet another contribution was Maria Theresa's solution of the succession crisis that had nearly destroyed the monarchy. Her marriage with Francis Stephen was unquestionably the greatest conjugal love-match in the dynasty's history. Together they had sixteen children during their first nineteen years of marriage (1737–56), a period during which the empress was pregnant two-thirds of the time and the Hofburg itself assumed the appearance of a nursery school. Only the onset of menopause ended the constant parade of new archdukes and archduchesses.

Yet, with the notable exception of her offspring, Austria's last baroque ruler contributed very little to the monarchy's development that was conceptually new. Admittedly, many of her early initiatives represented an advance in the government's application of the cameral sciences, which now extended beyond mercantile strategies designed to promote economic growth to assume more radical administrative and cultural dimensions. Yet historian Grete Klingenstein has shown that the ideas behind many of her reforms had already surfaced during her father's reign. What she provided was superior energy and determination that translated those ideas into action, together with a flexible pragmatism that always knew exactly when and where to push for change. Of course, like many of her predecessors (*except* her father), she was blessed with a motivation born of desperation. Not unlike a Martin Luther, Winston Churchill, or Abraham Lincoln, she was pushed to greatness by a crisis of survival that demanded nothing less; without a Frederick II to confront her, Maria Theresa would have probably done much less to change the monarchy's existing balance of domestic political forces or its cultural orientation.

However dramatic its results, the First Theresian Reform was hardly revolutionary in the tactics it employed. Although the central government had become much more assertive and efficient, it nevertheless continued to seek the consent and cooperation of the monarchy's estates, whenever possible. Generally speaking, the ruling classes responded, out of both a shared appreciation of the Prussian threat and a desire to retain the dynasty's favor, together with the patronage that stemmed from it. Where a consensus was not possible, such as in Hungary, Maria Theresa relented, thereby entrenching further the double standard that already existed between it and the *Erblande*. Only in Carinthia and the militarized districts of southern Hungary did she demonstrate a capacity for the methods of absolutism. There was, of course, some grumbling by the estates, displaced corporate officials, churchmen, and even peasants and townspeople who resented reductions in religious holidays. The British minister Keith found popular criticism of her clerical reforms so intense that "it would not be tolerated in the most free government in Europe." At one point an angry mob expressed its displeasure by pelting Haugwitz's residence with stones and excrement. Yet such manifestations of discontent paled by comparison with France, Spain, or Brandenburg-Prussia, where military force had to be employed at various stages of the centralization process. In the end Maria Theresa retained the trust, loyalty, and cooperation of ruling elites and their corporate bodies by seeking their cooperation, rather than their subjection.

Another reason for the muted opposition was that the empress pursued a limited agenda that conformed to her own conservatism. For all their intensity and success, her mercantile strategies deviated little from those employed under her father; she was as yet unexposed, or at least unsympathetic, to the free market ideas that had already begun to emerge elsewhere in Europe. Similarly, her secularization of censorship and elite education was driven by reason of state, not by the Enlightenment ideas that inspired some of her advisors; far from opposing censorship itself, she and her ministers actually strengthened the extensive, but characteristically ineffective system that had existed under Charles VI. For her the written word was primarily an instrument of social control rather than public enlightenment. Hence the Censorship Commission scrutinized textbooks to insure that they disseminated the proper moral and religious values. She even refused to create an academy of sciences because she feared that it might promote heresy. Nor did the recent curricular reforms persuade her to allow Protestants to receive degrees at any of the monarchy's universities.

Maria Theresa was, in fact, determined to use all available means to impose her rather rigid standards of Christian morality and religious orthodoxy. One example was her creation of a "chastity commission" to curb prostitution; she even insisted on denying promotions to army officers who visited brothels, despite her *Hofkriegsrat* president's retort that he would still be an ensign had the ban been in effect at the start of his career. The empress's decision to expel Prague's (and later all of Bohemia's) Jews was an early, but hardly isolated example of her religious intolerance. Although she eventually commuted their sentence to the far more constructive assessment of a fine, she did so only after the Bohemian estates had persuaded her that their expulsion would devastate the kingdom's economy. Her anti-Semitism was also evident in the sharp reduction in the government's patronage of Jewish financiers. Their exclusion compelled her to turn to foreign, largely Protestant creditors, but she apparently regarded them as the lesser of two evils.

Indeed, soon after the conclusion of peace she resumed her predecessor's efforts to eradicate the remaining pockets of Protestantism within the Austrian lands. In a scene reminiscent of past Reformation Commissions, she established a *Religionskommission* in March 1752 that levied heavy fines on anyone caught in possession of Protestant books; ultimately, it set up Conversion Houses (*Konversionshäuser*), to which all but the most elderly Protestants were committed for re-education by Catholic priests. Three months later a *Transmigrationpatent* ordered the forcible relocation of recalcitrant Protestants to Transylvania. The subsequent transfer was so badly handled that a quarter of the 2,664, mostly Upper Austrian, Protestants died in transit.

If Maria Theresa still adhered to the values of the Counter-Reformation, she was also a committed champion of feudal society. Although she felt obliged to place the military and civil service on a merit system, she did so reluctantly, preferring instead to base the appointment and advancement of officials solely on class rank. She was under no such constraints in the countryside, where she initially did nothing to stem the widening gap between the landed aristocracy and lesser nobility. In Bohemia the aristocracy continued to expand its control of the land; by mid-century it had bought out so many gentry families that only one hundred remained of the six hundred that had existed in 1620. In Hungary the diet went so far as to make a legal distinction between propertied and landless gentry, with the poorest nobles losing their tax exemption, county assembly seats, and office-holding rights. Nor was there any reason for the empress to inhibit the centuries-long transformation of the Bohemian and Hungarian landscape into great latifundia, run by a small group of aristocrats. If nothing else, it was far easier for her to enlist the support of a few powerful aristocrats through royal favor than to control an unwieldy and faceless mass of insecure gentry.

Admittedly the Theresian regime did prove somewhat more sensitive to the fate of the *Erblande*'s peasants, if only because it now subscribed more fully to the German cameralist notion of *Bauernschutz*, which sought to preserve them as the primary source of taxable income. Hence, the recent increases in the Contribution were divided equally between peasant-held "rustical" land and the heretofore untapped revenue from the nobles' demesne. New decrees forbade the nobility from resorting to its past habits of shifting its share of the Contribution from dominical to rustical land (1748), or from incorporating peasant plots into their demesne (1751). To prevent them from doing so, the government commissioned sophisticated land surveys that distinguished between rustical and dominical land. To ensure that each peasant household maintained what it judged a minimum living standard, it carefully calibrated the tax assessments for each plot of rustical land according to size, type (arable, pasture, gardens, vineyards, woods, even fishponds), and proximity to market; it was a measure of the cameralist penchant for precision that arable land was classified into nine discrete categories, according to fertility. By 1753 the government's new commitment to *Bauernschutz* also prompted it to begin inventorying the extent of *robot* labor.

Yet, having induced the *Erblande*'s nobles to shoulder roughly a quarter of the new Contribution, Maria Theresa was still unwilling to press her luck by confronting them directly over their continued abuse of the peasantry. When a royal commission reported that nobles were still shifting taxes, seizing rustical land, and increasing manorial obligations, she merely reissued new, equally unenforceable edicts. Then, in 1756 she ended the embarrassment by disbanding the commission itself. The fact remains, however, that neither Haugwitz's higher Contribution nor continued manorial oppression caused any major peasant uprisings within the *Erblande* during the first three decades of Maria Theresa's reign. As peasant revolts in southern Hungary (1753), Slavonia (1755), and Transylvania (1751, 1759) demonstrated, the worst forms of noble exploitation could still be found in the lands of St. Stephen.

The Diplomatic Revolution and the Seven Years' War

However much or little Maria Theresa undertook during the first reform period was determined not so much by Enlightenment notions of human freedom, equality, or justice, as they were by her perception of what would be necessary to win back Silesia. No sooner had she initiated her reforms, than she began contemplating renewing her struggle with Frederick II. During the spring of 1749 she convened the Privy Conference to consider the likely balance of forces in the next war with Prussia. She could be certain of support from Tsarina Elizabeth II (1741–62), who had concluded a defensive alliance with her in 1746 because she too feared the Prussian "usurper" and was unwilling to accept him as an equal player on the east European stage. The same could not be said for the Maritime Powers. After their humiliation in the last war, the Dutch were likely to remain neutral in any future conflict. Meanwhile the Conference recognized that the British would be unwilling to support the recovery of Silesia, especially if it detracted from the fulfilment of their own goal of reducing France. Of course, this was nothing new. Over the past half century her British ally had limited the monarchy's territorial acquisitions at Ryswick (1697), Carlowitz (1699), and Utrecht (1713), had failed to come to its assistance in the War of the Polish Succession (1733–8), and had recently forced it to give up valuable territory in Silesia, Milan, and occupied Bavaria. Nevertheless, of the seven men present, only the youngest and newest Conference member favored dispensing with the British alliance. Having been the chief Austrian negotiator at Aix-la-Chapelle, the brilliant 37-year-old Count Wenzel Anton von Kaunitz had witnessed "perfidious Albion" in action. The empress now backed Kaunitz, doubtless in the expectation that her domestic reforms would enable her to do without the subsidies that had previously held the monarchy captive to British interests.

There was, however, a second problem. Although Maria Theresa was prepared to dispense with her British ally, neither she nor her ministers felt that the monarchy could recover Silesia while making war with both France and Prussia. True Lorrainer that he was, Francis Stephen urged his wife to forget Silesia and to reconcile with Prussia for the purpose of attacking France. Instead the empress supported Kaunitz's proposal to seek a rapprochement with France. Kaunitz was, in fact, advocating a long-overdue revolution in Habsburg grand strategy that forsook the old battlegrounds of Italy and the Low Countries for the more proximate threat posed by Prussia. Like so many of Maria Theresa's innovations, her predecessors had contemplated an Austro-French alliance since the diminution of the French threat to the balance of power. Joseph I's ministers had first broached the idea in 1710, shortly after discovering Britain's impending desertion in the War of the Spanish Succession. During his brief alliance with Spain, Charles VI had encouraged Madrid to recruit France for a Habsburg-Bourbon pact against the Protestant powers. The empress herself had first mulled over that prospect in secret talks with the French in 1745, at a time when the British were forcing her to give up Silesia and Bavaria. Yet it was Maria Theresa who transformed abstract notions into concrete action by dispatching Kaunitz to Paris in the summer of 1750.

Although Kaunitz had won over the empress, he still had to convince the French that the two countries were no longer enemies. France too faced a new reality. It was no longer encircled by the Habsburgs and their clients, as it had been in the previous century. Furthermore, Frederick II had recently destroyed the prospect of a Habsburg-German monolith that it had feared since the sixteenth century. Great Britain was the real enemy and the battlefield was overseas, not in central Europe. Yet the need for a *renversement des alliances* was less urgent for Louis XV, whose ministers turned a deaf ear to Kaunitz's overtures. With her usual persistence Maria Theresa continued to encourage Kaunitz to the point of raising him to the new rank of state chancellor (*Staatskanzler*) and entrusting him with control of foreign policy. In the end it was her old British ally and her new Prussian enemy who pushed France into her arms. With the outbreak of fighting between French and British forces in America, George II concluded the Westminster Convention with Frederick II (16 January 1756). In return for helping to protect Hanover from French attack, Prussia gained British assurances that it would not fund an Austrian attack on Silesia. Frederick had effectively eliminated any remaining prospect of British help in recovering Silesia, but he had also enraged his French ally, which had not forgotten his numerous betrayals during the last war. Driven by anger and paranoia, Louis XV's ministers were now prepared to effect the Diplomatic Revolution that Kaunitz so ardently sought. They quickly concluded the First Treaty of Versailles (1 May 1756), a defensive alliance by which both countries promised to remain neutral in the event that the other became involved in a war and to provide 24,000 troops to defend it against attack by a third party.

Having secured French neutrality on such extraordinarily favorable terms, the empress now prepared to join with Russia in attacking Prussia in the spring of 1757. At the same time French, Russian, and Austrian diplomats attempted to enlist Sweden, Saxony-Poland, and other German states for the expanding anti-Prussian coalition. As the deadline approached, Maria Theresa began taking unobtrusive steps to place her army on a war footing. Her Russian ally was, however, less discreet in mobilizing its forces. Sensing that an attack was imminent, Frederick II accused Maria Theresa of having concluded an offensive alliance against him and demanded her assurances that she would not attack him in the near future. Never one to lie, she replied coyly – but truthfully – that she had not concluded an offensive alliance against Prussia. The Prussian king drew the obvious conclusion, telling his advisors that "if the empress is pregnant with war, then I shall offer the services of a midwife." Rather than await the attack he would strike first.

On 29 August 1756 Frederick II began the Seven Years' War by invading Saxony. His main objectives were to scare Russia into neutrality and to punish Saxony, which he wrongfully assumed had joined the anti-Prussian coalition. Instead, his attack on a virtually defenseless neutral country greatly multiplied the number and self-righteousness of his enemies. On the first anniversary of the Diplomatic Revolution, Austria and France concluded a Second Treaty of Versailles (1 May 1757), an offensive alliance in which France now pledged 129,000 troops and 12 million livres every year until Silesia had been recovered; in return for this largesse, Maria Theresa agreed to the partition of the Austrian Netherlands between Louis XV and his son-in-law, Duke Philip of Parma, who would then return Parma to Austria. An offensive alliance with Tsarina Elizabeth enlisted an additional 80,000 Russian troops; Russia would also receive territorial compensation for its efforts: Poland would cede Courland in return for acquiring East Prussia. Frederick's invasion of Saxony ensured that he would be placed under the imperial ban for breaking the peace, or *Reichsfriede*, within Germany. Over the next seven years the empire furnished 8 million fl. in taxes and fielded a 40,000-man imperial army to enforce the Regensburg Diet's mandate of *Exekution* against Frederick. With French help even the monarchy's old Swedish adversary joined the struggle in hopes of acquiring Prussian Pomerania. Against this overwhelming array of enemies, Frederick could only count on British money and auxiliaries from a few Protestant states like Hanover and Hesse-Cassel. Surely, Kaunitz had done his job well.

As had Haugwitz. Thanks to his interwar reforms, Maria Theresa's subjects now supported a massive military that reached 250,000 men by 1760. By then the tax burden had become sufficiently intense to justify widespread reports of ruined nobles and desperate peasants throughout the *Erblande*. Although Hungary paid only 17 percent of the taxes raised in the monarchy's core lands, contingents from the expanded Military Border more than doubled the kingdom's annual military contribution to 70–75,000 men. Meanwhile, the Austrian Netherlands provided 30 millions in cash and 26 millions in credit for a sovereign who had secretly consigned them to Bourbon rule. In 1762, the government even resorted to printing 12 million fl. in paper money – the first such issue in Austrian history. After sacrifices such as these, Maria Theresa's subjects surely must have appreciated that their country had become a great power at last.

With a half million men under arms, Kaunitz's great alliance should have been able to achieve what had now become the empress's ultimate goal of reducing Brandenburg-Prussia to its former rank of a middling German state. That Frederick II escaped the fate of the Winter King after White Mountain and Max Emanuel after Blenheim is partly attributable to his ruthless opportunism and military genius. Although he had misjudged Saxony's role in Kaunitz's pre-war machinations, he benefited enormously from the protection it offered his own dominions, as well as from the 50 million fl. that he extracted from its people. Following its conquest in the autumn of 1756, he even incorporated its troops (except officers) into the Prussian army. Operating from a compact geographical base formed by Brandenburg, Saxony, and Silesia, he had the advantage of interior defensive lines. By contrast, the Austrian, Imperial, French, Swedish, and Russian armies were literally scattered about the four directions of a compass. The Sudeten Mountains of northern Bohemia also posed a formidable obstacle to any Austrian descent on Silesia, while France and particularly Russia were hampered by their relative remoteness from Prussia itself.

Nor were the monarchy's coalition partners particularly motivated. Notwithstanding Kaunitz's genius for enlisting allies, the coalition was bound by little more than a common antipathy for Frederick II. The Habsburg monarchy was the only major country with a tangible interest in Prussia's demise. France's objectives lay primarily overseas and only re-motely in Hanover, whose conquest might afford it a bargaining chip in peace negotiations. Once the French recognized this, they negotiated a Third Treaty of Versailles (March 1759) that cut their commitments to a still con-siderable 100,000 troops and 6 million livres in subsidies. Yet, the uninter-rupted string of British overseas victories left them with little incentive to continue fighting. Admittedly, Tsarina Elizabeth was a devoted ally out of all proportion to Russia's own national interest. Within a short time, however, she began a tortuous battle with cancer that everyone realized would lead to the succession of the ardently Prussophile Grand Duke Peter. As the end drew closer, her generals and ministers were at pains to protect themselves from the wrath of her successor. Finally, except for Saxony, the German princes and Sweden had cast their lot against Prussia because they saw an opportunity to gain territory and influence by being on the winning side. None of them were especially interested in a long, indecisive war in which they would have to bear a significant share of the burden.

Given these parameters, Maria Theresa's own commanders should have
sustained immediate and unrelenting offensive operations against Prussia.
Even in the absence of battlefield victories, Frederick's outnumbered forces
could be overwhelmed by attrition alone. Yet once again the monarchy was
failed by its generals. The commander-in-chief, Field Marshal Daun, was a
proven master of defensive warfare who had saved Bohemia in 1757 by
crushing Frederick's army at the battle of Kolin (18 June). Yet, from the very
beginning of the war he stuck too closely to conventional eighteenth-century
tactics that stressed maneuver and discouraged risking a country's main army
in pitched battle. Although a small force of Hungarian and Military Border
troops briefly occupied Berlin during October, Daun failed to press his
advantage after Kolin. Within two months Frederick was able to recover and
turn back a Franco-Imperial invasion of Saxony at Rossbach (5 November)
and an Austrian thrust into Silesia at Leuthen (5 December). The following
campaign brought additional allied victories as Daun defeated Frederick
again at Hochkirch in Saxony (14 October 1758), the Swedes overran
Pomerania, and the Russians permanently occupied all of East Prussia. Yet
Silesia and almost all of Saxony were still in Prussian hands. One year later
the great Russo-Austrian victory at Kunersdorf (13 August 1759) cost
Frederick his main army and nearly his life, as a silver snuffbox in his coat
pocket absorbed what would have been a fatal bullet. Yet, when Daun failed
to assist the victorious Russians in administering the *coup de grâce*, they
withdrew their own forces in disgust, charging that Daun was forcing them to
do all the fighting.

Of course, Maria Theresa was partly responsible for failing to remove
Daun at a time when the monarchy needed a more aggressive military
commander. She later attributed her indecision to her "persistent loyalty" to
a devoted and otherwise competent man who had served her well in the past.
Although the demands and threats of her French and Russian allies soon
forced her to give greater freedom to other commanders, she was never able
to remove him from the field. Of course, even Daun's timidity could not
prevent the ring from closing ever tighter around Frederick. The next two
years witnessed the partial recovery of both Saxony and Silesia, including
their capital cities of Dresden and Breslau. Berlin was again subject to a brief
occupation, while the Russians and Swedes completed the 1761 campaign by
occupying all of Pomerania.

By then, however, time had finally run out. The anti-Prussian alliance
collapsed at the beginning of 1762 with the death of Tsarina Elizabeth II.
The new Tsar Peter III immediately concluded peace with Prussia, then took
steps to re-enter the conflict as Frederick's ally. Fortunately for Maria
Theresa, Peter was overthrown and murdered in July in a palace coup headed
by his own wife, Catherine. Nevertheless, the new Empress Catherine II

(1762–96) made clear that Russia would remain neutral. Russia's defection had already knocked Sweden out of the war. France's crushing defeats in Canada and India forced it to follow suit. When it concluded peace with Great Britain at the Treaty of Paris (3 February 1763), Maria Theresa had lost her last major ally. There was now no prospect of continuing the war. The Austrian army had already evacuated Silesia in the fall. The country itself was utterly exhausted from seven years of unremitting struggle, in which the empress's subjects had made sacrifices greater than at any time in the monarchy's history. In signing peace with Prussia at the Saxon hunting lodge at Hubertusburg (15 February 1763), Maria Theresa was obliged to recognize the *status quo ante bellum*. The only concession she won was Frederick's promise to vote for her son Joseph in the next imperial election. Never had the monarchy waged a war with so many advantages, so much to gain – and yet so little at risk. Its generals had even won most of the battles: only three of eight against Frederick himself, but all four major engagements fought against other Prussian commanders. Perhaps it was fitting that a state that had proven so well suited to defending itself against aggression should have made such an incompetent aggressor itself.

6 Discovering the people: the triumph of cameralism and enlightened absolutism (1765–1792)

Had the monarchy won the Seven Years' War and regained much or all of Silesia, contemporaries and historians alike could have pointed to a number of factors in its success: Kaunitz's Diplomatic Revolution had forged a seemingly invincible coalition against Prussia; Haugwitz's dramatic restructuring of taxation and administration had supported a huge increase in the size of the army; finally, notwithstanding Daun's shortcomings as a field commander, his military reforms had improved the quality and equipment of those troops. Instead, failure prompted another round of introspection as the empress and her ministers now carefully scrutinized the system that they had created. The reconquest of Silesia was no longer their immediate objective; repeated setbacks on the battlefield had finally persuaded Maria Theresa to accept its loss. Rather it was the monarchy's security against the almost certain threat of renewed Prussian aggression.

A cause for immediate concern was the state debt, which had more than doubled over the past fifteen years from 124 to 280 million fl. In the first half of the century, Anglo-Dutch financial aid had helped the *Hofkammer* to avert bankruptcy. Although French subsidies were neither as plentiful nor paid as punctually, they were still considerable and had come with fewer strings attached. Indeed, whereas the British had abruptly cut off all aid to Prussia at a critical point in the conflict, Versailles continued to make good on its arrears for at least eight years after the conclusion of peace. Nevertheless, France's lackluster performance during the war and, ultimately, its signing of a separate peace revived bitter memories of the monarchy's dependence on unreliable allies and the subsidies they provided.

The Second Theresian Reform

Administration and finance

As had so many of her predecessors, the empress began by undertaking a new round of administrative reforms. If Haugwitz had been the author of the first reform period, it was now the *Staatskanzler* Kaunitz who stepped forward from his foreign policy perch to restructure much of what Haugwitz had created. Even before the war's end there had emerged a consensus within the ministry that the Directory president's attempts to create a more rational administrative system had failed to eliminate the confusion that had long characterized Habsburg central government. Arguing that the monarchy still had no single central policy-making body, Kaunitz called for the creation of a United Chancery that would embrace all three of the monarchy's core lands, together with a Council of State (*Staatsrat*) to formulate internal policy for all of the Habsburg dominions. At the same time he recommended that finances be divided among no fewer than three offices: a reinvigorated *Hofkammer*, a Credit Deputation, and an Accounting Office (*Hofrechnungskammer*). Rather than wait for the end of hostilities, the empress implemented Kaunitz's system during the course of 1761. Both the Directory and the Internal Conference were abolished; of Haugwitz's creations only the Supreme Judiciary survived, although it was consolidated and made wholly independent.

The implementation of Kaunitz's reforms signaled his emergence as the monarchy's *de facto* prime minister. For Maria Theresa it was another long, but fruitful marriage of convenience. Like Bartenstein, Haugwitz, and so many of the Habsburgs' most gifted servants, Kaunitz was hardly an attractive personality. He was a prickly, sexually promiscuous hypochondriac who was so horrified of fresh air that he insisted on being carried to audiences in a closed sedan. He was also a committed proponent of Enlightenment ideas that the empress both feared and despised. Nevertheless, she now placed Kaunitz in near total command of state affairs. Not only did he remain in charge of foreign policy as State Chancellor, he also directed domestic policy as president of the newly created Council of State. Indeed, he successfully argued that no other Council member should head any other administrative body since that would foster administrative myopia and promote intramural jealousies between cabinet heads. The one exception was to be Kaunitz himself, whose continued control of the State Chancery would permit the government to coordinate domestic policy with the achievement of foreign policy objectives. Kaunitz also pointed out that, since the State Chancery enjoyed ultimate jurisdiction over the monarchy's outlying, "foreign" crown lands in Italy and the Netherlands, he was best equipped to represent them in the Council of State.

In fact, one of the goals of the second reform period was to induce Lombardy and Belgium to bear a larger share of the monarchy's tax burden. Kaunitz achieved considerable success in both crownlands by skillfully establishing a close, cooperative relationship with their ruling elites based on respect for their constitutional individuality. Under his tutelage, both paid Vienna much more in taxation than they received. He needed less finesse in his dealings with the newly named "grand principality" of Transylvania, whose Chancery also reported directly to him. Nor did the central government miss the opportunity to flex its muscles in the other parts of southern Hungary that it ruled directly. From 1765 the Military Border underwent extensive administrative and military restructuring, once again in response to concerns raised about the *Grenzers'* performance during the Seven Years' War. Meanwhile, the Illyrian Commission continued to serve as an effective vehicle for controlling Greater Hungary's Serb populations by reaffirming and protecting their religious privileges against almost continuous pressure from the kingdom's Catholic nobility. Beginning in 1769 it even promoted regular meetings of the Illyrian Church Congress, albeit only after packing it with loyal delegates, including twenty-five soldiers from the Military Border. Moreover, the empress obliged the first conclave to approve a new decree (1770) that sharply limited the secular privileges that Leopold I had first granted the Orthodox patriarch in 1690.

Not surprisingly, the second reform period had the least impact on Hungary proper. When it met in 1764 the diet rejected the competence of either the Council of State or the United Chancery. Although the *Staatsrat* persisted in secretly deliberating the kingdom's affairs, the empress reluctantly agreed to retain a separate Hungarian Chancery, alongside a renamed "United Austrian and Bohemian Chancery." As it had in the past, the Hungarian *Kammer* did remain subordinate to the *Hofkammer*, although the diet officially classified the relationship as one of "correspondence" rather than dependency. But the funds it administered remained less than optimal, especially after the diet agreed to a Contribution of only 3.9 million fl. Maria Theresa had always held out hope that her unfailing benevolence would goad Hungary into accepting a closer institutional union and a fair share of the Contribution. After the diet of 1764 she finally gave up.

Although the new administrative system was largely in place by 1766, the government continued to make adjustments until the end of the reign, prompted as it was by the uneasy feeling that neither confusion nor inefficiency had been wholly eliminated. Nevertheless, Kaunitz's system proved more durable than Haugwitz's. It also helped to perpetuate the steady rise in state revenue, which increased from 35 million fl. in 1763 to 50 million by the end of the reign. The treasury actually produced the first two balanced budgets in the monarchy's history in 1775 and 1777. Although the state debt also continued to mount, the growth in revenue ultimately made the government much less dependent on creditors and truly independent of foreign subsidies.

The government and the people

The latest restructuring of the central administration was a necessary first step in the Second Theresian Reform. Yet the most dramatic and revolutionary reforms involved a fundamental redefinition of the government's relationship to the people it ruled. Having abandoned the peasantry, bourgeoisie, and non-Catholics over a century ago, the government now rediscovered and addressed their needs in a series of domestic initiatives that included not only the *Erblande* but Hungary as well. Once again this remarkable about-face was motivated by power politics, specifically by the Theresian regime's awareness that the security of the state versus Prussia and other countries depended on its ability to promote and marshal the monarchy's resources better than it had in the past. Beginning with Ferdinand II, her predecessors had employed and favored the nobility and Catholic church as their primary instruments for state-building, much to the benefit of the aristocracy and Jesuits, but certainly to the detriment of society's less privileged elements.

Over the past half century cameralist authors like Schröder and Schierendorff had pointed out how this elitism limited the monarchy's military power by handicapping productivity and the taxable wealth it created. It was only now, however, that the loss of Silesia convinced the empress that social reform was necessary if the monarchy was to survive and compete in the rough and tumble world of great-power politics. Led by the German-émigré Justi and the Jewish-born convert Joseph von Sonnenfels (1733–1817), the current generation of Austrian cameralists carried home the message that a society's productivity – and its tax base – grew in direct proportion to the size, living standards, health, and happiness of its people. Moreover, they singled out agriculture and the peasantry for special attention, given the central role both played in defraying the Contribution.

By mid-reign Maria Theresa was totally committed to "sustaining the peasantry, as the most numerous class of subjects and the foundation and greatest strength of the state." Yet, to a certain extent her and her ministers' heightened concern for society's less privileged elements was motivated by additional considerations. One was Maria Theresa's genuine sympathy for her subjects' suffering. During the last fifteen years of her reign, the empress was somewhat less interested in international affairs and more dedicated to serving her people. The unsatisfactory outcome of the war helped move her in that direction. So did the sudden death of Francis Stephen in August 1765. She was so devastated by the loss that she did not make a public appearance for eight months, during which time she expressed her grief by calculating the number of hours that they had been married (precisely

385,744), by giving away all of her jewelry, and by opting to wear only black for the rest of her life. As a middle-aged widow who had already outlived most of her court contemporaries, Maria Theresa was prepared to delegate power to the men around her and less willing to resist their proposals.

Hence another factor that now loomed especially large was her advisers' espousal of Enlightenment ideas. The deaths of Haugwitz (1765), Daun (1766), and Bartenstein (1767) had opened the door for a group of younger and more liberal advisors, led by Kaunitz. Francis Stephen's sudden demise also ushered in the empress's son and heir, the newly elected Emperor Joseph II (1765–90). Like so many monarchs of his generation, Joseph II was not only a committed cameralist, but was also influenced by Enlightenment ideas. As a youth he had already received instruction in the works of central Europe's more moderate Enlightenment figures, such as Pufendorf and Muratori. The empress was, however, unable to shield him from the more radical Anglo-French ideas that circulated within the ministry and the court aristocracy. Nor could she keep Joseph from sharing his contemporaries' admiration for Europe's foremost "philosopher king," her nemesis Frederick II, whose domestic achievements and martial exploits he was eager to duplicate.

Of course cameralism was hardly incompatible with the Enlightenment, especially the central European *Aufklärung*. Both extolled the advantages of a secular, rational, educated society, that enjoyed a "free hand" in pursuing material well-being. Admittedly cameralists like Justi strove to attain "the happiness of the state," while the *philosophes* focused on the people. Yet the two coincided more often than not, especially since cameralism regarded a monarch's subjects as the state's most important element. For this reason, the empress had a good working relationship with her advisers, despite some abstract philosophical differences. Nor were ideas at the heart of the empress's conflicts with her son, especially since most of his projects co-incided with her own cameralist agenda. Rather, what exercised Maria Theresa most was her son's personality. Joseph II was no carbon copy of his father. On the positive side he was very intelligent, with a keen eye that enabled him to trace any problem quickly to its source. This perceptiveness, plus his boundless energy, made Joseph the facile advocate of daring and innovative ideas. It was, however, his awareness of these strengths that also made him an extraordinarily overbearing, persistent, and impatient individual who relished ridiculing those who did not share his gifts or ideas. Most important, his compulsive determination to carry out change as quickly and as thoroughly as possible conflicted with his mother's tendency toward moderation and compromise.

Nor was Joseph likely to wait patiently for his turn in the succession. He had no family of his own to divert his attention. His first, truly happy marriage to Isabella of Bourbon-Parma ended after just three years with her death from smallpox (1763); nor did either of their children survive childhood. A second, arranged marriage to an ugly Bavarian princess brought out the worst in his talent for ridiculing those less fortunate than himself. He readily reminded her of her shortcomings and even refused to sire an heir by her, insisting that "I would try to have children if I could put the tip of my finger on the tiniest part of her body that was not covered by boils." When smallpox again made him a widower in 1767 he decided to remain single, fulfilling his need for female companionship through platonic relationships with gracious, but reluctant, ladies and more intimate accords with Viennese prostitutes. Meanwhile, he left the dynasty's perpetuation to his brother, Grand Duke Peter Leopold of Tuscany, who rose to the challenge by fathering sixteen children, including twelve archdukes.

After her husband's death the empress announced that she and her son would rule jointly in a co-regency, but in practice Maria Theresa retained the final say in virtually all areas. There were some exceptions. As emperor Joseph directed German affairs. His mother also indulged his claim as emperor to dominion over military matters. Joseph made the most of the opportunity, working closely with *Hofkriegsrat* President Daun and his successor, Field Marshal Lacy, to make several constructive innovations, including the introduction of inspectors general, new drill and exercise manuals, and a more rational organization of military units. By 1772 he and Lacy had instituted Daun's plan for a Prussian-style canton system that permitted the army to assume direct control of recruitment from the estates. Finally, as his father's principal heir Joseph inherited and administered a considerable financial estate. Indeed, although Francis Stephen had proven an obtuse statesman and incompetent general, he had always been a businessman of considerable acumen, building a personal fortune worth 31 million fl. It was in recognition of his fiscal talents that the empress had actually entrusted her husband with managing the huge state debt, which he promptly consolidated, lowering interest on government bonds from 6 to 5 percent. Joseph put his inheritance to much the same use. He immediately committed nearly 19 millions to retiring some of the state debentures, which were then set afire in a public bonfire, while using the rest to lower interest on the balance to just 4 percent. Thanks to Joseph's intervention, annual savings on debt service totaled 870,000 fl. per year.

Beyond these clearly defined areas, there was constant friction between the conservative, discreet Maria Theresa and her headstrong son. She often yielded on relatively minor issues, but rarely on major ones. Thus she agreed to adjust the court's lifestyle to Joseph's egalitarian instincts. The stiff Spanish court protocol was eliminated because Joseph hated its formality and felt that the expensive Spanish mantles were beyond the means of less wealthy individuals. Gambling and hunting were also banned as wasteful manifestations of class privilege. By 1772 two of modern Vienna's most famous parks, the Prater and the Augarten, had been opened to public use for the first time. On the other hand the empress stood firm against her son's more far-reaching demand for an end to all tax immunities. Similarly, she agreed to streamline the central administration further by abolishing the essentially superfluous Transylvanian Chancery (1774), but she refused to consider his politically dangerous demand that Hungary, Lombardy, and the Austrian Netherlands be formally subordinated to the *Staatsrat*.

Joseph sublimated his frustration by devoting over 30,000 miles and a quarter of his time as co-regent to numerous fact-finding trips to virtually every corner of the monarchy. He often traveled incognito under the name "Count Falkenstein" in order to get a truer impression of how his subjects lived and felt about their government. His sympathy for the common people was no secret. When his presence was known he was invariably met by thousands of petitions. On at least two occasions he showed his support for agriculture and the peasants who pursued it by personally plowing the fields. This gesture quickly became a local legend among peasants, who presumably reveled in telling all comers that "Emperor Joseph II *schleppt* here." Although the empress also welcomed her son's absences from Vienna, he invariably returned to Vienna armed with first-hand knowledge that enhanced his influence and often obliged her to initiate additional reforms. The frequent confrontations led Maria Theresa to contemplate abdication and Joseph to consider exile in Italy. Yet they also helped push the empress toward a more progressive domestic agenda that served as a transition between the more traditionally Habsburg, aristocratic absolutism of the First Theresian Reform and the rather extreme form of enlightened absolutism that followed the co-regency.

If the empress and her advisers devised the Second Theresian Reform, it was empowered by a bureaucracy that was much more numerous and powerful than at the beginning of the reign, at least within the *Erblande*. The typical local *Beamte* was also much more concerned about his constituents' needs, thanks largely to Maria Theresa's earlier restructuring of elite education, which now paralleled most German institutions in its focus on the cameral sciences and exposure to the Enlightenment. Indeed, since 1755 Justi's lectures to future civil servants at the *Theresianum* had inspired him to publish central Europe's first and most influential textbooks on political economy. Eight years later, Sonnenfels became the University of Vienna's first professor of cameral science, a position he used to train future generations of Austrian officials. Indeed, by 1776 the cameral sciences had joined law as a required course of study for all civil service applicants. Nor was the acculturation of the monarchy's bureaucrats limited to the core lands. The cosmopolitan outlook of Milan's urban patriciate emboldened Kaunitz to stack its government with a remarkable group of Italian reformers, including Cesare Beccaria and Pietro Verri. Under their direction Lombardy soon emerged as a testing ground for some of Maria Theresa's bolder domestic initiatives.

Agrarian reform

Like reformers elsewhere in Europe, the Theresian regime tended to initiate changes only after they became aware of specific problems, often from information they received from conscientious local officials. The first major attempt at social reform came at the beginning of 1767, in response to nearly two years of mounting peasant unrest in the Hungarian lands. As usual the source of the problem was the nobility's widespread abuse of the existing laws, especially along the kingdom's relatively populous western frontier. The worst excesses involved *robot* service, which was still officially set at only fifty-two days per year for peasants working a standard plot, or "hide" (or 104 days if they employed no draft animals). Since most peasants owned less than a hide, they were supposed to perform proportionally less labor service, while landless cottagers were limited to as little as thirteen days' labor per year. In reality landlords had been extracting excessive levels of *robot* from all of their serfs since the onset of Habsburg rule. After appointing a commission to investigate the abuses, the empress promulgated a new *robot* patent for Hungary in January 1767. The *urbarium* (as *robot* patents were called in Hungary) was basically modeled after one she had given Slavonia in 1756, the year after its most recent peasant revolt. It prohibited landlords from adding to their demesne at their peasants' expense, while limiting the peasants' obligations to the standard fifty-two days per hide, together with the customary fees and tithes. Much as it had done in the *Erblande*, the government endeavored to strengthen enforcement by registering the peasants and their obligations, together with the breakdown between rustical and dominical lands.

In attempting to alleviate the suffering of the Hungarian peasantry, Maria Theresa was likely motivated primarily by humanitarian considerations, if only because the central kingdom was the one Habsburg dominion where the Contribution would not have increased significantly, even with an increase in the population's wealth or productivity. In any event, this first serious attempt at *Bauernschutz* in Hungary proper had little immediate impact on the peasants it was designed to protect: thanks to the shortage and relative powerlessness of royal officials there, it took eight long years before the government could fully implement the *urbarium*, which was then widely ignored by defiant landlords and the noble-dominated county assemblies.

Enforcement was, however, much less of a problem elsewhere in the monarchy. Once she had been aroused by conditions in central Hungary, the empress promptly turned her attention to the rest of the monarchy's core lands. In November 1769 she issued an *urbarium* for Transylvania, largely in response to Joseph's reports from the grand principality that "whole villages" of serfs were fleeing to Turkish territory in order to escape their Magyar landlords. Indeed, the *urbarium* helped to reduce *robot* service from four or more days, to a still considerable average of three days per week (156 per annum). By 1771 the government had also issued a new *Robotpatent* for Austrian Silesia after an extensive, three-year investigation conducted by local crown officials had ascertained that abuses were even worse there than in Hungary.

The government was eager to issue a similar patent for the rest of the Bohemian lands. The need for action was sharply underscored by the devastating central European famine of 1770–2, during which a quarter of a million Bohemian peasants starved to death while their landlords amassed huge profits exporting grain to Prussia and Saxony. Yet intense lobbying by the estates managed to divide the ministry and delay implementation until 1774. By then Maria Theresa was so frustrated and desperate to alleviate conditions that she actually proposed abolishing serfdom altogether. If such a dramatic step found no echo among her advisors, it was because they feared that it would reduce state revenue by undermining the Bohemian nobility's ability to pay taxes. Instead, Joseph persuaded her to employ the estates' counterproposal, by which peasants would negotiate individual contracts with their landlords; the government would impose a settlement only if the two parties failed to reach an agreement. Although the ensuing April 1774 patent appeared to be an equitable compromise, it failed to anticipate the superior leverage that landlords enjoyed in direct negotiations with their serfs. Nor did it meet the rising expectations of the Bohemian peasantry, which launched a massive revolt in the following spring.

The unarmed peasants were quickly dispersed by a 40,000-man field army. Nevertheless, given a second chance the empress now addressed their needs in the *Robotpatent* of August 1775. It established eleven, graduated levels of *robot* service, with the heaviest obligation set at three days per week. Although it was only intended for Bohemia, a virtually identical patent was soon issued for Moravia. Nor did the empress stop here. Over the next two years she sponsored a pilot project on two of her Bohemian estates that was designed to replace *robot* with free labor. The empress was driven by more than humanitarian considerations. State officials like the project's director, Franz Anton Raab, argued that compulsory labor service "violated the laws of nature." They also realized that free peasants would have the incentive to work harder and more efficiently, thereby producing more taxable wealth for themselves, their landlords, and the state. Indeed, the so-called Raab System released the peasants both from their personal subjection to their royal landlord and from the need to perform *robot* on her demesne lands. The demesne was then divided up among the peasants, who were free to farm it as free laborers in return for cash rents commensurate with the size of their holdings. As an added incentive peasants received long-term or hereditary leases on the land they worked. The pilot project was an unqualified success, with Raab reporting an immediate, 50 percent increase in the production from both estates. By the beginning of 1777 the empress felt sufficiently confident to extend the Raab System to other crown estates.

The government had somewhat less cause for alarm in the Austrian lands, which were neither as wealthy as greater Bohemia nor as oppressed by manorial obligations. Austrian peasants were not enserfed, as they were in the other core lands. *Robot* service was also less extensive. Lower Austrian landlords were less prone to exceed the customary limit of two days service per week, even before it was reconfirmed by a 1772 *Robotpatent*. Meanwhile, labor services were negligible in Upper Austria (fourteen days per year) and non-existent in the Tyrol and the western *Vorlande*. The exception was Inner Austria, where labor services were officially set at a crushing four days per week, growing to as many as six days during harvest. It was only at the end of 1778, after six years of difficult negotiations, that all but one of the Inner Austrian estates agreed to reduce *robot* to an average of three days per week (156 days per year). Even then Carniola held out. Once Croatia had received an *urbarium* in 1780, Carniola was the only Habsburg crownland in need of a *Robotpatent*. When it was finally issued in 1782 it conceded Carniola a limit of four days per week (208 days per year) – the highest in the monarchy.

The Theresian regime never seriously contemplated eliminating labor services altogether, if only because it was unwilling to deprive landlords of their property rights without compensation. Nonetheless, in reducing *robot* it turned back the clock on a century and a half of illegal encroachment by the landed nobility. Additional decrees addressed other age-old abuses. For example, many peasants regained the right to purchase and market goods independently of manorial businesses. Some also reacquired rustical land that had been seized by their landlords. Of course, the key to their improved position *vis-à-vis* their landlords was often better enforcement of existing laws rather than the implementation of new ones. Under Maria Theresa seigneurs were scrutinized as never before by crown officials as they exacted labor services, administered patrimonial justice, or conducted other manorial enterprises.

The empress did, however, sponsor several new initiatives that reflected the emphasis that the cameral sciences placed on developing a large and industrious population.[1] Thus she directed local officials to supervise pregnant girls to safeguard against infanticide or abandonment. She also offered marriage incentives – except to unemployed drifters, whom a March 1766 decree expressly forbid to wed. Lest newlyweds forget their obligation to work, another edict cut wedding celebrations from the customary three days to just one. The new emphasis on personal fertility and industry inevitably led the regime to place several restrictions on the Catholic church. The driving force behind them was the fiercely anti-clerical Kaunitz, who had already introduced several edicts in Lombardy that the empress now agreed to extend to the rest of the monarchy during 1771-2. At his instigation the government raised to 25 the age at which an individual could take monastic vows. It also placed a cap on the number of monks allowed in individual monasteries – sometimes at levels lower than the current membership. At the same time, laymen were discouraged from diverting work time to popular devotion through a further reduction in the number of religious holidays and pilgrimages. It even forbade a further increase in the thousands of religious brotherhoods that organized various devotional activities for their members.

Public education

Maria Theresa worked diligently to raise living standards among the monarchy's common people largely because she discerned a direct, causative link between peasant living standards, productivity, and state revenue. She was initially less convinced of the masses' need for an education. Although she established an Educational Commission (*Studienhofkommission*) for the *Erblande* in 1760, she gave it little attention during its first decade. Meanwhile, she entrusted the Hungarian school system to the ageing archbishop of Esztergom, to whom educational reform meant little more than closing down some Protestant academies. The impetus for action only came in 1769, when the bishop of Passau reported that his Austrian parishioners were not only woefully ignorant, but included significant numbers of crypto-Protestants. The vision of large numbers of heretics in the *Erblande* aroused the empress almost as much as an invading Prussian army.

It also gave the *Studienkommission* an excuse to pursue its own agenda for public education. Calling themselves the "Party of Enlightenment" (and their adversaries the "Men of Darkness") the commission was dominated by progressive minds like Swieten, Martini, and Sonnenfels. One of its newer members was Johann Anton von Pergen, a Kaunitz protégé on the *Staatsrat* and *Staatskanzlei* who had recently assumed the directorship of the Oriental

---

[1] An approximate population breakdown (in millions): Hungary, 9.7 (central Hungary, 6.5, Croatia, 0.7, Transylvania, 1.5, the Military Border, 1); Bohemia, 4.5; Austria, 4.3; Galicia and the Bukovina, 3.4; Belgium, 2.4; Lombardy 1.5.

Academy. In August 1770 Pergen submitted a lengthy memorandum to the empress that called for a thorough reform of the monarchy's educational system. Most radical was his proposal that lay teachers immediately replace all Jesuits and other clerics before the latter could inflict more cultural damage on future generations. Though Swieten convinced the empress to consider Pergen's proposal, she ultimately rejected it because it would have necessitated the importation of large numbers of Protestant teachers from Germany. Even those sympathetic to Pergen's proposal, like Swieten and Emperor Joseph, recognized that such a massive purge of the schools was far beyond the monarchy's financial and cultural resources.

Yet three years later Pope Clement XIV forced this very task on the monarchy when he dissolved the Society of Jesus. The suppression came in response to pressure from the Bourbon powers and Portugal, who resented Jesuit meddling in their national politics. Nevertheless the dissolution momentarily left the monarchy's *Gymnasien* and other secondary schools without teachers or administrators. Fortunately it also left the central government in control of the Jesuits' extensive wealth, which could now be used to defray the cost of a new, state-run educational system.

By 1773 the Theresian regime had a good idea of what the public schools' mission and methods should be. Once again the monarchy's leadership looked to neighboring lands for its cultural sustenance, this time by adopting the pietist teaching system employed in Prussian Silesia. To the pietists both schooling and literacy were instruments of social control. They reasoned that people would more readily obey authority if they did so out of inner conviction rather than out of fear of punishment. Of course, the monarchy's political and religious leadership was hardly inexperienced in the use of media to mold popular culture. Since the Counter-Reformation it had successfully impressed its values on the people not only through coercion, but through various forms of propaganda. Given the masses' illiteracy it had heretofore employed visual media, such as devotional display (religious processions, relics, art, and architecture) and the didactic plays staged by the Jesuits. Yet, as James Van Horn Melton has pointed out, the government was now prepared to use compulsory public education "to reconstitute popular culture on a more literate basis."

The projected school reform had a lengthy cultural agenda. Maria Theresa and clerical leaders like Archbishop Migazzi were eager to use mass literacy to reinforce Catholic orthodoxy. Their parallel concern for Christian morality was shared by others, like Sonnenfels, who had banned Vienna's bawdy popular comedies after becoming theater censor in 1770. Meanwhile, the ministry was primarily interested in enhancing the people's productivity by strengthening their sense of social responsibility. Once again it took its cue from the German pietists, who regarded the fulfilment of one's obligations to society and the state as a "moral imperative" that could be discharged by greater self-discipline and a stronger work ethic. Indeed, some officials even hoped to replace the subsistence mentality of the typical peasant with a profit motive that would incline him to work beyond the levels necessary to survive. Everyone also appreciated the vocational advantages that education offered. Finally, they valued instruction as a tool in preventing civil disobedience, although the threat of popular insurrection was hardly uppermost in their minds.

These objectives were embodied in two General School Ordinances that were issued for the *Erblande* (1774) and Hungary (1777). Their author was the Silesian bishop of Sagan, Ignaz Felbiger, who had already introduced pietist methods in the Catholic schools of his diocese and whom Frederick II now graciously granted leave to reform the school system of his Habsburg adversary. The ordinances established a three-tiered system. A compulsory elementary school, or *Trivialschule*, would give everyone basic instruction. In the countryside the focus would be on teaching peasant children religion, morality, and vocational skills; only urban elementary schools would stress the three R's. After that a middle school, or *Hauptschule*, in every district capital would give all burgher children a choice between vocational training and advanced academic preparation for the *Gymnasium*. Atop the system stood the *Gymnasium*, which remained an elite preparatory school for the university.

The Ordinances imposed an unprecedented degree of uniformity on the public schools. All instructors were required to receive training and certification at a specially dedicated normal school (*Normalschule*), one of which was established in the capital city of every Habsburg crownland. Each normal school also prepared teachers to employ standardized subject matter, teaching methods, and textbooks published on its premises. The curriculum included several pietist innovations. For example, teachers were expected to ask students to use reason and judgment to understand material, rather than to memorize it. Since not all students could be expected to progress at the same speed, they were divided into groups according to proficiency. Teachers were also expected to employ hourglasses in the classroom in order to instill their students with a sense of time and pace.

The General School Ordinances incurred considerable resistance from outside the ruling elite. Peasant parents resented sending their children to the schools instead of to the fields to work. Many lower clergy suspected that the pietists' curriculum and teaching methods would make people ungodly. Hungary's Protestant communities actually refused to adopt the ordinance in their schools because their leaders feared that a standardized curriculum might ultimately be used to undermine their faith. Nevertheless, the Theresian school reform proved an almost unqualified success. Although an initial shortage of lay teachers necessitated the retention of former Jesuits and other clergy, the number and percentage of secular teachers increased quickly as the normal schools turned out a steady stream of graduates. By 1780 the combination of new teachers and wealth acquired from the Jesuits had supported the establishment of 500 new schools within the *Erblande*. The gains were even more dramatic in the Hungarian lands, where half of the country's communities were without schools and only a quarter of all children in attendance. The most impressive strides came in relatively backward areas like the Banat, which more than doubled the number of schools from 183 in 1776 to 452 by 1782. Indeed, by the end of Maria Theresa's reign the monarchy boasted well over 6,000 schools and 200,000 students. By then it had passed its Prussian model in both the availability and quality of public education.

Sources of conflict: religion and the law

Maria Theresa's efforts to protect and educate the peasantry proceeded with a minimum of conflict within the government because there was a coincidence of interest between her, her son, and her ministers. Much less was accomplished, however, in those fields where the empress's conservatism precluded a consensus within the government. One such area was religious toleration. Thanks to men like Kaunitz and Joseph II, she was aware that intolerance hurt the economy through emigration and gave foreign countries like Protestant Prussia and Orthodox Russia unwelcome influence among her subjects. As a result both she and provincial authorities quietly tolerated Protestant businessmen and their dependants in places like the Austrian Netherlands, Trieste, and even Vienna, where as many as 2,000 resided by 1761. In 1778 she finally permitted the first Protestant to receive a degree at the University of Vienna. She made her most dramatic concession one year earlier, upon discovering a community of 10,000 Protestants in northern Moravia. With her son threatening to abdicate unless she granted them full toleration, she ultimately accepted Kaunitz's call for compromise by quietly granting them private worship. Repercussions were limited to the expulsion of a few ringleaders and the establishment of a new bishopric and forty Catholic churches.

Notwithstanding these concessions to "discreet tolerance," the empress remained resolute in her abhorrence of religious toleration. She continued to see it as a catalyst for disunity, telling her son that "he is 'no friend to humanity' who allows everyone his own thoughts." Indeed, she afforded the *Erblande*'s smaller, less important Protestant communities the same rough treatment that they had received earlier in her reign. Within the *Erblande* adult male heretics were sentenced to hard labor, drafted into the army, or expelled to Transylvania, which remained the one crownland where religious minorities could worship freely. Within Hungary proper, Lutheran towns were sometimes forced to observe Catholic holy days and elect Catholic magistrates. Even as she carried out her revolutionary education program, the empress withheld funding for Calvinist Latin schools, thereby forcing many of them to rely on private Swedish, Dutch, and British donations.

Even economic benefit was not sufficient to stay the empress's persecution of the Jews. With the support of the Croatian *Sabor*, she steadfastly rejected her son's and ministers' petitions to allow Jewish merchants to develop local trade within the Military Border. She also ordered that Vienna's Jews be placed in a ghetto, like their co-religionists in the monarchy's other cities. Five years of intensive lobbying and the passive resistance of her own ministers spared the community from relocation. Even then, however, the empress refused their petition to relax existing restrictions with the well-known retort that "I know of no greater plague than this race, which on account of its deceit, usury, and hoarding of money is driving my subjects to beggary."

Nor could Maria Theresa and her ministers agree on a program of legal reform. In 1766 she established a commission to codify the morass of edicts and regulations that comprised the monarchy's system of laws. She was, however, interested only in streamlining the existing code, not in making it more humane. That she refused to eliminate torture was most ironic, considering the enormous influence that her Milanese minister Cesare Beccaria had had on other governments, following the publication of his treatise *On Crime and Punishment* (1764). By 1767 the empress felt obliged to suspend work on the *Nemesis Theresiana*, after Kaunitz had objected to the code's explicit, illustrated procedures by which convicts could be impaled, broken on the wheel, or burned alive. Over the next decade her son led Sonnenfels, Martini, and Kaunitz in a determined lobbying effort against the retention of torture. The empress finally agreed to abolish it in 1776, although the criminal code was still not complete at the time of her death.

Foreign policy during the co-regency

Like domestic reform, Habsburg foreign policy during the co-regency represented the largely parallel but sometimes conflicting agendas of the empress, her son, and Kaunitz. Always the opportunist, the *Staatskanzler* was generally on the lookout for territorial acquisitions, especially if they could be achieved primarily by diplomatic means. Like his mother, Joseph II was largely driven by fear of Frederick II, and particularly by the prospect of a combined Prusso-Turkish attack on the monarchy. Yet his agenda for enhancing the monarchy's security included not only domestic reform but territorial expansion. As a result, Joseph and Kaunitz generally pursued a more aggressive foreign policy. The empress was not necessarily opposed to their activities or objectives, but she was the least motivated, especially when it involved unprovoked aggression. Yet none of the three envisioned armed conflict as a desirable or necessary extension of diplomacy.

One reason for this was the dearth of committed allies. Although France was still bound by a defensive alliance, its focus was almost exclusively on its overseas rivalry with Great Britain, rather than on continental affairs. Meanwhile the monarchy had lost the traditional constellation of countries that had assisted it militarily over the past century. The Diplomatic Revolution had ended not only the Anglo-Dutch alliance, but also the monarchy's credibility as a champion of the balance of power. The subsequent death of Tsarina Elizabeth had also terminated the long-standing Russian alliance and, with it, the chance of overwhelming Prussia in a future conflict. Finally, Prussia's emergence as the monarchy's virtual equal within Germany had all but eliminated the imperial crown as an instrument of Habsburg *Realpolitik*. By allying with France and continuing to persecute her non-Catholic subjects, Maria Theresa actually enhanced Prussia's pretensions to leadership among Germany's Protestant princes. The end of nearly a century of imperial resurgence was not lost on the co-regents. Although they still considered themselves German, they no longer identified with the *Reich* as a national political entity. Indeed, neither visited the empire or used its central institutions, except as transit points to other, more vital objectives.

Admittedly, the Second Theresian Reform had finally freed the monarchy from its former reliance on foreign allies. As the next conflict would demonstrate, the monarchy was fast approaching a wartime military establishment of well over 300,000 men. Nevertheless, when combined with the huge state debt, the cost of mobilizing such an army made it a financially prohibitive choice of last resort. Thus it remained more suitable as a deterrent to invasion than as an instrument for aggression. Notwithstanding Joseph's residual fear of Prussia and the Turks, the monarchy was, in fact, essentially secure from foreign invasion. Frederick II's central European agenda remained focused on defending his earlier conquest of Silesia, not in extending it deeper into the monarchy. Meanwhile, the Ottoman empire's steadily declining military power and French influence in Constantinople rendered the Turks less of a threat than at any time in the monarchy's history. The French alliance also gave the westernmost Habsburg possessions in the Netherlands, southwest Germany, and Italy an iron-clad guarantee against attack. Moreover, Maria Theresa quickly strengthened this security by concluding five marriage alliances with all of the Bourbon powers: she secured Spanish *infantas* for Joseph (1760) and her second son, Leopold, upon his succession as grand duke of Tuscany (1765); she also wedded three of her daughters to Ferdinand IV of Naples (1768), Ferdinand of Parma (1769), and the future Louis XVI of France (1770). In 1771 the empress fortified the dynasty's position in Italy still further by marrying her third eldest son, Ferdinand, to the heiress of the duke of Modena; when Ferdinand's son succeeded as duke in 1814 it was the first time in nearly three centuries that an Austrian Habsburg had inherited a foreign crown. In the meantime, frequent family conferences and Maria Theresa's voluminous, weekly correspondence with each of her dynastic surrogates ensured that the monarchy enjoyed considerable leverage wherever a Habsburg or Bourbon sat on the throne.

With the monarchy's western and southern frontiers thus secured, foreign policy during the co-regency focused on maintaining or improving the balance of power to the north and east *vis-à-vis* its Prussian adversary – and its former Russian ally. Ever since Peter the Great's victory over the Swedes at Poltava (1709) the monarchy's policy-makers had realized that Russian expansion might someday eclipse the fading Swedish and Turkish threats. Only Russia's eagerness to cooperate in Turkish and Polish affairs had assuaged those fears. All that had changed with Catherine II. The tsarina not only accepted Prussia's emergence as a third great power in eastern Europe, but decided to exploit the Austro-Prussian rivalry to achieve her own aggressive designs. Just one year after the end of the war she induced Frederick II to support her lover Stanislaus Poniatowski's election as king of Poland. By 1767 Catherine's progressive interference in the kingdom's affairs had led to a civil war in Poland, followed one year later by a Turkish declaration of war.

Vienna now saw Catherinian Russia as a loose cannon that might destroy its protective bastions in Poland and the Balkans. With Catherine's armies advancing deep into Turkish territory, Joseph and Kaunitz even entertained the notion of forming an unprecedented Austro-Prussian-Ottoman coalition against her. Both men met with Frederick II in a futile attempt to present a united front against Russian expansion. At their behest, Maria Theresa actually concluded an agreement with the Turks in 1771, by which she undertook to limit Russian territorial gains in exchange for the return of Little Wallachia to Habsburg rule. To overcome Austrian opposition, Catherine ultimately accepted Frederick II's proposal that Russia satisfy its territorial expectations at least partly at the expense of Poland; to counter-balance Russian inroads there, Prussia and Austria would also be compensated with Polish territory.

Maria Theresa's sense of justice initially inclined her to reject a plan that would victimize the totally innocent Poles. Only after it became clear that Frederick and Catherine were going to partition Poland with or without Austrian participation did she agree to accept territorial compensation. Even then she tried in vain to pressure Frederick into ceding part of Silesia, to which she felt the monarchy still had a legal right. She protested to her ministers that the impending partition was a "violation of every standard of sanctity and justice" and later told her son that it had taken ten years off her life. The thought of despoiling the Poles even brought her to tears. Yet, in the words of Frederick II, "the more she cried, the more she took." Not only did the partition help to limit Russia's march into the Balkans, it also rewarded the monarchy with Polish Galicia, which was easily the most valuable territorial award of the First Partition of Poland (1772). With 2.6 million people, Galicia was more populous than the combined acquisitions of Prussia and Russia. Nor was it the monarchy's only territorial gain. Following the Russo-Turkish peace of Kuchuk-Kainarji (1774), Joseph II enforced the monarchy's claim to compensation from the Turks. Instead of annexing Little Wallachia he chose the Bukovina, a small but strategic territory that enhanced communication between Hungary and the new Habsburg kingdom of Galicia. (see Map 4)

Admittedly, neither territory was a Slavic Silesia. Although they contained valuable minerals and rich farmland, both were extremely backward. Moreover, Galicia's wealth lay firmly in the hands of an oppressive nobility that had long since seized all of the Polish crown's domains and mines, and raised *robot* service to a crushing five days per week. Despite Roman or Greek Catholic majorities, both Galicia and the Bukovina contained sizeable Orthodox populations. To the empress's horror, Galicia's 225,000 mostly impoverished Jews more than doubled the monarchy's Jewish population; even Joseph remarked that the capital of Lemberg (Lvov) was a "new Jerusalem" whose 14,000-strong Jewish community was twice the size of Prague's and larger than the entire Jewish population of the Austrian lands. Nevertheless, the two new crownlands represented the monarchy's first net territorial gains in over half a century and provided a valuable buffer against Russia's westward advance. With the issuance of a new *Robotpatent* (1774) and the dispatch of large numbers of principally Czech-speaking officials, Galicia was gradually introduced to the benefits of the central European bureaucratic state.

Having successfully maintained the balance of power in the East, Joseph and Kaunitz were soon emboldened to strengthen the monarchy's position *vis-à-vis* Prussia within Germany. The occasion was the death of the childless Bavarian Elector Maximilian III Joseph on 30 December 1777. His cousin and successor, the Elector Palatine Charles Theodore (1742–99) had little desire to move his court from Mannheim to Munich, especially since he too had no legitimate sons to whom he could bequeath Bavaria. Even before Maximilian's death, Charles Theodore had offered to exchange his prospective inheritance for the much closer Austrian Netherlands. The

Habsburgs had also previously contemplated the strategic advantages of acquiring Bavaria, especially after its occupation by Austrian troops during the Wars of Spanish and Austrian Succession. At the end of the Seven Years' War Kaunitz had proposed a Bavarian–Belgian exchange as a way of compensating for the monarchy's failure to regain Silesia. With Maximilian's death Joseph argued that he could simply seize Bavaria as an escheated fief without compensating Charles Theodore in the Netherlands. Yet the empress decided that Kaunitz's plan for a formal exchange would be much less controversial and more likely to succeed without war. On 16 January the first Austrian troops entered the electorate, immediately after the chancellor's conclusion of a provisional accord with Charles Theodore.

Once again the monarchy held Bavaria within its grasp, this time with the approval of its legitimate ruler and the likelihood that it would become an integral part of the Habsburg monarchy. Unfortunately, Kaunitz's and Joseph's overconfidence now led them into a series of blunders. First, Kaunitz rejected reasonable Prussian demands that it be compensated with the eventual acquisition of the Hohenzollern duchies of Ansbach and Bayreuth; he then refused to take Frederick II's threats of armed intervention seriously, even after the king had ordered a general mobilization. Meanwhile, Joseph alienated his new subjects with his arrogance, as he did Charles Theodore by refusing to cede more than part of the Low Countries. By June 1778 Frederick had decided to intervene, ostensibly as the champion of the next Wittelsbach heir, Duke Charles of Zweibrücken. As he had so many times in the past, he made his point by entering Bohemia at the head of a Prussian army. This time Maria Theresa was ready for him. Despite months of maneuvering he failed to force his way past a 160,000-man Austrian field army, competently directed by Lacy, Laudon, and Joseph himself. Unable to enter the Bohemian plain, Frederick was forced to winter his forces in the Sudeten Mountains, where supply problems soon reduced both sides to fighting over frozen patches of potatoes.

By now, however, Maria Theresa was eager to end the so-called Potato War. She promptly accepted a Franco-Russian offer of mediation and concluded peace terms without even consulting her son. In the treaty of Teschen (13 May 1779) she relinquished all of Bavaria, except the right bank of the Inn River valley; she even recognized Frederick's eventual succession in Ansbach and Bayreuth, a concession that would have enabled the monarchy to keep all of Bavaria had it been granted one year earlier. Nevertheless, the empress now marked the conclusion of peace by holding a thanksgiving service at Vienna's St. Stephen's cathedral. She certainly was not celebrating the acquisition of the *Innviertel*, whose 100,000 inhabitants and 500,000 fl. in annual revenue were hardly worth the 100,000,000 fl. that the war had cost.

It is not difficult to appreciate Maria Theresa's decision to relinquish Bavaria. As in 1763, neither she nor Kaunitz wanted to fight Frederick II alone. If anything, the monarchy was more isolated now than it had been at the end of the Seven Years' War. Although the other great powers were officially neutral, none wanted to see the monarchy expand its frontiers. Even France secretly worked against its Austrian ally, despite public affirmations of support. Most of the German states also stood in opposition, Saxony to the point of assisting Prussia militarily. Yet, it is also possible that the empress could have succeeded in her long quest to redress the balance of power within Germany. Over the past four decades she had painstakingly built up the monarchy to the point where it could do so by making war on its own. Notwithstanding the crushing financial burden that it placed on the *Hofkammer*, the *Hofkriegsrat* was actually able to increase the army to the previously unthinkable level of 378,000 men for the 1779 campaign. And, like Prussia's army during the Silesian wars, it needed only to hold onto what it already possessed.

Joseph II and enlightened absolutism (1780–90)

The treaty of Teschen represented the latest, but also the last major humiliation that Joseph suffered at his mother's hands. Her death eighteen months later left him as sole ruler of the monarchy. Over the next nine years Joseph II put his stamp on it with an unprecedented barrage of domestic initiatives. Great reformer that she was, Maria Theresa had issued about 100 edicts per year during the co-regency; Joseph II now produced nearly 700 a year, or almost two a day. To some extent this flurry of activity stemmed from the emperor's pent up frustration after fifteen years as a figurehead co-regent; many of his reforms did, in fact, deal with residual problems that the empress had refused to confront. Several also reflected his desire to introduce Enlightenment ideas. Most notably, he embraced the utilitarian concept first expressed by Beccaria that the primary objective of government was to secure the welfare and happiness of the "greatest possible number" of its people. Yet Joseph II was not so much a "sorcerer's apprentice of the French *philosophes*" as he was a statebuilder bent on employing the often parallel strategies of the German cameralists. True to his central European pedigree, he was convinced not only that the state had a responsibility to help the people, but that the people had a reciprocal obligation to serve the state.

One thing that distinguished Joseph II from his predecessors was his compulsion for thoroughness. Previous Habsburgs had frequently resorted to half measures, and then only when they sensed that the monarchy's survival depended on it. By contrast, Joseph rarely distinguished between what was absolutely necessary and what was simply ideal. His aggressiveness went well beyond the pale of consensus politics that had heretofore characterized the relationship between the dynasty and the rest of the ruling elite: the nobility and church might agree to make sacrifices if they were crucial for the monarchy's survival, but not if they merely intended to make it stronger. To his credit, Joseph usually consulted his ministers and provincial officials before initiating major reforms. But he was not perturbed by the absence of a consensus. Nor was he deterred by any corporate constitutional powers, which he dismissed as mere instruments of privilege.

If anything, conservative opposition aroused yet another distinctive Josephine trait, namely, his spiteful penchant for humiliating anyone who disagreed with him. The gratuitous hostility that often filled his remarks and directives also contrasted sharply with the measured responses of previous rulers. Yet the extraordinary domestic stability and powerful army that Joseph had inherited from his mother afforded him the luxury of dispensing with the "Austrian Clemency" of previous, weaker regimes. No less important was Joseph's conclusion of an alliance with Catherine II in May 1781, just five months after his succession as sole ruler. Immediately thereafter he visited Louis XVI in Paris to repair the breach caused by the Bavarian conflict. Fortified in the West by France and the East by Russia, Joseph had ample reason to feel invulnerable to opposition both at home and abroad.

The first reforms

In addition to visiting Paris, Joseph spent much of 1781 on a whirlwind tour of his dominions, including his first trip ever to the Austrian Netherlands. His travels did not, however, deter him from initiating a number of major reforms during his first full year as sole ruler. He wasted no time in easing restrictions on freedom of expression. In February he sharply curtailed literary censorship. Publications could still be banned if they blasphemed the Catholic religion, subverted the government, or promoted superstition or immorality. But by centralizing censorship in the hands of Gerhard van Swieten's son, Gottfried (1733–1803), the emperor guaranteed an unparalleled degree of intellectual freedom. In fact, the *Theresianum*-educated Swieten was himself a former Berlin literary agent with a well-developed taste for erotic literature and major French *philosophes* like Voltaire. Despite a virtual flood of new publications, his commission quickly reduced the number of prohibited titles from well over 4,000 to about 900 a year. At Joseph's insistence it even permitted personal criticism of the emperor himself, including one scurrilous attack, entitled "The 42-Year-Old Ape." Joseph is reputed to have justified its publication with the retort that he would allow anyone to *say* whatever he pleased – so long as he was free to *do* whatever he pleased.

Joseph was also ready to expand toleration for the monarchy's religious minorities. In May he broadened educational and vocational opportunities for the Jews. In October he began issuing patents for each of his dominions that also eliminated a number of other humiliating restrictions. Most notably, the Jews were no longer compelled to wear distinctive dress (or have beards), to stay indoors on Sunday mornings, or pay the infamous *Leibmaut*, a tax that was levied only on Jews and cattle. October also witnessed Joseph's proclamation of the Edict of Toleration for his Protestant and Orthodox subjects. Private worship was now granted them everywhere in the monarchy, as was permission to build churches and parochial schools in communities of at least one hundred families. Both Christian minorities were also permitted to buy and sell land, attend a university, join a guild, or enter the civil service.

Joseph had taken a major step toward giving his subjects a higher degree of literary and religious freedom than anywhere else in Catholic Europe. Yet he encountered opposition at virtually every level of society. The Edict of Toleration was so unpopular among Roman Catholics that provincial officials left their own names off the posted proclamations. Meanwhile, Christians of all persuasions derided Joseph as "emperor of the Jews." Despite his earlier support for educational and clerical reform, Archbishop Migazzi denounced the edicts, while many lesser churchmen and civil officials tried to sabotage them at the local level. Early in 1782 Pope Pius VI expressed his concern by visiting Vienna and meeting with Joseph and Kaunitz. Joseph proved a gracious host and made some minor concessions on religious toleration. He was, however, less flexible on other issues. Just before the pope's visit he had begun to suppress all contemplative monastic orders, preserving only those foundations that performed useful functions like farming, teaching, and charity work. Over the next five years he seized 738 of the monarchy's 2,047 abbeys, including 55 percent of those in the *Erblande* and a staggering 75 percent of those in Hungary; 27,000 out of a total of 65,000 monks and nuns were now obliged to choose between a more productive career or retirement on a government pension.

In seizing a third of the monarchy's monasteries, Joseph was merely continuing his mother's policy of converting non-productive religious activities and church wealth to more useful economic purposes. Much more original and radical was Joseph's decision to assert his control over the church hierarchy itself, with the intention of guiding its use of teaching and pastoral activities. The emperor was largely influenced by a sincere desire to improve the quality of religious instruction, perhaps with an eye toward countering the appeal of Protestantism. Yet what has come to be known as "Josephinism" (or "Josephism") was an inevitable step in the state-building process. During the Counter-Reformation the Habsburgs had given the church a free hand in its use of media, because their work reinforced its drive for a culturally uniform and politically loyal society. A century later the more rigorous demands of state-building required a more rational and secular society. Since the church was unlikely to accept such a change in direction, state control became necessary in order to continue to use the church as an instrument of social control.

State control began at the top of the church hierarchy. Beginning in 1781 all bishops were required to give an oath of allegiance to the crown; those bishops who resided outside the monarchy were deprived of any diocesan jurisdiction within its borders. The pope himself was forbidden to issue bulls or even to communicate with the monarchy's churchmen without first submitting all documents for prior clearance. He even lost control over the remaining monasteries, which were now placed under the authority of the nearest bishop. Yet Josephinism also extended to the local level to the point of defining – and generally improving – the contact between priests and parishioners. Beginning in 1782 parish boundaries were radically redrawn in order to place people as close as possible to the nearest available church. Using the proceeds from the monasteries it had seized, the state assumed responsibility for all clerical salaries. Although high churchmen suffered a slight reduction in their princely salaries, common priests were paid far better and more regularly.

They also got a better education. In March 1783 Joseph decreed that all novices receive six years of instruction at one of half a dozen specially created general seminaries. To be sure the new curriculum emphasized religion and morality, but it also attempted to combat superstition by teaching math, natural sciences, and history, and even offered practical courses on agricultural and teaching techniques. When budgetary and enrollment pressures forced Joseph to shorten the curriculum to just four years, it was theological instruction in dogma, polemics, and the Bible that were eliminated. Indeed, Joseph's commitment to secularization extended beyond religious instruction to the sacrament of marriage, which now became a civil contract that could be entered into without the services of a clergyman; even the grounds for divorce were expanded to include impotence, adultery, criminal conviction, and desertion.

The professionalization of the clergy was actually preceded by a parallel reform of the judiciary. A September 1781 decree required that all judges and lawyers receive extensive legal training and pass rigorous qualifying examinations. Judges were also given much higher salaries, thereby reducing the temptation to accept bribes. By 1787 Joseph had completed the transition to a modern judicial system by issuing a new criminal code. The so-called *Allgemeines Gesetzbuch* upheld for the first time the Enlightenment concept of equality before the law; in practice noble-born offenders actually suffered stiffer penalties on the grounds that their wealth and upbringing gave them less excuse to break the law. The new code also eliminated the barbaric vestiges of the *Nemesis Theresiana*. Suspects could no longer be tortured, or even threatened with physical punishment. Although whipping and branding were still assessed in exceptional circumstances, punishment of convicts was generally limited to imprisonment. Similarly, capital punishment was retained for its deterrent value, but was assessed only for the most gruesome crimes. Thus only one convict was executed within the Austrian lands during Joseph's reign, while the emperor actually removed a Hungarian judge who persisted in executing criminals.

The judicial reforms afforded special attention to the peasants, as befitted the indispensable role they played in producing taxable wealth. A 1 September 1781 patent awarded them free legal aid in any litigation against their lords; by contrast landlords had to bear their own expenses, as well as the costs of legal aid if the peasant won the case. The establishment of professional standards had the additional effect of excluding the seigneur from presiding over the manorial court except in the rare instances when he held the proper credentials. Even when they decided against the peasant, the 1781 patent prohibited manorial courts from levying fines or jail terms in excess of eight days, without review by crown officials.

The most important peasant legislation came exactly two months later, in the form of two patents issued on 1 November 1781. One was the so-called Emancipation Patent, which abolished serfdom in the Bohemian lands. It essentially awarded Bohemia's peasants the same rights already enjoyed by their countrymen in the Austrian archduchies: they could now leave the manor, buy and sell land, marry, or begin a new trade simply by notifying their landlord. The patent's extension to Inner Austria and Galicia (April–July 1782) left Hungary as the only Habsburg crownland where serfdom still existed. On the same day that he emancipated Bohemia's peasants, Joseph issued a Land Purchase Patent that gave the monarchy's peasants the right to secure hereditary tenure over the land they worked. Many a peasant had, in fact, already purchased this security from his landlord, only to be evicted anyway. The patent not only reaffirmed the tenure of such "bought-in" peasants, but gave anyone the right to buy-in for a modest price. Henceforth, landlords could evict only those peasants who were severely in debt – and then only with the permission of crown officials.

With the patents of 1781 Joseph took a decisive step toward establishing the economic freedom and security of the monarchy's peasants. Yet they represented only the first steps of the emperor's agrarian program. With the success of the Raab System it was only a matter of time before Joseph moved against *robot* service outside the crown's own domain lands. That time came with the Directive Regulation of March 1783. The monarchy's peasants were now given the option of commuting *robot* service in the fields by paying the landlord a regular sum in cash or crops. Having lost their captive work force, landlords were now directed to apportion their demesne land among their peasant tenants, who could work it in exchange for a freely negotiated wage. Although peasants still performed other, relatively minor forms of obligatory service, the 1783 Directive eliminated compulsory fieldwork in every dominion except Galicia. Although Joseph opted not to confront his Polish nobles on this issue, he did issue a new patent one year later that reduced *robot* service in Galicia from five to three days per week.

The elimination of field *robot* proved a troublesome task. To no one's surprise, some landlords protested that the commutation fees were set too low. At the same time, however, many peasants suddenly stopped performing other forms of obligatory service because they were convinced that Joseph would soon eliminate them as well. There were also problems in administering the reform. To the peasants' dismay Raab's successor, Count Johann Paul von Hoyer, responded to pressure from the nobility by granting less favorable terms than those in effect on the crown's domains. Thus, he raised commutation fees, reduced the length of contracts to only three to six years, and restricted peasant access to those farm buildings and equipment that were located on former demesne land. Joseph finally replaced Hoyer in February 1785, in response to mounting peasant unrest and the insistence of his own ministers and local officials.

By then, however, an additional crisis had surfaced in Transylvania. In October 1784, as many as 30,000 peasants rose in rebellion. They raised the usual demands: the abolition of serfdom, a reduction in manorial burdens, and the redistribution of noble land among peasants. Yet, whereas they killed hundreds of nobles, the peasants were hardly in revolt against the crown. Their leader, Vasile Nicula Horia, had already visited Vienna three times, where he had sensed Joseph's genuine concern and commitment for the peasants' welfare. Hence he and his followers genuinely believed that they were merely carrying out the emperor's instructions against the nobility. Nor was Joseph eager to use force. Much as Maria Theresa had done in 1775, he attempted to resolve matters with a minimum of violence, to the point of having Orthodox priests accompany his troops as they marched through the countryside. Once Horia realized his error, he disbanded his forces. That did not save him or the other ringleaders, whom Joseph ordered broken on the rack, then drawn and quartered. The emperor did, however, appoint a special commission to investigate the peasantry's grievances. On 22 August 1785 a new *urbarium* addressed their needs by abolishing serfdom throughout the Hungarian crownlands.

The collapse of consensual politics

It is fair to say that the opening years of Joseph's reign had been a *tour de force*. Not only had he accomplished a great deal, but he had enlisted the support of the great majority of his subjects. The monarchy's unprivileged elements had every reason to agree with Sonnenfels, who happily informed his students that all of Joseph's subjects were now "citizens." Indeed, the emperor had also captured the imagination of the monarchy's intellectual elite of academic and civil officials, regardless of social rank. Of course not everyone was pleased with everything that he had done. Religious toleration and the establishment of a state church rankled many Catholic clergy and laymen alike, while the elimination of serfdom and field *robot* worried the landed nobility. Yet public criticism and passive resistance only encouraged the emperor to intensify his relentless quest for a more perfect state.

Ever since the Rákóczi Revolt (1703–11), every attempt at administrative reform had stopped short of threatening the regional autonomy and diversity of the various Habsburg lands. Nowhere had this been more true than in Hungary. Despite the Magyar nobility's refusal to grant her fiscal requests, Maria Theresa had gone out of her way to disarm their lingering distrust by pandering to their personal ego and national pride. During the last half of her reign she had named several magnates to high military, diplomatic, and court positions, while creating a Royal Hungarian Bodyguard (1760) and Order of St. Stephen (1764) for the sole purpose of honoring individual Magyar nobles. She had even appealed to the diet's political sensibilities by placing Croatia's officials under Hungarian administrative oversight and by surrendering both Fiume (1776) and the Banat (1778) to direct Hungarian control. This policy of *douce violence* had, in fact, created considerable goodwill between the Magyar nation and its "benevolent queen."

Nor had Joseph damaged his own stock within Hungary when he reincorporated Transylvania into Hungary and transferred the royal capital from Pressburg to Buda in 1784. Both moves were, however, merely administrative efficiencies. By then he was ready to undertake radical administrative and agrarian reforms that all but destroyed the consensus and mutual trust that had heretofore existed within the monarchy's ruling elite. In 1784 he announced that German would be the official language for all government business within the monarchy's core lands. He gave civil servants up to three years to learn the language or lose their jobs. To facilitate the transition, German became the principal language of instruction at both the secondary and university level, as well as in the newly created general seminaries. At the same time Joseph began to draft wholly new administrative districts outside the *Erblande*. Once again efficiency was a factor, but even more important was his desire to circumvent those provincial authorities that had long used their position to block the crown's domestic initiatives. He turned first to Transylvania, where the privileged Saxon estates had successfully resisted his attempt to extend civil equality to the Romanian Orthodox peasantry. In July 1784 he abolished the special status of

Transylvania's three privileged nations and the counties that represented them in the diet. In their place he created eleven new administrative districts whose borders cut across existing ethnic boundaries. One year later he replaced Croatia's and central Hungary's counties, together with the elected officials who ran them. In their stead he created ten roughly equal administrative districts, each headed by a royally appointed commissar. Nor did Joseph have any use for Hungary's parliamentary bodies. Although his mother had already reduced the Croatian *Sabor* to little more than a ceremonial body, he disbanded it in 1785. Meanwhile he never convened the Hungarian diet, despite the Magyar nobility's appeals for a coronation diet and the confirmation of their constitutional liberties.

A similar fate awaited the monarchy's Italian and Belgian lands. In 1786 Joseph abolished Milan's council of state and senate, together with its numerous municipal privileges. In their place he created a unified Lombard administration for Milan and Mantua. At its head stood an all-powerful governing council that directed eight, newly created administrative districts, each of which was run by a crown-appointed commissar. Joseph completed his administrative coup in January 1787 by replacing the Low Countries' historic provinces with a system of nine districts, each of which was headed by an intendant and subdivided into smaller units run by royal commissars. He also deprived the estates and municipalities of their extensive legislative power, while compelling them to register all imperial edicts. Joseph's drive for conformity also included the introduction of conscription in the Netherlands, as well as the Tyrol, despite the latter's historic exemption from military service.

Whereas administrative restructuring deprived the nobility of its political power, the emperor's new agrarian initiatives promised to destroy its economic well-being. The physiocrats had long argued that, since agriculture was the sole source of a nation's wealth, governments should base all of their revenue on a single, uniformly assessed tax on arable land. Joseph had resolved to do just that. In 1784 he ordered a new cadaster of all of the monarchy's arable land, with the intention of making it the basis for future taxation. The earlier commutation of field *robot* had reduced the need to distinguish between rustical and dominical land, especially since Joseph intended to tax both at the same rate. Nevertheless the new cadaster proved an enormously difficult and time-consuming task. Although he compensated for the lack of experienced surveyors by employing army engineers and even peasants, the job dragged on through the end of the decade.

By then Joseph had issued another, even bolder edict. The Tax and Agrarian Regulation of 10 February 1789 decreed that, with the implementation of the new cadaster, peasants who farmed rustical land would pay no more than 30 percent of their income in taxes, including 12 percent to the state and a total of 18 percent to the landlord, church, and community. This was a major windfall for those who were covered by the edict, since the typical peasant devoted over 70 percent of his crops to taxes. It also represented a significant sacrifice for those who had previously lived off their labor. Although the *Erblande*'s peasantry had heretofore paid 42 percent of its income in state taxes, Joseph expected to make up most of the shortfall by taxing previously unsurveyed plots and by collecting higher levies from outside the hereditary lands. Of course landlords had less reason for optimism. Although rustical peasants were few in number in the Bohemian and Hungarian lands (only 20 percent in Bohemia proper), many landlords sensed that Joseph would later extend the Regulation to dominical peasants. If that ever happened, estate incomes would be cut in half.

In fact, the Regulation represented a significant departure from past initiatives. Like his mother and so many enlightened monarchs elsewhere, Joseph had heretofore endeavored to protect all of his subjects from the ill effects of his reforms, including privileged groups like the nobility, clergy, and Catholic laity. Even when he abolished serfdom and commuted field *robot*, Joseph had expected that landlords would be amply compensated by the higher productivity of a free and happier peasantry. Now several of his ministers objected to the Regulation because it expropriated the landlords' property rights without offering any hope of adequate compensation. One of Joseph's most strident critics was Karl von Zinzendorf, the president of the Tax Regulation Court Commission that was responsible for devising the new tax scheme. The stinging memorandum that he submitted in February 1788 not only spoke of the landlord's property rights but accused the emperor of acting too hastily in implementing the project before various problems could be ironed out. Although Joseph immediately removed Zinzendorf, the Austro-Bohemian Chancellor Chotek continued the fight until 5 February 1789, when he resigned rather than sign the Regulation into law. With its proclamation the scene shifted from Vienna to the countryside. The outcry was loudest in Galicia and Hungary, where the nobility stood to lose the most from a cap on manorial fees. Meanwhile the peasants did not help their case by withholding all tax payments for several months, because they were convinced that further reductions were on the way. The emperor finally agreed to delay implementing the regulation until the end of 1790, partly because the new cadaster was not likely to be completed much before then.

This briefly quieted noble opposition within most of the hereditary lands. But it did little to appease the ruling elite in peripheral dominions like the Tyrol, Lombardy, and Belgium. Here the burning issue was not peasant taxes but the restoration of political autonomy. Joseph's most recent administrative changes had greatly reduced the number of paid government officials, together with the formidable power they wielded. They had also exposed him as a foreign despot, who acted arbitrarily without even consulting his own officials. Already in 1785 Pietro Verri had protested Joseph's disdain for Milan's separate identity by retiring from public service. Farther north Tyrolean officials pressed for the restoration of the county's traditional exemption from compulsory military service. True to their long tradition of unconditional loyalty to the dynasty, the Milanese patriciate and Tyrolean regime contented themselves with muted expressions of concern. The Austrian Netherlands was rather less restrained. By 1787 an alliance of clerics, nobles, and burghers had launched a massive display of civil disobedience. Seminary students demonstrated against the introduction of state-run General Seminaries. The estates of Brabant refused to pay taxes. Pamphleteers compared Joseph with ageless tyrants like Attila and Nero, as well as their old nemesis, the duke of Alba. Although Joseph's representatives initially gave in to the malcontents' demands, the dispatch of reinforcements permitted him to restore order and withdraw all the concessions that they had made. Yet many opposition leaders simply took refuge in the nearby bishopric of Liège, where they began to organize an armed insurrection.

The situation was just as explosive in Hungary, the one crownland where both tax reform and political autonomy were compelling issues. The Magyars were the one ethnic group within the core lands that seriously objected to the imposition of German as the official language of administration. Although they accepted Joseph's argument that Latin was a dead language, they now insisted that it be replaced by Magyar, rather than German. Taken together with the abolition of the kingdom's traditional governmental institutions, they charged Joseph with launching a systematic program of Germanization that would ultimately destroy them as a nation. In response the Magyar nobility quickly revived their county assemblies for the purpose of joining Belgium in an armed rebellion against Habsburg rule.

By themselves neither the Belgian revolt nor the budding Magyar conspiracy represented an insurmountable threat, especially given the imposing size of the Austrian army. As in the past, only foreign intervention on their behalf could threaten the monarchy's constitutional and territorial integrity. Yet Joseph's aggressive foreign policy had also exposed it to outside intervention. As with his domestic policy, the emperor committed his first missteps at mid-reign. Toward the end of 1784 he attempted to eliminate the remaining extraterritorial rights that the Dutch enjoyed in the Austrian Netherlands. He easily secured their withdrawal from the Barrier fortresses, which had become an anachronism in the aftermath of the Austro-French alliance. The Dutch stood firm, however, when he threatened war if they did not end their 200-year blockade of the Scheldt estuary and the once great port of Antwerp. By the treaty of Fontainbleau (November 1785) the Dutch paid Joseph an indemnity of 10 million fl., but the Scheldt remained closed.

Having failed to liberate Belgium's commercial lifeline, Joseph then made a second attempt to trade the Austrian Netherlands for Bavaria. During 1785 he enlisted Elector Charles Theodore by promising him all of the territory except Luxemburg, which he offered to France in return for its diplomatic support. In addition Joseph pledged to raise the elector to the sovereign rank of king of Burgundy, a title that he hoped would also induce the support of Charles Theodore's troublesome heir presumptive, Duke Charles August of Zweibrücken. The whole project fell apart, however, when Joseph reneged on his promise to give Luxemburg to the French, who promptly withdrew their support and informed Prussia of the project. Frederick then used this new evidence to convince the leading German princes that Joseph posed a threat to the empire's territorial integrity. By July 1785 he had joined Hanover and Saxony in a League of Princes (*Fürstenbund*) dedicated to protecting the German states against the emperor's designs. Within a year the league had eighteen members, including Zweibrücken and the Catholic archbishop-elector of Mainz.

With these two projects Joseph had acquired the unenviable reputation of an habitual expansionist – and an ineffectual one at that. As a result Prussia not only was motivated to oppose Joseph's every move but could be certain of finding allies who felt that it was both necessary and possible to frustrate his plans for expansion. It was Joseph's misfortune that he was now perceived as an aggressor even where he had no aggressive intent. In August 1787 the Ottoman empire declared war on the monarchy's Russian ally. Although the Russian alliance represented a formidable weapon against the Turks, Joseph had little interest in acquiring their sparsely populated, disease-ridden dominions. He preferred instead to use the alliance to control Catherine the Great's advance into the Balkans, as well as to help deter another Prussian invasion. Yet, as in 1737, the Ottoman attack compelled him to go to war in the Balkans, despite the widespread domestic unrest within his dominions.

Although Frederick II had recently died, his successor Frederick William II (1786–97) did everything in his power to turn the conflict into a nightmare. First he induced Sweden to invade Russia from Finland, thereby preventing Catherine's main field army from assisting her ally in the Balkans. With over 200,000 of the monarchy's 350,000-man army at his disposal, Field Marshal Lacy had the tools to face the Turks alone. Yet, like Daun before him, Lacy was a good administrator but irresolute commander. During 1788 his failure to prevent the Turks from invading the Banat prompted Joseph to assume personal command of the army. Perhaps the emperor hoped to win for himself the epithet "the Great" that military conquests had bestowed on Frederick and Catherine. Instead, the marshy terrain of the lower Danube immobilized the army with dysentery, typhus, and malaria, while ruining the emperor's health. In his weakened state Joseph soon contracted tuberculosis, which compelled him to return to Vienna.

His departure left the army in the hands of the gifted Field Marshal Laudon. During the course of 1789 Laudon captured both Bosnia and Serbia, including Belgrade, while a separate force occupied most of Moldavia. At the same time, a Russo-Austrian army under Marshal Suvorov conquered Wallachia and its capital of Bucharest. So rapid was the allied advance that Kaunitz now pressed Joseph to consider partitioning the Balkans with Russia, even though it meant replacing the Turks with a much more powerful neighbor. They need not have worried. With the Austrian army tied down in the Balkans, Frederick William now seized the opportunity to destroy his Habsburg adversary once and for all. At the beginning of 1790 he concluded an offensive alliance with the Sultan; with the spring thaw a Prussian army would invade Bohemia. Even before concluding the alliance he sent money and *agents provocateurs* to stir up trouble in Hungary and the Low Countries. Confident of Prussian help, many Magyar nobles began calling for a diet to dethrone the Habsburgs; Frederick William even suggested replacing them with the pro-Prussian duke of Saxe-Weimar. At the same time, the Belgian exiles in Liège re-entered the Austrian Netherlands at the head of a small army. By the end of 1789 they had expelled all Austrian forces from the western half of the country. Although Luxemburg remained under Habsburg control, the other estates now declared their independence as the *États belgiques unis*.

The emperor reacted to the first reports of trouble with a mixture of incredulity and determination. He could not understand how his subjects could oppose reforms that were expressly designed for their benefit. At the heart of his incomprehension was his inability to appreciate how people could prefer traditional ways over what was rational. Nor was he willing to tolerate such unreasonable behavior. At the end of 1787 the Belgian revolt prompted him to reimpose political censorship throughout the monarchy. Soon thereafter the public hangman was conducting book burnings in Brussels's main square. In May 1789 the emperor imposed a duty on all periodicals in order to limit the number and influence of his critics. Two months later he closed down one Viennese newspaper that had been particularly hostile. Joseph also gave considerable latitude to the industrious Count Pergen, who distinguished himself as secret police chief by spying on private citizens and feeding him weekly reports on the public mood.

Yet none of these measures addressed the underlying causes of political unrest. By years' end the rush of developments in Belgium and Hungary, as well as his rapidly failing health, inclined him to reconsider his course. To his brother and heir, Leopold, he confessed that "I am unfortunate in everything I undertake . . . I no longer dare to have an opinion and put it into effect." He began modestly enough by announcing that he would convene the Hungarian diet for the purpose of hearing its grievances and being formally crowned; in the interim he promised to adhere to the kingdom's constitution. Yet once he had learned of the impending Prussian attack, Joseph's retreat became a rout. At the end of January he revoked his administrative reforms, thereby ending his crusade to convert the monarchy into a highly centralized *Beamtenstaat*. He also restored the Croatian *Sabor* and ordered the crown of St. Stephen returned to Buda after an absence of two and a half centuries. Meanwhile, to avoid a two-front war he resolved to seek an accommodation with the sultan and king of Prussia. Three weeks later death deprived Joseph of the opportunity to make further amends. From his deathbed he composed his own epitaph, "Here lies Joseph II, who failed in everything he undertook."

Leopold II (1790–2)

The "revolutionary emperor" left his successor with a monumental task. Belgium had already severed all ties with the monarchy, with Hungary threatening to follow suit. There was also considerable unrest in the hereditary lands, thanks primarily to the higher taxes and prices caused by the Turkish war. With most of the army tied down in the Balkans, there was little prospect of frustrating the Prussians or the domestic insurrections they had helped inspire. Nor could the monarchy expect any assistance from its Russian and French allies. With a two-front war of her own in Finland and the Balkans, Catherine II was in no position to send additional forces to Germany. Meanwhile, Louis XVI had been totally immobilized by the outbreak of the French Revolution during the previous summer. Like Maria Theresa half a century earlier, Joseph's successor needed to move quickly and adeptly if he was to keep his inheritance intact.

Once again, however, the monarchy was saved by its rulers' ability to adapt to the situations that they inherited. Like his late brother, Leopold was a child of the Enlightenment. During his twenty-five-year reign as Tuscan Grand Duke Peter Leopold (1765–90) he had established an enviable record as an enlightened reformer. He was, however, more like his mother in his willingness to compromise and accept constitutional checks on royal authority. Recently he had even devised plans to grant his Tuscan subjects a constitution based on that of Pennsylvania that would have limited his own lawmaking powers. Perhaps most important, Leopold was an adept negotiator, with a devious talent for playing one side off against another. He now wasted no time in undoing the damage done by Joseph's more controversial initiatives. He abolished the Tax Regulation Court Commission (22 March), thereby removing the 30 percent cap on peasant taxes before it could be implemented. He also returned responsibility for raising and collecting of taxes to the estates. One week later he repealed military conscription in the Tyrol. He further mollified the Tyroleans and Catholic conservatives elsewhere by eliminating the general seminaries and even restoring a few monasteries. In May Leopold made his most important concession by giving landlords the right to refuse *robot* commutation; they and their peasants would now be left to negotiate (or refuse) contracts by mutual agreement, without the participation of government officials. Although Leopold urged the nobles to treat their subjects well, the decree guaranteed that they would once again enjoy an upper hand in dealing with their peasants. Except for its continuation of free legal aid, the crown now withdrew from the business of actively protecting the peasants to a more passive role of "refereeing" disputes that came to its attention.

Not surprisingly, the reinstatement of *robot* service was met by muted protests from enlightened officials and brief resistance from some peasants. Leopold's strategic retreat did, however, quickly reassure the monarchy's conservative and traditional elements. The resulting calm also gave him more room to maneuver in his negotiations with Frederick William II of Prussia. During March Leopold had informed the king of his willingness to renounce territorial gains in the Balkans. By July his diplomats had obtained at Reichenbach a Prussian pledge not to attack the monarchy or foment rebellion among his subjects. The convention also facilitated Leopold's election as Holy Roman emperor two months later. In exchange for these concessions, Leopold was obliged to conclude peace with the Turks on the basis of the *status quo ante bellum*. Although the peace talks dragged on for nearly a year, the resulting treaty of Sistova (August 1791) returned all of Laudon's conquests except for the Danube river town of Orsova and a 450-square-mile strip of mountainous terrain along the Bosnian–Croatian border.

The Reichenbach convention and the impending peace with the Ottoman empire left the emperor free to confront his rebellious Hungarian and Belgian subjects. He was also able to strengthen his hand further by skillfully exploiting tensions within each country. When he convened the Hungarian diet in September, he had no trouble reforging the dynasty's traditional alliance with the magnates, whose privileges were being challenged by the more numerous gentry. He also secured the support of the Serbs by convening the Orthodox National Church Council and admitting the first Orthodox clerics and nobles to the diet. In his greatest coup, Leopold persuaded the Croatian estates to merge with the Hungarian diet, a move that enhanced both parties' influence in the diet's deliberations. When the diet adjourned he had conceded little more than the restoration of the constitutional relationship that existed at the death of Maria Theresa.

Moreover, in appointing his son Alexander to fill the long-vacant post of palatine, Leopold not only appeased the diet but assured himself of the loyalty of the kingdom's highest official. He was no less successful in the Low Countries, where the country's clergy and nobility had fallen out with more democratic elements inspired by the French Revolution. By exploiting this rift and his own repudiation of Joseph's decrees, Leopold was able to re-establish his authority by the end of 1790 – just twelve months after the estates' independence declaration.

In less than a year Leopold had rescued the monarchy from the specter of yet another life struggle. The price had been high. Gone was the 30 percent tax ceiling for peasants, *robot* commutation, the general seminaries, and military conscription in the Tyrol and Belgium. The prospects of an extensive Balkan empire had also disappeared. Nevertheless, by his deft handling of the crisis the new emperor had also saved much of his brother's legacy. The peasants were now personally free; the clergy was more committed to serving its parishioners' needs; religious minorities enjoyed greater toleration; the educational system and censorship had been secularized; the law had become more just and humane. Moreover, thanks to Leopold's intervention, Joseph's stature would attain mythic proportions among future generations of civil officials, intellectuals, peasants, and persecuted national and religious minorities.

Nor did Leopold rest on these accomplishments. Once order had been restored, he revived a number of enlightened innovations. He lifted most of Joseph's restrictions on free speech, including the duty on newspapers. He also ordered Count Pergen to release the handful of political opponents whom the police had detained and admonished them to afford due process to anyone accused of criticizing or conspiring against the government. When Pergen resigned in protest, Leopold replaced him with Sonnenfels, who promptly expanded police responsibilities for providing social services, while resuming the lengthy task of legal codification. Leopold also actively courted the monarchy's underprivileged elements. He made significant overtures to Hungary's Protestants and Serbs, for whom he promptly established an Illyrian Chancery. He also promoted an increase in burgher representation in the Bohemian, Styrian, and Hungarian diets. He even planned to resume the process of commuting *robot* service on the nobles' demesne as soon as his position had become sufficiently secure. Like his brother, Leopold realized that each of these innovations would anger that combination of nobles and Catholics that comprised the bulk of the monarchy's ruling elite; unlike his brother, he had the political skill to mobilize the country's unprivileged majority to strengthen his hand in any future confrontation with them.

The Habsburg monarchy at the end of the Old Regime

In just two years Leopold II had preserved the greater part of Joseph's legacy, while averting the very real prospect of internal rebellion and foreign invasion. Having escaped catastrophe, the monarchy and its people were in a much stronger position than at any time in the past. Quite aside from the political achievements of the past half-century, they had attained other attributes of the major states and societies of western Europe.

The economy had grown considerably, thanks in no small part to the government's policies. Just as the numerous urbarial reforms had helped increase agricultural productivity, more conventional mercantile initiatives had had a positive impact on manufacturing and commerce. The monarchy's transportation network had improved steadily, as Maria Theresa and her son continued Charles VI's devotion to dredging rivers and building new roads. They also strengthened native industries by continuously raising barriers against foreign imports, most notably with a 1764 tariff imposed against Silesian goods and a truly comprehensive list of prohibitive duties established by Joseph in 1784. The domestic economy also benefited from the concurrent adoption of more liberal mercantile strategies that reflected the growing influence of Joseph, Kaunitz, and other ministers during the final decade of the co-regency. Their most dramatic success came in 1775, when Maria Theresa eliminated all internal tolls within the hereditary lands, except the Tyrol (which still relied on the transit trade between Italy and Germany). The empress did, however, achieve a closer commercial union with the Austrian Netherlands in 1777, albeit after nine years of negotiations. When Joseph integrated Galicia into the customs union in 1784, he created one of Europe's largest free trade zones.

Nor was the customs union the government's only step toward free enterprise. In 1776 it contemplated eliminating virtually all guild privileges. Although the empress was still reluctant to take such a dramatic step, Joseph II ended their exclusive privileges immediately after his succession. He even abolished some guilds outright and converted their property to public use. The empress and her son also pushed the monarchy's new industries to compete in a free market, with a minimum of government financial assistance. Business subsidies were reduced from a peak of 1 million fl. in 1770 to a mere 250,000 by 1786. Although both monarchs still exempted new enterprises from taxes during startup periods, Joseph afforded them only minor tax breaks thereafter and refused to take over troubled concerns.

This eclectic combination of protection and *laissez-faire* appears to have benefited the monarchy's industrial enterprises. In Bohemia and Moravia the number of workers involved in manufacturing nearly doubled to 750,000 in the fifteen years after the creation of the customs union; one in every six people in Greater Bohemia now worked at least part of the time for an industrial enterprise. The growth was even more rapid in Lower Austria, which quintupled its industrial workforce to nearly 100,000 in the first two decades after the Seven Years' War.

Although the *Erblande* was one of the continent's foremost iron producers and also exported glass, porcelain, and paper products, most of the growth in manufacturing was still concentrated in the textile industry. Indeed, the number of Bohemian and Moravian textile mills nearly quadrupled, from twenty-four to ninety-five, during the reigns of Joseph II and Leopold II. With over 10,000 workers, Linz possessed one of the continent's largest and most important wool factories. Lower Austria had become a major cotton producer; by 1790 a factory in Schwechat originally founded by Charles VI employed 3,306 workers. Even the Tyrolean town of Imst boasted a single concern with 7,000 wool and flax workers.

As usual Hungary remained the odd land out. After the Seven Years' War Maria Theresa rejected the advice of some of her liberal advisors, who urged her to promote new industries there, so long as they did not compete directly with those of the *Erblande*. She justified her position by arguing that industrial development would only benefit the same aristocrats who had defeated her request for a substantially higher Contribution in the 1764 diet. Hence, she excluded the kingdom from the Court Commercial Council that had been founded in 1762. She also refused to countenance a customs union with the other core lands, arguing that import and export duties were the only way she could legally compel the Hungarians to bear a more equitable share of the monarchy's taxes; it also made no fiscal sense to permit the lightly taxed Hungarians to develop industries that might undercut Austrian producers who were providing the *Hofkammer* with vital revenue. The hereditary lands' own manufacturers were, in fact, the primary beneficiaries. The customs union of 1775 not only protected their industries from Hungarian competition, but also lowered the tariff on their Hungarian exports to a maximum of 5 percent; at the same time, prohibitive export tariffs deprived the kingdom's grain, wine, and livestock producers of their traditional markets in Venice, Poland, Saxony, and Prussian Silesia, thereby compelling it to deliver its foodstuffs to the *Erblande*. Indeed, by 1790, 87 percent of Hungarian exports and 85 percent of its imports were with the Austrian and Bohemian crownlands.

By contrast the *Erblande* enjoyed considerable foreign outlets for its products. The expansion was especially noticeable in the south, which realized Charles VI's dream of a seaborne export trade. By 1769 the monarchy had no fewer than twenty-five consulates developing commercial relations throughout the Mediterranean world, including fifteen within the Turkish empire. Intercourse with the Ottoman dominions doubled from

1771 to 1788, growing to about 20 percent of foreign trade. Even the Hungarian crownlands were encouraged to trade with the Ottomans, either via the Danube or through Fiume, which was ceded to the kingdom and declared a free port in 1776. Of course, the Adriatic trade remained focused in Trieste, which boasted 20,000 people and fifty manufacturing concerns by 1786; fully a third of the monarchy's exports now passed through the port. Perhaps most remarkable were the monarchy's commercial ventures in the Indian Ocean. Though shorn of its imperial charter, the Ostend Company was revived by its private investors. Thanks largely to its efforts, there were a dozen Habsburg merchant ships sailing the East Indies by 1763. Over the next two decades still other enterprises briefly established colonies in Mozambique, India's Malabar Coast, and the Nicobar Islands.

Steady economic expansion had been accompanied by a corresponding increase in population, especially in the monarchy's towns. Thanks largely to the combined growth of industry and government, fully 15 percent of the *Erblande*'s nine million people now lived in urban centers. Vienna itself housed over 200,000 people, nearly 300,000 counting its suburbs. Meanwhile, Prague's 80,000 inhabitants made it twice the size of any other city in the monarchy's core lands. Industrialization stimulated even greater population growth in the countryside, where there was less guild competition and an ample supply of cottage labor. Rural manufacturing had the greatest demographic impact on property-poor peasants, who could now support larger families with the wages they earned. Cottage labor also enabled their children to start a family at an earlier age, thereby further accelerating population growth. Nor should we overlook the positive effect of the Bohemian *Robotpatent* of 1775, which afforded the typical cottager more work time by cutting his labor service in half. Indeed, the combined effects of rural enterprises and urbarial reform help explain why Greater Bohemia's population rose by 50 percent after mid-century, compared to 10 percent in the Austrian lands.

Hungary's continued demographic resurgence demands a different explanation. Obviously, eight decades of peace had enabled the kingdom to recover from the unnaturally low population levels that obtained at the beginning of the century. During that period the towns tripled in size, partly because of the re-establishment of an artisan class, but also because many peasants chose to dwell in population centers. According to the 1787 census, central Hungary was the only Habsburg dominion with six cities of over 20,000 inhabitants. Pressburg still ranked first with 30,000 inhabitants, but Joseph II's transfer of the central government to Buda in 1784 soon boosted the twin cities of Buda and Pest to a combined population of 50,000. Yet, as in the *Erblande*, most real growth occurred in the countryside, which still held 95 percent of its 10 million people. By 1792 the century-long influx of half a million colonists and an equal number of Balkan immigrants had repopulated the kingdom's southern and eastern frontiers. At 1.5 million inhabitants, Transylvania had nearly doubled in size since 1711. Meanwhile, the south central districts watered by the Tisza, Sava, and Lower Danube had grown tenfold over the same period to over 700,000 people, thanks in part to two more waves of settlers brought in by Joseph II and Leopold II.

With 26 million people and an expanse of 247,000 square miles, the monarchy was nearly as populous as France and larger than any other country, except Russia. Admittedly, population growth can be a mixed blessing unless it is accompanied by parallel increases in food supply. The century-long increase had, in fact, reduced levels of nutrition in densely populated areas. In Vienna bread prices had risen by a third between 1730 and 1780, while meat consumption declined substantially. Army recruiting records even suggest that the average height of Maria Theresa's Bohemian and Lower Austrian subjects dropped by two inches during the course of her reign. By then, however, the cumulative effect of the government's domestic policies had helped to overcome the subsistence crisis and insure the further growth of an industrial workforce. Improved working conditions helped the peasants to grow more food, just as better roads facilitated its delivery to urban centers. Meanwhile, Joseph II's abolition of serfdom and most guild privileges insured a continuous stream of workers for manufacturing jobs.

As it had in the past, wealth and prosperity manifested itself in cultural display. Maria Theresa and her sons played an important, if finite role in supporting the arts and letters. Although the empress finally completed Schönbrunn and patronized the court opera and ballet, she actually reduced the court and theatrical extravagances of her baroque predecessors by a quarter. She opted not to employ Johann Sebastian Bach because he was a Protestant and suggested that retaining the puckish Wolfgang Amadeus Mozart would be "unprofitable" and "degrading" to the civil service. Instead, the court served as a home for other important, though admittedly less gifted composers. The *Hofkapellmeister* Antonio Salieri (1750–1825) became one of Europe's most popular composers of comic opera. Although he initially hewed to the Italian operatic forms and libretti of Metastasio, Court Composer Christoph Willibad Gluck (1714–87), soon remolded the medium by making it more theatrical and introducing French vaudeville elements. Meanwhile, the prolific son of Maria Theresa's court embroiderer, Karl Ditters von Dittersdorf (1739–99), made his mark by introducing the light-hearted *Singspiel* to the European stage.

Even before the empress's death, Vienna had superseded Elector Charles Theodore's court at Mannheim as the European center of symphonic music. The triumph of the Vienna Classical Style was most readily evident in the music world's adoption of four-movement symphonies written in the sonata allegro form. It was also instrumental in attracting Wolfgang Amadeus Mozart (1756–91), after he had been literally kicked out of the employ of Salzburg's archbishop (or arch-boobie, as he put it). Arriving in 1781, he became Joseph II's court composer after Gluck's death in 1787. The young Ludwig van Beethoven arrived five years later, securing a position in the court orchestra. Admittedly, the dynasty had much less experience or interest in promoting literature, which was judged a less effective vehicle for enhancing the dynasty's prestige. Nevertheless, Joseph II deserves some of the credit for the accomplishments of Joseph von Sonnenfels, whose state-sponsored efforts to improve German prose contributed to the development of modern German. Although Sonnenfels never achieved the prominence of German writers like Lessing and Goethe, he became the undisputed standard bearer of the Austrian *Aufklärung*.

Despite these achievements, private patronage remained the key to discovering and developing artistic expression within the monarchy. Thus the Bavarian-born Gluck had begun his music career in the service of the Bohemian Lobkovic, whom his father served as a forester; both he and Ditters were later introduced to court circles through the patronage of the prince of Saxe-Hilburghausen. In addition to valuable introductions, the Princes Lobkovic and Lichnowsky provided Beethoven with free lodging and start-up funds. Until the end of the century most concerts were performed in the salons of the city's aristocrats, such as the Princes Lichnowsky and Rasumofsky, who staged them on a weekly basis. Nor was the aristocracy alone in its patronage. During Joseph II's reign many of the city's untitled nobles, wealthy commoners, and government officials like Gottfried van Swieten hosted concerts in their homes. At Swieten's instigation a group of two dozen music patrons formed a Consortium of Associated Gentlemen (*Gesellschaft der Associierten Cavaliere*) that sponsored numerous concerts, including an oratorio performed each winter by members of the court's orchestra and chorus.

The monarchy's contribution to the arts was, of course, not limited to Vienna. In Hungary alone Maria Theresa's long reign witnessed the construction of 200 noble palaces, most of them in the new classical and rococo styles. Moreover, it was at the Esterházy family's massive new palaces at Fertöd and Eisenstadt that their *Kapellmeister* Franz Joseph Haydn (1732–1809) composed and performed most of his work. Only after three decades in their service (1761–91) and two subsequent concert tours of London did he become a dominant figure in Vienna's music circles. Haydn's triumphant London performances underscore a major evolutionary step in the monarchy's history: whereas it had traditionally adopted the religious, political, mercantile, and philosophical systems of other societies, it had now emerged as a major contributor to European cultural heritage. Admittedly the visual arts of the Austrian high baroque had spread to Catholic central Europe, but the music of Gluck, Salieri, Haydn, and Mozart was being performed all over Europe. And the best was yet to come.

Moreover, the monarchy's artists were appreciated not only by foreign audiences but also by a broader segment of its own population. Nowhere was this more evident than in Hungary, where prosperous nobles, who had previously rejected the magnates' opulent lifestyle as a foreign threat to their nation's culture, now imitated them in constructing palaces, complete with theaters and music ensembles. The kingdom's wealthier towns also founded their own orchestras and German-language theaters that offered the first secular alternative to the crudely improvised performances that were popular among the masses. Thanks in part to the advent of public education and Joseph II's removal of censorship, the number of printing presses had tripled over the past three decades, which in turn helped sustain a surge in the number of newspapers and reading clubs. There is even some evidence that the growth of mass literacy may have created a reading audience among the more prosperous elements of the peasantry.

That the political and philosophical discourse had also changed was evident by the foundation of scores of masonic lodges that served as a meeting-place for reform-minded civil, academic, and military officers, as well as for private nobles, burghers, and clerics. Within the Austrian lands as many as 80 percent of higher public officials were freemasons. By 1780 Hungary boasted 30 lodges, with about 900 members. Unlike most central European rulers, Joseph II never warmed to their presence since he regarded them as a potential source of domestic opposition. In 1785 the exposure of the so-called Illuminati conspiracy in neighboring Bavaria inspired him to place limits on masonic activities. Nevertheless, Joseph's policies enjoyed broad support, within both the lodges and the intelligentsia as a whole. Most fell into one of two categories. One shared Sonnenfels's faith in the populist absolutism of Joseph's highly disciplined *Beamtenstaat*, even to the point of challenging the crownlands' feudal constitutions. While supporting the emperor's objectives, a second group felt that his unwillingness to heed advice or tolerate institutional checks on his power had led the monarchy to the verge of despotism. One of its spokesmen was Joseph Richter, whose satiric journal, the *Eipeldauer Briefe*, offered sympathetic, but critical commentary of his methods and policies. That Richter spoke for a broad and influential cross-section of the ruling elite is evident from the subsidy that he received from Pergen's secret police following the succession of Leopold II. Whereas both groups essentially supported the government, they were flanked by more hostile elements: large numbers of conservative nobles and clergy who had never accepted enlightened absolutism, especially in Hungary, Belgium, and Galicia, as well as a tiny number of republicans who envisioned eliminating the monarchy altogether. There is no question, however, that fifty years of bureaucratization, secular education, and populist reform had reshaped the greater part of the monarchy's ruling elite in its own image.

Of course, the monarchy itself was hardly a unified state. Despite Joseph II's attempts at administrative centralization, it still comprised no fewer than seven discrete political entities, including the territorially discontiguous Netherlands and Lombardy, and the largely unassimilated Galicia and Bukovina. In some ways the tactical demands of statebuilding had actually encouraged the central government to promote even greater diversity. The "southern strategy" that it had pursued over the past century had essentially created two Hungarys: the independent-minded northern counties that looked to the diet for leadership, and a more compliant, tightly controlled southern tier represented by the extensive Military Border system, Transylvania, Croatia, and (since 1791) the Illyrian Chancery. More recently, the increasing stress on literacy as an instrument of social control had impelled Maria Theresa and her successors to promote the monarchy's many "peasant languages" in schools, universities, printed media, and government business. The government's promotion of the vernacular languages helped pave the way for several "national awakenings," most notably among the Magyars and Czechs. Admittedly, these movements operated primarily on an aesthetic plain that did not undermine their loyalty to the dynasty and the state it had created. Nonetheless, this remarkable resilience of political and cultural diversity retarded the evolution of a single identity among the monarchy's peoples, except in their common allegiance to the dynasty. Even as foreign diplomats and academics increasingly referred to this dynastic ensemble as "Austria" or "Austrian," the Habsburgs' own subjects still restricted these terms to the two Danubian archduchies or, at most, to the dynasty's German lands; otherwise, they continued to identify themselves by the specific dominion into which they had been born.

At the same time, however, the monarchy was gradually laying the foundations for a "corporate soul" that would transcend different regions and language groups. After centuries of secundogenitures and split inheritances, the Pragmatic Sanction had finally visualized a single sovereign entity. The abrupt end of the dynasty's hegemony in the Holy Roman empire had helped Maria Theresa, her sons, and their German-speaking subjects to distinguish between their German roots and their loyalty to a separate Habsburg commonwealth. The massive bureaucratic and military establishment that they created to defend it served as a powerful vehicle for integrating the monarchy's other ethnic groups, including the Magyar nation, which had readily begun dispatching its forces to conflicts fought well beyond its own frontiers. That the monarchy's military commanders, civil officials, merchants, and public affairs journals communicated in German did not overly concern the other language groups, which accepted its utility as an instrument of communication and social mobility. The evolution of a common elite culture that leaned heavily on German did not forestall the parallel development of other national cultures. Thus, the Baroque monarchy that had been forged by an alliance of crown, church and aristocracy was now supported by a much broader constituency that included an educated elite, a professional bureaucracy, and an imposing military establishment that literally spoke the same language.

Having weathered the turbulence caused by the opposition to Joseph II, the Habsburg monarchy had fewer unresolved problems than at any time – either in its past or in its future. As a result it was well prepared to face the formidable military, economic, and cultural challenges of the next generation. Thanks to the industrial infrastructure in the *Erblande*, Lombardy, and Belgium, it was economically comparable to the continent's other major states and was poised to enter the industrial revolution. Its intellectual life had rejoined the western-European mainstream for the first time since the advent of the Counter-Reformation. Its systems of education and justice were models for the rest of the continent. Although its political and administrative system still did not approach the ideal envisioned by Joseph II, it was far more efficient, honest, and responsive than most other European governments. It had also become a strong vehicle for raising large amounts of revenue. The 87.5 million fl. that poured into the *Hofkammer*'s coffers in 1788 was nearly twice that of its Prussian rival and almost equal to the £12 million raised by the British exchequer at the height of the War of American Independence. Although Louis XVI still collected appreciably more revenue than his Habsburg brother-in-law, the emperor had much more money at his disposal after debt service than did bankrupt France. If the government was still mired in debt, it was no longer because of an incompetent administration system, but rather because of the *Hofkriegsrat*'s talent for pushing the military's size beyond the *Hofkammer*'s ability to pay. With a wartime strength of roughly 400,000 men, it now had the largest standing army that Europe had seen since the age of Louis XIV.[2] Relative to the other states and societies of the continent, the Habsburg monarchy was neither weak, nor backward, nor in decline. But, then again, the world around it was about to change.

---

[2] The numbers tabulated by P. G. M. Dickson suggest about 315,000 front-line troops, 75,000 *Grenzer*, and 20,000 artillery, engineer, and other special units. Its interwar level of 300,000 (1791) was also considerably higher than the peacetime military establishments of Prussia (195,000), Russia (224,000), and France (182,000).

7   The age of revolution (1789–1815)

It has long been customary to regard the French Revolution as a great event in western civilization, a defining moment in the development of world democracy that sounded the death-knell of monarchy. Today a great many scholars see it as at best a mixed blessing, both for France and for the continent as a whole. But it was worse than that. Far from heralding the end of monarchy, it gave new life to conservative forces by permitting them to blame the Enlightenment for the Revolution's unfortunate legacy of domestic terror and international aggression. The French Revolution was nothing short of a catastrophe for the monarchy, not because it was ideologically hostile to the Habsburg state, but because it unleashed hugely powerful, aggressive forces that prompted much of the monarchy's ruling elite to cast off Enlightenment values that now became linked to the French enemy in favor of the reassuring safety of an outmoded feudal order.

The twilight of the Old Regime, 1789–94

Of course, the domestic political turmoil of the past three years had closely coincided with the outbreak of the French Revolution. Yet events in France had virtually no impact on the government's handling of their own domestic crises. Neither Joseph II nor Leopold II viewed the Revolution as a direct threat. They did not expect it to spread to the monarchy's core lands, if only because the sources of opposition in the two countries came from diametrically opposite directions: whereas the Belgian revolt and Hungarian conspiracy articulated the privileged elite's opposition to Joseph II's populism and rationalization of traditional institutions, the French nation was driven by the need for a more just and efficient form of government. In beating a hasty retreat from his most controversial innovations, Joseph and his brother were merely trying to appease the monarchy's traditional ruling elite, not avert a popular revolution comparable to the one in France.

To a certain extent both emperors and many of their academic and civil officials welcomed the Revolution as an endorsement of their own domestic policies. Joseph II was quick to note that he had already instituted most of the

National Assembly's legislation within his own realms, even if he was less pleased by the reception his reforms had received. Leopold II viewed the collapse of Louis XVI's authority as a reaffirmation of his own constitutional principles and an "urgent warning to all sovereigns to treat their subjects with great consideration." The two emperors even expressed their disdain for the émigrés who fled France after the storming of the Bastille: Joseph by expelling them from the Austrian Netherlands, Leopold by ignoring their incessant pleas for support against the new French government.

What concerned both men most about the Revolution was its effects on the monarchy's international position. Although they took solace from Kaunitz's prediction that France would henceforth be incapable of acting aggressively toward its neighbors, they also feared that it would be in no position to discharge its commitments as an ally. In reality, the Habsburg–Bourbon alliance had never been popular in France, which remembered its humiliation in the Seven Years' War, the subsequent despoliation of its Polish and Turkish allies, and Louis XVI's hapless marriage to the emperors' sister, Marie Antoinette. Yet Leopold now urged the royal couple to work with the National Assembly and accept its draft of a new constitution, knowing that reconciliation with the nation was the best way to save both them and the alliance from ruin. Instead, they ignored his counsel and lost everything in their futile flight to Varennes in June 1791.

The demise of the Austro-French alliance severely undermined the monarchy's position in eastern Europe. It had already forced Leopold to relinquish Laudon's Balkan conquests at Reichenbach and Sistova. Even though the treaties had extricated the monarchy from any imminent danger, Leopold knew that France was no longer available as a counterpoise to Prussian or Russian expansionism. Catherine's Balkan designs remained a source of concern, especially since she remained at war with the Turks. Meanwhile, the most immediate danger came from Prussia, which was now set on annexing part of Poland. In characteristic fashion Leopold attempted to preserve that kingdom's territorial integrity by dealing with both sides. Once again he demonstrated his penchant for populist politics by supporting the ongoing efforts of Polish patriots to strengthen the kingdom's constitution. But he also cultivated closer ties with Prussia, hoping thereby to enlist its support in protecting Poland against Russia – and the Bourbon royal family against the National Assembly.

The result was the notorious Pillnitz Declaration (27 August), in which Leopold and Frederick William II announced that they were willing to act in concert with their fellow monarchs in forcibly restoring Louis XVI's position as king. There is no question that Berlin valued the proclamation as a handy pretext for annexing French territory. The emperor and his ministers were also confident that any war with France could be won quickly. Yet Leopold was only bluffing, hoping that tough talk would simultaneously keep Prussia preoccupied in the West and protect the French royals by shaping the behavior of the National Assembly. He knew that Great Britain's reluctance to join a European concert rendered the proclamation a dead letter. His decision to reduce the Austrian army by 25,000 men also suggests that he neither wanted nor expected war. Indeed, news of Louis XVI's belated acceptance of the French constitution (13 September) prompted the emperor to replace his threat of intervention with a call for a "Concert of Observation" by the great powers; it also delighted Kaunitz, who still hoped to revive the Austro-French alliance that he had created. Unfortunately, Leopold's motives were not so evident to the new, more radical Legislative Assembly that had been created by France's constitution. A war party soon emerged that exploited a number of minor squabbles and the threat of invasion to unite the country behind them. On 20 April the Legislative Assembly declared war on the emperor.

At the eleventh hour Leopold anticipated the outbreak of hostilities by concluding a formal alliance with Prussia on 7 February. Yet he never had to face the consequences of his confrontation with revolutionary France. He died suddenly on 1 March 1792 – killed by his doctors, who had repeatedly bled him for a respiratory ailment. Nor did the 80-year-old Kaunitz, who was soon driven from office by the advocates of a Prussian alliance against France. Instead, the burden fell on Leopold's 24-year-old son and successor, Francis II (1792–1835). The new sovereign was not without his strengths. He was a cultivated, virtuous, and reasonably intelligent man, whose affable and unpretentious nature earned him the immediate and lasting affection of his subjects. He was also extremely conscientious. Like Joseph II, he had prepared for his eventual succession by travelling extensively throughout his future dominions. When in Vienna he spent little time or money on court extravagances, choosing instead an austere daily regimen that included long hours at his desk. The young sovereign did, however, lack the self-confidence that comes with experience. Consequently, he made no immediate changes in course, in either foreign or domestic matters.

Kaunitz's resignation left foreign policy in the hands of Philip Cobenzl and Anton Spielmann, both of whom were avid proponents of the Prussian alliance. Their tenure at the *Staatskanzlei* would, however, be brief and disastrous. Prussia remained every bit as predatory and unreliable as it had been under Frederick the Great. Whereas Francis's war aims were limited to restoring Louis XVI and securing Prussian approval for a Belgian–Bavarian exchange, Prussia was intent on being compensated for its intervention with new acquisitions, either in the Rhineland or in Poland. Although Catherine II joined the alliance, she promptly committed her forces to an invasion of Poland, rather than to war against France. As a result, the monarchy was assisted in the west by only a few thousand émigrés, 6,000 Hessian auxiliaries, and 40,000 Prussians under the aged duke of Brunswick.

The allies expected that such a force would be more than adequate to march on Paris. But Brunswick's ill-advised manifesto (25 July) threatening "unforgettable vengeance" if the French offered resistance or mistreated their royal family helped rally the French nation against their enemies. Their first victims were Louis XVI and Marie Antoinette, who were imprisoned following Jacobin-led riots on 10 August. Next came Brunswick, whose poorly prepared forces were turned back by the rag-tag French army at Valmy (20 September). The National Convention celebrated the news by formally ending the monarchy one day later. Its forces now went on the offensive, seizing much of the Rhineland during October and the Austrian Netherlands one month later. The news from the east was no better. Having been denied any spoils in France, Prussia promptly joined Russia in dismembering Poland. Vienna's opposition to the Second Partition (23 January 1793) was totally without effect, except in guaranteeing its own exclusion from the proceeds.

Having recognized the folly of the Prussian alliance, Francis removed Cobenzl and Spielmann by the customary means of transferring them to other posts. For the next eight years, the difficult job of confronting revolutionary France and the equally aggressive Prussians and Russians was born by Franz Maria Baron Thugut. This typically hardworking, but humorless career diplomat had been quick to appreciate revolutionary France's great military potential, as well as Prussia's unsuitability as a partner in opposing it. Fortunately, the French made it easy for Thugut to find more appropriate allies: their occupation of Belgium and the Rhineland had quickly aroused the Maritime Powers and the German states; meanwhile, the execution of Louis XVI (21 January 1793) provided further motivation to Europe's crowned heads. By the end of March the monarchy was part of a formidable coalition reminiscent of the Grand Alliance against Louis XIV: aside from Great Britain, the Netherlands, the Habsburg monarchy and the Holy Roman empire, it included British client states like Portugal, Sardinia, and numerous German princes with troop subsidy treaties, as well as the remaining Bourbon monarchies of Spain, Naples, and Parma. Most important, unlike Prussia and Russia, the so-called First Coalition (1793–7) generally shared the Habsburg monarchy's desire to uphold the status quo by maintaining legitimate frontiers and governments. Thus, while Prussia and Russia devoted the spring of 1793 to devouring half of Poland, Coalition forces quickly retook the Austrian Netherlands and most of the Rhineland from the French.

Francis's early domestic policies reflected a similar continuity in outlook. In a more stable political environment the young emperor would have doubtless sustained the enlightened agenda of his immediate predecessors. Like them he criticized the landed nobility's exploitation of the peasantry as both shortsighted and inhumane. Barely a month into his reign he decided to carry out his father's project for a resumption of mandatory *robot* commutation. At the beginning of 1793 the Lower Austrian estates even accused the government of "Jacobin tendencies" because of its unwillingness to abandon some of Joseph II's agrarian reforms. Indeed, one element that had not changed was the army of civil officials which was destined to retain its Josephinian outlook until well into the next century.

The men around Francis were, however, more conservative and less capable of innovative thinking than previous ministries. Led by his childhood tutor, Count Colloredo-Waldsee, they were hesitant to play Leopold's difficult and devious game of appealing simultaneously to the monarchy's privileged and unprivileged elements. Above all they feared that a continuation of his predecessors' populist policies would inspire rising expectations among the masses and opposition from the estates. To avoid a renewal of domestic chaos while the monarchy was at war made good sense; it also led to a more one-sided, conservative agenda that re-enlisted the privileged classes' support for the struggle against France. Thus, at the last minute Francis's advisors dissuaded him from issuing the *robot* commutation order, thereby keeping it voluntary; as a result, compulsory labor service made a comeback within the Habsburg lands as landlords let existing commutation contracts lapse once they came up for renewal. The emperor also dropped his father's plans for broader town and peasant representation in the various diets. In return for securing additional assistance from the Hungarian diet, he sacrificed the Illyrian Chancery and recent privileges granted to the kingdom's Protestants. Even the church hierarchy received a valuable concession with the abolition of the regime's supervisory Commission for Ecclesiastical Affairs.

However unfortunate we may judge Francis's retreat, it did have the desired effect of sustaining internal order and enlisting the estates' support for the war effort. Within Hungary, "enlightened" and feudal nobles alike joined the rest of the monarchy's elites in rallying behind the government, especially after the French Revolution entered its radical phase. The beheading of Louis XVI and, nine months later, Marie Antoinette appalled all segments of the population. Although the ensuing wars of the next decade were not popular, they caused little unrest or popular protest in the countryside, if only because harvests were very good and grain prices high. When people criticized the government it was the "war baron" Thugut rather than the emperor, whose popularity remained intact.

Francis's reluctance to launch additional reforms did prompt a few dozen enlightened nobles and officials to yearn for a republican revolution. The

Austrian Jacobins were, however, neither well organized nor united by a single agenda. Notwithstanding the suspicions of police officials and some Marxist historians, most were not Jacobins at all, but merely frustrated Josephinians. One leading figure, the Hungarian Ignaz von Martinovics, did seek a republic but one dominated by the gentry in which the peasantry would still pay their feudal dues! Moreover, any expectations of a popular revolution were totally unrealistic. By the summer of 1794 they had done little more than sing the *Marseillaise* and dance around "liberty trees" that they had planted in and around cities like Graz and Vienna.

The emperor did take some precautions against the spread of revolution. At the beginning of 1793 he banned all secret societies and French publications, while placing strict limits on all French nationals. He not only rehired Pergen, but sanctioned the secret trial and sustained imprisonment of at least four individuals for making politically injudicious remarks. Others were detained for shorter periods, including the famed hypnotist Franz Anton Mesmer, who was eventually deported for defending the revolution (though not the Jacobins) in a talk with his Viennese landlady. Yet, during the opening years of the reign neither Francis nor his ministers were particularly alarmed by police reports of these activities. They resisted Pergen's more extreme requests, which included the outright expulsion of French and other undesirable foreigners, the removal of public officials and university faculty who were sympathetic to the ideals of the revolution, and even the authority to deny due process to anyone suspected of treasonous activity. Instead, the civil courts generally followed the government's lead in refusing to condemn individuals for expressing revolutionary, or even pro-French views.

The turning point came during the summer of 1794, after an Austrian army lieutenant, Franz Hebenstreit, delivered a "drunken diatribe" to a police agent in which he divulged a plot to overthrow the monarchy. It also came to light that Hebenstreit had developed a mobile artillery piece, which his accomplices had smuggled to France for use against the Austrian cavalry. The invention was not quite the technological equivalent of a cruise missile, consisting as it did of a standard gun barrel, adorned with pikes and mounted on baby carriage wheels. However infantile Hebenstreit's plans may have been, they did constitute treason. Many of the forty-five individuals who were arrested with him were guilty of little more than inflammatory rhetoric. This too was construed as treason now that the monarchy was at war with republican France. While Hebenstreit and three other soldiers were tried by military courts, Francis ordered that the remaining defendants be afforded due process in a series of public trials. The resulting Jacobin Trials yielded forty convictions; Martinovics, Hebenstreit, and seven others were subsequently executed, while the remainder received lengthy prison terms.

The failure of the coalitions, 1793–1805

The government's willingness to punish its dissidents so severely reflected the outbreak of war hysteria and paranoia within its ranks. The monarchy was, in fact, just entering a twelve-year period during which it led no fewer than three anti-French coalitions to defeat. Much of France's success stemmed from its resort to a *levée en masse* (August 1793), which had given it overwhelming numerical superiority on the battlefield. By the end of 1794 its citizen armies had not only retaken the Rhineland and the Austrian Netherlands, but had even conquered the United Provinces. One by one, the monarchy's allies began coming to terms with the French. Although Prussia briefly contributed some forces to the Coalition, it soon concluded a separate peace (March 1795) in return for France's promise to compensate it for its Rhenish losses. Within a year most of the emperor's German allies had also deserted him in return for comparable promises from the French. The news was no better in the Mediterranean, where France's successes forced the capitulation of both Spain (June 1795) and Sardinia (April 1796). The only other major land power left in the Coalition was now Russia, which had recently joined the monarchy and Prussia in consummating the Third Partition of Poland. Yet its remoteness and the succession of a new tsar prevented it from committing its forces in the West.

Despite its lack of powerful allies, the Austrian army fought successfully in 1796, especially in Germany, where the emperor's brother, Charles, won a series of brilliant victories. But the First Coalition finally collapsed one year later, following Napoleon Bonaparte's conquest of all of northern Italy. On 17 October the emperor accepted the peace terms that Bonaparte offered in the treaty of Campo Formio. He recognized France's dramatic expansion to the Rhine, as well as the creation of the puppet Batavian Republic in the northern Netherlands and the Cisalpine Republic in northern Italy. Although he was forced to surrender Belgium and most of Lombardy, the monarchy was compensated with the former republic of Venice, including Dalmatia. Before handing Venice over to Francis, Bonaparte's forces stripped it of everything useful, including its priceless manuscript collections, artworks, even the four bronze stallions from atop St. Mark's Cathedral, and the gondolas from its canals.

Campo Formio proved little more than a truce. The French government felt that Bonaparte had treated the monarchy too leniently. Indeed, when combined with its new Polish province of West Galicia, the acquisition of Venice had actually increased the monarchy to its greatest extent ever. There were even those in Vienna who were convinced that the loss of its outlying Belgian and Italian lands would actually strengthen the monarchy by streamlining it. Yet the most devastating losses lay just beyond its frontiers.

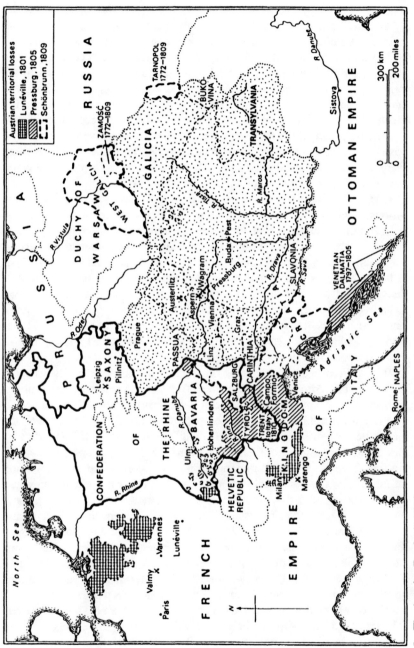

Austrian territorial losses
Lunéville, 1801
Pressburg, 1805
Schönbrunn, 1809

RUSSIA

DUCHY OF WARSAW

ZAMOŚĆ
1772–1809

WEST GALICIA

GALICIA

TARNOPOL
1772–1809

BUKO-VINA

TRANSYLVANIA

R. Vistula

PRUSSIA

R. Oder

SAXONY

Leipzig

Pillnitz

Prague

CONFEDERATION OF THE RHINE

PASSUA

Austerlitz

Aspern

Wagram

R. Tisza

Vienna

Buda Pest

Pressburg

R. Drava

SLAVONIA

CROATIA

R. Maros

R. Sava

VENETIAN DALMATIA
1797–1805

OTTOMAN EMPIRE

Sistova

Adriatic Sea

Linz

Graz

CARINTHIA

BAVARIA

Hohenlinden

Ulm

Danube

SALZBURG

TYROL

TRENT
1810

Campo Formio

Venice

MILAN KINGDOM

Marengo

ITALY

Rome

NAPLES

HELVETIC REPUBLIC

R. Rhine

Valmy

Varennes

Lunéville

Paris

FRENCH

EMPIRE

North Sea

N

300 km
200 miles

5   The Austrian Empire in 1812

The addition of over a million more Polish subjects was hardly worth the 1,000-mile border that the monarchy now shared with Prussia and Russia. Nor was Venice adequate compensation for the end of three centuries of Habsburg hegemony in the peninsula. Worst of all, France's conquest of the Rhine dealt a deathblow to imperial power within Germany. In return for deserting the Coalition, Prussia and other German states were now compensated for their Rhenish losses with the promise of territories elsewhere in the *Reich*. This could only mean the absorption of those ecclesiastical and smaller lay principalities that had traditionally been the emperors' most loyal vassals. At the same time larger states like Prussia, Bavaria, and Württemberg were now beholden to France, rather than to the emperor. In just five years, the monarchy had lost three of its four foreign buffers.

It is not difficult to appreciate Thugut's eagerness to forestall the provisions of Campo Formio. Even before its final implementation could be worked out, further French aggression against neutral Switzerland, the Papal States, and the Ottoman empire enabled him to piece together a Second Coalition (1799–1801) that included both Great Britain and Russia. At first, Admiral Nelson's victory at Aboukir Bay and Austro-Russian successes in Italy deluded the allies into contemplating a march on Paris. The Coalition collapsed, however, after Tsar Paul (1796–1801) clashed with his Austrian and British allies over strategy. By 1800 the twin defeats at Marengo (4 June) and Hohenlinden (2 December) had effectively eliminated any chances of revising the Campo Formio settlement.

With a French army advancing on Vienna, the emperor finally accepted the inevitable. Although he held on to Venice, the treaty of Lunéville (9 February 1801) now consigned the rest of peninsular Italy and the Rhineland to French control. As additional compensation, the monarchy received the bishoprics of Passau, Brixen, and Trent, while the displaced Habsburg princes of Tuscany and Modena were awarded Salzburg and part of Austrian Swabia. Two years later an imperial commission formalized the elimination of the empire's ecclesiastical states, most of its smaller lay principalities, and all but six of its forty-eight free cities. As France's new head of state, Bonaparte bound the princes of Württemberg, Baden, and Hesse-Cassel closer to him by obliging Francis to make them imperial electors; although Francis also made Salzburg an electorate, the newly configured empire now counted just four Catholic princes among its nine electors. The first Protestant electoral majority ever was, however, hardly a source for concern in Vienna. The Holy Roman empire was now as good as dead.

The defeat of the Second Coalition spelled the end of Thugut's career. The task of dealing with France's military dictator now fell to Colloredo and Ludwig Cobenzl. It was not long before Bonaparte aroused in them the same apprehension that had inspired Thugut. In May 1804 he crowned himself

Napoleon I, emperor of the French. The possibility now arose that the Holy Roman empire's eventual dissolution would place Francis behind both Napoleon and Tsar Alexander in princely rank. Francis responded on 11 August by declaring himself "hereditary emperor of Austria," by which he meant all of the remaining Habsburg dominions. Nearly three centuries after its creation, the Danubian commonwealth finally rested under a single crown. What worried the emperor's ministers most was Napoleon's progressive creation of puppet states in Germany, Italy, and Spain. Fearing that the new Austrian empire might be next, Cobenzl concluded a defensive pact with Russia at the end of 1804.

Though intended as a deterrent, the alliance actually made war inevitable by provoking Napoleon and by emboldening the tsar to press for a resumption of hostilities. Napoleon's decision to anoint himself king of Italy (May 1805) pushed the emperor and his ministers over the edge. Once again the monarchy's statesmen had allowed themselves to be dragged into an unwanted – and ultimately unsuccessful – conflict by the need to hold onto their more aggressive Russian ally. Great Britain soon joined them by contributing the usual combination of subsidies and sea power. But Cobenzl suffered a key setback when he was unable to convince Prussia to risk war against France. Indeed, if the Third Coalition (1805–7) differed from its two predecessors, it was that virtually all of the remaining German states were now firmly allied with their French benefactor.

The outcome was all too familiar. The Austrian General Mack failed to make good on his pledge "to triumph or die" fighting the French when his 60,000-man army was captured by Napoleon at Ulm (20 October 1805). Although Nelson destroyed the Franco-Spanish fleet at Trafalgar just one day later, neither British ships nor the promise of Russian assistance were of much help. On 12 November Napoleon entered Vienna, the first foreign enemy to do so since Matthias Corvinus 320 years before. Francis still had a chance of winning the war. A Russian army under general Kutuzov had recently reached Bohemia; a second force under the emperor's brother, Archduke Charles, was also on its way from Italy. Both field armies were larger than Napoleon's own forces. Yet, in their eagerness to defeat the French, Francis and the Russian Tsar Alexander ordered Kutuzov to attack Napoleon without waiting for the archduke's army to arrive. The ensuing battle of the three emperors, better known as Austerlitz (2 December), was perhaps Napoleon's most brilliant and decisive victory.

Francis immediately concluded an armistice, followed by the formal peace at Pressburg (26 December). This time Napoleon was far less lenient. Although the monarchy acquired Salzburg, it now lost Venice (to Italy), the rest of its Swabian lands (to Württemberg), and the Tyrol, the Vorarlberg, and the recently acquired bishoprics of Passau, Brixen, and Trent (to

Bavaria). It was also required to pay an indemnity of forty million livres. Napoleon even contemplated forcing Francis to abdicate in favor of the Archduke Charles, but dropped the idea when the archduke expressed no interest in the offer. Francis was, however, forced to recognize Bavaria, Württemberg, and Baden as fully sovereign states. On 12 July 1806 Napoleon finally delivered the *coup de grâce* to the Holy Roman empire by uniting his German satellites in a new Confederation of the Rhine (*Rheinbund*). In response to pressure from Napoleon and his German clients, Francis formally dissolved the Holy Roman empire four weeks later, 1,006 years after its creation by Charlemagne. Yet the last act in the German tragedy was reserved for Prussia. Napoleon had recently given it Hanover in return for its continued neutrality. But soon after Austria's defeat he turned on Prussia, forcing it into a short, suicidal conflict. After a single afternoon on the battlefields of Jena and Äuerstädt (14 October 1806), Napoleon was able to take away over half of its territory and subject the rest to a French army of occupation.

Francis could take grim satisfaction from Prussia's fate. If the French Revolution and Napoleon had killed the Holy Roman empire, it was Prussia that had doomed it to destruction by undermining the emperor's leadership. Together with Russia, it also bore primary responsibility for France's destruction of the European balance of power. Although all of the great powers had been slow to realize exactly how dangerous and powerful France had become, Prussia had repeatedly allowed itself to be seduced into neutrality by the prospects of Polish and German territory. Only Great Britain had shared the emperor's determination to stop France and had expressed that commitment by advancing considerable subsidies to the monarchy and other coalition members. But French control of the Low Countries and the co-option of its German client states prevented the British from fielding an army of their own. Thus, in contrast to the wars it fought against Louis XIV, the Austrian army had been compelled to bear the brunt of the military operations. This would have posed no problem had it been fighting a more conventional, mercenary army. It had a number of competent commanders. The Archduke Charles was an especially gifted tactician who had stopped the French at the Rhine during the first two conflicts and defeated them in Italy during the third. Moreover, the rank and file was well trained and equipped, certainly better than any of its predecessors. Nevertheless, no conventional force could stand alone against France's larger, more aggressive citizen armies, at least so long as its commanders adhered to the traditional tactics of preserving their manpower and supply lines.

The monarchy during the revolutionary age

Although the defeat of the three coalitions had inflicted considerable territorial and strategic losses on the monarchy, the greatest casualty was the enlightened political culture that had emerged over the past generation. Twelve years of military disasters had not only forced the government to suspend controversial domestic innovations that might spur opposition from its traditional ruling elite or rising expectations among the common people. They had also created a link in Francis's mind between the ideas of the Enlightenment and the demonstrable evils of the French Revolution. As a result, anyone who advocated a return to populist absolutism risked being labeled a freemason or Jacobin sympathizer, even if his intention was to strengthen the monarchy against France. This was not the first time that a threat to the monarchy's security had forced a major catharsis in its political culture. Two centuries earlier the danger of internal conflict had convinced men like Ferdinand II to end religious toleration and embrace the Counter-Reformation as an instrument of social control. More recently, the sudden emergence of the Prussian threat had inspired Maria Theresa and Joseph II to jettison the feudal *Ständestaat* in favor of a more efficient, tightly centralized bureaucratic state. The Franciscan reaction did not constitute an outright rejection of the Enlightenment, if only because many of his ministers and most civil officials retained the populist mind-set of his predecessors. Like Francis himself, they continued to yearn for greater social justice, even as they sacrificed it to the more immediate need for domestic and external security. But then again, the desire for social justice has always been a recessive trait in governments obsessed with their own survival.

Another casualty of the Franciscan reaction was intellectual freedom. Francis had already revived censorship shortly after the onset of hostilities. Newspapers had been prohibited from reporting about events in France or printing anything that might place the revolutionaries in a favorable light. Reading rooms and circulating libraries had been shut down. Even literary journals were banned in order to prevent them from discussing prohibited books. The police also redoubled its efforts to prevent the formation of organizations that might conspire against the government. The monarchy's masonic lodges were suppressed, as were all learned societies except those engaged in promoting agriculture. Even music ensembles of more than two instruments required prior police approval before they could perform. Following the defeat of the Second Coalition all state employees – even members of the royal family – were obliged to swear that they did not belong to a secret society. Nor were Francis's ministers and family members exempted from the army of police informers who now infiltrated every echelon of society. At the same time, censorship was extended to virtually everything written, including even the inscriptions on fans, toys, and snuff-boxes. By 1803 a "Re-Censoring Commission" had begun reviewing all books that had been approved between 1780 and the restoration of censorship in 1792. Roughly 2,500 were subsequently banned. People were even prohibited from inheriting the libraries of dead relatives until they had been screened by the police.

To his credit, Francis never allowed his fear of revolution to undermine his respect for the law. He used Pergen's police mainly to gather information on public opinion and prevent possible conspiracies, rather than to imprison political opponents. At his insistence, the police were not allowed to use intercepted letters as evidence against their authors or addressees. In fact, convictions were few and the sentences fairly light. The question arises, however, whether any action was necessary. Notwithstanding widespread apprehension at the highest levels of government, the monarchy was in no imminent danger of succumbing to a Jacobin revolution. When he retired in 1804 even Pergen was convinced that the threat of revolution had long since passed. Unfortunately, so had much of the intellectual growth of the previous generation. Of Vienna's many political periodicals, only the *Wiener Zeitung* survived the turn of the century. Meanwhile, censorship helped to reduce the number of Hungarian newspapers from eighteen (1792) to just four (1805).

One concept in which Austria's leaders retained complete confidence was the rationally organized, efficiently run bureaucratic state. Although everyone was aware of Napoleon's genius and the superiority of France's citizen armies, the men around Francis believed that victory could still be achieved by the all-too-familiar resort to administrative reform. In their relentless push for change, Colloredo and Cobenzl received crucial assistance from among Francis's eight younger brothers. Several of the archdukes were more talented than Francis. Their royal blood also afforded them the luxury of criticizing the emperor's shortcomings. Some of them objected to his refusal to revive Joseph's populist reforms, such as *robot* commutation or the Tax and Agrarian Regulation of 1789. But they focused their criticism on his failures as an administrator. In his first fifteen years as emperor Francis had issued twenty-four thick volumes of ordinances, among them Sonnenfels' long-awaited Criminal Code in 1803. Yet his arduous work habits had singlehandedly slowed the pace of government. He not only refused to delegate decisions to subordinates, but tended to agonize over even the most trivial matters. With as many as 2,000 reports piled on his desk at one time, it was sometimes years before some matters were acted on.

Far from welcoming their views, Francis distrusted his brothers to the point of spying on them. He also disappointed their expectations of being included at the highest levels of policy-making. The one exception was Archduke Charles. Although Francis wrongly suspected that Charles might still want to replace him as emperor, the archduke's successes on the battle-field afforded him leverage to force some innovations. In 1802 he convinced Francis to combine foreign, domestic, and military affairs in a single State and Conference Ministry. By establishing a joint policy-making body, the archduke and his supporters hoped to acquire the same comprehensive overview of the monarchy's affairs that was enjoyed by the emperor. Instead the *Staatskonferenzministerium* proved too cumbersome and was eventually obliged to relinquish its oversight of foreign affairs. The archduke achieved somewhat better success in his capacity as director of the *Hofkriegsrat*. It proved a task of Herculean proportions. Upon assuming control in 1801 he found a mountain of 154,000 unpaid bills and 33,000 unanswered petitions for pensions and supplies. He also discovered that no fewer than forty-eight different officials were needed to process a typical document, a ritual that he was able to cut by half. Within a year he had also reduced the enlistment period from life to a mere ten to fourteen years, because it was both inhumane and had left the monarchy with an army of old men.

The most intractable problem confronting the monarchy was not administrative, but financial. The staggering cost of fighting revolutionary France had increased annual expenditures to roughly double the average state income of 75 million fl. During Francis's first decade as emperor, the *Hofkammer* was compelled to finance a deficit of over 400 million fl. Half of the shortfall was added to the state debt, which went from 417 to 613 million fl. between 1793 and 1801. The rest was met by printing over 200 million fl. in paper money. The result was inflation, which the French aggravated by flooding the monarchy with additional millions in counterfeit banknotes. Although the government used the brief period of peace to redeem some of the notes, the Third Coalition brought a further spiral in prices; by 1805 the cost of living had nearly trebled in just four years.

People living on fixed incomes, such as pensioners and government employees, were hurt most by the wartime inflation. One police report estimated that only one in five petty officials could afford to buy meat for their families. Yet spiraling prices proved a boon to the monarchy's peasant majority, especially those who owed money or had commuted *robot* service into cash. Together with their landlords, they also benefited from grain prices that quadrupled between 1799 and 1806. Inflation was sustained in part by massive requisitions by the Austrian military, which now provided a major stimulus for both agriculture and industry. As the army's primary source of food, Hungary experienced the greatest agrarian boom in its history. Croatia used the demand for uniforms to become a producer of merino wool, for both domestic and foreign military consumption. Indeed, the overall value of the monarchy's exports increased by two-thirds between 1790 and 1804. Most of the growth came from the hereditary lands, which continued the industrial expansion that had begun in the 1780s. After 1800 its well-established textile industry grew at an annual rate of 5 percent. Six years later Napoleon's continental blockade against Great Britain provided a further boost by creating a huge captive market for the *Erblande*'s industrial products.

Stadion and Metternich, 1805–15

Despite its military defeats and the recent loss of 3 million people in the treaty of Pressburg, the Austrian empire was still a great economic and military power. Until the 1805 campaign its core lands had not even been occupied by foreign troops. Furthermore, with the possible exception of West Galicia, the emperor's subjects remained steadfastly loyal. None of this was lost on the new foreign minister, Count Philip Stadion. Like all Austrian statesmen of the past half-century, Stadion advocated further administrative reform. But he also felt that Francis could defeat Napoleon only by enlisting the support of all segments of the population. He hoped to achieve this by reviving the double game first employed by Leopold II: the government would reassure the ruling elite by reaffirming its traditional institutions and privileges, but would also play to the masses by integrating them into the empire's power structure. Francis readily endorsed a number of administrative changes by recreating the *Staatsrat*, delegating some authority to his brothers, and placing the talented Galician-Irishman Joseph O'Donnell in control of state finances. But, in contrast to Baron Stein's Prussia, he limited his appeal for popular support to meaningless public gestures. Thus he promised to allow freer intellectual life and talked about the great "inner strength" that would come from the cooperation of all elements of society. He refused, however, to reduce police power or increase local autonomy.

It was not long before news from abroad prompted Francis to reconsider the popular appeal of Stadion's agenda. Napoleon's ill-considered decision to invade Portugal (November 1807) and place his brother on the Spanish throne (May 1808) reminded Francis of the risks of coexisting with Napoleonic France. In the words of the Archduke Charles, "There can no longer be any question what Napoleon wants – He wants everything!" Furthermore, the resulting Spanish revolt against the French occupation suggested that Austria might be able to lead a popular war of liberation in central Europe. Finally, the Austrian ambassador to Paris, Count Metternich, reported that Napoleon's latest aggression had inspired opposition at the highest levels of the French government. With Stadion, the archdukes, and his own wife clamoring for action, Francis now prepared for war.

In May 1808 the emperor approved plans for mobilizing popular support for a war of liberation – at least among the peoples of the hereditary lands. Austrian propagandists avidly spread news of the successful Spanish resistance to Napoleon. Patriotic journals mobilized public support by praising the accomplishments of the cameralist Austrian state. A single article in the newly established *Vaterländische Blätter* enumerated "culture, welfare, public peace and security, public instruction, religious life, the arts and sciences, trade, industry and agriculture, crafts and poor relief." Others mentioned the rule of law, and social mobility attainable through ennoblement and equal access to careers in administration, the army, and the church. To build a sense of national identity, the government began to stress a common history, not only in the journals but in the public schools and in several historical museums founded in the major cities. Francis and his wife even worked to build military enlistments by touring the *Erblande* amid patriotic displays of support. At the urging of the liberal Archduke John, the army accommodated its citizen soldiers in a newly established national militia, or *Landwehr*, which he hoped would politicize the nation by merging all social elements into a single fighting force. Stadion articulated his design by entrusting the organization of individual units to the provincial nobility, while dividing the overall command among several of the archdukes. Once they had enlisted, volunteers were further inspired by patriotic war songs that were translated from German into each of the hereditary lands' Slavic languages. Stadion's campaign struck a chord among the *Erblande*'s population. Large numbers of men joined the *Landwehr*, including many students and others who were otherwise exempt from military service.

Notwithstanding its appeal to all of the *Erblande*'s language groups, the government made a special effort to inspire German national feeling against the French. Stadion employed exiled German publicists, like Friedrich von Gentz and Friedrich Schlegel, to whip up support not just within the *Erblande* but throughout Germany. Here too Archduke John played an important part by fomenting a popular insurrection in the Tyrol against Bavarian rule. By contrast, the government was more circumspect about encouraging popular support from the rest of the Austrian empire. There was no attempt to extend the *Landwehr* to Galicia and West Galicia, mainly because of Napoleon's immense popularity among the Poles. Nor was Francis especially eager to summon the Hungarian diet. When he convened it at Pressburg, the diet quickly rejected the idea of extending the *Landwehr* to Hungary, but did surprise him by offering 60,000 troops for a period of three years – a 50 percent increase over previous levels. Once again, however, the diet's expressions of support proved more valuable than the *insurrectio*, which never exceeded a fifth of the forces promised.

Despite Hungary's meager contribution, the empire was still able to field an army of 300,000 men, no small accomplishment for the thrice-defeated and truncated monarchy. The French empire and its numerous satellites had twice that number of troops at their disposal. Nevertheless, the war party expected that Napoleon would be tied down in the Iberian peninsula, where the British had landed forces in support of the Spanish *guerrillas*. It could also count on Britain's promise of a second diversion in the Low Countries, together with a 5 million subsidy. In October Prussia's promise to join forces had reinforced Stadion's hopes for a war of liberation in central Europe, during which Napoleon's German and Italian auxiliaries would either defect or fight without enthusiasm. Upon his return from Paris, Ambassador Metternich even suggested that Russia would join the new coalition, or that anti-war sentiment in France might force Napoleon to come to an accommodation.

By the time spring arrived, any notion of an allied coalition had collapsed. Napoleon had not only scattered the Spanish *guerrillas* and their British allies, but had returned to Paris, where he quickly suppressed opposition within his government. Not only did Russia remain neutral, but Prussia repudiated its earlier promise of military aid. Although the British made good on their subsidies, their amphibious diversion at Flushing was both late and dismally unsuccessful. True to their Habsburg heritage, the Tyrolean peasantry successfully rose against their new Bavarian overlord. But less serious uprisings elsewhere in Germany were quickly suppressed by Napoleon's client princes. Instead of participating in a fourth anti-French coalition, the Austrian army was now obliged to face Napoleon and his German and Italian auxiliaries all by itself.

Whatever chance Austria had of defeating Napoleon was doomed by the tactics pursued by the Archduke Charles. Unlike the rest of his brothers, Charles had opposed the war because he realized that one more defeat might spell the end of the monarchy. This fear now led him to pursue a defensive strategy throughout the campaign, thereby making victory impossible. Although the *Landwehr* fought well in the war's opening engagements, its units were soon demoralized by the enemy's progress. Indeed, the fall of Vienna (13 May 1809) quickly replaced popular enthusiasm for the war with relief that peace would soon be at hand. One observer reported that the eagerness with which the city's women rushed to accommodate the French soldiers "made Vienna look like Sodom and Gomorrah." Archduke Charles's victory at Aspern (21 May) – Napoleon's first battlefield defeat – did little to change the empire's prospects, primarily because the archduke was unwilling to risk his forces by pursuing the enemy. When Napoleon rebounded with the hard-fought victory at Wagram (6 July), the archduke rushed to sign an armistice while his army was still intact.

Although Charles's defeatism enraged his brother, news of the British fiasco at Flushing left Francis with no alternative but to conclude yet another unfavorable peace. Having now lost four wars to revolutionary France, the emperor seriously considered abdicating as a means of attaining more favorable peace terms. In fact, the French negotiator Champagny hinted that dividing the Austrian, Bohemian, and Hungarian lands among three archdukes might provide the best guarantee for peace. Yet Napoleon never considered partitioning the Habsburg monarchy, let alone dissolving it altogether. The same man who had destroyed the thousand-year *Reich*, dethroned the princes of Germany, Italy, and Spain, and created countless new entities, shared the conventional wisdom of those before him that the monarchy was a European necessity. His foreign minister Talleyrand had advised him on the morrow of Austerlitz that, "Your Majesty can now eliminate the Austrian monarchy or reestablish it. [But] this conglomeration of states must stay together. It is absolutely indispensable for the future well-being of the civilized world."

The treaty of Schönbrunn (14 October 1809) reflected Napoleon's judgment that Austria should be severely punished, but retained as a European power. He took away its entire coastline by annexing Croatia west of the Sava River and all of Inner Austria, except Styria and eastern Carinthia. He also rewarded his allies by ceding Salzburg and the *Innviertel* to Bavaria, and West Galicia to the Polish duchy of Warsaw; even Russia received the small Galician district of Tarnopol as a reward for having remained neutral. That Napoleon decided against giving all of Galicia to the Poles or establishing an independent Hungary suggests that he intended Austria to serve as a counterpoise to Russia. He did, however, further degrade its ability to make war against him by levying an 85 million franc indemnity and limiting its army to 150,000 men.

Defeat also brought the downfall of the war party. Although Stadion and Archduke Charles resigned voluntarily, Francis went one step further by prohibiting his *generalissimus* from participating in all public affairs. If the other archdukes were spared the humiliation, they also lost most of their influence over state affairs. For the next quarter century, Francis left no doubt about who was in control and what he expected from the men who served him. His determination was not lost on Stadion's successor, Clemens Wenzel Count Metternich. Contrary to his reputation as a staunch reactionary, Metternich was very much a product of the Enlightenment. The son of a freemason, he was notably secular in outlook and a convinced advocate of enlightened absolutism. One of his associates claimed that his favorite motto was "everything for the people, nothing by the people," a formula that he preferred to execute while respecting historically distinct and diverse institutions. But Metternich also knew his place. Although he did not share Francis's rejection of the Enlightenment and the populist reforms it had inspired, he realized that the emperor would sooner change ministers than his policies. Having carefully climbed to the top of the career ladder, he had no intention of causing his own fall by being out of step with Francis's domestic agenda.

Metternich's mission as foreign minister was clear enough. The latest peace treaty had reduced the empire by another 3.5 million subjects and left state finances in a shambles. In addition to a 700 million fl. debt and the latest indemnity, the *Hofkammer* had had to support a crushing six-month military occupation. A sixfold increase in paper currency – to 1.437 million fl. – had reduced banknotes to only a twelfth of their face value. Unable to get private credit, the government was forced to declare its first bankruptcy ever in 1811. To save money the army had to be reduced to well below the 150,000 maximum set by the peace treaty. If revolutionary France was to be defeated, another country would have to assume the lead, and the risks that went with it.

The need to avoid offending Napoleon was so great that Austria was now reduced to the status of a French satellite. The *Landwehr* was disbanded at his request. Metternich even urged Francis to offer Napoleon the hand of the 18-year-old Archduchess Maria Luisa; the wedding took place in April 1810, even though both father and daughter detested him. One year later Metternich suppressed Austrian newspaper reports of French reverses in Spain to forestall public displays of support for their enemies. Soon thereafter he dissuaded Francis from concluding what would have been another potentially fatal defensive alliance with Russia. Instead, he negotiated Austria's first alliance with revolutionary France in March 1812. When the Grand Armée invaded Russia three months later, it was supported by an independent corps of 30,000 Austrians under Prince Karl Philip Schwarzenberg.

Schwarzenberg was chosen to command because he had the diplomatic experience that would be necessary to carry out Metternich's strategy: to promote French goodwill by participating in the campaign, but to keep alive the option of joining a subsequent anti-French coalition by avoiding active hostilities with the Russians. By the following summer, the Grand Armée's destruction by the Russian winter had led to the formation of a Fourth Coalition (1813–15); comprising Russia, Prussia, Sweden, Great Britain, Spain, and Portugal, it was the first anti-French alliance in which Austria had not been a founding member. Although Schwarzenberg had already concluded a cease-fire with the tsar in January, Metternich proceeded with extreme caution. Austria could not risk provoking a French attack before its own forces could mobilize. Hence, when he discovered that Archduke John was organizing another Tyrolean uprising, he had him interned and his accomplices arrested. He even offered to mediate a peace settlement between the belligerents that would have preserved France's Rhine frontier. Only after Napoleon rejected these terms – and the allies had accepted Austria's war aims – did the emperor declare war on France (12 August).

The Austrian army that took the field in the fall of 1813 was poorly trained and equipped. Many soldiers were without shoes, muskets, or uniforms; some even marched to the front in their underwear. But it also numbered

568,000 men, easily the largest in the coalition. More than half of these troops now joined the 570,000-man allied field army, to which Schwarzenberg was named supreme commander. And they fought well in the subsequent campaign that culminated in the decisive victory at Leipzig (16–19 October). Deserted at last by the German princes, Napoleon was now doomed by a four to one advantage in allied forces. The following spring brought the march on Paris that everyone had expected two decades earlier. On 31 March 1814 the city fell to a foreign invader for the first time in over thirteen centuries. Napoleon's abdication followed eleven days later.

As they marched on Paris, the allies issued a proclamation in which they reassured the French nation that its postwar borders would still be larger than they had ever been under the Bourbons. If the proclamation was in marked contrast with the infamous Brunswick Manifesto of 1792, it was because Metternich had obliged Prussia and Russia to place a stable balance of power ahead of territorial gain. This implied not only retaining France as a great power, but preventing Russia from replacing it as a threat to European security. When the great peace conference convened in Vienna, it restored most of the countries and international frontiers that had existed before the wars. There were unavoidable exceptions: Poland, an early casualty of the revolutionary wars, could not be restored because that would have come at expense of the victorious allies. The only difference was that Russia received most of the lands that had been parceled out to Prussia and Austria in 1795. Prussia got much of the Rhineland and northern Saxony as compensation. In fact, both countries emerged from the Congress considerably larger than they had been in 1792.

By contrast, the Austrian empire in 1815 was only slightly larger and more populous than at the outbreak of the revolutionary wars. This was partly due to the coalitions and defeats that it had sustained while Prussia and Russia were expanding in the East. Indeed, Austria had fought revolutionary France for 108 months, roughly twice as long as either of them. Another reason was that its aims were more strategic than territorial. For much of the past century its leaders had worked to consolidate the far-flung dominions that had been acquired during the War of the Spanish Succession. Metternich now accomplished this by making the monarchy wholly contiguous for the first time in its history. Although the monarchy essentially reassumed its pre-revolutionary configuration, it forsook far-off Belgium and its ancient, but scattered Swabian lands for Venice and the adjoining prince-bishoprics of Salzburg, Brixen, and Trent. In addition to its concern for the balance of power, Metternich also addressed the monarchy's long-standing interest in maintaining regional security beyond its frontiers: in Italy it not only directly ruled the new kingdom of Lombardy-Venetia, but benefited from the restoration of the Habsburg duchies of Modena and Tuscany, as well as the

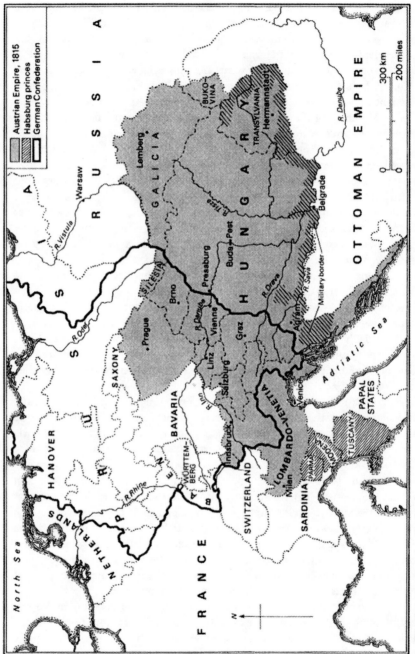

6 The Austrian empire 1815

essentially innocuous Spanish Bourbons; even though Prussia remained a virtual equal within Germany, the emperor was still its titular head as president of the newly formed German Confederation. Moreover, in the best traditions of Habsburg statecraft Metternich reinforced the restored international order with an alliance system that embraced every major European power.

If the Quadruple Alliance was different from past coalitions, it was because it was primarily directed against the threat of domestic revolution, rather than foreign aggression. Hence the overriding criticism of Metternich: Whereas few historians have disputed his diplomatic genius, most have criticized him for having tried to reinstitute the Old Regime without taking into account the new currents that had begun to transform the European world. Actually, the Austrian empire would have been far better off if he *had* restored the situation that obtained in the Habsburg lands on the eve of the French Revolution. A combination of cameralist and Enlightenment ideas had convinced a generation of monarchs, ministers, and common bureaucrats that populist reform was not only ethically, but practically correct. The resulting program of domestic reform had won the gratitude of the peasantry and various religious and ethnic minorities; it had also co-opted much of the nobility and bourgeoisie through education and government employment in the ever-expanding bureaucratic state. Their joint patronage of the arts and participation in reading clubs, masonic lodges, and salon society attested to their empowerment by the state, not their alienation from it.

The young Emperor Francis never grasped the breadth of this emerging national consensus and the patriotism that it engendered. Even the great resilience that the monarchy demonstrated during the revolutionary wars failed to convince him that revolutionary subversion was unlikely to occur within his own dominions. Despite multiple military defeats and Francis's own fear of Jacobinism, the progressive political culture of the pre-revolutionary generation survived in Count Stadion and many of the archdukes, the mass of faceless bureaucrats, and the legions of *Landwehr* volunteers. Only the defeat of 1809 and the advent of the Metternich System ended any chance of returning to Leopold II's condominium of populist politics and corporate institutions.

8   Decline or disaggregation?

Francis surely merits the criticism he has received. But he also deserves to be evaluated in a broader historical context that distinguishes between the achievements of the first half of his reign and the inertia of the second. Almost without exception, the early modern Habsburgs had achieved their greatest successes in the process of addressing major security crises that they had inherited from their predecessors. And more often than not those crises came in the person of foreign adversaries. In restructuring and reorienting the monarchy the Emperors Ferdinand were inspired less by divine inspiration than by the successive gauntlets thrown down by the Winter King, Gustavus Adolphus and Cardinal Richelieu. The massive territorial gains of Leopold I and his sons owed more to the miscalculations of Kara Mustafa and Louis XIV than to the tactical genius of Prince Eugene. And it was the ruthless Frederick the Great who obliged Maria Theresa and her sons to abandon the Baroque world for the secular rationalism of the cameralists and *philosophes*; if the "great empress" was unique in launching a second Theresian reform period in the last half of her reign, it was because she failed to eliminate the Prussian threat in the Silesian wars. By 1815 Francis I had also saved the monarchy from a formidable foe. Just five years into Metternich's ministry, the monarchy had not only vanquished Napoleon but attained a higher level of security than at any time since the reign of Charles VI. To the south it was the undisputed hegemon in both Italy and the Balkans, where its former Bourbon and Ottoman adversaries now looked to it for their own security. To the north, Prussia and Russia were closer and more powerful than ever before, but the Napoleonic nightmare had instilled in them a healthy appreciation for secure frontiers, based on international law and cooperation, while the fear of France had inspired a half-century of Hohenzollern deference to Habsburg leadership in Germany.

It is no coincidence that the last two decades of Francis I's reign bore a certain resemblance to those of Charles VI. Rather than resume the statebuilding process, both rulers focused on strengthening the dynasty's legitimacy, Charles by securing foreign and domestic acceptance of the Pragmatic Sanction, Francis by the vigilant application of censorship, backed by a system of international congresses. Meanwhile, the imperial capital celebrated the latest triumph over France with a new surge in population and patronage that fueled another golden age of fine and performing arts; if there was a difference between High Baroque and *Biedermeier*, it was that the intimate world of aristocratic patronage now coexisted with massive public concert audiences that attested to a growing economy and middle class. There was, in fact, much more substance to Franciscan Austria than to the delicate façade of Charles VI's second Habsburg empire. Aside from the avoidable crisis of 1848, Austria did not face a single life struggle during the long century between the appointment of Metternich and the death of Emperor Francis Joseph (1848–1916).

And that was the problem. The absence of a credible foreign threat removed the one incentive that had consistently informed and activated the domestic policies of Francis's forebears. Thus it was at the moment of its greatest triumph that the Austrian empire commenced a century-long "decline" that ultimately led to its defeat and dissolution in 1918. In reality it was more a process of disaggregation, during which the monarchy shed one after another of the five distinctive attributes that had given the early modern Habsburg enterprise its unique *raison d'être*.

1   The role of the dynasty

The complex and hazardous world of central European politics had heretofore demanded almost constant vigilance from the Austrian Habsburgs. Although not all of the early modern rulers were exceptionally intelligent, energetic or talented, they managed nonetheless to adapt to a steady variety of imposing challenges by drafting solutions that were sometimes bold and always practical. The three nineteenth-century Habsburgs provided no such leadership, principally because the absence of internal or external threats suggested that further innovation was unnecessary. Rather than embrace new currents and developments, they regarded them with diffidence or suspicion. The promotion of industry slowed, while land reform stopped altogether; urbanization, literacy, even higher living standards were seen more as potential threats than as ready opportunities. Near the end of his life Francis I was so confident in the monarchy's security that he perpetuated the status quo by insisting on the natural succession of his mentally incompetent son, Ferdinand I (1835–48). Only Ferdinand's total failure to forestall or limit the subsequent revolutions of 1848 forced a change with his abdication in favor of his nephew. Alas, over the next seven decades Francis Joseph accumulated an unenviable record for making poor choices or delaying the implementation of more suitable alternatives until it was too late for them to succeed.

2   Conflict or consensus?

As early as the sixteenth century the Habsburgs had learned all about the advantages of consensual politics, whether with prospective foreign allies, their German vassals, or the monarchy's own regional elites; collaborating with them brought strength and legitimacy, ignoring them risked diplomatic isolation or armed rebellion. Thus, within a decade of his succession, Ferdinand II had laid the foundation for the "triarchy" of aristocracy, church, and crown that comprised the Habsburg ruling establishment until the middle of the next century. Even when Maria Theresa felt compelled to restructure the monarchy, she made sure to enlist the grudging consent of the *Erblande*'s aristocratic and clerical elites, which understood that the most likely alternative was the more ruthless military efficiency of Protestant Prussia; at the same time, she wisely refrained from implementing major reforms in those peripheral possessions where they were less welcome. By contrast, rulers like Leopold I and Joseph II who violated the contractual basis of Habsburg absolutism were ultimately obliged to retrace their steps in the face of formidable revolts in Hungary or Belgium. With the outbeak of the revolutionary wars, Franciscan absolutism was initially accepted because it represented the best defense against the more compelling threats of Jacobinism and French imperialism. The Metternich System was, however, deeply resented by all segments of monarchy's educated elite, including not only conservative clerics and feudal nobles, but a generation of civil officials whom Sonnenfels had taught to embrace the populist absolutism of Emperors Joseph II and Leopold II. Yet Francis judged – correctly – that the Austrian empire could be ruled without consensus, because there was no longer a credible threat of foreign intervention, even from Prussia. His autocratic legacy extended well beyond the caretaker regime of Ferdinand I into a decade of "neo-absolutism" under Francis Joseph. When embarrassing military defeats finally moved Francis Joseph to try "a little parliamentarism" he did so not by searching for a broad political consensus, but by engaging in divisive interest-group politics that sacrificed the general interest in favor of slender, working majorities in a deeply divided parliament. In this way democracy manifested itself as conflict and chaos, rather than as consensus and cooperation.

3   The problem of diversity

Surely the early modern Habsburgs would have preferred a more unified and homogenous commonwealth. Their championship of the Counter-Reformation was, after all, designed to achieve religious uniformity by coercing Protestants into Catholics, Orthodox into Uniates, and Jews into ghettoes. They also worked doggedly to centralize and consolidate the administration of a discontiguous patrimony of many kingdoms, each of which had its own laws and privileges. On occasion they even attempted to minimize the monarchy's geographic diversity, whether by absorbing enclaves in Silesia and Upper Hungary, appending territorial scraps like the *Innviertel* and Bukovina, or exchanging remote provinces like Sardinia, the Swabian enclaves, and Belgium for more contiguous ones. But the early modern Habsburgs never regarded the monarchy's linguistic or ethnic diversity as a threat to its integrity. Instead, they readily employed military force to acquire even more ethnically diverse dominions in Italy, the Low Countries, the northern Balkans, or southern Poland. Nor did they hesitate to colonize the depopulated lands of southern Hungary with a patchwork pattern of settlers from all over the continent. They need not have worried. Aside from a mass exodus by Ottoman Hungary's Muslim communities, the newly acquired populations accepted their place in the Habsburg commonwealth, together with the waves of settlers who became their neighbors. There were no "age-old" rivalries, even when there was blood to be shed. Hence, in wartime Croat and Serb *Grenzer* fought side by side as skirmishers ahead of regular German and Czech infantry units whose flanks were protected in turn by squadrons of Hungarian hussars. Even when they revolted against the emperor, his subjects were impelled by opposition to feudal dues, religious persecution, or lost corporate privileges, not by animosity toward one another.

The ready acceptance of diversity strengthened the monarchy by permitting it to expand well beyond its medieval, German core. Of course, as it doubled in size and quadrupled in population, the proportion of Germans fell by half from nearly 60 percent in 1618 to rather less than 30 percent two centuries later. But the monarchy adapted to this changing demography. From the very beginning, the media of social control – whether the devotional literature of the Counter-Reformation or the secular schoolbooks of the Enlightenment – were disseminated in a multitude of indigenous languages. The freedom to choose helped prevent language from becoming a source of conflict between ethnic groups; in the meantime, German further entrenched its position as the most common medium of inter-ethnic communication, not because it was required by the state but because it served the self-interest of the upwardly mobile. When Joseph II issued his ill-advised language ordinance for public officials, he briefly considered Czech in deference to the monarchy's large Slavic population, but settled on German simply because it was most widely spoken among the educated classes. As late as 1809, Stadion's patriotic popular appeals against Napoleonic France were published in many of the monarchy's languages, thus justifying his boast to the emperor that "We have created a nation!"

In reality, ethnic diversity did not become a problem until Francis I and his successors made it into one by misconstruing language as the sole source of national identity. Perhaps they were too close to the maelstrom of nationalism to recognize that a "national idea" could be forged from a shared cultural and territorial identity, rather than solely from a common language. Having failed to appreciate the distinction, they forewent the opportunity to construct a common, transethnic "Austrian" identity for their peoples, relying instead on a loyalty to the emperor himself, plus a certain residual faith in the dynasty's original German constituency. One consequence of this fear of ethnic diversity was that it mortgaged the monarchy's ability to resume its historic march into the Balkans. For the better part of two centuries the Hohenzollerns had adhered to the dictum that a country that ceases to expand must contract. Yet, as early as 1804 Francis rejected the first of two overtures by the Ottoman Serbs to place themselves under Habsburg rule. He subsequently directed his commanders along the Military Border to take various steps to preserve the fragile stability of the Turkish empire. The decision proved a fateful oversight, since it transformed the Ottoman Balkans from an avenue for ready expansion into what ultimately became the lethal instrument of the Habsburg monarchy's ultimate demise.

4   The Habsburg monarchy and Germany

The nineteenth-century Habsburgs would have still been interested in acquiring more Germans, given the the genuine, historic ties between them and the indispensable role that the German language played in holding the monarchy together. Alas, Prussia had not only foreclosed that option during the Silesian wars, but followed it up in 1866 by unceremoniously expelling them and the *Erblande* from Germany. Admittedly the affiliation with Germany had frequently distracted the dynasty from the statebuilding process within its own dominions; it had also compelled Vienna to choose between East and West, as it recruited allies or allocated the monarchy's own finite military resources. But this had been a positive dilemma between competing opportunities. Expulsion from Germany deprived the monarchy of valuable allies in the West at a time when it confronted growing threats elsewhere. Ultimately, its diplomats decided that they could not do without German support, concluding a Dual Alliance (1879) with its old Prussian adversary and the new German empire that it had fashioned in 1871. But the center of gravity in the traditional Austro-German alliance had shifted: from Vienna, where it had been throughout the early modern period, to Berlin, which set its own course, with fatal consequences for both empires.

5   Diplomacy and the formation of the monarchy

It was with the Dual Alliance that the Habsburg monarchy lost the last of those five distinctive traits that had made it so distinctive – and successful – in the early modern period. It survived for another century, despite the revolutions of 1848 and major defeats in 1859 and 1866, primarily because it retained its *raison d'être* in the eyes of its subjects and the other great powers. Indeed, the monarchy weathered each of the great crises of the early modern period not only because it won victories on the battlefield, but because both its people and its neighbors had an interest in its survival; even in defeat, the actions of men like Frederick the Great in 1742, Napoleon in 1809, Nicholas I in 1849, and Bismarck in 1866 suggest that its enemies also regarded it as a European necessity. Even the fatal Prussian embrace of 1879 had been motivated by Bismarck's realization that the monarchy's survival was in Germany's best interest, as both a buffer and a client for Germany. Of course, it was this perversion of the early modern relationship with Germany that doomed the monarchy. By 1918 dependence on Europe's looming German hegemon flatly contradicted its role as a major counterpoise in balance of power politics. Simply put, there were those among its people and foreign adversaries who no longer saw the Danubian monarchy as an indispensable solution to the problems of central Europe. Perhaps they should have.

Bibliography

The following summary is not intended as a comprehensive bibliography of the field or even of the titles I employed in writing this book. Instead it is presented here as a guide for further reading, including numerous titles that have appeared since the publication of the first edition.

I   GENERAL

Except for Jean Bérenger, *History of the Habsburg Empire*, I: *1273–1700* (London, 1994), II: *1700–1918* (London, 1997), those general treatments that cover the early modern monarchy are now somewhat dated. The most comprehensive and authoritative remains Hugo Hantsch, *Die Geschichte Österreichs* (Vienna, 1951). Robert A. Kann, *A History of the Habsburg Empire 1526–1918* (London and Berkeley, 1974) is more complete and accurate than Victor-Louis Tapié, *The Rise and Fall of the Habsburg Monarchy* (New York, 1971). Kann and Zdenek David, *The Peoples of the Eastern Habsburg Lands, 1526–1918* (Seattle, 1984) is a carefully compiled study that gives individual attention to each nationality of the Habsburg core lands, except the Germans and Italians. R. J. W. Evans, *The Making of the Habsburg Monarchy 1550–1700: an Interpretation* (Oxford, 1979) is indispensable for understanding the alliance between crown, aristocracy, and church during the Counter-Reformation and the distinctiveness of Habsburg culture. Ernst Wangermann, *The Austrian Achievement 1700–1800* (London, 1973) provides a very readable survey for the following century, principally from a social and cultural perspective. A more comprehensive narrative is available in Hanns Leo Mikoletzky, *Österreich: Das grosse 18. Jahrhundert* (Vienna 1967) and *Das entscheidende 19. Jahrhundert: Geschichte, Kultur und Wirtschaft* (Vienna, 1972). Charles Ingrao, ed., *The State and Society in Early Modern Austria* (West Lafayette, In., 1994) examines various aspects of the monarchy's religious, cultural, economic, social, and diplomatic history from the mid-sixteenth to the eighteenth centuries.

Anton Schindling and Walter Ziegler, eds., *Die Kaiser der Neuzeit, 1519–1918* (Munich, 1990) provides a collection of biographical sketches for each of the Habsburg emperors. The best general treatment of social developments is Ernst Bruckmüller, *Sozialgeschichte Österreichs* (Vienna, 1985). Eduard Winter, *Frühaufklärung* (Berlin, 1966) and *Barock, Absolutismus und Aufklärung in der Donaumonarchie* (Vienna, 1971) remain the best comprehensive treatments of intellectual developments in the Austrian, Bohemian, and Hungarian lands. For aspects of the Counter-Reformation there is Anna Coreth, *Pietas Austriaca: Österreichische Frömmigkeit im Barock*, 2nd edn (Munich, 1982), and the first half of R. A. Kann, *A Study in*

Austrian Intellectual History: From Late Baroque to Romanticism (New York, 1960), which focuses on the prominent court preacher, Abraham à Sancta Clara

CORPORATE INSTITUTIONS

Increasing scholarly interest in ruling elites and corporate institutions is reflected in the number of recent studies of the Habsburg estates. R. J. W. Evans and Trevor Thomas, eds., *Crown, Church and Estates: Central European Politics in the Sixteenth and Seventeenth Centuries* (London, 1991) includes several relevant articles by leading scholars. Dietrich Gerhardt, ed., *Ständische Vertretungen in Europa im 17. und 18. Jahrhundert* (Göttingen, 1974) includes an excellent article on the eighteenth-century estates by György Bonis. For the various Austrian estates, there is Herbert Hassinger, "Die Landstände der österr. Länder ... im 16. und 18. Jht.," *Jahrbuch des Vereins für Landeskunde von Niederösterreich und Wien*, 2 (1964); Christine Mueller, *The Styrian Estates in Transition, 1740–1848* (New York, 1987); Franz Quarthal, *Landstände und landständisches Steuerwesen in Schwäbisch-Österreich* (Stuttgart, 1980); David Luebke, *His Majesty's Rebels: Communities, Factions and Rural Revolt in the Black Forest, 1725–1745* (Ithaca, 1997); and Miriam Levy, *Governance and Grievance: Habsburg Policy and Italian Tyrol in the Eighteenth Century* (West Lafayette, In., 1988). Eila Hassenpflug-Elzholz, *Böhmen und die böhmischen Stände in der Zeit des beginnenden Zentralismus* (Vienna, 1982) provides a comprehensive analysis for the mid-eighteenth century.

ECONOMIC DEVELOPMENTS

There is no comprehensive economic history of the Habsburg dominions. For the seventeenth century various parts of the monarchy are covered by Antoni Maczak *et al.*, *East Central Europe in Transition from the Fourteenth to the Seventeenth Century* (Cambridge, 1985), and in John R. Lampe and Marvin R. Jackson, *Balkan Economic History, 1550–1950: From Imperial Borderlands to Developing Nations* (Bloomington, 1982). Charles VI's reign is treated by Herman Freudenberger, "Economic Progress during the Reign of Charles VI," in Jürgen Schneider, ed., *Wirtschaftskräfte in der europäischen Expansion: Festschrift für Hermann Kellenbenz* (Bamberg, 1978).

Several scholars have examined the beginnings of industrialization, most notably John Komlos, *Nutrition and Economic Development in the Eighteenth-Century Habsburg Monarchy* (Princeton, 1990) and "Institutional Change under Pressure: Enlightened Government Policy in the Eighteenth-Century Habsburg Monarchy," *Journal of European Economic History*, 15 (1986); the opening chapter of David Good, *The Economic Rise of the Habsburg Empire 1750–1914* (London and Berkeley, 1984); and Herman Freudenberger, "An Industrial Momentum in the Habsburg Monarchy," *Journal of Economic History*, 12 (1983), and "The Woolen Goods Industry of the Habsburg Monarchy in the Eighteenth Century," *ibid.*, 20 (1960). Freudenberger has also contributed to our knowledge of the all-important Bohemian lands with *The Industrialization of a Central European City: Brno and the Fine Woollen Industry in the Eighteenth Century* (Edington, 1977), and "Industrialization in Bohemia and Moravia in the Eighteenth Century," *Journal of Central European Affairs*, 19 (1960), as has Arnost Klima, "Agrarian Class Structure and Economic Development in Pre-industrial Bohemia," *Past & Present* 85 (1979), "Industrial Development in Bohemia, 1648–1781," *ibid.* 11 (1957), "Industrial Growth and Entrepreneurship in the Early Stages of Industrialization in the Czech Lands," *Journal of European Economic History*, 6 (1977), and "The Role of Rural Domestic Industry in Bohemia in the Eighteenth Century," *Economic History Review*, 2nd Series: 27 (1974).

II   INDIVIDUAL CROWNLANDS

The Hungarian crownlands have attracted considerable attention during recent decades. The most up-to-date general surveys are Erwin Pamlényi, *A History of Hungary* (Budapest 1973; London, 1975), and Peter Sugar, Peter Hanák, and Tibor Frank, eds., *A History of Hungary* (Bloomington, 1990). The eighteenth century is particularly well covered by Henrik Marczali, *Hungary in the Eighteenth Century* (Cambridge, 1910, reprinted 1971) and Domokos Kosáry, *Culture and Society in Eighteenth-Century Hungary* (Budapest, 1987). Although Stefan Pascu, *A History of Transylvania* (Detroit, 1982) provides a useful survey, the best one-volume treatment of the principality is Gábor Barta *et al.*, *History of Transylvania* (Budapest, 1994). Despite its title, Keith Hitchins, *The Rumanian National Movement in Transylvania, 1780–1849* (Cambridge, Mass., 1969) includes an excellent eighteenth-century background. Stanko Guldescu, *The Croatian-Slavonian Kingdom 1526–1792* (The Hague, 1970) is a very readable, if somewhat biased study. Gunther E. Rothenberg, *The Austrian Military Border in Croatia 1522–1747* (Urbana, 1960) and *The Military Border in Croatia 1740–1881* (Chicago, 1966) remain the definitive works on that fascinating institution, while Eva Faber, *Littorale Austriaco: Das österreichische und kroatische Küstenland 1700–1780* (Graz, 1995), provides a comparable service for the monarchy's Adriatic dominions.

The rest of the Habsburg dominions have received substantially less attention, at least in English. For the Habsburg capital and its court there is Ilse Barea, *Vienna: Legend and Reality* (London, 1966) and John Spielman, *The City and the Crown* (West Lafayette, In., 1993). Karl Bosl, *Handbuch der Geschichte der böhmischen Länder* (Stuttgart, 1974), as well as Ludwig Petry, Josef Menzel, and Winfried Irgang, *Die Geschichte Schlesiens, 2: Die Habsburgerzeit 1526–1740* (Sigmaringen, 1988) provide a comprehensive treatment of these dominions. Mikulás Teich, ed., *Bohemia in History* (Cambridge, 1998), features several articles on the early modern period. Dino Carpanetto and Giuseppe Ricuperati, *Italy in the Age of Reason* (London, 1987), devotes four chapters exclusively to Lombardy and Tuscany, while Stuart Wolff, *A History of Italy, 1700–1860: The Social Constraints of Political Change* (London, 1979) focuses mainly on the Habsburg principalities' cultural elites. For somewhat broader coverage there is Heinrich Benedikt, *Kaiseradler über dem Apennin: die Österreicher in Italien 1700 bis 1866* (Vienna, 1964) and Adam Wandruszka, *Österreich und Italien im 18. Jahrhundert* (Munich, 1963). For the Austrian Netherlands there is Heinrich Benedikt, *Als Belgien österreichisch war* (Vienna, 1965), Hervé Hasquin, ed., *La Belgique autrichienne, 1713–1794* (Brussels, 1987), and C. Bruneel, "The Spanish and Austrian Netherlands, 1585–1780," in J.C.H. Blom and E. Lamberts, eds., *History of the Low Countries* (Providence, 1998).

III   THE THIRTY YEARS' WAR (1618–1648)

Geoffrey Parker, *Europe in Crisis, 1598–1650* (Ithaca, N.Y., 1979) presents a reasonably broad, up-to-date profile of the European scene, including the General Crisis.

For the war itself, C. V. Wedgwood, *The Thirty Years War* (London, 1938, reprinted 1981) provides a superbly written, thorough account of the conflict and its leading personalities. Robert Bireley, *Religion and Politics in the Age of the Counter-Reformation: Emperor Ferdinand II, William Lamormaini, S.J., and the Formation of Imperial Policy* (Chapel Hill, 1981) studies the interaction between the emperor and his Jesuit confessor through 1635. The aforementioned Evans and Thomas, *Crown, Church and Estates* includes several studies of the monarchy during the Thirty Years' War, including Robert Bireley's provocative essay, "Ferdinand II: Founder of the Habsburg Monarchy." Karin MacHardy, "The Rise of Absolutism and Noble Rebellion in Early Modern Habsburg Austria, 1570–1620," *Journal of Comparative History*, 34 (1992) focuses on the evolving alliance between crown, nobility, and church in Lower Austria. For the Habsburg military, see John Mears, "The Thirty Years' War, the 'General Crisis' and the Origins of a Standing Army in the Habsburg Monarchy," *Central European History*, 21 (1988). Gary Nichols, "The Economic Impact of the Thirty Years' War in Habsburg Austria," *East European Quarterly*, 23 (1989) briefly surveys the effects of the conflict. Hermann Rebel, *Peasant Classes: The Bureaucratization of Property and Family Relations under Early Habsburg Absolutism, 1511–1636* presents an innovative study of peasant families during the uprising of 1626.

IV   THE BAROQUE MONARCHY (1648–1740)

Oswald Redlich, *Weltmacht des Barock*, 4th edn (Vienna, 1961) and *Das Werden einer Grossmacht*, 4th edn (Vienna, 1962) are still the most thorough surveys of the politics of the period 1648–1740. Jean Bérenger, *Finances et absolutisme* (Paris, 1975) contains much useful information on the interaction between the crown and the monarchy's corporate bodies under Leopold I. John Spielman, *Leopold I of Austria* (New Brunswick, 1977) is a very useful survey. For the reign of Joseph I, see Charles Ingrao, *In Quest and Crisis: Emperor Joseph I and the Habsburg Monarchy* (West Lafayette, In., 1979). The long wait for a biography of the last male Habsburg has now ended with Bernd Rill, *Karl VI: Habsburg als barocke Grossmacht* (Vienna, 1992), although John Stoye, "Emperor Charles VI: The Early Years of the Reign", *Royal Historical Society Transactions*, 12 (1962) remains the only English-language treatment of any part of the reign. For the impact of Charles VI's famous testament see Charles Ingrao, "The Pragmatic Sanction and the Theresian Succession: A Reevaluation," in *Etudes danubiennes*, 9 (1993), an earlier version of which appears in William McGill, ed., *The Habsburg Dominions under Maria Theresa* (Washington, Pennsylvania, 1980).

MINISTERS AND ADVISORS

Henry F. Schwarz, *The Imperial Privy Council in the Seventeenth Century* (Cambridge, Mass., 1943) presents a rather dry but comprehensive look at that body and the men whom it embraced. For Leopold's economic advisors there is John Spielman and S. J. Miller, *Cristóbal de Rojas y Spínola [American Philosophical Society Transactions, 52 (Philadelphia, 1962)]* and Louise Sommer, *Die österreichischen Kameralisten in dogmengeschichtlicher Darstellungen* (Vienna, 1925, reprinted 1967). Derek McKay, *Prince Eugene of Savoy* (London, 1977) is a superior substitute for Max Braubach's massive, five-volume *Prinz Eugen von Savoyen* (Munich, 1963). Nicholas Henderson, *Prince Eugen of Savoy* (New York, 1964) is a handy, but less authoritative study. For other key ministers there are Hugo Hantsch, *Reichsvizekanzler Friedrich Karl Graf von Schönborn (1674–1746)* (Augsburg, 1929); J. Hrazky, "Johann Christoph Bartenstein," *Mitteilungen des österreichischen Staatsarchivs* [*MÖSA*], 11 (1958); and Brigitte Holl, *Hofkammerpräsident Gundaker Thomas Graf Starhemberg und die österreichische Finanzpolitik der Barockzeit (1703–1715)* (Vienna, 1976). John Stoye, *Marsigli's Europe 1680–1730: the Life and Times of Luigi Ferdinando Marsigli, Soldier and Virtuoso* (New Haven, 1994) provides a marvelously rich tapestry of the age, as seen through the life, work, and intellect of a Habsburg career diplomat, soldier, and scientist.

HUNGARY AND THE TURKS

Ladislas Baron Hengelmüller, *Hungary's Fight for National Existence* (London, 1913) is a very well-written, if somewhat chauvinistic account of the first half of the Rákóczi Revolt; Orest Subtelny, *Domination of Eastern Europe* (Gloucester, 1986) places the uprising in an east-European context, while Charles Ingrao, "Guerrilla Warfare in Early Modern Europe: the Kuruc War (1703–1711)," in Gunther E. Rothenberg and Béla Király, eds., *War and Society in East Central Europe*, 1 (New York, 1979) analyzes it from a military perspective. *Acta Historica*, 22 (1976), 27 (1981), 33 (1987) contain numerous specialized articles in English, German, or French on the kingdom's social, economic, and political history. For the siege of Vienna there is Thomas Barker's definitive *Double Eagle and Crescent* (Albany, 1967) and the shorter, very readable John Stoye, *The Siege of Vienna* (New York, 1965). The continuing Austro-Turkish conflict under Charles VI is covered by the somewhat journalistic Lavender Cassels, *The Struggle for the Ottoman Empire 1717–1740* (London, 1966) and the more scholarly but engaging Karl Roider, *The Reluctant Ally: Austria's Policy in the Austro-Turkish War, 1737–1739* (Baton Rouge, 1972).

IMPERIAL AND FOREIGN POLICY

Charles Ingrao, "Habsburg Strategy and Geopolitics during the Eighteenth Century," in Gunther E. Rothenberg and Béla Király, eds., *War and Society in East Central Europe*, 2 (New York, 1982) visualizes the broader structures and strategic concerns that helped predetermine foreign policy throughout the century. Michael Hughes, *Law and Politics in Eighteenth-Century Germany: The Imperial Aulic Council in the Reign of Charles VI* (Woodbridge, Suffolk and Wolfeboro, N.H., 1988) analyzes not only how the *Reichshofrat* functioned but how its judgments were affected by the emperor's German and foreign policy. For the monarchy's troubled relationship with the Maritime Powers there is Jeremy Black, "When Natural Allies' fall out: Anglo-Austrian relations, 1725–1740" *MÖSA*, 36 (1983).

V   REFORM AND ENLIGHTENED ABSOLUTISM
(1740–1792)

There is nothing in any language remotely comparable to Alfred von Arneth's monumental ten-volume *Geschichte Maria Theresia's* (Vienna, 1863–76, reprinted

Osnabrück, 1971). Nevertheless, Edward Crankshaw, *Maria Theresa* (London, 1969), William McGill, *Maria Theresa* (New York, 1972), and especially C. A. Macartney, *Maria Theresa and the House of Austria* (London, 1969) are all useful biographies. For the great empress's consort, see Georg Schreiber, *Franz I. Stephen: An der Seite einer grossen Frau* (Graz, Vienna, and Cologne, 1986). Her stormy relationship with her son and heir is just one of the contributions of Derek Beales, *Joseph II: In the Shadow of Maria Theresa* (Cambridge, 1987). There are no fewer than three brief, excellent studies of Joseph, one by Paul Bernard, *Joseph II* (New York, 1968) and two by T. C. W. Blanning, *Joseph II and Enlightened Absolutism* (London, 1970), which is somewhat more sympathetic to his Enlightenment agenda, and *Joseph II* (London 1994), which focuses on his destructive compulsiveness in rationalizing an intrinsically irrational, but wholly functional Habsburg patrimony. For Leopold II's early years as grand duke of Tuscany, see Eric Cochrane, *Florence in the Forgotten Centuries, 1527–1800* (Chicago, 1973). Otherwise there are only two German-language biographies, Adam Wandruszka, *Leopold II*, 2 vols. (Vienna, 1963–65) and the more recent but less scholarly Helga Pehem, *Leopold II: Herrscher mit weiser Hand* (Vienna, Graz, and Cologne, 1987).

MINISTERS AND ADVISORS

Franz Szabo, *Kaunitz and Enlightened Absolutism, 1753–1780* (Cambridge, 1995) provides a definitive account of the Enlightenment mindset that spurred the great chancellor's domestic projects and policies, while Paul Bernard, *From the Enlightenment to the Police State: The Public Life of Johann Anton Pergen* (Urbana, 1991) deftly examines the many official careers of the founder of the Austrian secret police. For the two Swietens, there is Frank Brechka, *Gerhard van Swieten and his World 1700–1772* (The Hague, 1970) and Ernst Wangermann, *Aufklärung und staatsbürgerliche Erziehung: Gottfried van Swieten als Reformator des österreichischen Unterrichtswesens 1781–1791* (Munich, 1978). The second half of the aforementioned R. A. Kann, *A Study in Austrian Intellectual History* focuses on Joseph von Sonnenfels, while Christine Lebeau, *Aristocrates et grands commis la Cour de Vienne (1748–1791): Le mod le français* (Paris, 1996) examines the link between French Enlightenment ideas and the mindset of high officials like Karl and Ludwig von Zinzendorf.

WAR AND DIPLOMACY

For most of this century there were no English-language treatments of the Silesian wars, except for several informative articles on Anglo-Austrian relations in Richard Lodge, *Studies in Eighteenth-Century Diplomacy 1740–1748* (London, 1930). That gap has now been partially filled with the appearance of two fine surveys, Reed Browning, *The War of the Austrian Succession* (New York, 1993) and M. S. Anderson, *The War of the Austrian Succession, 1740–1748* (London, 1995). Max Braubach, *Versailles und Wien von Ludwig XIV. bis Kaunitz* (Bonn, 1952) is still the best account on the origins and realization of the Diplomatic Revolution. For the first two partitions of Poland, see Herbert Kaplan, *The First Partition of Poland* (New York, 1972) and Robert H. Lord, *The Second Partition of Poland* (Cambridge, Mass., 1915, reprinted New York, 1969). Karl Roider, *Austria's Eastern Question* (Princeton, 1982) is particularly valuable for attempts to balance Russian expansion and

Ottoman decline under Maria Theresa and her sons. Paul Bernard, *Joseph II and Bavaria* (The Hague, 1965) handles Joseph II's repeated attempts to absorb the strategic Wittelsbach electorate. For his relations with the British, see Jeremy Black, "British Policy towards Austria, 1780–1793," *MÖSA*, 42 (1992). Christopher Duffy, *The Army of Maria Theresa* (Vancouver, 1977) and *The Wild Goose and the Eagle: A Life of Marshal von Browne, 1705–1757* (London, 1964) are two very readable studies of the Theresian military establishment. Paul W. Schroeder, *The Transformation of European Politics, 1763–1848* (Oxford, 1994) affords a penetrating analysis of the monarchy's difficulties confronting the expansionist designs of Frederick II and Catherine II.

FISCAL, LEGAL AND SOCIAL POLICY

P. G. M. Dickson, *Finance and Government under Maria Theresia 1740–1780* (Oxford, 1987) is a two-volume work of monumental scholarship that contains a wealth of information in meticulous detail. Henry E. Strakosch, *State Absolutism and the Rule of Law: The Struggle for the Codification of Civil Law in Austria 1753–1811* (Sydney, 1967) deals with legal reform, while Paul Bernard *The Limits of Enlightenment: Joseph II and the Law* (Urbana, 1979) focuses on Joseph II's meddlesome dealings with it. Agrarian reform is best studied by individual crownland, through Edith Link, *The Emancipation of the Austrian Peasant 1740–1798* (New York, 1949, reprinted 1974); William Wright, *Serf, Seigneur and Sovereign: Agrarian Reform in Eighteenth-Century Bohemia* (Minneapolis, 1966); and Béla Király, "Maria Theresa's Hungarian Serf Reforms," in the aforementioned William McGill, ed., *The Habsburg Dominions under Maria Theresa*. For Habsburg political economy, see Helen Liebel [-Weckowicz], "Free Trade and Protectionism under Maria Theresa and Joseph II," *Canadian Journal of History*, 14 (1979).

RELIGION, EDUCATION AND CULTURE

Grete Klingenstein, *Staatsverwaltung und kirchliche Autorität im 18. Jahrhundert: Das Problem der Zensur in der theresianischen Reform* (Munich, 1970) traces the secularization of censorship, while suggesting some continuity between the reigns of Charles VI and Maria Theresa. James Van Horn Melton, *Absolutism and the Eighteenth-Century Origins of Compulsory Schooling in Prussia and Austria* (Cambridge, 1988) is a provocative and well-written comparative analysis of school reform. Paul Bernard, *Jesuits and Jacobins: Enlightenment and Enlightened Despotism in Austria* (Urbana, 1971) profiles political and social commentary under Joseph II. Virtually all of the work on Josephinism is in German, most notably Elisabeth Kovacs, *Katholische Aufklärung und Josephinismus* (Munich, 1979); and Eduard Winter, *Der Josephinismus: die Geschichte des österreichischen Reformkatholizismus 1740–1848* (Berlin, 1962). Joseph Karniel, *Die Toleranzpolitik Kaiser Josephs II.* (Gerlingen, 1986) is especially valuable for Joseph II's policies toward the Jews, as is William McCagg, *A History of the Habsburg Jews, 1670–1918* (Bloomington, 1989). There are also two fascinating, specialized studies, Hilde Spiel, *Fanny von Arnstein: a Daughter of the Enlightenment, 1758–1818* (New York, 1991), which profiles secular life and culture among Vienna's Jewish elite, and Lois Dubin, *The Port Jews of Habsburg Trieste: Absolutist Politics and Enlightenment Culture* (Stanford, 1998). For contemporary attitudes and reactions to government policy, there is also Charles O'Brien, *Ideas of Religious Toleration at the Time of Joseph II* [*American Philosophical Society Transactions*, 59] (Philadelphia, 1969).

There are several useful profiles of music and patronage, most notably Giorgio Pestelli, *The Age of Mozart and Beethoven* (Cambridge, 1984), which focuses principally on the Habsburg lands, and Mary S. Murrow, *Concert Life in Haydn's Vienna* (Stuyvesant, N.Y., 1989). There is no dearth of studies on the monarchy's great composers. For Haydn there is Karl Geiringer, *Haydn: a creative life in music* (3rd edn, Berkeley, 1982), as well as a chapter in Rebecca Gates-Coon, *The Landed Estates of the Esterházy Princes* (Baltimore, 1994). John Rosselli, *The Life of Mozart* (Cambridge, 1998) is both compact and accessible, while Nicholas Till, *Mozart and the Enlightenment: Truth, Virtue and Beauty in Mozart's Operas* (New York, 1995) is somewhat more provocative and sophistocated. Bruce Alan Brown, *Gluck and the French Theatre in Vienna* (Oxford, 1991) makes a convincing case for its subject's considerable, if less monumental, genius and impact. Among the plethora of Beethoven biographies are David W. Jones' new, compact *The Life of Beethoven* (Cambridge, 1998), and Elliott Forbes' revised edition of the more definitive *Thayer's The Life of Beethoven*, 2 vols. (Princeton, 1991).

INDIVIDUAL CROWNLANDS

There are several informative accounts for the reigns of Joseph II and Leopold II, especially Éva Balázs, *Hungary and the Habsburgs: an Experiment in Enlightened Absolutism* (Budapest, 1997), which is more comprehensive than the title suggests, profiling personalities and policymaking in Vienna as they impacted the Hungarian crownlands; Béla Király, *Hungary in the Late Eighteenth Century* (New York, 1969); the aforementioned Rebecca Gates-Coon, *The Landed Estates of the Esterházy Princes* (Baltimore, 1994); Robert J. Kerner, *Bohemia in the Eighteenth Century* (New York, 1932, reprinted 1969); Walter Davis, *Joseph II: an Imperial Reformer for the Austrian Netherlands* (The Hague, 1974); and Janet L. Polasky, *Revolution in Brussels, 1787–1793* (Brussels and Hanover, N.H., 1987). Hamish Scott, *Enlightened Absolutism: Reform and Reformers in Later Eighteenth-Century Europe* (Basingstoke, 1990) includes two stimulating articles by R. J. W. Evans, "Maria Theresa and Hungary" and "Joseph II and Nationality in the Habsburg Lands." Grete Klingenstein, "The Meaning of Austria' and Austrian' in the Eighteenth Century," in Robert Oresko, G.C. Gibbs, and H.M. Scott, eds., *Royal and Republican Sovereignty in Early Modern Europe: Essays in Memory of Ragnhild Hatton* (Cambridge, 1997) carefully traces the finite evolution of the Austrian state idea.

VI   AUSTRIA IN THE REVOLUTIONARY ERA (1792–1815)

Both C. A. Macartney, *The Habsburg Empire 1790–1918* (New York and London, 1968) and Hanns Leo Mikoletzky, *Österreich: Das entscheidende 19. Jahrhundert* (Vienna, 1972) begin with excellent sections on the early revolutionary era. The only modern treatments of Francis II/I, are William C. Langsam, *Francis the Good: The Education of an Emperor, 1768–1792* (New York, 1949) and Heinrich Drimmel, *Kaiser Franz: Ein Wiener übersteht Napoleon* (Vienna, 1981). There are, however, several good studies of the men around the emperor, most notably Karl Roider,

Baron Thugut and Austria's Response to the French Revolution (Princeton, 1987); Gunther E. Rothenberg, *Napoleon's Great Adversaries: The Archduke Charles and the Austrian Army, 1792–1814* (Bloomington, 1982); Hellmuth Rössler, *Graf Johann Philipp Stadion: Napoleons deutscher Gegenspieler*, 2 vols. (Vienna and Munich, 1966); William C. Langsam, "Count Stadion and the Archduke Charles," *Journal of Central European Affairs*, 6 (1946); Henry Kissinger, *A World Restored: Metternich, Castlereagh, and the Problems of Peace 1812–22* (Boston, 1973); Enno Kraehe, *Metternich's German Policy*, 2 vols. (Princeton, 1963–83); and Paul Bernard's aforementioned biography of Pergen. Various aspects of the monarchy's reception of the French Revolution are treated in Ernst Wangermann, *From Joseph II to the Jacobin Trials*, 2nd edn (London, 1969); T. C. W. Blanning, *The Origins of the French Revolutionary Wars* (London and New York, 1986); Kinley Brauer and William Wright, eds., *Austria in the Age of the French Revolution* (Minneapolis, 1991); F. Gunther Eyck, *Loyal Rebels: Andreas Hofer and the Tyrolean Uprising of 1809* (Lanham, Md., 1986); Frida Knight, *Beethoven and the Age of Revolution* (London, 1973); William C. Langsam, *The Napoleonic Wars and German Nationalism in Austria* (New York, 1930).

Index

NEW APPROACHES TO EUROPEAN HISTORY

Printed in the United States
153933LV00003B/46/A